JOHN WILLIS'

DANCE WORLD

1977

Volume 12

1976–1977 SEASON

CROWN PUBLISHERS, INC.
One Park Avenue
New York, N.Y. 10016

TO

DAME MARGOT FONTEYN

Prima Ballerina Assoluta of the world. Her ethereal beauty, musical sensitivity, exquisite line, and impeccable artistry have made her one of the greatest ballerinas of this century. The world has embraced her with love and admiration, showered her with well-deserved accolades, and encouraged her to achieve one of the lengthiest performing careers in the history of ballet.

Page Left: all pictures of Margot Fonteyn (clockwise from top left) with Robert Helpmann in "The Sleeping Beauty," with Michael Somes in "Dante Sonata," with David Blair in "The Sleeping Beauty," with Rudolf Nureyev in "Giselle," in "Swan Lake," with Rudolf Nureyev in "Swan Lake," with Robert Helpmann at curtain call (June 22, 1976) of "The Merry Widow" (Beverley Gallegos Photo), with Rudolf Nureyev in Martha Graham's "Lucifer" (Martha Swope Photo), with Rudolf Nureyev in "Marguerite and Armand," with Rudolf Nureyev in "Romeo and Juliet," in "Les Sylphides," "Swan Lake," center: 1975 portrait

MAYA PLISETSKAYA
in Maurice Bejart's "Isadora"
(Beverley Gallegos Photo)

CONTENTS

EDITOR: JOHN WILLIS

Assistant Editor: Ron Reagan

Staff: Joseph Burroughs, Alberto Cabrera, Frances Crampon,
Maltier Hagan, Stanley Reeves, William Schelble

Staff Photographers: Beverley Gallegos, Ron Reagan, Lyn Smith,
Van Williams

DANCE PROGRAMS ON BROADWAY

BILLY ROSE THEATRE
Opened Wednesday, June 9, 1976.*
The Paul Taylor Dance Foundation presents:

PAUL TAYLOR DANCE COMPANY

Artistic Director-Choreographer, Paul Taylor; Administrator, Richard J. Alderman; Music Director, John Herbert McDowell; Lighting Design, Jennifer Tipton; Rehearsal Mistress, Bettie deJong; Wardrobe Supervisor, Beth Rappaport

COMPANY

Carolyn Adams	Ruth Andrien
Bettie deJong	Linda Kent
Eileen Cropley	Lila York
Nicholas Gunn	Robert Kahn
Monica Morris	Victoria Uris
Elie Chaib	Christopher Gillis

REPERTOIRE

(All choreography by Paul Taylor) "Public Domain" (John Herbert McDowell), "Big Bertha" (St. Louis Melody Museum Band Machines/McDowell), "Esplanade" (Bach), "Aureole" (Handel), "Tablet" (David Hollister), "Runes" (Gerald Busby)
WORLD PREMIERE: Wednesday, June 9, 1976 "Cloven Kingdom" (Arcangelo Corelli/Henry Cowell/Malloy Miller/John Herbert McDowell, Paul Taylor; Headpieces, John Rawlings; Women's Costumes, Scott Barrie; Men's Formal Wear, After Six; Lighting Design, Jennifer Tipton) danced by the company

General Manager: Robert Yesselman
Press: Michael Alpert, Marilynn Le Vine, Warren Knowlton, Randi Cone
Stage Managers: Rosemary Cunningham, Tony Marques

* Closed June 20, 1976 after limited engagement of 16 performances.

Sue Cook, Kenn Duncan, Ron Reagan Photos

**Left: Robert Kahn (top), Elie Chaib,
Nicholas Gunn, Christopher Gillis in "Cloven Kingdom"**

**Linda Kent, Nicholas Gunn
in "Runes"**

**Carolyn Adams, Eileen Cropley
in "Public Domain"**

6

Bettie deJong, Carolyn Adams in "Big Bertha"
Top Left and below: "Esplanade" Top Right and below: "Runes"

Opened Tuesday, June 22, 1976.*
Hurok by arrangement with the Australian Ballet Foundation presents:

THE AUSTRALIAN BALLET
with
MARGOT FONTEYN
in
"The Merry Widow"

By Franz Lehar; Scenario and Staging, Robert Helpmann; Choreography, Ronald Hynd; Design, Desmond Heeley; Musical Adaptation, John Lanchbery; Administrator, Peter F. Bahen; Director, Sir Robert Helpmann; Associate Directors, Ray Powell, Bryan Ashbridge; Musical Director, John Lanchbery; Conductors, Alan Abbott, Alan Barker; Coordinator, Daisy Hill; Choreologist, Barbara Nimmo; Asisstant Ballet Master, Colin Peasley; Stage and Lighting Director, Christopher Maver; Head Technician, Chris Grieve; Wardrobe, Frances Towers, John Langmaid; Wardrobe Supervisor, Deborah Musgrove; Lighting Supervisor, John Gleason

COMPANY

PRINCIPALS: Alan Alder, Lucette Aldous, Walter Bourke, Alida Chase, Kelvin Coe, Marilyn Jones, Jonathan Kelly, Maria Lang, John Meehan, Ray Powell, Marilyn Rowe
SOLOISTS: Dale Baker, Janne Blanch, David Burch, Susan Dains, Hilary Debden, Paul de Masson, Ai-gul Gaisina, Joseph Janusaitis, Josephine Jason, Michela Kirkaldie, Rex McNeil, Robert Olup, Anthony Pannell, Colin Peasley, Paul Saliba, Ross Stretton, Janet Vernon, Christine Walsh
CORYPHEES: Mark Brinkley, Julie da Costa, Chrisa Kermidas, Leigh Matthews, Graeme Murphy, Valmai Roberts
ARTISTS: Glenda Allen, Stephen Baynes, Paul Cini, Amanda Clerke, Allan Cross, Michael Curry, Sheree da Costa, Irena Fogerty, Carol Green, Deborah Lerine, Angus Lugsdin, William Pepper, Terese Power, Danilo Radojevic, Martin Raistrick, Lucinda Sharp, Olga Tamara, Meryl Tankard, Nina Thomson, Dennis Trinder, Abril Ward
　　Performed in three acts. The action takes place in Paris in 1905.

Company Manager: William Orton
Press: Sheila Porter, Susan Bloch, William Schelble
Stage Managers: Michael Williams, Francis Croese

* Closed July 3, 1976 after limited engagement of 15 performances. Dame Margot Fonteyn danced 12 performances, Marilyn Rowe danced 3.

Beverley Gallegos, Martha Swope Photos

**Right: Lucette Aldous, John Meehan
Above: Margot Fonteyn**

John Meehan, Margot Fonteyn,
Kelvin Coe

Margot Fonteyn, John Meehan

MINSKOFF THEATRE

Opened Tuesday, November 9, 1976.*
Hurok presents:

DUTCH NATIONAL BALLET

Artistic Director, Rudi van Dantzig; Administrative Director, Anton Gerritsen; Choreographer/Regisseur, Hans van Manen; Choreographer/Designer, Toer van Schayk; Ballet Mistress, Christine Anthony; Ballet Masters, Ivan Kramar, Heinz Manniegel, Reuven Voremberg; Conductors, Lucas Vis, Omri Hadari; Production Manager/Stage Director, Dhian Siang Lie; Coordinator, Johan Mittertreiner; Press, Dick Hendriks, Anna Marijke Diderich-Pijper; Wardrobe Supervisor, Joop Stokvis

COMPANY

Maria Aradi, Olga de Haas, Sonja Marchiolli, Alexandra Radius, Monique Sand, Han Ebbelaar, Henny Jurriens, Zoltan Peter, Francis Sinceretti, Ronald Snijders

Laurel Benedict, Aina Bilkins, Erna Droog, Sonja Geerlings, Judith James, Rebecca Ross, Mea Venema, Jeanette Vondersaar, Joanne Zimmerman, Clint Farha, David Loring, Jan Willem de Roo, Pieter Roowaan

Marie-Josette Aerts, Joke van Bergen, Anneke van Brakel, Monique Diederen, Annemieke Goldewijk, Rowena Greenwood, Gerri Heevel, Ingrid Jense, Annelies Knoop, Reni Kohne, Liliane Kuyer, Nicolette Langestraat, Anja Licher, Annemarie Norton, Corrice Rijkuiter, Jane Ryan, Karin Schnabel, Charlotte Sturgess, Hlif Svavarsdottir, Valerie Valentine, Loes van Veen Marion Venema, Margriet van Waveren, Anna Bonnie Wilmans, Carmela Zegarelli

Jimmy Ameland, Stephen Baranovics, Jacques Barkley, Ad Berbers, John Brown, Joseph Carman, Philip Clyde, Ben Eggers, Charles Flanagan, Arnold Goores, Wim Koelma, Leon Koning, Graham Lustig, Raymond Ottenhoff, Jaime Petty, Boudewihn Pleines, Lazaro Prince, Wade Walthall, Rob van Woerkom

Ilse van Berkel, Marina Camby, Anne Genne, Cecile Genne, Josiane Geys, Annabel Helmore, Sanne Jacobsen, Angailika MacArthur, Sophia Meermans, Vicki Summers, Julie Towers, Ricardo Anemaet, Fred Berlips, Leo Besseling, Simon de Mowbray

REPERTOIRE

"Metaphors" (Daniel-Lesur, Hans van Manen), "Twilight" (John Cage, Hans van Manen), "Epitaph" (Gyorgy Ligeti, Rudy van Dantzig), "First Aerial Station" (Louis Spohr, Toer van Schayk), "Ginastera" (Alberto Ginastera, Rudi van Dantzig), "Adagio Hammerklavier" (Beethoven, Hans van Manen), "Before, During and After the Party" (Gilius van Bergeyk, Toer van Schayk)

Company Manager: William Orton
Press: Rima Corben, Norman Lombino
Stage Managers: Dhian Siang Lie, Liesbeth Visser

* Closed Nov. 14, 1976 after limited engagement of 8 performances.

Jorge Fatauros Photos

Right: Alexandra Radius, Han Ebbelaar in "Twilight"
Above: "Epitaph" Top: "Before, During and After the Party"

Sonja Marchiolli, Francis Sinceretti, Han Ebbelaar, Alexandra Radius in "Metaphors"

Henny Jurriens, Monique Sand in "Adagio Hammerklavier"

Francis Sinceretti, Han Ebbelaar in "Metaphors"
Above: "Ginastera"

Alexandra Radius, Han Ebbelaar (also above)
in "Adagio Hammerklavier" Top: "Epitaph"

DUTCH NATIONAL BALLET

MINSKOFF THEATRE
Opened Tuesday, January 18, 1977.*
The Cunningham Dance Foundation, Inc. presents:

MERCE CUNNINGHAM
& DANCE COMPANY

Artistic Director-Choreographer, Merce Cunningham; Musical Adviser, John Cage; Artistic Adviser, Jasper Johns; Resident Designer, Mark Lancaster; Lighting Supervisor, Richard Nelson; Administrator, Richard Svare; Rehearsal Assistant, Chris Komar; Sound, John Fulleman; Wardrobe Supervisor, Ann Goodson

COMPANY
Merce Cunningham

Karole Armitage	Meg Harper
Louise Burns	Chris Komar
Ellen Cornfield	Robert Kovich
Morgan Ensminger	Julie Roess-Smith
Lisa Fox	Jim Self

REPERTOIRE: "Summerspace" (Morton Feldman, Cunningham), "Solo" (John Cage, Cunningham), "Rebus" (David Behrman, Cunningham), "Torse" (Maryanne Amacher, Cunningham), "Signals" (David Behrman/Joe Kubera/David Tudor, Cunningham), "Sounddance" (David Tudor, Cunningham), "Squaregame" (Takehisa Kosugi, Cunningham)
PREMIERE: On Tuesday, January 18, 1977 "Travelogue" (John Cage, Merce Cunningham; Scenery, Costumes and Lighting, Robert Rauschenberg)

Company Manager: William Orton
Press: Gurtman & Murtha Associates, Meg Gordean
Stage Managers: Charles Atlas, Suzanne Joelson, Andy Tron

* Closed January 23, 1977 after limited engagement of 6 performances.

Herb Migdoll, J. L. Vartoogian Photos

Top Right: Merce Cunningham in "Rebus"
(Jack Mitchell Photo)

**Jim Self, Morgan Ensminger, Julie Roess-Smith
in "Torse" Above: "Travelogue"**

**Chris Komar, Morgan Ensminger, Ellen Cornfield
in "Signals" Above: Cunningham in "Travelogue"**

URIS THEATRE
Opened Tuesday, March 22, 1977.*
The National Opera of Belgium (Maurice Huisman, Director) presents:

BALLET OF THE 20th CENTURY

Artistic Director-Choreographer, Maurice Bejart; Administrator, Anne Lotsy; Assistant Artistic Directors, Robert Denvers, Jorge Donn, Daniel Lommel; Ballet Master, Jose Pares; Stage Director, Maurice Bivort; Lighting, Allan Burrett; Sound, Leo Van Horenbeeck; Wardrobe, Elizabeth Desmaret; Executive Producer, Mel Howard; Production Manager, Joe Calvan; Assistant, John Jonas

COMPANY

Angele Albrecht, Axelle Arnouts, Frankie Arras, Hitomi Asakawa, Anouchka Babkine, Mohamed Bahiri, Jean-Paul Balmer, Alain Baran, Sophie Baule, Maurice Bejart, Beatrice Berger, Marilyn Berlander, Jean-Michel Bouvron, Anne Breuer, Kym Cassiman, Suzy Caufield, Tom Crocker, Catherine Dethy, Martine Detournay, Jorge Donn, Judith Eger, Marie Fernandez, Michel Gascard, Dominique Genevois, Lynn Glauber, Christiane Glik, Tim Golliher, Daryl Gray, Dyane Gray-Cullert, Micha Von Hoecke, Philippe Horekens, Igor Ivanoff, Sherry Kowtko, Jacques Leclercq, Yann Le Gac, Jean-Marie Limon, Philippe Lizon, Daniel Lommel, Patrice Malguy, Richard Majewski, Nurio Mamiya, Maguy Marin, Ivan Marko, Claude Mazodier, Paul Melis, Shonach Mirk, Michele Mottet, Piotr Nardelli, Josyane Note, Jan Nuyts, Jose Pares, Thierry Parmentier, Bertrand Pie, Rita Poelvoorde, Catherine Pouillon, Monet Robier, Quiny Sacks, Doris Schaefer, Robert Secondi, Thierry Sirou, Christiane Sturnich, Philippe Talard, Patrice Touron, Lutgart Vanderstraeten, Catherine Verneuil, Jeannot Vinclair, Gerard Wilk, Andrzej Ziemski
GUEST STARS: Suzanne Farrell, Maya Plisetskaya, Luciana Savignano

REPERTOIRE

"Firebird" (Stravinsky, Maurice Bejart), "Le Sacre du Printemps" (Stravinsky, Bejart), and *NY PREMIERES* of "Golestan" (Traditional Iranian, Bejart), "Isadora" (Liszt/Chopin/Beethoven/Schubert/ de Lisle/Scriabin, Bejart) danced by Maya Plisetskaya, "Marimba: A Trance Dance" (Steve Reich, Lar Lubovitch), "Ce Que L'Amour Me Dit" (Mahler, Bejart), "Le Marteau sans Maitre" (Boulez, Bejart), "Song of a Wayfarer" (Mahler, Bejart), "Bolero" (Ravel, Bejart), "Fold by Fold" (Boulez, Bejart), "Rhapsodie" (Ravel, Micha Van Hoecke), full-length "Notre Faust" (Bach, Bejart), "No Exit" (Bartok, Bejart), "Leitmotiv" (Craig Steven Shuler, Robert Weiss)

Company Manager: Charles Eisler
Press: Tom Kerrigan
Stage Manager: Francky Arras

* Closed April 3, 1977 after limited engagement of 15 performances.

Dupont, Beverley Gallegos, Colette Masson Photos

12

Maya Plisetskaya
in
"Isadora"

Daniel Lommel, Jorge Donn in "Songs of a Wayfarer"
Top Left: Yann LeGac, Maurice Bejart in "Notre Faust"

Ivan Marko in "Firebird" Above: "Le Sacre du
Printemps" Top: Jorge Donn, Suzanne Farrell
in "No Exit" (Sonate a Trois)

Luciana Savignano, Jorge Donn in "Ce Que
L' Amour Me Dit" Top: Jorge Donn in
"Notre Faust"

URIS THEATRE

Opened Tuesday, March 1, 1977.*
James Nederlander and S. A. Gorlinsky present:

NUREYEV
with
Vivi Flindt   Johnny Eliasen
Anne Marie Vessel

Orchestra conducted by Stanley Sussman; Decor and Costume Supervision, Rouben Ter-Arutunian; Lighting Supervision, John B. Read; Production Management, TAG Foundation; Wardrobe Supervisor Stephanie Cheretun; Executive Producer, Lillian Libman; Assistant, Louise Porter; Bethany Beardslee, Soprano; Robert Kaufman, Pianist; William Metcalf, Baritone

PROGRAM

"Pierrot Lunaire" (Arnold Schoenberg, Glen Tetley), "Songs of a Wayfarer" (Gustav Mahler, Maurice Bejart), "The Lesson" (George Delerue, Flemming Flindt)

Company Manager: Jerry Livengood
Press: Sheila Porter

* Closed March 20, 1977 after limited engagement of 24 performances.

Beverley Gallegos Photos

**Top Right: Vivi Flindt, Rudolf Nureyev
in "Pierrot Lunaire"**

14   **Rudolf Nureyev, Anne Marie Vessel
in "The Lesson"**

**Rudolf Nureyev, Johnny Eliasen in "Songs of a Wayfarer"
Above: Nureyev, Vivi Flindt in "The Lesson"**

PALACE THEATRE
Opened Thursday, April 7, 1977.*
The Broadway Palace Theatre Company in association with Sheldon Soffer presents:

LES BALLETS TROCKADERO DE MONTE CARLO

Artistic Directors, Peter Anastos, Natch Taylor; Scenery Supervised by Robert Randolf; Lighting Design, Jennifer Tipton; Regisseuse, Betteann Terrell: Program Director, Peter Anastos

COMPANY

Peter Anastos (Olga Tchikaboumskaya), Natch Taylor (Alexis Ivanovitch Lermontov/Suzina LaFuzziovitch), Zamie Zamora (Zamarina Zamarkova), Shawn Avrea (Eugenia Repelskii), Leland Walsh (Ida Neversayneva), Brent Mason (Dame Margaret Lowin-Octeyn/William Vanilla), Joel Paley (Bertha Vinayshinsky), William Toth (Vera Namethatunova), Mark Pollini (Santuzza Popolini), Michael Haimson (Natalia Marionetskaya), Lance Hunter (Olga Plushinskaya), Keith Glancy (Xenia Zlotmachinskaya)

REPERTOIRE

"Le Lac des Cygnes (Swan Lake)" (Tchaikovsky, Gasparinetti/Ivanov), "Phaedra/Monotonous #1148" (AC/DC, Shawn Avren), "The Dance of Liberation of the American People in Homage to Isadora Duncan, the Greatest American Patriot since Betsy Ross, Barbara Fritchie and Sacagawea" (Tchaikovsky, Olga Plushinskaya), "Go for Barocco" (Bach, Anastos), "Les Sylphides" (Chopin, Alexandre Minz/Fokine), "Spring Waters" (Rachmaninoff, Betteann Terrell), "The Dying Swan" (Saint-Saens, Terrell), "Ecole de Ballet" (Pastiche, Anastos), "Pas de Quatre" (Pugni, Gasparinetti), "Isadora in Bayreuth" (Richard Wagner, St. Vitus), "Don Quixote" (Minkus, Anastos)
WORLD PREMIERES: "Les Oiseaux D'Or" (Tchaikovsky, Betteann Terrell after Petipa), "Yes, Virginia, Another Piano Ballet". (Chopin, Peter Anastos) both Thursday, April 7, 1977, and "Giselle Act II" (Adolphe Adam, Peter Anastos) on Tuesday, April 12, 1977.

General Manager: Eugene McDougle
Press: Michael Alpert, Marilynn LeVine, Warren Knowlton

* Closed April 17, 1977 after limited engagement of 12 performances.

Kenn Duncan Photos

Top Right: "Don Quixote"

"Swan Lake"

"Swan Lake"

LUNT-FONTANNE THEATRE
Opened Monday, May 16, 1977.*
The Martha Graham Center for Contemporary Dance presents:

MARTHA GRAHAM DANCE COMPANY

Artistic Director-Choreographer, Martha Graham; General Director, Ron Protas; Rehearsal Director, Linda Hodes; Costumers, Sharon Hollinger, Kathi Horne; Production Assistant, Glenn Ostergaard; Conductors, Robert Irving, Stanley Sussman; Settings: Isamu Noguchi, Arch Lauterer, Leandro Locsin; Lighting Design, Jean Rosenthal, Nicholas Cernovitch; Costumes: Martha Graham, Halston; Associate Artistic Directors, Linda Hodes, Ron Protas

COMPANY

William Carter, David Chase, Mario Delamo, Janet Eilber, Margot Fonteyn, Diane Gray, Phyllis Gutelius, Diana Hart, Bonnie Oda Homsey, Yuriko Kimura, Pearl Lang, Peggy Lyman, Daniel Maloney, Lucinda Mitchell, Elisa Monte, Eric Newton, Rudolf Nureyev, Peter Sparling, Tim Wengerd

Christine Dakin, Susan McLain, Henry Yu, Mary Collins, Jacquelyn Buglisi, Sharon Filone, Don Foreman, Dindi Lidge, Jeanne Ruddy, Sally Trammell, Sharon Tyers, George White

REPERTOIRE

(All choreography by Martha Graham except where noted)
"Adorations" (Albeniz/Frescobaldi), "Errand into the Maze" (Menotti), "Primitive Mysteries" (Horst), "Appalachian Spring" (Copland), "El Penitente" (Horst), "Diversion of Angels" (Dello Joio), "Seraphic Dialogue" (Dello Joio), "Deaths and Entrances" (Johnson), "Phaedra" (Starer), "Frontier" (Horst), "Lamentation" (Kodaly), "Plain of Prayer" (Lester), "Dark Meadow" (Chavez), "Romeo and Juliet Balcony Scene Pas de Deux" (Prokofiev, Kenneth MacMillan) danced by Margot Fonteyn and Rudolf Nureyev, "The Wise Virgins" (Bach/Walton, Frederick Ashton) danced by Margot Fonteyn

WORLD PREMIERES: Tuesday, May 17, 1977 of "O Thou Desire Who Art About to Sing" (Meyer Kupferman, Martha Graham; Costumes, Martha Graham; Lighting, Nicholas Cernovitch) danced by Elisa Monte and Tim Wengerd; Tuesday, May 24, 1977 of "Shadows" (Gian Carlo Menotti, Martha Graham; Costumes, Halston; Lighting, Nicholas Cernovitch) danced by Janet Eilber, Peter Sparling, Diane Gray, Eric Newton

General Manager: Cynthia Parker
Press: Betty Lee Hunt, Maria Pucci, Fred Hoot
Stage Manager: Robert Neu

* Closed June 11, 1977 after limited engagement of 32 performances.

**Top Left: Margot Fonteyn, Nureyev in
"Romeo and Juliet Pas de Deux"**

**Peter Sparling, Janet Eilber in "Seraphic Dialogue"
Above: Peggy Lyman in "Frontier"**

Rudolf Nureyev, Pearl Lang in "El Penitente"
(Beverley Gallegos Photo)

Diane Gray, Rudolf Nureyev in "El Penitente"
Top: Margot Fonteyn in "The Wise Virgins"
(Beverley Gallegos Photos)

Phyllis Gutelius in "Letter to the World"
Top: Gutelius, Eric Newton in "Deaths and Entrances"

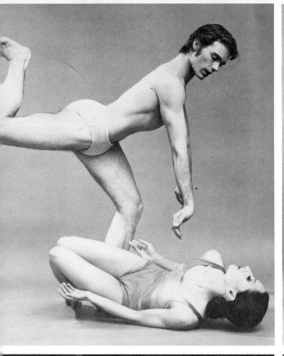

Diane Gray, Tim Wengerd in "Appalachian Spring"
Top: Tim Wengerd, Elisa Monte in "O Thou Desire . . ."

MARTHA GRAHAM DANCE COMPANY

Yuriko Kimura in "Diversion of Angels"
Top: Elisa Monte, Tim Wengerd in "O Thou Desire
Who Art about to Sing"

Peter Sparling, Janet Eilber in "Plain of Prayer"
Top: Rudolf Nureyev in "Appalachian Spring"

Margot Fonteyn in "The Wise Virgins" *(Beverley Gallegos Photo)* **Top: Mario Delamo, Diane Gray in "Seraphic Dialogue"**

LINCOLN CENTER PROGRAMS

METROPOLITAN OPERA HOUSE
Opened Monday, June 7, 1976.*
In association with Ballet Theatre Foundation (Justin Colin, President), Hurok presents:

AMERICAN BALLET THEATRE

Directors, Lucia Chase, Oliver Smith; Associate Director, Antony Tudor; Assistant Director, Enrique Martinez; Music Director, Akira Endo; Regisseur, Dimitri Romanoff; Conductor, Tibor Pusztai; Ballet Mistress, Fiorella Keane; Resident Lighting Designer, Nananne Porcher; Ballet Masters, Michael Lland, Scott Douglas, Jurgen Schneider; Props, Alan Price; Wardrobe, Robert Holloway, May Ishimoto, Robert Boehm; Production Associate, Marian Kinsella; Production Assistant, Dana Bruce; Administrative Assistant, Bentley Roton

COMPANY

Mikhail Baryshnikov, Karena Brock, Erik Bruhn, Fernando Bujones, William Carter, Eleanor D'Antuono, Vladimir Gelvan, Marcia Haydee, Gelsey Kirkland, Ted Kivitt, Natalia Makarova, Yoko Morishita, Ivan Nagy, Dennis Nahat, Terry Orr, Marcos Paredes, John Prinz, Lynn Seymour, Martine van Hamel, Sallie Wilson, Gayle Young

Buddy Balough, Warren Conover, Starr Danias, Kristine Elliott, Nanette Glushak, Jolinda Menendez, Hilda Morales, Kirk Peterson, Frank Smith, Marianna Tcherkassky, Clark Tippet, Charles Ward, Rebecca Wright

Elizabeth Ashton, Victor Barbee, Carmen Barth, Amy Blaisdell, Nina Brzorad, Miguel Campaneria, David Cuevas, George de la Pena, Rebecca Drenick, Peter Fonseca, Susan Frazer, Cynthia Gast, Rodney Gustafson, Melissa Hale, Aurea Hammerli, Cynthia Harvey, Kenneth Hughes, Janne Jackson, Roman Jasinski, Marie Johansson, Susan Jones, Francia Kovak, Linda Kuchera, Elaine Kudo, Lisa Lockwood, Charles Maple, Sara Maule, Ruth Mayer, Eric Nesbitt, Christine O'Neal, Gregory Osborne, Michael Owen, Janet Popeleski, Berthica Prieto, Leigh Provancha, Cathryn Rhodes, Lisa Rinehart, Miguel Sanchez, Richard Schafer, Raymond Serrano, Janet Shibata, Christine Spizzo, David Wallach, Denise Warner, Patricia Wesche, Sandall Whitaker, Cheryl Yeager

REPERTOIRE

"Giselle" (Adam, David Blair), "La Bayadere" (Minkus, Petipa/Natalia Makarova), "Romeo and Juliet" (Delius, Tudor), "Shadowplay" (Koechlin, Tudor), "Petrouchka" (Stravinsky, Fokine), "Pillar of Fire" (Schoenberg, Tudor), "Gemini" (Hans Werner Henze, Glen Tetley)
AMERICAN PREMIERES: "The Sleeping Beauty" (Tchaikovsky, Mary Skeaping after Petipa; Sets and Costumes, Oliver Messel) on Tuesday, June 15, 1976 with Natalia Makarova, Mikhail Baryshnikov, Martine van Hamel, Dennis Nahat, Yoko Morishita, Fernando Bujones. "Le Sacre du Printemps" (Stravinsky, Glen Tetley; Scenery and Costumes, Nadine Baylis; Lighting, John B. Read) on Monday, June 21, 1976 with Mikhail Baryshnikov, Martine van Hamel, Clark Tippet and company.

General Manager: Daryl Dodson
Company Manager: Herbert Scholder
Press: Sheila Porter, Norman Lombino, Charles France, Ellen Levene, Elena Gordon
Stage Managers: Dan Butt, Jerry Rice, Peter Gardner

* Closed June 26, 1976 after limited engagement of 24 performances. On Tuesday, June 29, 1976 opened at New York State Theater for 47 additional performances, closing Aug. 7, 1976. Additions to the repertoire were: "Swan Lake" (Tchaikovsky, David Blair), "Push Comes to Shove" (Haydn, Tharp), "Brahms Quintet" (Brahms, Nahat), "Jardin aux Lilas" (Chausson, Tudor), "Rodeo" (Copland, deMille), "Fall River Legend" (Gould, deMille), "Other Dances" (Chopin, Robbins), "Les Sylphides" (Chopin, Fokine), "Le Spectre de la Rose" (Weber, Fokine), "Epilogue" (Mahler, Neumeier), "Three Virgins and a Devil" (Respighi, deMille), "The Leaves are Fading" (Dvorak, Tudor), "Fancy Free" (Bernstein, Robbins), "Medea" (Barber, Butler), "At Midnight" (Mahler, Feld), "Billy the Kid" (Copland, Loring), "Concerto" (Shostakovich, MacMillan), "La Sylphide" (Lovenskjold, Bournonville), "Pas de Duke" (Ellington, Ailey), "Les Noces" (Stravinsky, Robbins), "Etudes" (Riisager, Lander), "The River" (Ellington, Ailey), *COMPANY PREMIERE* on July 8, 1976 of "Texas Fourth" (Harvey Schmidt/Traditional, Agnes de

Mille; Scenery, Oliver Smith; Costumes, Christina Giannini; Lighting, Nananne Porcher; Conductor, Michael Sasson), and *WORLD PREMIERE* on Monday, July 12, 1976 of "Once More, Frank" (Frank Sinatra, Twyla Tharp) danced by Miss Tharp and Mikhail Baryshnikov.

Spring Season at Metropolitan Opera House: Monday, April 18–June 11, 1977. (56 performances). Cynthia Gregory rejoined the company, and additional artists were John Meehan, Alexander Minz, and Leslie Browne. To the repertoire were added *COMPANY PREMIERES* of "Firebird" (Stravinsky, Christopher Newton after Fokine/Diaghilev; Design, Nathalie Gontcharova) danced by Natalia Makarova and Ivan Nagy on Tuesday, April 26, 1977. "Voluntaries" (Poulenc, Glen Tetley) with Natalie Makarova, Clark Tippet, Leslie Browne on Monday, May 2, 1977. *NY PREMIERE* on Wednesday, May 18, 1977 of "The Nutcracker" (Tchaikovsky, Mikhail Baryshnikov; Scenery, Boris Aronson; Costumes, Frank Thompson; Lighting, Jennifer Tipton) with Marianna Tcherkassky, Mikhail Baryshnikov, Alexander Minz. It had its world premiere in Washington, D.C., on Dec. 21, 1976.

Martha Swope, Beverley Gallegos Photos

Top: Mikhail Baryshnikov, Natalia Makarova
Below: Charles Ward, Cynthia Gregory
in "The Sleeping Beauty"

Marianna Tcherkassky, Terry Orr in "Billy the Kid" Above: Leslie Browne in "The Nutcracker" Top: Tcherkassky, Baryshnikov in "Nutcracker"

Martine van Hamel, Baryshnikov in "Push Comes to Shove" Above: Clark Tippet, van Hamel, and Top: Natalia Makarova in "Le Sacre du Printemps"

Leslie Browne in "Voluntaries"
(Beverley Gallegos Photo)

Eris Nesbitt, Rebecca Wright in "Texas Fourth"
Top: Martine van Hamel in "The Sleeping Beauty"
(Martha Swope Photos)

AMERICAN BALLET THEATRE

Marianna Tcherkassky, Ivan Nagy in "La Bayadere"
Top: Lynn Seymour, Fernando Bujones in "Romeo
and Juliet"
(Kenn Duncan Photo)

Natalia Makarova, Eric Bruhn in "Firebird"
Top: Cynthia Gregory in "Swan Lake"
(Beverley Gallegos Photos)

AMERICAN BALLET THEATRE 23

Mikhail Baryshnikov, Natalia Makarova in "Giselle"
Top: Charles Ward, Gelsey Kirkland in "Leaves are
Fading" *(Beverley Gallegos Photo)*

Mikhail Baryshnikov in "Petrouchka"
(Beverley Gallegos Photo)   Top: Yoko Morishito

AMERICAN BALLET THEATRE

Martine van Hamel in "Push Comes to Shove"
Top: "The Sleeping Beauty"
(Martha Swope Photos)

Natalia Makarova
in "The Sleeping Beauty"

AMERICAN BALLET THEATRE

LIBRARY & MUSEUM OF PERFORMING ARTS
Saturday, June 12, 1976*
Performing Arts Foundation, Inc. (Herman Rottenberg, President)
presents:

PHILIPPINE DANCE COMPANY OF NEW YORK
in
"Pamana: A Bicentennial Offering"

Artistic Director-Choreographer, Ronnie Alejandro; Executive Director, Bruna P. Seril; Technical Director, Chuck Golden; Stage Manager, Lee Horsman; President, Ramon de Luna; Producer, Herman Rottenberg

COMPANY

Melen Acaac, Veda Agus, Ronnie Alejandro, Joy Coronel, Josie Espartero, Bennie Felix, Kristin Jackson, Ramon de Luna, Maxie Luna, Ruth Malabrigo, Don Marasigan, Jun Pascual, Kathy Serio, Eddie Sese, Vicky Tiangco, Rosemarie Valdes, Vicky Valdes

PROGRAM

(All choreography by Ronnie Alejandro) "Polkabal," "Timawa," "Panuelo de Amor," "Paypay de Manila," "Jota Cavitena," "Malong-Malong," "Tarjata Sin Kagukan," "Singkil," "apApayao Maidens," "Kalinga Wedding Dance," "Anihan," "Binasuan," "Itik–Itik," "Subli," "Pandanggo sa Ilaw," "Tinikling"
* Program repeated July 13, 1976 at NY Chamber of Commerce Great Hall of Fame, Aug. 29, 1976 at Lincoln Center Out-of-Doors Festival.

Philippine Dance Company
(Ely Pascual Photo)

LIBRARY OF PERFORMING ARTS/LINCOLN CENTER
June 21–25, 1976 (5 performances)

OLD MOVIES & NEW FRIENDS

Choreographed and Directed by Nat Horne; Producer, Albert B. Reyes; General Manager, Sarah J. Miley; Accompanist, Rodger Swarth; Announcer, Mark Leff

COMPANY

David McCauley	Nat Horne
Freda Scott	Lynne Fursa
Carol Baxter	Susan Streater
Linda Buckley	Joyce Hanley

PROGRAM: "Bottoms Up," "Hemaway," "Nobody Does It Like Me," "Maple Leaf Rag," "Send in the Clowns," "Sandwiches Again," "Salsa," "Ain't Misbehavin'," "Happy Session Blues," "Friends," "Somewhere," "Burgerland," "Thank Heaven for You," "Bottoms Up"

Left: Susan Streater, Nat Horne
(Ron Reagan Photo)

LINCOLN CENTER PLAZA
Monday, August 30, 1976*
Lincoln Center Community Street Theater presents:

LAURA VELDHUIS DANCE COMPANY

Artistic Director-Choreographer, Laura Veldhuis; Technical Director, Joop Veldhuis; Narrator, Frank Albert

COMPANY

Cynthia Breidenbach, Julia Gale, Paul Kessman, Lee Michelsen, Laura Veldhuis, Bruce Weitzmon

PROGRAM

AN ODE TO AMERICANS: "Those Who Loved the Land and Sky First" (Louis W. Ballard), "Those Who Came to Build" (Gustav Mahler), "Those Who Removed Their Bondage" (Paul Robeson), "All Who Made America" (Aaron Copland)
* Program was repeated Tuesday, Sept. 7, 1976 in Central Park Mall.

Laura Veldhuis in "Ode to Americans"
(Susanne Faulkner Stevens Photo)

METROPOLITAN OPERA HOUSE
Opened Monday, June 28, 1976.*
Hurok presents:

RUSSIAN FESTIVAL OF MUSIC AND DANCE

Produced and Staged by Igor Moiseyev; with the Piatnitsky Choir, Dancers and Orchestra; dancers from the Georgian State Dance Company, the Ukrainian Dance Company, Dance Ensemble of the Northern Nations; Komuzisty Chamber Ensemble; Artists from The Ruvin Philharmonic, The Tadzhik Republic; Romen Trio, and Pantomime Artists Natalia and Oleg Kiriushkin

General Manager: John H. Wilson
Press: Sheila Porter, Norman Lombino

* Closed July 17, 1976 after limited engagement of 24 performances.

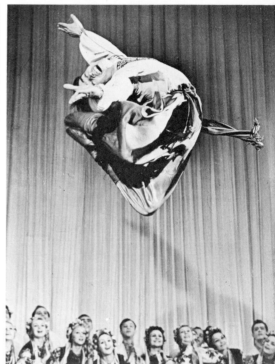

METROPOLITAN OPERA HOUSE
Opened Tuesday, July 20, 1976.*
Hurok presents:

NATIONAL BALLET OF CANADA
with
RUDOLF NUREYEV

Artistic Director, Alexander Grant; Production Director, Dieter Penzhorn; Musical Director-Conductor, George Crum; Ballet Mistress, Joanne Nisbet; Ballet Master, David Scott; Repetiteurs, Hazaros Surmeyan, Lorna Geddes, Charmain Turner; Wardrobe Supervisor, James Ronaldson; Administrator, Gerry Eldred; Associate Conductor, John Goss

COMPANY

PRINCIPALS: Vanessa Harwood, Mary Jago, Karen Kain, Nadia Potts, Veronica Tennant, Frank Augustyn, Stephen Jefferies, Charles Kirby, Tomas Schramek, Sergiu Stefanschi, Hazaros Surmeyan
SOLOISTS: Victoria Bertram, Colleen Cool, Rashna Homji, Gloria Luoma, Linda Maybarduk, Wendy Reiser, Mavis Staines, Joel Dabin, Jacques Gorrisen, James Kudelka, Clinton Rothwell, David Roxander, Ann Ditchburn, Cynthia Lucas, Miguel Garcia, Constantin Patsalas
CORPS: Yolande Auger, Susan Bodie, Lorna Geddes, Valerie Iles, Susan Keen, Jennifer Laird, Stephanie Landry, Daphne Loomis, Caitlan Maggs, Karin Mawson, Esther Murillo, Patricia Oney, Jennifer Orr, Theresa Padvorac, Heather Ronald, Katherine Scheideger, Barbara Szablowski, Karen Tessmer, Charmain Turner, Valerie Wilder, Jane Wooding, Gizella Witkowsky, David Allan, Luc Amyot, John Aubrey, Sean Boutilier, Victor Edwards, Albert Forister, David Gornik, Paul Jago, Anton Kaloczy, Thomas Nicholson, Peter Ottmann, Colin Simpson, Raymond Smith
GUEST ARTISTS: Carla Fracci, Rudolf Nureyev

REPERTOIRE

"The Sleeping Beauty" (Tchaikovsky, Rudolf Nureyev after Petipa), "Monument for a Dead Boy" (Jan Boerman, Rudi van Dantzig), "La Sylphide" (Lovenskjold/Crum, Bournonville), "Swan Lake" (Tchaikovsky, Erik Bruhn), "Giselle" (Adam, Peter Wright after Coralli/Perrot/Petipa), "Four Schumann Pieces" (Schumann, Hans van Manen) *(U.S. Premiere)*

Company Manager: Hamish Robertson
Press: Sheila Porter, Norman Lombino, Mary Jolliffe
Stage Managers: Dieter Penzhorn, Lawrence Beevers, Ernest Abugov, Bernard Fox

* Closed August 8, 1976 after limited engagement of 23 performances.

Beverley Gallegos, Andrew Oxenham Photos

**Left Center: Nadia Potts and corps de ballet
in "Swan Lake"**

**Sergiu Stefanschi, Vanessa Harwood
in "Swan Lake"**

**Frank Augustyn, Karen Kain in "Swan Lake"
Top Left: Rudolf Nureyev, Carla Fracci
in "Sleeping Beauty"**

David Allan, Yolande Auger in "Monument for a Dead Boy" Above: Veronica Tennant in "La Sylphide" Top: Alexander Grant in "Sleeping Beauty"

Karin Kain, Rudolf Nureyev in "Four Schumann Pieces" Above: "Giselle" Top: Veronica Tennant, Nureyev in "The Sleeping Beauty"

NEW YORK STATE THEATER
Opened Tuesday, August 10, 1976.*
City Center of Music and Drama presents the Alvin Ailey City Center Dance Theater in:

AILEY CELEBRATES ELLINGTON

Artistic Director-Choreographer, Alvin Ailey; Associate Artistic Director-Ballet Master, Ali Pourfarrokh; Musical Director-Conductor, Joyce Brown; Guest Conductors, Mercer Ellington, Tibor Pusztai; Produced by Dance Theater Foundation (Edward Lander, Executive Director); Operations Director, R. Robert Lussier; Lighting Supervisor, Chenault Spence; Wardrobe Master, Duane Talley; Managerial Coordinator, Lois Framhein; Sound Consultant, Abe Jacob; Assistant to Ailey/Lander, Harry Caldwell; Production Manager, Ralph McWilliams

COMPANY

Sarita Allen, Enid Britten, Sergio Cal, Masazumi Chaya, Ulysses Dove, Valerie Feit, Meg Gordon, Judith Jamison, Melvin Jones, Mari Kajiwara, Anita Littleman, Jodi Moccia, Michihiko Oka, Carl Paris, Beth Shorter, Warren Spears, Estelle Spurlock, Clive Thompson, Marvin Tunney, Elbert Watson, Dudley Williams, Donna Wood, Peter Woodin, Tina Yuan
GUEST ARTISTS: Duke Ellington Orchestra directed by Mercer Ellington, Brother John Sellers, Mikhail Baryshnikov, American Ballet Theatre, Alvin Ailey Repertory Workshop

REPERTOIRE

"Night Creature" (Duke Ellington, Alvin Ailey), "Blues Suite" (Traditional, Ailey), "The Mooche" (Ellington, Ailey), "Caravan" (Michael Kamen/Duke Ellington, Louis Falco), "The River" (Ellington, Ailey) with American Ballet Theatre, "Cry" (Coltrane/Nyro, Ailey), "Echoes in Blue" (Ellington, Milton Myers), "Liberian Suite" (Ellington, Lester Horton/James Truitte), "Love Songs" (Hathaway/Simone, Ailey), "Reflections in D" (Ellington, Ailey), "Revelations" (Traditional, Ailey), "Road of the Phoebe Snow" (Ellington/Strayhorn, Talley Beatty), "Streams" (Miloslav Kabelac, Ailey), *PREMIERE* Friday, Aug. 12, 1976 of "Three Black Kings" (Ellington, Ailey), and the Alvin Ailey Repertory Workshop performances of "Afro-Eurasian Eclipse" (Ellington, Raymond Sawyer), "Deep South Suite" (Ellington, Dianne McIntyre), "Forty" (Ellington, Gus Solomons, Jr.), "New Orleans Junction" (Ellington, Alvin McDuffie), "Still Life" (Ellington, Cristyne Lawson), "Games" (Traditional, Donald McKayle)

Company Manager: R. Robert Lussier
Press: Gurtman & Murtha, Meg Gordean
Stage Managers: Kevern R. Cameron, Donald Moss

* Closed Aug. 22, 1976 after limited engagement of 16 performances.

Johan Elbers Photos

Dudley Williams, and above with Elbert Watson, Clive Thompson in "Three Black Kings"

Clive Thompson, Tina Yuan in "Three Black Kings"

Masazumi Chaya, Donna Wood, "Blues Suite"
Above: "Road of the Phoebe Snow" Top: "The Mooche"

Judith Jamison, Clive Thompson in "Liberian Suite"
Above: Jamison in "Caravan" Top: Carl Paris, Mari Kajiwara, Warren Spears in "Echoes in Blue"

NEW YORK STATE THEATER
Opened Wednesday, November 16, 1976.*
City Center of Music and Drama, Inc. presents:

NEW YORK CITY BALLET

General Director, Lincoln Kirstein; Ballet Masters, George Balanchine, Jerome Robbins, John Taras; Assistant Ballet Masters, Rosemary Dunleavy, Tom Abbott; Music Director-Principal Conductor, Robert Irving; Associate Conductor, Hugo Fiorato; Costumer, Karinska; Wardrobe Supervisors, Sophie Pourmel, Leslie Copeland; Company Manager, Patricia Avedon Turk; Stage Managers, Ronald Bates, Kevin Tyler, Roland Vazquez; General Manager, Betty Cage; Assistant Manager, Edward Bigelow; Wardrobe Mistress, Dorothy Fugate; Wardrobe Master, Larry Calvert; Assistant to Mr. Balanchine, Barbara Horgan; Administrative Assistant, George Fernandez; Technical Director, Ronald Bates; Press, Virginia Donaldson, Leslie Bailey

COMPANY

PRINCIPALS: Jacques d'Amboise, Karin von Aroldingen, Anthony Blum, Jean-Pierre Bonnefous, Suzanne Farrell, Allegra Kent, Sara Leland, Adam Luders, Peter Martins, Kay Mazzo, Patricia McBride, Francisco Moncion, Peter Schaufuss, Helgi Tomasson, Violette Verdy, Edward Villella
SOLOISTS: Merrill Ashley, Bart Cook, Susan Hendl, Deni Lamont, Robert Maiorano, Teena McConnell, Marnee Morris, Colleen Neary, Shaun O'Brien, Frank Ohman, Susan Pilarre, Christine Redpath, Robert Weiss
CORPS: Muriel Aasen, Debra Austin, John Bass, Tracy Bennett, Bonita Borne, Elyse Borne, Victoria Bromberg, Leslie Brown, Jilise Bushling, Maria Calegari, Stephen Caras, Victor Castelli, Hermes Conde, Gail Crisa, Richard Dryden, Daniel Duell, Joseph Duell, Gerard Ebitz, Renee Estopinal, Nina Fedorova, Elise Flagg, Laura Flagg, Wilhelmina Frankfurt, Susan Freedman, Jean-Pierre Frolich, Judith Fugate, John Grensback, Lauren Hauser, Lisa Hess, Nichol Hlinka, Linda Homek, Richard Hoskinson, Dolores Houston, Kipling Houston, Elise Ingalls, Sandra Jennings, William Johnson, Jay Jolley, Deborah Koolish, Lourdes Lopez, Laurence Matthews, Catherine Morris, Peter Naumann, Kyra Nichols, Bruce Padgett, Delia Peters, Bryan Pitts, Terri Lee Port, Lisa de Ribere, David Richardson, Francis Sackett, Paul Sackett, Stephanie Saland, Lilly Samuels, Peter Schetter, Marjorie Spohn, Carol-Marie Strizak, Richard Tanner, Ulrik Trojaborg, Nolan T'Sani, Sheryl Ware, Heather Watts, Garielle Whittle, Sandra Zigars

REPERTOIRE

(All choreography by George Balanchine except where noted) "La Source" (Delibes), "Sonatine-Ravel" (Ravel), "Agon" (Stravinsky), "Who Cares?" (Gershwin/Kay), "Jewels: Emeralds (Faure), Rubies (Stravinsky), Diamonds (Tchaikovsky)." "Bugaku" (Mayuzumi), "Duo Concertant" (Stravinsky), "Square Dance" (Vivaldi/Corelli), "Dances at a Gathering" (Chopin, Robbins), "Firebird" (Stravinsky, Balanchine/Robbins), "Chaconne" (Gluck), "Union Jack" (Kay), "Swan Lake" (Tchaikovsky), "Afternoon of a Faun" (Debussy, Robbins), "Western Symphony" (Kay), "Swan Lake" (Tchaikovsky), "Afternoon of a Faun" (Debussy, Robbins), "Western Symphony" (Kay), "Coppelia" (Delibes, Balanchine/Danilova), "The Cage" (Stravinsky, Robbins), "The Nutcracker" (Tchaikovsky), "Symphony in Three Movements" (Stravinsky), "Tzigane" (Ravel), "Divertimento 15" (Mozart), "Stravinsky Violin Concerto" (Stravinsky), "Tchaikovsky Suite No. 2" (Tchaikovsky, d'Amboise), "Ma Mere L'Oye" (Ravel, Robbins), "Four Temperaments" (Hindemith), "Symphony in C" (Bizet), "Episodes" (Webern), "In G Major" (Ravel, Robbins), "Stars and Stripes" (Sousa/Kay), "An Evening's Waltzes" (Prokofiev, Robbins), "The Concert" (Chopin, Robbins), "In the Night" (Chopin, Robbins), "Brahms-Schoenberg Quartet" (Brahms/Schoenberg), "Goldberg Variations" (Bach, Robbins), "The Steadfast Tin Soldier" (Bizet), "La Sonnambula" (Rieti/Bellini), "Fanfare" (Britten, Robbins), "Concerto Barocco" (Bach), "Don Quixote" (Nabokov), "Other Dances" (Chopin, Robbins), "Valse-Fantaisie" (Glinka)
PREMIERES: Thursday, Feb. 3, 1977 of "Bournonville Divertissements: Ballabile from Napoli, Pas de Deux from Kermesse in Bruges, Pas de Trois from La Ventana, Flower Festival Pas de Deux, Pas de Sept from "A Folk Tale" (Helsted/Lumbye/Paulli, Bournonville; Staged by Stanley Williams)

* Closed Feb. 20, 1977 after 58 performances. Because of a musicians' strike performances were suspended for 5 weeks from Dec. 13, 1976 to Jan 25, 1977. The spring season opened Tuesday, May 3, 1977 and closed July 3, 1977 after 72 performances. Additions to the company were Toni Bentley, Paul Boos, Carole Divet, Peter Frame, Sean Lavery, Leslie Roy, Noelle Shader, and missing from the roster were Violette Verdy, Teena McConnell, Marnee Morris, and Leslie Brown. Jorge Donn was a guest artist.
ADDITIONS TO THE REPERTOIRE: "Le Baiser de la Fee" (Stravinsky), "Cortege Hongrois" (Glazounov), "Dybbuk Variations" (Bernstein, Robbins), "Harlequinade" (Drigo), "A Little Musical" (Stravinsky, Robbins) formerly "Dumbarton Oaks", "A Midsummer Night's Dream" (Mendelssohn), "Monumentum Pro Gesualdo and Movements for Piano and Orchestra" (Stravinsky), "Pas de Deux Meditation" (Tchaikovsky), "Tarantella" (Gottschalk/Kay), "Raymonda Variations" (Glazounov), "Scotch Symphony" (Mendelssohn), "Serenade" (Tchaikovsky), "Le Tombeau de Couperin" (Ravel), "La Valse" (Ravel), "Variations Pour Une Porte et Un Soupir" (Henry), "Watermill" (Ito, Robbins)
WORLD PREMIERE: Thursday, June 23, 1977 of "Vienna Waltzes" (Johann Strauss/Franz Lehar/Richard Strauss, George Balanchine; Conductor, Robert Irving; Costumes, Karinska; Scenery, Rouben Ter-Arutunian; Lighting, Ronald Bates) danced by the company. *NY PREMIERE:* Friday, June 17, 1977 of "Etude for Piano" (Scriabin, Balanchine; Costumes, Christina Giannini) a pas de deux danced by Patricia McBride and Jean-Pierre Bonnefous.

Martha Swope Photos

Top Right: Jorge Donn, Suzanne Farrell in "Vienna Waltzes" Below: Peter Martins (center) in "Vienna Waltzes"

Bart Cook, Sara Leland Above: Kay Mazzo,
Peter Martins Top: Sean Lavery, Karin
von Aroldingen all in "Vienna Waltzes"

Patricia McBride, Helgi Tomasson
Above and Top: "Vienna Waltzes"   33

"Bournonville Divertissements" Top Left: Merrill Ashley, Robert Weiss, Kyra Nichols
Below: Peter Martins, Suzanne Farrell Top Right: Patricia McBride, Helgi Tomasson
Below: Adam Luders, Muriel Aasen, all in "Bournonville Divertissements"

NEW YORK CITY BALLET

Gerard Ebitz, Kyra Nichols, Maria Calegari, Merrill Ashley, Peter Martins,
Colleen Neary, Sean Lavery in "Divertimento #15"

Maria Calegari, Kipling Houston,
Karin von Aroldingen in "Serenade"

Peter Schaufuss, Patricia McBride
in "Tchaikovsky Pas de Deux"

NEW YORK CITY BALLET 35

Bart Cook, Peter Martins, Daniel Duell, Heather Watts, Suzanne Farrell, Wilhelmina Frankfurt
in "The Goldberg Variations" Top: (L) Bart Cook, Merrill Ashley in "Square Dance" (R) Heather
Watts, Adam Luders in "Symphony in C"

NEW YORK CITY BALLET

Suzanne Farrell, Jorge Donn in "Meditation" *(Beverley Gallegos Photo)* **Top: Lawrence Matthews, Wilhelmina Frankfurt in "Western Symphony"**

Peter Schaufuss, Allegra Kent in "Episodes" Top: Renee Estopinal, David Richardson in "Bugaku"

NEW YORK CITY BALLET

Sheryl Ware in "Coppelia" Above: Jean-Pierre
Bonnefous in "Four Temperaments"

38   NEW YORK CITY BALLET

Muriel Aasen in "Union Jack" Above: Heather
Watts, Daniel Duell, Bonita Borne in "Jewels"
Top: Peter Martins, Suzanne Farrell in
"Afternoon of a Faun"

LIBRARY & MUSEUM OF PERFORMING ARTS
Friday, October 15, 1976

VIJA VETRA
in
"Dances of India"

LIBRARY & MUSEUM OF PERFORMING ARTS
Friday, November 12, 1976

VIJA VETRA
in
"Meditations"

A program of modern dance improvisations with music and poetry.

Nichol Hlenka in "Harlequinade"
Top: "Dances at a Gathering"
Right Center: "Chaconne"

DANCE PROGRAMS AT NEW YORK CITY CENTER

CITY CENTER 55th STREET THEATER
Opened Wednesday, October 13, 1976.*
The Foundation for the Joffrey Ballet (Anthony A, Bliss, Chairman; John C. Waddell, President) in association with the 55th Street Dance Theater Foundation (Howard M. Squadron, Chairman) presents:

THE JOFFREY BALLET
Twentieth Anniversary

Artistic Director-Choreographer, Robert Joffrey; Associate Director-Choreographer, Gerald Arpino; General Administrator, Peter S. Diggins; Music Director, Seymour Lipkin; Ballet Master, Scott Barnard; Conductor, Sung Kwak; Lighting Designers, Thomas Skelton, Jennifer Tipton; Associate Ballet Mistresses, Diane Orio, Diana Cartier Taylor; Associate Ballet Masters, Dermot Burke, Paul Sutherland; Production Supervisor, Penelope Curry; Executive Assistant, Mary Whitney; Staff Associates, Susan Higgins, Warren Rudd; Costume Supervisors, John Allen, Dorothy Coscia; Staff Assistants, Laurie Abramson, Carolyn Clarke

COMPANY

Cynthia Anderson, Charthel Arthur, Lisa Bradley, Francesca Corkle, Amy Danis, Ann Marie de Angelo, Ingrid Fraley, Susan Frazer, Rachel Ganteaume, Charlene Gehm, Jan Hanniford, Denise Jackson, Krystyna Jurkowski, Miyoko Kato, Carol Messmer, Pamela Nearhoof, Diane Orio, Beatriz Rodriguez, Donna Ross, Trinette Singleton, Lisa Slagle, Carole Valleskey, Berissa Welles, Jodi Wintz Darrell Barnett, Dermot Burke, Gary Chryst, Richard Colton, Robert Estner, Tom Fowler, Luis Fuente, Jerel Hilding, Christian Holder, Gregory Huffman, Jeffrey Hughes, Philip Jerry, Andrew Levinson, Kevin McKenzie, Roberto Medina, Dennis Poole, Paul Shoemaker, Russell Sultzbach, Paul Sutherland, Robert Thomas, William Whitener, Craig Williams

REPERTOIRE

"Square Dance" (Corelli/Vivaldi, Balanchine), "Feast of Ashes" (Surinach, Ailey), "Cakewalk" (Hershy Kay/Louis Moreau Gottschalk, Ruthanna Boris), "Olympics" (Toshiro Mayuzumi, Arpino), "Sea Shadow" (Michael Colgrass, Arpino), "Deuce Coupe II" (Beach Boys, Tharp), "Reflections" (Tchaikovsky, Arpino), "N.Y. Export: Op. Jazz" (Robert Prince, Robbins), "Drums, Dreams and Banjos" (Foster, Arpino), "Fanfarita" (Chapi/Wright, Arpino), "Astarte" (Crome Syrcus, Joffrey), "Tchaikovsky Pas de Deux" (Tchaikovsky, Balanchine), "The Relativity of Icarus" (Gerhard Samuel, Arpino), "Trinity" (Alan Raph/Lee Holdridge, Arpino), "Weewis" (Stanley Walden, Sappington), "As Time Goes By" (Haydn, Tharp), "Opus '65" (Macero, Sokolow), "Rodeo" (Copland, deMille), "Moves" (Robbins), "Viva Vivaldi!" (Vivaldi, Arpino), "The Moor's Pavane" (Purcell, Limon), "Kettentanz" (Strauss, Arpino), and *WORLD PREMIERE* Thursday, Oct. 21, 1976 of "Orpheus Times Light" (Jose Serebrier, Gerald Arpino; Set and Costumes, Willa Kim; Lighting, Thomas Skelton; Conductor, Jose Serebrier), and Wednesday, Nov. 3, 1976 of "Happily Ever After" (Snuffy Jenkins/Pappy Sherrill and the Hired Hands/Charlie Poole and the North Carolina Ramblers/Richard Peaslee, Twyla Tharp; Costumes, Santo Loquasto; Lighting, Jennifer Tipton)

Company Managers: Hans Mortig, Mindy Forman
Press: Robert Larkin, Ken Marini
Stage Managers: Richard Thorkelson, Pat Ballard, Tom Bucher

* Closed Nov. 7, 1976 after limited engagement of 31 performances. Returned for additional two weeks (Dec. 21, 1976–Jan. 2, 1977) and 16 performances. Limited repertoire consisted of "Pineapple Poll" (Sullivan, Blair after Cranko), "Petrouchka" (Stravinsky, Fokine), "The Dream" (Mendelssohn/Bartholdy, Ashton), "Rodeo" (Copland, deMille). The company's spring season (March 23–April 17, 1977) was canceled,

40   Cynthia Anderson, Christian Holder
in "Orpheus Times Light"

Top Left: Ingrid Fraley, Christian Holder,
Robert Thomas, Tom Van Cauwenbergh in
"Orpheus Times Light"

Ingrid Fraley, Miyoko Kato Above: Darrell
Barnett, Jerel Hilding, Robert Thomas,
Tom Van Cauwenbergh in "Orpheus Times Light"

Beatriz Rodriguez, Russell Sultzbach in "Rodeo"
Top: Ann Marie De Angelo in "Happily Ever
After" (title changed to "Cacklin' Hen")

Gary Chryst, Christian Holder
in "The Moor's Pavane"

Luis Fuente, Ann Marie De Angelo in "Fanfarita"
Top: "Drums, Dreams and Banjos"

JOFFREY BALLET

Denise Jackson, Kevin McKenzie in "Tchaikovsky Pas de Deux" Top: "Reflections"

Denise Jackson, Paul Sutherland in "Kettentanz"

JOFFREY BALLET

"Rodeo" Top Left: Kevin McKenzie, Denise Jackson in "The Dream"
Top Right: Dennis Poole in "Pineapple Poll" Below: "Trinity"

JOFFREY BALLET

Gregory Huffman in "Rodeo" Above: "Moves"
Top: "Square Dance"

Donna Cowen, Pamela Nearhoof in "Viva Vivaldi!"
Top: Russell Sultzbach in "The Relativity
of Icarus"

JOFFREY BALLET

45

**Donna Wood, Carl Paris
in "Blood Memories"**

Opened Wednesday, December 1, 1976.*
Dance Theater Foundation (Edward Lander, Executive Director) in association with 55th Street Dance Theater Foundation (Howard M. Squadron, Chairman) presents:

ALVIN AILEY AMERICAN DANCE THEATER

Artistic Director-Choreographer, Alvin Ailey; Musical Director-Conductor, Joyce Brown; Guest Conductor, Howard Roberts; Lighting Supervisor, Chenault Spence; Operations Director, R. Robert Lussier; Wardrobe Supervisor, Ann Goodson; Wardrobe Master, Duane Talley; Managerial Coordinator, Lois Framhein; Administrative Assistant, Arthur Fisher; Artistic Director Alvin Ailey Repertory Ensemble, Sylvia Waters

COMPANY

Charles Adams, Sarita Allen, Marla Bingham, Enid Britten, Sergio Cal, Masazumi Chaya, Ulysses Dove, Judith Jamison, Melvin Jones, Mari Kajiwara, Anita Littleman, Jodi Moccia, Michihiko Oka, Carl Paris, Beth Shorter, Warren Spears, Estelle Spurlock, Clive Thompson, Marvin Tunney, Elbert Watson, Dudley Williams, Donna Wood, Peter Woodin, Tina Yuan
GUEST ARTISTS: Brother John Sellers, George Tipton, Bernard Thacker, Alvin Ailey Repertory Ensemble

REPERTOIRE

"Three Black Kings" (Duke Ellington, Alvin Ailey), "Liberian Suite" (Ellington, Lester Horton/James Truitte), "Caravan" (Ellington/Michael Kamen, Louis Falco), "Gazelle" (David Newman/Art Blakey/Yusef Lateef, George Faison), "Cry" (Alice Coltrane/Laura Nyro/Voices of East Harlem, Ailey), "Revelations" (Traditional, Ailey), "Rainbow 'Round My Shoulder" (Arranged by Robert de Cormier and Milton Okun from John and Alan Lomax Collection, Donald McKayle), "Blues Suite" (Traditional, Ailey), "After Eden" (Lee Hoiby, John Butler), "The Road of the Phoebe Snow" (Ellington/Strayhorn, Talley Beatty), "Portrait of Billie" (Billie Holiday/Butler), "Songs for Young Lovers" (Popular, Judith Willis), "Journey" (Charles Ives, Joyce Trisler), "Myth" (Stravinsky, Ailey), "The Lark Ascending" (Ralph Vaughan Williams, Ailey), "Night Creature" (Ellington, Ailey), "Missa Brevis" (Zoltan Kodaly, Jose Limon), "Deep South Suite" (Ellington, Dianne McIntyre) with Alvin Ailey Repertory Ensemble, and *WORLD PREMIERES* of "Facets" (Bessie Smith/Ethel Waters/Dinah Washington/Lena Horne/LaBelle, John Butler; Costumes, Jane Greenwood; Lighting, Thomas Skelton; Decor, Irving Milton Duke) danced by Judith Jamison (Wednesday, Dec. 1, 1976), "Hobo Sapiens" (Stevie Wonder/Billy Preston, George Faison; Decor, Irving Milton Duke; Lighting, Shirley Prendergast) danced by Dudley Williams (Tuesday, Dec. 7, 1976), "Blood Memories" (Howard Roberts, Donald McKayle; Design, Vittorio Capecce; Costumes, Hugh Sherrer; Lighting/Projections, Chenault Spence; Conductor, Howard Roberts) danced by the company (Thursday, Dec. 9, 1976)

Company Manager: Lois Framhein
Press: Gurtman and Murtha, Meg Gordean
Stage Managers: Ralph McWilliams, Peter H. Brown

* Closed Dec. 19, 1976 after limited engagement of 23 performances. Returned Wednesday, May 4, through May 22, 1977 for 23 additional performances. New members of the company were Alistair Butler, Dianne Maroney, Michele Simmons. Guest Stars from National Ballet of Cuba were Maria Elena Llorente, Lazaro Carreno dancing "El Rio y El Bosque," and "Plasmasisi" Additions to the repertoire were "According to Eve" (George Crumb, John Butler), "Love Songs" (Donny Hathaway/Nina Simone,Ailey), *Company Premieres* of "Coverage II" (Tape, Rudy Perez) and "Countdown" (Madaline Gray, Rudy Perez) both danced by Clive Thompson; *NY Premieres* of "Ancestral Voices" (Tape, Cecil Taylor, Dianne McIntyre; Design, Romare Bearden) danced by the company, "Crossword" (Burt Allcantata, Jennifer Muller; Design, Randy Barcelo; Lighting, Richard Nelson) danced by the company (May 4, 1977), and *WORLD PREMIERE* May 4, 1977 of "The Wait" (Antonio Vivaldi, Milton Myers; Lighting, Chenault Spence) danced by Judith Jamison.

**Top Left: Judith Jamison in "Facets"
Left Center: "Blood Memories"**

*Photos by Jack Vartoogian, Ron Reagan, William Burd,
Ellen Gibbs Chiemiego, Jack Mitchell, Charles Slatkin,
Alan Bergman, Donald Moss, Fred Fehl, Mario Ruiz*

"Ancestral Voices" also above
(Ron Reagan Photos) Top: Dudley
Williams in "Hobo Sapiens"

Maria Llorente, Lazaro Carrena in "El Rio y El
Bosque" Above: Mari Kujiwara in "Journey"
Top: Clive Thompson in "Coverage"

Elbert Watson, Donna Wood in "Road of the Phoebe Snow" Top: Tina Yuan in "Gazelle"

"Crosswords" Above: Dudley Williams in "Caravan" Top: Clive Thompson in "Countdown"

48

ALVIN AILEY DANCE THEATER

**Donna Wood in "Gazelle" Above: "Night Creature"
Top: Judith Jamison in "The Wait"**

**Mari Kajiwara, Melvin Jones, Judith Jamison
in "Revelations" Above: Michihiko Oka, Tina
Yuan in "After Eden" Top: "Portrait of Billie"**

CITY CENTER 55 STREET THEATER
Opened Wednesday, January 5, 1977.*
Ballet Theatre Foundation (Justin Colin, President) in association with
City Center of Music and Drama presents:

AMERICAN BALLET THEATRE

Directors, Lucia Chase, Oliver Smith; Associate Director, Antony Tudor; Assistant Director, Enrique Martinez; Music Director, Akira Endo; Regisseur, Dimitri Romanoff; Ballet Masters, Michael Lland, Scott Douglas, Jurgen Schneider; Conductor, Patrick Flynn; Lighting, Nananne Porcher; Assistant Ballet Master, Terry Orr; Production Associate, Marion Kinsella; Production Assistant, Dana Bruce

COMPANY

Karena Brock, Fernando Bujones, William Carter, Eleanor D'Antuono, Cynthia Gregory, Gelsey Kirkland, Ted Kivitt, Natalia Makarova, Yoko Morishita, Ivan Nagy, Terry Orr, Marcos Paredes, John Prinz, Marianna Tcherkassky, Clark Tippet, Martine van Hamel, Charles Ward, Sallie Wilson, Gayle Young
Warren Conover, George de la Pena, Kristine Elliott, Nanette Glushak, Marie Johansson, Ruth Mayer, Jolinda Menendez, Hilda Morales, Michael Owen, Kirk Peterson, Richard Schafer, Frank Smith, Rebecca Wright
Brian Adams, Elizabeth Ashton, Victor Barbee, Carmen Barth, Michelle Benash, Amy Blaisdell, Nancy Collier, Fanchon Cordell, David Cuevas, Laurie Feinstein, Peter Fonseca, Cynthia Gast, Meg Gordon, Rodney Gustafson, Aurea Hammerli, Cynthia Harvey, Alina Hernandez, Janne Jackson, Roman Jasinski, Susan Jones, Francia Kovak, Elaine Kudo, Lisa Lockwood, Charles Maple, Sara Maule, Eric Nesbitt, Gregory Osborne, Berthica Prieto, Cathryn Rhodes, Lisa Rinehart, Maia Rosal, Miguel Sanchez, Raymond Serrano, Janet Shibata, Kristine Soleri, Christine Spizzo, Carla Stallings, David Wallach, Denise Warner, Patricia Wesche, Sandall Whitaker, Cheryl Yeager

REPERTOIRE

"Coppelia" (Delibes, Martinez), "Giselle" (Adam, Blair)

General Manager: Daryl Dodson
Press: Charles France, Ellen Levene, Elena Gordon
Stage Managers: Dan Butt, Jerry Rice, Peter Gardner

* Closed Jan. 30, 1977 after limited engagement of 28 performances.

Martha Swope, Beverley Gallegos, Kenn Duncan Photos

**Fernando Bujones
in "Coppelia"**

**Ted Kivitt, Cynthia Gregory Top Left:
Clark Tippet, Martine Van Hammel
in "Coppelia"**

Marianna Tcherkassky, Ivan Nagy
Top: Cynthia Gregory, Ted Kivitt
in "Giselle"

Eleanor D'Antuono, Ted Kivitt Above:
Cynthia Gregory Top: Jolinda Menendez
in "Giselle"

51

CITY CENTER 55th STREET THEATER
Opened Wednesday, March 9, 1977.*
Original Ballets Foundation, Inc. in association with 55th Street Dance
Theater Foundation, Inc. presents:

ELIOT FELD BALLET

Artistic Director-Choreographer, Eliot Feld; Administrator, Cora
Cahan; Assistant, Catherine Paull; Assistants to Mr. Feld, Christine
Sarry, George Montalbano; Administrative Assistant, Candace Ler-
man; Wardrobe Master, Kristina Kaiser; Sound, Roger Jay; Pia-
nists, Gladys Celeste Mercader, Peter Longiaru; Lighting Design,
Thomas Skelton

COMPANY

Michael Auer, Arturo Azito, Helen Douglas, Mona Eigh, Eliot Feld,
Richard Gilmore, Michaela Hughes, Cynthia Irion, Charles Ken-
nedy, Edmund LaFosse, Remus Marcu, Linda Miller, Gregory
Mitchell, George Montalbano, Mark Morris, Jennifer Palo, Shirley
Reevie, Christine Sarry, Jeff Satinoff, Paul Stewart, Susan Rowe,
Gwynn Taylor
GUEST ARTIST: Mikhail Baryshnikov

REPERTOIRE

"Harbinger" (Prokofiev, Feld), "The Gods Amused" (Debussy,
Feld) "The Consort" (Dowland/Neusidler/Others/Jaffe, Feld),
"Intermezzo" (Brahms, Feld), "The Real McCoy" (Gershwin,
Feld), "At Midnight" (Mahler, Feld), "A Soldier's Tale" (Stra-
vinsky, Feld), "Waves" (Spiegel, Posin) "Tzaddik" (Copland, Feld),
"Cortege Parisien" (Chabrier, Feld) "Excursions" (Barber, Feld),
and *WORLD PREMIERES* of "Variations on 'America' " (Charles
Ives/William Schuman, Eliot Feld; Costumes, Willa Kim; Lighting,
Thomas Skelton; Conductor, Gerard Schwarz) on Wednesday,
March 9, 1977 danced by Mikhail Baryshnikov and Christine Sarry,
"A Footstep of Air" (Beethoven, Eliot Feld; Costumes, Willa Kim;
Lighting, Thomas Skelton; Conductor, Gerard Schwarz) on Satur-
day, March 12, 1977 danced by the company.

Company Manager; G. Warren McClane
Press: Merle Debuskey, Susan L. Schulman, William Schelble
Stage Managers: John H. Paull III, Bruce Goldstein, Zack
Arkontaky

* Closed March 20, 1977 after limited engagement of 13 performances.

Herb Migdoll Photos

"Harbinger"

**Richard Gilmore, Eliot Feld, John Sowinski
in "Tzaddik" Top Left: Mikhail
Baryshnikov, Christine Sarry in "Variations
on America"** *(Beverley Gallegos Photo)*

Helen Douglas, Edmund LaFosse, Linda Miller
in "Gods Amused" Above: Christine Sarry in
"Excursions" Top: "Harbinger"

George Montalbano, Linda Miller in "Intermezzo"
(Lois Greenfield Photo) Top: Michael Hughes, Eliot
Feld in "The Real McCoy"

53

BROOKLYN ACADEMY DANCE PROGRAMS

BROOKLYN ACADEMY OF MUSIC/OPERA HOUSE
Opened Tuesday, October 20, 1976.*
The Brooklyn Academy of Music presents:

PENNSYLVANIA BALLET

Director, Barbara Weisberger; Artistic Director, Benjamin Harkarvy; General Manager, Timothy Duncan; Artistic Administrator, Richard Carter; Music Director, Maurice Kaplow; Ballet Mistress, Fiona Fuerstner; Ballet Masters, Robert Rodham, William Thompson; Lighting Design, David K. H. Elliott; Costume Supervisor, E. Huntington Parker; Wardrobe Mistress, Lillian Avery; Assistant Conductor, Daniel Forlano; Solo Pianist, Martha Koeneman; Assistant Manager, Judith von Scheven

COMPANY

Brian Andrew, Dana Arey, Elaine Austin, Marcia Darhower, William DeGregory, Gregory Drotar, Jeffrey Gribler, Tamara Hadley, Mark Hochman, Linda Karash, David Kloss, Dane LaFontsee, Cherylyn Lavagnino, Barry Leon, Sherry Lowenthal, Michelle Lucci, James Mercer, Adam Miller, Melissa Mitchell, Edward Myers, Anya Patton, Melissa Podcassy, Robin Preiss, Constance Ross, Barbara Sandonato, Janek Schergen, Missy Yancey
GUESTS ARTISTS: Martine van Hamel, Burton Taylor

REPERTOIRE

"Adagio Hannerklavier" (Beethoven, Hans van Manen), "Raymonda Variations" (Glazounov, Balanchine), and *NY Premieres* of "For Fred, Gene and M-G-M" (Aaron Copland, Benjamin Harkarvy), "Four Men Waiting" (Saint-Saens, Harkarvy), "Under the Sun" (Kamen, Sappington), "Eakins' View" (Charles Ives, Rodney Griffin)

Press: Charles Ziff, Kate MacIntyre, Amy R. Karash
Stage Managers: Rosemary Cunningham, Lawrence E. Sterner, Tom Hinsdale

* Closed October 24, 1976 after limited engagement of 7 performances. Returned April 26 - May 1, 1977 for 7 additional performances. The repertoire included "Concerto Grosso" (Handel, Charles Czarny), "Recital for Cello and Eight Dancers" (Bach, Harkarvy), "Allegro Brillante" (Tchaikovsky, Balanchine), "Under the Sun" (Kamen, Sappington), "The Moor's Pavane" (Purcell, Limon), "Grand Pas Espagnol" (Moszkowski, Harkarvy), "Serenard" (Tchaikovsky, Balanchine), and *NY Premiere* of "From Gentle Circles" (Dvorak, Harkarvy)

Ron Reagan Photos

Michelle Lucci (C) in "Under the Sun" Top Right: Dane LaFontsee, Marcia Darhower in "For Fred, Gene and M-G-M"

**"Eakins View"
Above: "Raymonda Variations"**

54

BROOKLYN ACADEMY OF MUSIC/PLAYHOUSE
December 9–19, 1976 (8 performances)
Sheldon Soffer presents:

LES BALLETS TROCKADERO DE MONTE CARLO

Artistic Directors, Peter Anastos, Natch Taylor; General Manager, Eugene McDougle; Lighting Design-Technical Director, Druth McClure; Regisseuse, Betteann Terrell; Press, Anne Obert Weinberg

COMPANY

Olga Tchikaboumskaya (Peter Anastos), Alexis Lermontov and Suzina LaFuzziovitch (Natch Taylor) Natasha Veceslova and Aubrey Smythe-Wickes (Clinton W. Smith), Zamarina Zamarkova (Zamie Zamora), Dame Margaret Lowin-Octeyn (Brent Mason), Ida Neversayneva (Leland Walsh), Bertha Vinayshinsky (Joel Paley), Noximova (William Curtis Gooden), Vera Namethatunova (William Toth), Ludmilla Redrova-Komova

REPERTOIRE

"Swan Lake" (Tchaikovsky), "Spring Waters" (Rachmaninoff), "The Dying Swan" (Saint-Saens), "Go for Barocco" (Bach), "Les Biches" (Poulenc), "Les Sylphides" (Chopin), "Phaedra/Monotonous" (AC/DC), "Harlequinade Pas de Deux," "Ecole de Ballet" (Pastiche), "Sweetsweatsuitsuite"

Kenn Duncan Photos

"Go for Barocco"

"Swan Lake" and also above

BROOKLYN ACADEMY OF MUSIC/LEPERCQ SPACE
February 24–27, 1977 (4 performances)
The Brooklyn Academy of Music presents:

CHUCK DAVIS DANCE COMPANY

Artistic Director-Choreographer, Chuck Davis; Musical Director-Master Drummer, Yomi Yomi Awolowo; Ballet Master, Ibraheim Camara; Stage/Production Manager, N'Goma Vyeit Vyusi; Wardrobe Mistress, Juanita Tyler; Press, Elsie Washington; Management, Bess Pruitt Associates; Administrative Assistant, Audrey Benjamin

COMPANY
Chuck Davis

Marilyn Banks
Onika Bgemon
Lansana Diarrah

Normadien Gibson
Juanita Tyler
Charles Wynn

REPERTOIRE: "Dyembe & Chant," "Molu Yamee," "Konkoba," "Shakeres," "Yarabi," "Isicathulo," "Ritual," "Sea Ritual," "Women's Dance," "Watutsi," "KalunJi-Yi," "Bantaba," "Homge"

Chuck Davis Dance Company
(Irene Gertik Photo)

55

Twyla Tharp in "Sue's Leg"

Christine Uchida, Jennifer Way, Shelley
Washington in "Hodge Podge"

Christine Uchida, Raymond Kurshals, Shelley
Washington, Richard Colton in "Mud"

BROOKLYN ACADEMY OF MUSIC
May 12–22, 1977 (12 performances)
The Brooklyn Academy of Music presents:

TWYLA THARP AND DANCERS

Director-Choreographer, Twyla Tharp; Administrators, Christine Estes, Arthur O'Connor; Costumes, Santo Loquasto, Kerrmit Love, Robert Huot; Lighting Design, Jennifer Tipton; Press, Charles Ziff, Kate MacIntyre

COMPANY

Twyla Tharp	Christine Uchida
Rose Marie Wright	Raymond Kurshals
Tom Rawe	Richard Colton
Jennifer Way	Kimmary Williams
Shelley Washington	Joseph Lennon

GUEST ARTISTS: Sara Rudner, Kenneth Rinker, Gary Chryst, Paul Simon

REPERTOIRE

"The Hodge Podge" (Paul Simon, Tharp), "The Bix Pieces" (Bix Biederbecke, Tharp), "Country Dances" (Traditional, Tharp), "Cacklin' Hen" (Folk, Tharp), "Half the One Hundreds" (Tharp), "Sue's Leg" (Fats Waller, Tharp), "The Fugue" (Tharp), and *WORLD PREMIERE* of "Mud" (Mozart, Tharp; Costumes, Santo Loquasto) on Thursday, May 12, 1977.

Tom Rawe, Twyla Tharp, Rose Marie Wright,
Kenneth Rinker in "Sue's Leg"

THE CUBICULO

Artistic Director, Philip Meister; Managing Director, Elaine Sulka; Business Manager, Barbara Crow; Program Coodinators, John Dudich, Dinah Carlson; Technical Director, William Lambert; Press, Dinah Carlson

THE CUBICULO

Monday & Tuesday, June 21 & 22, 1976

GELMAN/PALIDOFSKY DANCE THEATRE: Artistic Directors, Linda Gelman, Meade Palidofsky; Dancers, Greta Buck, Linda Gelman, Barbara Smith Kerwin, Jean Morgan, Meade Palidofsky, Pamela Ross, Paul Zuckerman; Lighting, John B. North; Production Coordinator, Paul Zuckerman; Production Assistant, David Rothenberg. PROGRAM: "3 Dialogues for 2 Voices and 2 Bodies" (Palidofsky, Gelman/Kerwin/Morgan), "Midwest/Summer" (Palidofsky), "Occurrences and Connections" (Gelman), "Cat's Cradle" (Greta Buck/Mead Alidofsky, Gelman), "Six Impossible Things before Breakfast" (Palidofsky, Gelman)

Monday & Tuesday, June 28 & 29, 1976

BRUCE PACOT AND DANCE COMPANY: Jane Benedict, Jane Comfort, Gail Conrad, John DeWees, Ellen Ducker, Peter Greggitt, Ann Hohn, David Malamut, Mitzi Maxwell, Cynthia May, Iris Olshin, Bruce Pacot, Robin Shimel, Maria Valdez; Choreography, Bruce Pacto. PROGRAM: "Premonition," "Wheatfields," "Triptychs" (*Premiere*)

Friday & Saturday, July 2 & 3, 1976

EIKO & KOMA in "White Dance"

Monday & Tuesday, July 5 & 6, 1976

CUBICULO DANCE RETROSPECTIVE: "Other Times" choreographed and danced by Sally Gross; "Brahms Variations on a Theme by Paganini" choreographed and danced by Dianne Hulburt; "Phosphate" performed by Eva DeKievit; "Shimmy Sh-ush" choreographed by Sheila Sobel and danced by her with Marlene Novitsky; "Beginning" (Carl Michaelson) choreographed and danced by Betsy Wetzig; "Alone" (Collage) choreographed and danced by Gael Stepanek;

Friday & Saturday, July 9 & 10, 1976

CUBICULO DANCE RETROSPECTIVE II: "Energy" (Paul Horn) choreographed and performed by Betty Martyn; "In the Spirit of Isadora" (Schumann) choreographed and danced by Judith Saltz; "Ichthyosauria" (Klausmeyer) choreographed and danced by Kent Baker; "Dimensions of Conflict" (Bartok) choreographed and danced by Judith Schmukler; "To Fred and the Late Show" (Ruby Brass) choreographed and danced by Judith Saltz; Excerpt from "Wintershape" (Carlos) choreographed and danced by Kent Baker; "Josephine Bracken" (Stockhausen, Alejandro) danced by Rika Burnham; "The Keeper" (Pennison) choreographed and danced by Marleen Pennison

Monday & Tuesday, October 18 & 19, 1976

KATHRYN PAPALE DANCE COLLECTION: Pamela Smith, Kathryn Papale, Judith Phelps; Choreography by Kathryn Papale; Costumes, Judith Phelps. PROGRAM: "Probe," "When They Dress Like That They're Asking for Trouble," "Puck 'n' High Heels"

OIBRE EALAIN DANCE COMPANY: David-John Basque, Deidre Glasheen, Kristin Moore, Georgina Sculco. PROGRAM: "Crossings," "Outlist"

Friday & Saturday, October 22 & 23, 1976

A BAKER'S HALF DOZEN: Kent Baker, Roberta Diamond, Joan Gedney, Jody Oberfelder, Dale Orrin, Dale Thompson; Director-Choreographer, Kent Baker; Lighting, Craig Evans; Assistant, Patricia Evans; Costumes, Kent Baker, Joan Gedney. PROGRAM: "Doily" (Bernard Herrmann) "Gallery"

Monday & Tuesday, October 25 & 26, 1976

JUDE BARTLETT AND DANCERS: Ellen Jacob, Janna Jensen; Choreography, Jude Bartlett; Lighting, Michael Kasper. PROGRAM: "Sunny Satie" (Satie), "Swimmers" (Ives), "Six Bagatelles" (Webern), "Nemesis" (Schuman), "Nightshift" (Copland)

Friday & Saturday, October 29 & 30, 1976

"Dances with Words" choreographed by FRANCES ALENIKOFF; Director, Edward M. Cohen; performed by Dalienne Majors, Myrna Packer, Frances Alenikoff, Kenneth Fischer, Tod Miller. PROGRAM: "I Don't Want to Kiss Your Mouth of Salt," "The One of No Way" (Charlie Morrow), "Zero Sum" (Steven Shea); Lighting, Bob Lampel; Stage Managers, Andy Lopata, Paul Leavin

Top Right: Eiko and Koma in "White Dance"
(R) Marleen Pennison Below: Bruce
Pacot in "Triptychs"
Right Center: Kent Baker in "Doily" *(Sandy Geis Photo)*

Dalienne Majors, Myrna Packer, Frances Alenikoff in "I Don't Want to Kiss . . ." *(Don Manza Photo)*

THE CUBICULO

Monday & Tuesday, December 6 & 7, 1976

JORGE SAMANIEGO WORKS IN CONCERT with Elizabeth Gottlieb, Nancy Cruz, Kenneth Macdonald, Sandra Lynn, Laura Lange, Allen Sobek, Lee Larkin. PROGRAM: "Opus Four Women" (Beethoven, Samaniego), "Take Two" (Beethoven, Elizabeth Gottlieb), "Arrived" (Prokofiev, Samaniego), "Prologue" (Voices, Samaniego); Costumes, Samaniego; Lighting, Emily Jefferson

Monday & Tuesday, December 13 & 14, 1976

SHEILA SOBEL & THE MWC DANCE COMPANY: Sheila Sobel, Laura McCarthy, Jane Regan, Patricia Usakowska, Judith Benari, Viva Beck, Cindy Kanewischer, Diann Krevsky, performing "Shimmy SH-ush" and *Premiere* of "Moving Road Song"

THOMAS HOLT DANCE ENSEMBLE: Thomas Holt, Lucinda Gehrke, Norbert DuBois, Allan Seward, Ann Moser, Carol Elsner Frezza, JoAnne Kuhn performing "Duet for Summer" (Holdridge), "In Autumn to Romp" (Bartok), "The Conception of the Nativity" (Handel); Choreography by Thomas Holt

Friday & Saturday, December 17 & 18, 1976

TWO OF A FASHION: CANDICE CHRISTAKOS & GAEL STEPANEK performing "Downtown Blues" (Jim Kweskins Jug Band, Stepanek), "In Escape" (Krumb, Donald Blumenfield), "Le Danser" (Jane Birkin, Stepanek), "3 A.M." (Thomas Dillow, Christakos), "Madrigal" (Dillow, Christakos), "Portrait of 3" (Mozart/Average White Band, Stepanek)

Monday & Tuesday, January 24 & 25, 1977

SERENA & DANCERS in "Daughters of a Vanished Sultan": Artistic Director-Choreography, Serena; Dancers: Julia Baldachino, Diana Castellon, Lerma Chen, Zoe Dixey, Nina Grand, Mary Lydon, Amelia Martinez, Linda Mills, Claudia Murphy, Jill Paznik, Hertha Poje, Joy Silver, Jan Vanture, La Donn Amato, Helen Adams, Phyllis Finley, Cail Menchenfreund, Michele Russo, Linda Thomas, Billie Warren

Friday & Saturday, January 28 & 29, 1977

WORKWITH DANCERS COMPANY: David Briggs, Nancy Hill, Dianne McPherson Hulburt, Dennis Kocjan, Jacqueline McKannay, Rosemary Newton, Susan Osberg, Catherine D. Sullivan; Lighting-Stage Manager, Myra Koutzen. PROGRAM: "Danses Sacree et Profane" (Debussy, David Briggs), "Twone Verse/Quartet" (Traditional, Dianne McPherson Hulburt), "Brambles" (Scriabin, Susan Osberg), "Street Scene" (Bartok, Hulburt), "Incantations to Emily" (Copland, Osberg), "Stravinsky's Violin Concerto" (Stravinsky, Briggs), "A Night at the Bijou" (Collage, Osberg)

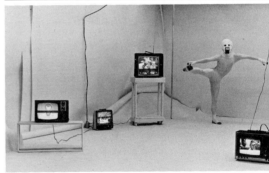

Monday & Tuesday, January 31 & February 1, 1977

ELLEN GOLDMAN & SANDY JAMROG in Concert: "Shepherds Hey" (Grainger, Jamrog), "Shadows" (Robert Kogan, Goldman), "Hymn" (Judy Collins/Joshua Rifkin, Jamrog), "Silverpoint" (Sound Effects/Bob Rosen, Goldman), "Two/One" (Murooka, Jamrog), "Jitterbug" (Stockhausen, Goldman)

Friday & Saturday, February 4 & 5, 1977

ELAINE SUMMERS DANCE & FILM COMPANY: Program: "City People Moving" (Carmen Moore), "What Does She Think She Is Doing?" "Energy Changes" "Interchange" (Philip Corner, Summers), "Tumble Dance" (McDowell), "Two Girls Downtown Iowa," "Theater Piece for Chairs and Ladders," "Iowa Blizzard '73," "Country Houses," "Mini-Illuminated Workingman"

Friday & Saturday, February 11 & 12, 1977

REYNALDO ALEJANDRO & LESLIE JANE with Michael Kane, Penny Hutchinson, Cassandra Crowley, Pamela Schick, Rika Burnham, Jose Rizal, Rodgee Cao, Priscilla Brownlee, Jane Battipaglia; Lighting and Set, Guy J. Smith; Stage Manager, Shirley McPherson. PROGRAM: "Sehnsucht" (Mahler, Leslie Jane), "Sumasampalataya" (Michael Dadap, Alejandro), "Song to a Seagull" (Joni Mitchell, Jane), "OOSei-San" (Partch, Alejandro), "To the Flowers of Heidelberg" (Bo Lawergren, Alejandro), "Josephine Bracken" (Stockhausen, Alejandro), "Cycle" (Stravinsky, Jane), "Salome" (Lou Harrison, Alejandro)

Monday & Tuesday, February 14 & 15, 1977

SATORU SHIMAZAKI and Dancers: Barbara Finney Berkey, Nancy Hall, Juliet Neidish, Susan Peters, Susan Tamlyn, Robbie Tessler, performing "Dance Gallery" (choreography, Satoru Shimazaki)

Top: MWC Dance Company in "Shimmy Sh-ush"
(Barnet Silver Photo)
Below: Reynaldo Alejandro Dance Theater

Serena
Above: Satoru Shimazaki

THE CUBICULO

Monday & Tuesday, March 28 & 29, 1977
Seven Solo Dances by KATHY DUNCAN accompanied by Tom Johnson: "Aba," "Shoe Shift," "Along a Line," "Broken Mirror Waltz," "Fall Wall," "Counting Ceremony," "Running out of Breath"

Friday & Saturday, April 1 & 2, 1977
THE CLEAR MIME COMPANY: Inese Brunins, Donna Jacobson, Susan McCarthy, Lynn Sonneman, Helene Webb, performing "Glass House" (John Barone), "The Dancer" (Brian D. J. Flahive, Susan McCarthy), "The Look Game" (Music Boxes, McCarthy)
ANA MARIE FORSYTHE COMPANY: Jane Hedal, Richard R. Pierlon, Ana Marie Forsythe, Carlos A. Duran, Lynn Frielinghaus, Theodore Pollen III, Nedra Marlin-Harris performing "A Time of Darkness" (Boulanger, Forsythe), "Grand Pas de Deux Moderne" (John D. Parkinson, Forsythe), "El Baile" (Santana, Forsythe)

April 4–6, 1977 (3 performances)
THE PUMP PARABLE (Burling McAllester) with John Bernd, Judy Burrows, David Freelander, Janice Geller, Aviva Glass, Keith Goodman, Drew Hoag, Mimi Huntington, Didi Levy, Bob Marinaccio, Bur McAllester, Molly McGuire, Fran Parker, Marta Renzi, Mark Weiboldt

Friday & Saturday, April 8 & 9, 1977
KARIN ADIR performing an evening of mime and comedy
CLEAR DANCE LINES COMPANY: Artistic Director, Sheila Kaminsky; Co-Artistic Director, Helen Adams; Company, Sheila Kaminsky, Helen Adams, Martha Caust, Rika Burnham, Barbara Salmon, performing "Reverberations" (Crumb, Kaminsky), "Rites" (Kabuki, Kaminsky), "Little Fallings" (Ashley, Adams) "Free-Space" (Collage, Kaminsky), "Markings" (Randall McClellan, Kaminsky/Adams), "Take 4" (Xenakis/Oliveros, Kaminsky)

Tuesday & Wednesday, April 11 & 12, 1976
BILL KIRKPATRICK in "Dangerous Rhythm" with Bob McDowell, Patricia Yenawine, Eva Vazquez, Gael Stepanek, performing "Fit to Be Tied" (Tape, Kirkpatrick), "Retainer" (Kirkpatrick), and *Premieres* of "Introductory Offer" (Leo Kraft, Kirkpatrick), "Maneuvers" (Kirkpatrick), "Dangerous Rhythm" (Biederbeck/Freddie Taylor/others, Kirkpatrick)

Monday & Tuesday, May 16 & 17, 1977
JAZZ DANCE THEATRE: Director-Choreographer, Jean Sabatine; Lighting, Pamela Chestek; Costumes, Montez King; Dancers: Mary Lou Belli, Susan Belli, Aida DeQuick, Jeff French, David G. Hodge, Martha Kent, Rob Lehman, Deborah Girasek, Thomas P. O'Leary, James Smith, Audrey Tischler, William Morgan, Jean Sabatine, performing "Junk Yard Punk" (Selected, Sabatine), "Impressions of the Blues" (Yusef Lateef, Sabatine), "Nameless Hour" (Davis/Cobham/Ellington, Sabatine), "Anne Boleyn" (Wakeman, Sabatine), "Affair" (Evans, Sabatine), "Impasse" (Hancock/Lateef/Laws, Sabatine), "Trilogy" (Grover Washington, Jr./Bob James, Sabatine)

Thursday - Saturday, May 19–21, 1977
MARLEEN PENNISON and Dancers: Thomas Wilkinson, Peter Bass; Lighting Design, Blu; Stage Managers, Holly Johnson, Technical Director, Ron Daley; Press, Dinah Carlson; Choreography, Marleen Pennison. PROGRAM: "Bethena Before" (Scott Joplin), "Bethena After" (Joplin), "One Dance in the Shape of a Couple" (Pennison), "In Absentia" (*Premiere*), "The Keeper" (Sound Mix), "River Road Sweet" (Hawley/Lewis/Miller, Pennison)

Monday & Tuesday, May 23 & 24, 1977
ROLANDO JORIF DANCE COMPANY: Gloria Bailen, Beverley Ann Brown, Martin Cofsky, Rolando Jorif, Juliana Rabal, performing "Songs" (Odetta/Robeson), "Novella" (Hageman), "B's Boogie" (Buck Hammer/Benny Goodman)

May 26–28, 1977 (3 performances)
MICHAEL SULLIVAN DANCE COMPANY: Kevin Keenan, Michaele Sallade, Michael Sullivan (Choreographer), Phoebe Neville (Guest Artist) dancing "Ice," "Little of This Little of That" (Bach), "I'm OK, You're. . . .(Wagner), "304" (Beaver/Krause); Lighting Design, Ron Daley; Stage Manager, Tom Lyons; Company Manager, Kaylyn Sullivan

Monday & Tuesday, May 30, June 1, 1977
JUNKO KIKUCHI & VICTORIA LARRAIN with Pilar Urreta, Felix Lindrey, Jonas Dalbecchi, dancing "Breeze" (Junko Kikuchi), "Latin American Fragments" (Barbieri, Lorrain)

Top Right: Ana Marie Forsythe *(Susan Cook Photo)*
Below: Rolando Jorif (on floor)

Victoria Larrain
Above: Junko Kikuchi
(Thomas Haar Photo)   59

DANCE UMBRELLA

ROUNDABOUT STAGE ONE
October 27–31, 1976 (7 performances)
Dance Umbrella (Michael Kasdan, Administrator) presents:

CONTEMPORARY DANCE SYSTEM

Artistic Director, Daniel Lewis; Resident Choreographer, Anna Sokolow; Musical Director, Stanley Sussman; Lighting Design, Edward Effron; Conductor, David Fein; Stage Manager, David Rosenberg; Rehearsal Director, Nancy Scattergood Jordan; Press, Meg Gordean

COMPANY

Pierre Barreau
Matthew Diamond
Randall Faxon
Laura Glenn
Peter Healey

Hannah Kahn
Daniel Lewis
Jim May
Victor Vargas
Teri Weksler

REPERTOIRE

"Nightspell" (Priaulx Rainier, Doris Humphrey), "Steps of Silence" (Anatole Vieru, Anna Sokolow), "And First They Slaughtered the Angels" (Berlioz/Pachelbel/Ussachevsky, Daniel Lewis), "The Waldstein Sonata" (Beethoven, Jose Limon/Lewis), "Debussy Dance" (Debussy, Hannah Kahn), "Day on Earth" (Aaron Copland, Doris Humphrey/Lewis), "Rooms" (Kenyon Hopkins, Sokolow), "Dead Heat" (Collage, Matthew Diamond)

ROUNDABOUT STAGE ONE
November 2–7, 1976 (4 performances)
Dance Umbrella presents:

KEI TAKEI'S MOVING EARTH

Artistic Director-Choreographer, Kei Takei; Lighting, Vincent Lalomia; Costumes, Kei Takei; Stage Manager, Skip Winitsky; Production Director, Maldwyn Pate; Administrative Assistant, Donald Moore; Set, Maxine W. Klein; Press, Meg Gordean

COMPANY

Amy Berkman, Richmond Johnstone, Regine Kunzle, John de Marco, John Parton, Maldwyn Pate, Marta Renzi, Joseph Ritter, Lloyd Ritter, Joan Schwartz, Kei Takei, Laurie Uprichard, Howard Vichinsky, John Vinton, Avi Davis

PROGRAM

"Light Part 9," "Light Part 10," "Light Part 12"

**Top Right: Pierre Barreau, Hannah Kahn
in "Nightspell" (Contemporary Dance System)**

Kei Takei's Moving Earth in "Light Part 9"
(Don Manza Photo)

ROUNDABOUT STAGE ONE
November 3–7, 1976 (4 performances)
Dance Umbrella presents:

JAMES CUNNINGHAM
and
THE ACME DANCE COMPANY

Artistic Director-Choreographer, James Cunningham; Associate Artistic Director, Lauren Persichetti; Lighting Design, Raymond Dooley; Executive Director, William Holcomb; General Manager, Robert Marinaccio; Stage Managers, Ron Cappa, Edward Heffernan

COMPANY

Jane Comfort
Michael Deane
Barbara Ellmann

Candice Prior
Ric Rease
Ted Striggles

PROGRAM: "Aesop's Fables" (Vincent Persichetti, James Cunningham/Lauren Persichetti; Costumes, Paul Steinberg; Masks, Gary Finkel, Ross Klahr), "Apollo and Dionysos: Cheek to Cheek" (Collage, James Cunningham/Lauren Persichetti; Costumes, William Florio)

**Candice Prior, Barbara Ellmann, James Cunningham
in "Apollo and Dionysos"**
(Joel Gordon Photo)

ROUNDABOUT STAGE ONE
November 9, 11, 13, 14, 1976 (4 performances)
Dance Umbrella presents:

PHYLLIS LAMHUT DANCE COMPANY

Director-Choreographer, Phyllis Lamhut; Lighting, Jon Garness; Decor, Dennis Cady; Technical Director, Jon Knudsen; Production Manager, Bruce Hoover; Press, Gurtman and Murtha Associates, Meg Gordean; Set, George Trakas; Costumes, Frank Garcia; Company Coordinator, Joan Gedney

COMPANY

Phyllis Lamhut	Thomas Evert
Kent Baker	Kathleen Gaskin
Donald Blumenfeld	Steven Iannacone
Diane Boardman	Jody Oberfelder
Diane Elliot	Natasha Simon
Patrice Evans	Vic Stornant

PROGRAM: "House" (Reich, Lamhut), "Hearts of Palm" (Arranged Sound, Lamhut), and *PREMIERE* of "Brainwaves" (Ed Arragne and the Silva Mind Control, Phyllis Lamhut; Costumes, Dennis Cady, Frank Garcia)

ROUNDABOUT STAGE ONE
November 10–14, 1976 (4 performances)
Dance Umbrella presents:

ROD RODGERS DANCE COMPANY

Artistic Director-Choreographer, Rod Rodgers; Executive Director, Leon B. Denmark; Administrative Assistant, Helen Royall; Lighting Design, George Vaughn Lowther; Stage Manager, Roger Overton; Press, Priscilla Chatman, Gurtman and Murtha Associates, Meg Gordean

COMPANY
Rod Rodgers

Shirley Rushing	Noel Hall
Ramon Colon	Thomas Pinnock
Tamara Guillebeaux	Leslie Innis
Enrico Labayen	Jeanne Moss

PROGRAM: "Creature" (Herbie Hancock, Shirley Rushing), "Intervals One" (Gwendolyn Watson, Rod Rodgers), "Intervals II" "Visions . . . of a new blackness" (Selected, Rodgers), "Freedome! Freedom" (Coleridge Taylor-Perkinson), "Rhythm Ritual" (Rod Rodgers)

Rod Rodgers Dance Company in "Rhythm Rituals" *(Jack Harr Photo)* Top: Thomas Evert, Vic Stornant, Kent Baker, Steven Iannacone in "Brainwaves" *(Tom Caravaglia Photo)*

ROUNDABOUT STAGE ONE
November 16–21, 1976 (5 performances)
Dance Umbrella presents:

DON REDLICH DANCE COMPANY

Director-Choreographer, Don Redlich; Lighting Design-Stage Manager, Mark Litvin; Assistant Stage Manager, Dennis Dugan

COMPANY
Jennifer Donohue
Irene Feigenheimer
Don Redlich
Barbara Roan
Billy Siegenfeld

PROGRAM: "Patina" (Besard/Caruso/Galilei/Gianoncelli, Redlich; Costumes, Margaret Tobin), "Rota" (George Crumb, Hanya Holm; Costumes, Sally Ann Parsons), "Traces" (Traditional American Folk, Redlich), and *PREMIERE* of "Lake of Fire" (Arranged, Don Redlich; Costumes, Sally Ann Parsons, Jim Meares) danced by the company.

ROUNDABOUT STAGE ONE
November 17–21, 1976 (3 performances)
Dance Umbrella presents:

ANNABELLE GAMSON

An evening of solo dances reconstructed by Annabelle Gamson from the works of Isadora Duncan and Mary Wigman; Lighting Design, Thomas Skelton; Costumes, Kitty Daly; Stage Manager, Mark Litvin; Manager, Chris Ashe; Press, Meg Gordean

PROGRAM

"Valse Brillante" (Chopin, Duncan), "Prelude" (Chopin, Duncan), "Piano Interlude" (Scriabin, Duncan), "Mother" (Scriabin, Duncan), "Etude" (Scriabin, Duncan), "Pastoral" (Will Goetze, Wigman), "Dance of Summer" (Goetze, Wigman), "Agave I" (Elliot Carter, Gamson), "Agave II" (Carter, Gamson), *World Premiere* of "Five Easy Dances" (Shostakovich, Gamson)

**Don Redlich Dance Company
in "Traces"**

ROUNDABOUT STAGE ONE

February 16–20, 1977 (7 performances)
Dance Umbrella (Michael Kasdan-Michael O'Rand, Administrators) presents:

DAN WAGONER AND DANCERS

Artistic Director-Choreographer, Dan Wagoner; Administrative Assistant, Eric Weinberger; General Manager, Frank Wicks; Lighting, Jennifer Tipton; Pianist, Michael Sahl; Stage Manager, Joan Devine; Press, Meg Gordean

COMPANY

Christopher Banner	Sally Hess
Heidi Bunting	JoAnn Jansen
Robert Clifford	George Montgomery
Regan Frey	Dan Wagoner

Understudies: Diann Sichel Perrelli, Mark Taylor

REPERTOIRE: "Allegheny Connection" (George Montgomery, Dan Wagoner) *World Premiere* on Wednesday, Feb. 16, 1977, "Songs" (Mendelssohn/Grieg/Brahms/Dvorak, Wagoner) *NY Premiere* on Feb. 16, 1977, "A Dance for Grace and Elwood" (Carole Weber/Robert Sallier, Wagoner), "Taxi Dances" (Popular/Michael Sahl, Wagoner), "Broken Hearted Rag Dance" (Scott Joplin, Wagoner), "Summer Rambo" (Bach, Wagoner), "Brambles" (Montgomery, Wagoner), "A Sad Pavane for These Distracted Times" (Thomas Tomkins, Wagoner)

ROUNDABOUT STAGE ONE

February 22–27, 1977 (7 performances)
Dance Umbrella presents:

LAR LUBOVITCH DANCE COMPANY

Artistic Director-Choreographer, Lar Lubovitch; Lighting Design, Craig Miller; Assistant, Tina Charney; Stage Manager, Karen De Francis; Press, Gurtman and Murtha, Meg Gordean

COMPANY

Rob Besserer	Charles Martin
Laura Gates	Mari Ono
Gerri Houlihan	Aaron Osborne
Harry Laird	Susan Weber
Lar Lubovitch	Christine Wright

PROGRAM: "Whirligogs" (Luciano Berio, Lubovitch), "Exhultate Jubilate" (Mozart, Lubovitch), "Les Noces" (Stravinsky, Lubovitch)

Timothy Knowles, Senta Driver, Michaele Sallade in "Matters of Fact"
(Linda Adamson Photo)

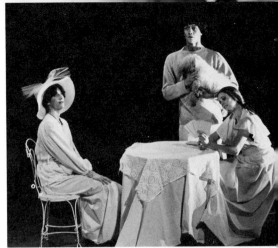

ROUNDABOUT STAGE ONE

Saturday matinee, February 26, 1977
Dance Umbrella presents:

RACHEL LAMPERT AND DANCERS

Choreography, Rachel Lampert; Lighting, Nicholas Wolff Lyndon; Costumes, Patricia McGourty; **DANCERS,** Rachel Lampert, Holly Harbinger, Alfredo Gonzales, Michael Blue Aiken, Kimberly Dye, Erica Everett, Eugene Roscoe, Merian Soto dancing "Issue" (Ivanovici), "Home" (Haydn); Press, Meg Gordean

SARA RUDNER with WENDY ROGERS

dancing *Premiere* of "November Duets/Molly's Suite" (Peggy Stern, Sara Rudner; Costumes, Robert Kushner; Lighting, Nicholas Wolff Lyndon; Pianist, Peggy Stern)

HARRY

dance and other works by Senta Driver: "Matters of Fact" and *Premiere* of "Gallery" (John Fahey/Patsy Cline/Bobby Bare) performed by Timothy Knowles, Michaele Sallade, Genevieve Weber, Senta Driver

ROUNDABOUT STAGE ONE

Saturday, February 26, 1977 (1 performance)
Dance Umbrella presents:

HARRY

Senta Driver
Michaele Sallade
Timothy Knowles
Genevieve Weber

All works by Senta Driver; Lighting Design, Robin Kronstadt; Stage Manager, Karen deFrancis; Press, Meg Gordean
PROGRAM: "Matters of Fact," "Gallery" (John Fahey/Patsy Cline/Bobby Bare) assisted by members of management and service organizations

Top: Dan Wagoner Dancers in "Summer Rambo" *(Ron Reagan Photo)* **Below: Lar Lubovitch Dance Company in "Whirligogs"** *(Oleaga Photo)*

MEREDITH MONK/THE HOUSE

Conceived, Directed and Choreographed by Meredith Monk and Ping Chong; Lighting Design, Beverly Emmons; Music, Meredith Monk; Text, Ping Chong; Scenic Consultant, Pat Woodbridge; Stage Managers, Bob Seder, Lauren Barnes; Technical and Sound Director, Tony Giovannetti; Assistant Choreographer, Gail Turner.

COMPANY

Meredith Monk, Ping Chong, Tone Blevins, Blondell Cummings, Spalding Gray, Sybille Hayn, Paul Langland, Steve Lockwood, Lee Nagrin, Mary Schultz, Daniel Ira Sverdlik, Gail Turner, Pablo Vela and John Bernd, Margot Corrigan, Ellen Goldsmith, Andrea Goodman, Jeannie Hutchins, Genny Kapuler, Eva Maier, Terry O'Reilly, Monica Solem, Mark Sovocool, Barry Talesnick, Tom Wilkinson
PROGRAM: "Paris/Chacon/Venice/Milan: A Travelogue" in three acts. (no photos submitted)

MERCE CUNNINGHAM & DANCE COMPANY

Artistic Director-Choreographer, Merce Cunningham; Costumes and Lighting, Mark Lancaster; Musical Adviser, John Cage; Artistic Adviser, Jasper Johns; Production Supervisor, Charles Atlas; Administrator, Richard Svare; Stage Mangers, Suzanne Joelson, Andy Tron

COMPANY

Merce Cunningham

Karole Armitage	Meg Harper
Louise Burns	Chris Komar
Ellen Cornfield	Robert Kovich
Morgan Ensminger	Julie Roess-Smith
Lisa Fox	Jim Self

REPERTOIRE: (one "Event" performed each night in chronological order) "Event #186 with Company and Joan LaBarbara," "Event #187 with Company and John Cage," "Event #188 with Company and John Cage," "Event #189 with Company and Meredith Monk," "Event #190 with Company and Annea Lockwood," "Event #191 with Company and David Tudor"

Top Right: Merce Cunningham, Karole Armitage, Julie Roess-Smith, Robert Kovich, Chris Komar in "Squaregame" *(Herb Migdoll Photo)*

KATHRYN POSIN DANCE COMPANY

Artistic Director-Choreographer, Kathryn Posin; Associate Director, Lance Westergard; Technical Director, Edward Effron; Stage Manager, David Rosenberg; Executive Director, William Holcomb; General Manager, Robert Marinaccio; Press, Meg Gordean

COMPANY

Kathryn Posin

Dian Don Chen	Ricky Schussel
William Gornel	Lance Westergard
Holly Reeve	Marsha White

PROGRAM: "Waves" (Laurie Spiegel, Posin), and *Premieres* of "Soft Storm" (Kirk Nurock, Kathryn Posin; Costumes, A. Christina Giannini) danced by the company, and "In a Crystal Palace" (Mozart/Daniel Lentz/Couperin, Lance Westergard; Set, Peter Kluge, Robert Parsekian; Costumes, Peggy Schierholz) danced by the company

PHOEBE NEVILLE DANCE COMPANY

Director-Choreographer, Phoebe Neville; Lighting Design, Nicholas Wolff Lyndon; Composer-Musician, Carole Weber; KLS Management; Production Supervisor, Craig Miller; Technical Director, Jon Knudsen; Press, Gurtman and Murtha Associates, Meg Gordean

COMPANY

Susan Saskia Emery
Jeannie Hutchins
Phoebe Neville
Tryntje Shapli

PROGRAM: "Mosaic" (Meredith Monk, Neville), "Tigris" (Carole Weber, Neville), "Oracles" (Eleanor Hovda, Neville)

Kathryn Posin Dance Company in "Waves" *(Joel Gordon Photo)*

63

RIVERSIDE DANCE FESTIVAL
November 4, 1976–May 31, 1977

Director, James Van Abbema; Technical Directors, Robert Brenner and Mary E. Brachmann; Artistic Director, Anita L. Thomas

THEATRE OF THE RIVERSIDE CHURCH
November 4–7, 1976 (4 performances)
New Dance Group Studio and Mid Man Dance Foundation present:

JOYCE TRISLER DANSCOMPANY
in
"The Spirit of Denishawn"

Artistic Director-Choreographer, Joyce Trisler; Pianist, John Colman; Lighting Design, Chenault Spence; Staged by Klarna Pinska; Costumes adapted from designs by Pearl Wheeler; Stage Managers, Bill Burd, Douglas Drew, Oscar Ruiz; Sound, Robert Momchilov; Tapes, Jon Bowden

COMPANY

Elaine Anderson, Miguel Antonio, Jacqulyn Buglisi, Nancy Colahan, Ralph Farrington, Don Foreman, Marry Gorrill, Anne-Marie Hackett, Kate Johnson, Laurie Kaplan, Clif de Raita

PROGRAM

"Techniques of Denishawn" (Colman), "Second Arabesque" (Debussy, Ruth St. Denis/Doris Humphrey), "Dance in Space" (Chaminade, Humphrey/Pinska), "Brahms Waltzes" (Brahms, St. Denis), "Liebestraum" (Liszt, St. Denis), "Bach" (Bach, Ted Shawn), "Sonata Pathetique" (Beethoven, St. Denis/Humphrey), "Nautch" (Cadman, St. Denis), "Gnosienne" (Satie, Shawn), "Red & Gold Sari" (Stoughton, St. Denis), "Spear Dance Japonesque" (Louis Horst, Shawn), "Soaring" (Schuman, St. Denis/Humphrey)
Returned for 6 additional performances Feb. 2–6, 1977.

THEATRE OF THE RIVERSIDE CHURCH
November 11–14, 1976 (4 performances)
Hava Kohav Theatre/Dance Foundation presents:

PLAYTHING OF THE WIND

Conceived, Choreographed and Performed by HAVA KOHAV; Music, G. Watson/Villa-Lobos/Bach/Vivaldi/Mozart; Film Editor, Larry Revene; Stage Managers, Edward M. Greenberg, Joan Shapiro; Lighting Design, Edward M. Greenberg; Assistant Manager, Thomas Beller;

THEATRE OF THE RIVERSIDE CHURCH
November 18–21, 1976 (4 performances)
Riverside Theatre Dance Festival presents:

MULTIGRAVITATIONAL AERODANCE GROUP

Artistic Director, Stephanie Evanitsky; Assistant Artistic Director, Robert Fiala; Costumes, Nils Eklund, Stephanie Evanitsky; Lighting Design, Jon Garness

PERFORMERS

Suellen Epstein	Donald Porteou
Kay Gainer	Barbara Sal
Arthur-George Hurray	Bronya Weinber

PROGRAM: "Homage to Picasso II—Inflame" (Richard Hayman Evanitsky), "Aerodance Rituals," "Buff Her Blind—to Open the Light of the Body" (Hayman, Evanitsky)

Members of Multigravitational Aerodance Group in "Homage to Picasso" *(Ric Schreiber Photo)*

Top: Joyce Trisler Danscompany *(Lois Greenfield Photo)*
Below: Hava Kohav in "Plaything of the Wind"

CLIFF KEUTER DANCE COMPANY

Artistic Director-Choreographer, Cliff Keuter; Costume Designer, A. Christina Giannini; Lighting Design, Edward Effron; Sets, Walter Nobbe; Musical Director, John Herbert McDowell; Managing Director, Alan Kifferstein; Press, Kaylyn Sullivan

DANCERS

John Dayger	Ernest Pagnano
Joan Finkelstein	Michael Tipton
Cliff Keuter	Susan Whelan
Ellen Kogan	Karla Wolfangle

PROGRAM: "Plaisirs D'Amour" (Collage, Cliff Keuter), "Field" (Mahler, Keuter), "Interlude" (Collage, Keuter), "Tetrad" (Stravinsky, Keuter)

THEATRE OF THE RIVERSIDE CHURCH
December 2–5, 1976 (4 performances)
Riverside Dance Festival and New Dance Group Studio present:

SOPHIE MASLOW DANCE COMPANY

Director-Choreographer, Sophie Maslow; Assistant, Stanley Berke; Lighting Design, Bill Burd; Stage Manager, Oscar Ruiz; Costume Designs, Bernard Johnson; Executive Director, Harry Rubenstein

COMPANY

Stanley Berke	Karen Lashinsky
Kimberly Dye	Priscilla Lenes
Glenn Ferrugiari	Faye Fujisaki Mar
Ana Marie Forsythe	Nedra Marlin-Harris
Lynn Frielinghaus	Theodore Pollen III
Thomas Glantz	Jerome Sarnat

PROGRAM: "Songs for Women" (*Premiere*) and "Songs for Men" (Bartok, Sophie Maslow), "Such Sweet Thunder" (Duke Ellington, Maslow), "Decathlon Etude" (Gottschalk, Maslow)

Karla Wolfangle, Susan Whelan, Ernest Pagnano, Cliff Keuter in "Tetrad" *(Ron Reagan Photo)*

THEATRE OF THE RIVERSIDE CHURCH
December 15–19, 1976 (6 performances)
Riverside Dance Festival presents:

ENTRE-SIX DANCE COMPANY

Artistic Director-Choreographer, Lawrence Gradus; Administrative Director, Jacqueline Lemieux; Assistant Director, Christine Clair; Designer, Nicole Martinet; Lighting, Kenneth Ferencek, Trevor Parson

COMPANY

Dominique Giraldeau	Francois Beaulieu
Fabyenne Gosselin	Jacques Drapeau
Shelley Osher	Pierre Lemay

PROGRAM: "Sentiments" (Ravel, Lawrence Gradus), "Nonetto" (Bohuslav Martinu, Gradus), "Three Pieces from a Children's Program" (Stravinsky/Strauss, Gradus), "Toccata" (Britten, Gradus)

THEATRE OF THE RIVERSIDE CHURCH
January 6–9, 1977 (4 performances)
Riverside Dance Festival presents:

ANNABELLE GAMSON
An Evening of Solo Dances

PROGRAM: "Five Waltzes" (Brahms, Isadora Duncan), "Mother" (Scriabin, Duncan), "Etude" (Scriabin, Duncan), "Pastoral" (Will Goetze, Mary Wigman), "Agave I & II" (Elliott Carter, Annabelle Gamson), "Five Easy Dances" (Shostakovich, Gamson), "First Movement: (Mozart, Gamson)
Lighting Design-Stage Manager, Bill Burd; Manager, Christopher Ashe
Sunday, January 9, 1977

DANCES BY ISADORA DUNCAN

"Water Study" (Schubert), "Prelude" (Chopin), "Mazurka" (Chopin), "Waltz" (Chopin), "Valse Brilliante" (Chopin), "Dance of the Furies" (Gluck), "Waltzes" (Brahms), "Mother" (Scriabin), "Etude" (Scriabin)

Entre-Six Dance Company, and above
(Derek Dunn Photos)

THEATRE OF THE RIVERSIDE CHURCH
December 9–12, 1976 (5 performances)
Riverside Dance Festival (James Van Abbema, Director) presents:

CHIANG CHING DANCE COMPANY

Artistic Director, Chiang Ching; Pianist, Adolovni Acosta; Stage Managers, David Kissel, Michael Smart, Beverly Borough; Lighting Design, David Kissel, Pat Stern

COMPANY
Chiang Ching

Sharon Hom Chaing
Ma-Tzi-Foon
Paula Gallagher

Francis Marsh
Philip Matsu
Terry Richards

REPERTOIRE: "Extrapolation" (Traditional/William Moy, Chiang Ching), "Yang Kuan" (Chou Wen-Chung, Ching), "Nostalgia" (Hsu Tsang-Houei, Ching), "Between" (John Bischoff, Ching), "All in Spring Wind" (Wen-Chung, Ching), "Androgyny" (Wen-Chung, Al Chung/Liang Huang), "Shen" (Tona Scherchen, Ching), "Three Folk Songs" (Wen-Chung, Ching), "On the Steppes" (Traditional Mongolian, Ching), "Nostalgia" (Hsu Tsang-Houei, Ching), "Moments from Chinese Past" (Chinary Ung, Ching)

THEATRE OF THE RIVERSIDE CHURCH
Januray 12–14, 1977 (3 performances)
Riverside Dance Festival presents:

LUISE WYKELL AND COMPANY

Artistic Director-Choreographer-Costume Designer, Luise Wykell; Lighting Design, Jon Garness; Stage Manager, Jon Garness; Production Assistant, Phyllis SanFilippo; Tapes, Gale Ormiston

COMPANY

Luise Wykell, Jane Alsen, Mari Rustad, Judith Silverman, Sandra Seymour, Susan Creitz, Steven Iannacone, Richard Biles, Janis Brenner, Sharon Spanner, Jane Durbin, Valery Farias, Rosemary Newton

PROGRAM

"Goldenrod" (Tonto's Expanding Handband, Wykell), "Chrome Green" (Arranged/Ormiston, Wykell), "Ultramarine Blue" (Horn, Wykell), "The Game" (Selected, Wykell)

THEATRE OF THE RIVERSIDE CHURCH
Saturday & Sunday, January 15 & 16, 1977 (3 performances)
Riverside Dance Festival presents:

REBECCA
A Dancemime Concert

PROGRAM: "Babe" (Prokofiev), "Playtime" (Glazounov), "Girl" (Jay Friedman/Robert Roman), "The Lady" (Chuck Mymit), "Delusion" Schumann), "Onstage" (Mozart), "Enticement" (Halffter), "Temptation," "Resistance" (Yusef Lateef), "Greed," "Nightime" (Lateef), "Carnival" (Mymit) Costumes, Maria Ferreira; Lighting, Jon Garness

THEATRE OF THE RIVERSIDE CHURCH
January 20–23, 1977 (4 performances)
Riverside Dance Festival presents:

JOAN LOMBARDI/VIC STORNANT AND DANCERS

Managing Director, Jan Michell; Lighting Design-Stage Manager, Jon Garness; Artistic Adviser, George Hudacko; Technical Assistant, Tom Rogowsky

DANCERS

Christine Strazza, Elyssa Paternoster, Felicia Norton, Tara Mitton, Felice Dalgin, Alison Morgan, Lisa Baranof, Stephanie Rothenberger, Joan Lombardi, Alex Dolcemascolo, Harry Laird, Miguel Lopez, Chester Roberts, Vic Stornant

PROGRAM

"Some Time Here, Some Times There" (Gershwin, Stornant), "Foggie's Foxtrot" (Collage, Lombardi), "All the Way Around and Back" (Collage, Lombardi), "Sketches" (Collage, Stornant), "Resignation," "Ambivalence," "Film Solo" (Collage, Stornant), "Segaki" (Walter Carlos, Lombardi)

Joan Lombardi Dancers in "Segaki" *(Lois Greenfield Photo)*
Above: Rebecca

Top: Chiang Ching Dance Company
Below: Luise Wykell Company
(Norman Ader Photo)

THEATRE OF THE RIVERSIDE CHURCH
January 27–30, 1977 (5 performances)
Riverside Dance Festival presents:

MURIEL COHAN
& PATRICK SUZEAU

PROGRAM: "Aquarelle" (Shostakovich, Patrick Suzeau), "Caligula" (Choreography, Muriel Cohan), "Collage" (Nikos Skalkottas, Suzeau), "Dress-Up" (Shostakovich, Cohan), "Poems of Lorca" (George Crumb, Cohan/Suzeau)

Lighting Designer-Stage Manager, Barbara Rosoff; Assistant Marge Smilow

THEATRE OF THE RIVERSIDE CHURCH
March 31–April 3, 1977 (4 performances)
Riverside Dance Festival presents:

DIANE BOARDMAN
& ROBERT SMALL

with Kent Baker, Diane Elliot, Jeffrey Bickford, Pamela Francis, Dale Thompson, Susan Creitz, Shawn Hiers, Janis Brenner, Kathleen Gaskin, Jeffrey Eichenwald; Lighting Design, James Van Abbema; Stage Manager, Peter Koletzke; Technical Director, Richard Talcott; Technical Assistant, Lori Ziesemer; Press, Dianne Markham

PROGRAM

"Divertimento" (John Addison, Robert Small), "Cambiozoan" (Morton Subotnik, Diane Boardman), "Set Up" (Selected, Boardman), "Tight, Down, Light" (Mimaroglu, Small), "Two Alone" (Dockstader/Robb/Mimaroglu, Small), "Fusion/FFiusssiioonn/-Fission" (Stockhausen/Braxton/Brubeck, Boardman)

THEATRE OF THE RIVERSIDE CHURCH
April 6, 8, 10, 1977 (3 performances)
Riverside Dance Festival presents:

NEW YORK DANCE QUINTET

Artistic Director-Choreographer, Greg Reynolds; Lighting Designers, Jennifer Tipton, Gary Grill, Jill Heller; Stage Manager, Jill Heller; Music Adviser, John Herbert McDowell

COMPANY
Greg Reynolds, Schellie Archbold, Holly Fairbank, Peggy Levine, Vicki Piper, Tom Laskaris, Oliver Freed

PROGRAM
"O Luminous Flux" (Bach, Greg Reynolds), "Down Home" (Ives, Reynolds), "Brother Sun/Sister Moon" (Pat Moffitt, Reynolds), "The Passion according to Mary" (Selected, Reynolds)

THEATRE OF THE RIVERSIDE CHURCH
April 7, 9, 10, 1977 (3 performances)
Riverside Dance Festival presents:

CLAUDIA GITELMAN/ALICE
TEIRSTEIN

PROGRAM: "Pastita" (Telemann, Claudia Gitelman; "Excerpts from Homage to Mahler" (Mahler, Hanya Holm) performed by Claudia Gitelman and Terry Kaelber; "Sunday Dances" (Paul Petersky, Gitelman) performed by Candice Christakos, Patricia Payne, Dale Thompson, Dorian Petri, and Claudia Gitelman; "Fox-Trot" (Richard Einhorn, Alice Teirstein) performed by Bruce Block, Kathy Kramer, Michael Ciccetti, Marta Renzi; "Solo" (Stanley Walden, Teirstein) performed by Art Bridgman, Michael Ciccetti, Anita Feldman, Olgalyn Jolly, Madeleine Perrone; "Inside Sam" (Gerald Otte, Gitelman) performed by Jeffrey Fox, Patrick Ragland

Top Right: Muriel Cohan, Patrick Suzeau
Below: Diane Boardman, Robert Small

Claudia Gitelman (*Norman Ader Photo*) **Above: New York Dance Quintet members**
(*Jonathin Atkin Photo*)

67

THEATRE OF THE RIVERSIDE CHURCH
April 13, 15, 17, 1977 (3 performances)
Riverside Dance Festival presents:

VIRGINIA LAIDLAW
DANCE THEATRE

Artistic Director-Choreographer, Virginia Laidlaw; Lighting Design-Stage Manager, Jon Garness; Technical Assistant, Arthur Chu

COMPANY

Virginia Laidlaw, Mark DeGarmo, Susan Gillis, Kathleen Heath, Reenie Linden, Judy Steel, Jill Feinberg, Elissa Kirtzman, Wanda Pruska, Djuna Moran, Gale Ormiston

PROGRAM

"Place" (Web Terhune, Virginia Laidlaw), "Other Parts Other Places" (Web Terhune/Elton John, Laidlaw), "Sweetheart Suite" (Irin Peollot, Laidlam)

THEATRE OF THE RIVERSIDE CHURCH
April 14, 16, 17, 1977 (3 performances)
Riverside Dance Festival presents:

RICHARD BILES DANCE COMPANY

Artistic Director-Choreographer-Costume Design, Richard Biles; Lighting Design-Stage Manager, Jon Garness; Technical Assistant, Geoffrey Hood

COMPANY

Richard Biles, Jane Durbin, Shawn Hiers, Sharon Spaner, Marjorie Myles, Peggy Vogt, Donna Evans, Geoffrey Hood, Jane Alsen

PROGRAM

"Black and White Dances" (Mozart/Kucera/Riegger/Kahn/Jones, Biles), "Solo in Three Parts" (Malec/Reibel/Farrari, Biles), "The Pale" (Eddie Gomez/Jeremy Steig, Biles)

Virginia Laidlaw
(Arthur Chu Photo)

THEATRE OF THE RIVERSIDE CHURCH
April 20–23, 1977 (4 performances)
Riverside Dance Festival presents:

RIRIE-WOODBURY DANCE
COMPANY

Artistic Directors, Shirley Ririe, Joan Woodbury; General Manager, Susan Salazar; Company Manager, Colleen Langford; Technical Director-Designer, Robert Allen; Stage Manager-Media Designer, Nicholas J. Cavallaro; Costumes, Maureen Winterton, Barry Lunn, Donna Sheya

COMPANY

Phyllis Haskell	Shirley Ririe
Doris Hudson	Lynn Walter Topovski
Robin Edward Johnson	Joan Woodbury
Suzanne Renner	Dennis Wright

REPERTOIRE: "Forest Dreams" (Art Lande, Tandy Beal), "June, Where Are You?" (Nyle Steiner, Loabelle Mangelson), "Incantation" (John LaMontaine, Joan Woodbury), "Paper Piece" (Nyle Steiner, Shirley Ririe), "Fabrik" (Miriam Brunner, Woodbury), "Deeper and to the Right" (Nyle Steiner, Edd Pelsmaker), "Striped Celebrants" (Alwin Nikolais), "Clouds" (Byrd/Moskowitz, Ririe), "Affectionate Infirmities" (Mozart, Woodbury), "Play It as It Rings" (Collage, Ririe/Woodbury), "Overlay" (Kenneth Garburo, Mangelson), "Obliquities" (John Cage, Ann Brunswick), "Duet from Fall Gently on Thy Head" (Bach, Cliff Keuter), "Prisms" (Steiner, Ririe)

THEATRE OF THE RIVERSIDE CHURCH
April 27–May 1, 1977 (6 performances)
Riverside Dance Festival presents:

JOYCE TRISLER DANSCOMPANY

Artistic Director-Choreographer, Joyce Trisler; Lighting Design, Chenault Spence; Stage Manager, Oscar Ruiz; Assistant to Miss Trisler, Nancy Long

COMPANY

Nancy Colahan, Anne-Marie Hackett, Laurie Kaplan, Nancy Long, Eileen Price, Miguel Lopez, Lonne Moretton, Clif de Raita, Stephen Shawn, Leslie Watanabe

PROGRAM

"Four Temperaments" (Hindemith, Trisler), Excerpts from "The Spirit of Denishawn": Single and Double Scarf Techniques (Colman), Gnosienne (Satie, Shawn), Dance in Space (Chaminade, Humphrey/Pinska), Brahms Waltz (Brahms, St. Denis), Liebestraum (Liszt, St. Denis), Spear Dance Japonesque (Horst, Shawn), Soaring (Schumann, St. Denis/Humphrey), and *PREMIERE* of "Argot" (Selected, Donald McKayle)

Members of Joyce Trisler Danscompany
(John Dady Photo)
68 Above: Ririe-Woodbury Dance Company

THEATRE OF THE RIVERSIDE CHURCH
May 5–8, 1977 (4 performances)
Riverside Dance Festival (James Van Ebbema, Director) presents:

RUDY PEREZ DANCE THEATRE

Artistic Director-Choreographer, Rudy Perez; Lighting Design-Stage Manager, Kenneth F. Merkel; Administrative Director, Peter Obletz; Sound, Russell Krum

COMPANY
Rudy Perez

Laura Delano	Tara Mitton
Paco Garcia	Elyssa Paternoster
Steven Gray	Edwin Rupert
Katherine Liepe	Harry Streep III

PROGRAM: "New Annual" (Collage, Rudy Perez), "System" (Arranged Sounds, Perez), "Rally (or Variation on a Theme for a Small Space with Less People)" (Arranged, Perez), and *Premiere* of " . . . Just For the Sake of It" (Arranged Sounds and Music, Rudy Perez; Costumes, Kenneth Wampler)

THEATRE OF THE RIVERSIDE CHURCH
May 12–15, 1977 (4 performances)
Riverside Dance Festival presents:

MIMI GARRARD DANCE COMPANY

Artistic Director-Choreographer, Mimi Garrard; Lighting Designer-Stage Manager, Jon Garness; Company Manager, David Yaksic; Special Effects, James Seawright

COMPANY

Mimi Garrard	Gael Stepanek
Gale Ormiston	Gary Davis
Joanne Edelmann	Alexander Wang
Jill Feinberg	Antonia Beh

PROGRAM: "P's and Cues" (Mozart, Garrard), "Brazen" (Ghent, Garrard), "Dreamspace" (Trimble, Garrard), and *Premiere* of "ARC" (Semegen, Garrard) performed by the company

THEATRE OF THE RIVERSIDE CHURCH
May 18–22, 1977 (6 performances)
Riverside Dance Festival and New Dance Group presents:

SOPHIE MASLOW DANCE COMPANY

Artistic Director-Choreographer, Sophie Maslow; Lighting Design, Chenault Spence; Stage Managers, Oscar Ruiz, Michaelanthony Cheatham, Patrick Casey; Assistant to Miss Maslow, Stanley Berke

COMPANY

Diane Chavan, Kimberly Dye, Lynn Frielinghaus, Karen Lachinsky, Nedra Marlin-Harris, Liz Rosner, Stanley Berke, Glenn Ferrugiari, Elmore Cisco James, Theodore Pollen III, Jerome Sarnat, Perry Souchuk

PROGRAM

"The Village I Knew" (Gregory Tucker/Samuel Matlowsky, Sophie Maslow), "Decathlon Etude" (Gottschalk, Maslow), and *Premiere* of "La Noche de los Mayas" (Sylvestre Revueltas, Anna Sokolow; Costumes, Zoe)

THEATRE OF THE RIVERSIDE CHURCH
May 26–29, 1977 (4 performances)
The Committee for the Isadora Duncan Centenary in co-production with the Riverside Dance Festival presents:

THE DANCE OF ISADORA DUNCAN

Soloists Hortense Kooluris, Gemze de Lappe, Julia Levien, Sylvia Gold, with the Isadora Duncan Centenary Dance Company: Adrienne Barouth, Lori Belilove, Jeanne Bresciani, Julia Keefer, Judy Ann Landon, Cynthia R. Millman, Susan Sparkman, Hedy Weiss, and children Devon Levine, Melissa Mignone, Mary Lynn Morris, Naomi Wittes

PROGRAM

"Excerpts from Dance Preparation Classwork" (Julia Levien), "Schubert: Slow March, Tanze, Moment Musical," "Strauss: Southern Rose Waltzes," "Gluck: Dances from the opera Orpheus," "Scriabin: Two Etudes," "Chopin: Prelude, Mazurka, Polonaise"

Hortense Kooluris, Julia Levien of Isadora Duncan
ncers *(Arnold Genthe Photo)* **Above: Sophie Maslow Dance Co.**
(Jane Rady Photo)

Top: Rudy Perez in "System" *(Sandy Geis Photo)*
Below: Mimi Garrard Dance Company

MISCELLANEOUS NEW YORK PROGRAMS

AMERICAN THEATRE LABORATORY
May 14–16, 1976 (4 performances)
Dance Theater Workshop presents:

JANET SOARES COMPANY

Director-Choreographer, Janet Soares; Lighting Design, Jennifer Herrick Jebens; Costumes, Meg Kozera

COMPANY

Hannah Kahn, Linda Roberts, Jessica Fogel, Carol Hess, Shaw Bronner, Martha Wiseman, Emily Andrews

PROGRAM: "Scaramouche I, II, Trois Rag—Caprices II" (Darius Milhaud, Soares), "Risks and Pleasures" (Collage, Soares), "singing low songs . . . and even thinking . . . dancing" (Cat Stevens, Soares), and *Premiere* of "Cameo" (Bach, Soares).

DANSPACE
Opened Tuesday, June 1, 1976.*

DOUGLAS DUNN/LAZY MADGE

Artistic Director-Choreographer, Douglas Dunn; performed by Ellen Webb, Daniel Press, Dana Roth, Diane Frank, Michael Bloom, Ruth Alpert, Jennifer Mascall, Susan Strickland, David Woodberry, Christina Grasso Caprioli, Douglas Dunn
* Moved June 3, 1976 to 541 Broadway for performances through June 20, 1976.

Right: **Douglas Dunn** (*Nathaniel Tileston Photo*)
Top: **Janet Soares** (*Lois Greenfield Photo*)

MARYMOUNT THEATRE
June 2–6, 1976 (5 performances)

2nd CENTURY DANCERS

Artistic Director-Choreographer, Ronn Forella; Executive Director, William Gatewood; Rehearsal Director, Dean Badolato; Executive Secretary, Anna Maria Fanizzi; Production Supervisor, Richard Winkler; Stage Manager, Arthur Karp; Assistant to Mr. Winkler, James Chaleff; Lighting, Richard Winkler

COMPANY

David Gibson, George Giraldo, Frank Mastrocola, Rodney Pridgen, Joseph Pugliese, Clare Culhane, Anita Ehrler, Linda Haberman, Nancy Stewart

PROGRAM

"Molly" (Biff Rose, Forella), "The Villain" (Crown Heights Affair, Forella) and *PREMIERES* of "Ever Since" (Bach/interpreted by Jacques Loussier Trio, Forella), "Melissa" (Barry Manilow, Forella), "Los Gatos Triste" (Chuck Mangione, Forella), "Please" (Buddy Rich, Forella), "Collage" (Billy Cobham, Forella).

AMERICAN THEATRE LABORATORY
June 3–13, 1976 (15 performances)
Dance Theater Workshop presents:

DTW RETROSPECTIVE

REPERTOIRE: "Winesburg Portraits:" (Jeff Duncan), "Birdwatch" (Itornay), "Dreams" (Sokolow), "Bach 5th Clavier Concerto (Duncan), "Do Not Want To Kiss Your Mouth of Salt" (Alenikoff), "Errands" (Bauman), "Cloud Song" (Cohen), "Arcade" (Perez), "Days" (Posin), "Palimpsest" (Jowitt), "Skating to Siam" (J. Cunningham), "Please" (Summit), "Light Part 5" (Takei), "The Black" (Wilson), "Poison Variations" (Keen).

James Cunningham in "Skating to Siam"
70 Above: 2nd Century Dancers in "Collage"
(*Ron Reagan Photos*)

ST. PETER'S CHURCH
June 3–5, 1976 (3 performances)
The Mel Wong Dance Foundation presents;

BREATH

Choreographed by Mel Wong; Music, Denman Maroney; Lighting Design, Andy Tron; Stage Manager, Dara Candi Lamb

COMPANY

Louise Burns, Timothy Gallaghan, Susan Emery, Valerie Farias, Alan Good, Melinda Gros, Jo Ann Jansen, Karen Levey, Rosalind Newman, Nanna Nilson, Karen Shields, Mel Wong

WASHINGTON SQUARE CHURCH
June 3–5, 1976 (3 performances)

WENDY OSSERMAN DANCE COMPANY

Artistic Director-Choreographer, Wendy Osserman; Technical Director-Lighting Design, Vince Laloma; Stage Manager, Bren Bowen; Production Coordinator, Marilyn Atlas; Press, Madeleine Landolt, Ellen Barrett, Manuel Fernandez, Richard DePasquale

COMPANY

Ellen Barrett, Richard DePasquale, Gary Easterling, Maggie Higgs, Meredith Johnson, Chris Stevens, Deirdre Towers, Bruce Weitzmon, Lelia Wingrove, Davida Wittman, Nancy Zendora

PROGRAM

"Dream Animal" (Lloyd McNeill/Pink Floyd, Wendy Osserman), "L'Essence" (Lloyd McNeil) choreographed and danced by Madeleine Landolt, "Still Me" (Lloyd McNeill, Osserman), "Sinfonia" (Luciano Berio, Carol Egan), "New Quartet" (McNeill, Osserman), "Cycles" (Balinese gamelan/Tibetan Bells, Osserman), "Danceritualgames" (Andre Nadelson, Manuel Fernandez/Wendy Osserman)

Top Right: Mel Wong
Below: Ellen Barrett, Deirdre Towers,
Nancy Zendora, Lelia Wingrove of Wendy
Osserman Dance Company *(Ron Reagan Photo)*

HIGH SCHOOL OF PRINTING AUDITORIUM
Saturday, June 5, 1976

HIGH SCHOOL OF PERFORMING ARTS GRADUATION PROGRAM

MODERN MAJORS: Millie Borges, Sabrina Davis, Rhonda Edmonds, Phenecia Folkes, Barbara Gordon, Andrea Havelin, Lois Hewitt, Deborah Paliukaitus, Ivelisse Pacheco, Judith Smart, Phillip Wright, Pia De Silva, Troy Jackson, Michele Mullings, Tamara Richards, Justine Zollo, Wanda Dryer, Daryl Richardson, Ricky Stotts, Allison Williams, Mindy Horowitz, Evelyn Levy
BALLET MAJORS: Leslie Halpern, Lucy Popper, Pamela Risenhoover, Annette White, Karen Ackerman, Mary Beblowski, Barbara Ellioraga, Donna Landtwig, Ora Torres, Roman Greller
GUEST ARTIST George de la Pena, SPA '74, Courtesy American Ballet Theatre.

PROGRAM: "Koon Joong Moo" (traditional, Sun Ock Lee), "In The Spirit of the Jota" (Band music of Aragon, Spain, Matteo), "What Now?-the inevitable senior dilemma" (Paul Hindemith, Stephanie Zimmerman), "Water Study" (Doris Humphrey reconstructed by Charlotte Wile from the Labanotation score by agreement with the Dance Notation Bureau, Inc; assisted by Penny Frank), "A Light Wind" (Giovanni Pergolesi, performed by SPA Senior String Ensemble; Choreography by Penny Frank), "Show Stopper" (Marvin Hamlisch, Suzanne Walker), "Vahine" (Traditional, Robert Powell), "Valse Fantaisie" (Glinka, Balanchine; staged by Victoria Simon, assisted by Dorothy Fiore), "Congolese Wedding" (Congolese Traditional, Pearl Primus; staged by Mary Waithe; Drummers: Butch Orville, Earl Stewart; Singers: Debra Hayes, Pia De Silva)

"A Light Wind" by High School of Performing
Arts Graduation class *(Ron Reagan Photo)*

Laura Veldhuis
(Ron Reagan Photo)

MUSEUM OF NATURAL HISTORY
Saturday & Sunday, June 5–6, 1976 (6 performances)

LAURA VELDHUIS DANCE COMPANY

Artistic Director-Choreographer, Laura Veldhuis; Technical Director, Joop Veldhuis; Narrator, Frank Albert

COMPANY

Cynthia Breidenbach, Julia Gale, Paul Kessman, Lee Michelsen, Laura Veldhuis, Bruce Weitzmon

PROGRAM: "Mood in Dance II"

THEATRE OF THE RIVERSIDE CHURCH
June 5–13, 1976

ZSEDENYI BALLET COMPANY
in
"Coppelia"

Music, Leo Delibes; Choreography and Direction, Karoly Zsedenyi; Scenic Design, Charles Barnes; Lighting Design, Jon M. Garness; Production Manager, Kitty Bozic; Stage Manager, Jon M. Garness; Company Manager, Kitty Blozic; Technical Assistant, Rob Brenner; Production Assistants, Terry Bell, Maurice Ackroyd, John Robertshaw III

COMPANY

Elizabeth Kim, Susanna Organek, Mark Franko, Brian Hughes, Anke Junge, Sylvia Palumbo, Linda Sloboda, Genie Joseph, Robert Chipok, Francoise Davis, Cesar Bujosa, Maurice Ackroyd

Mark Franko, Elizabeth Kim of Zsedenyi Ballet in "Coppelia"
(Ronald Berman Photo)

ST. CLEMENT'S THEATRE
June 10–13, 1976 (4 performances)

MARCUS SCHULKIND DANCE COMPANY

Artistic Director-Choreographer, Marcus Schulkind; Co-Artistic Director, Elisa Monte; General Manager, Charles Moody; Lighting Design-Stage Manager, John Knudsen; Press, Susan Knapp; Costumes, Elisa Monte

COMPANY
Marcus Schulkind

Gloria Chu	Paul Gifford
Stephanie Herman	Monica Johansson
Elisa Monte	Christine Wright

PROGRAM: "Big Bird" (Scarlatti, Schulkind), "Lambent" (Beethoven, Schulkind), "Onus" (Crumb, Schulkind), "Ladies' Night Out" (Beatles, Schulkind), "The Fred and Barbara Section" (Fred Coffin, Schulkind), "Affettuoso" (Telemann, Schulkind), "A Piece of Bach" (Bach, Schulkind)

72 WOOSTER STREET
June 10–27, 1976 (8 performances)
Soho Performing Artists present:

MUSIQUE PLANANTE & NEW DANCES

COMPANY: Anthony Nunziata, Barbi Leifert, Kevan Cleary, Michelle Berne, Paloma Anthony, Robert Cheasty, Roberto Sandoval, Sylvia Mocroft, and musicians Horacio Vaggione, Elisabeth Wiener

PROGRAM: "Endings" (Vaggione/Wiener, Mocroft, Berne), "Ritual" (Vaggione/Wiener, Cleary), "Jail" (Cheasty/Nunziata/Cleary), "Oural" (Vaggione/Wiener), "Triage" (Vaggione/Wiener, Cleary)

Marcus Schulkind Dance Company in "A Piece of Bach"

Patricia Hruby

**Monica Diaz of Chamber Dance
Group in "Coppelia"**
(Ron Reagan Photo)

Frances Alenikoff in "Fingers"
(Don Manza Photo)

TERRA FIRMA
Friday & Saturday, June 11 & 12, 1976 (2 performances)

ONE PLUS ONE

Patricia Hruby
Deborah Riley

PROGRAM: "Solo" choreographed and danced by Deborah Riley; "Discontents" (Dennis Kita) choreographed and danced by Patricia Hruby; "Untitled Duet" (Terry Mohn, Deborah Riley) danced by Patricia Hruby, Deborah Riley; "Solo with Cloth and Chair" choreographed and danced by Deborah Riley; "Detail from Bird" (Vivaldi/Bird Songs) choreographed and danced by Patricia Hruby; "Album" (Catherine Hall, Patricia Hruby) danced by Patricia Hruby, Deborah Riley

BRANDEIS AUDITORIUM
Monday, June 14, 1976

THE CHAMBER DANCE GROUP

Artistic Director, Nanette Bearden; Costumes and Lighting, Michael Purris assisted by Sheila Nowosadko; Production Manager, Hank Frazier; Photography, Ron Reagan.

COMPANY

Toni Ann Gardella, Robert Chiarelli, Jim Roberts, John Bate, Elain Monn, Mark Trares, Lance Hunter, Monica Diaz, Jack Tully, Lisa Bendelac, Christine Cordon, Laima Drobavicius, Linda Parker, Sheila Nowosadko, Patrick McCord, Natch Taylor.

PROGRAM

"Coppelia" (Delibes, Saint-Leon/staged by Marian Horosko), PREMIERE of "Four of One & One of Another" (15th Century music, Marvin Gordon)

MARYMOUNT THEATRE
Monday, June 14, 1976

SOLARIS

Artistic Director, Henry Smith; Administrative Director, Edwin Bayrd; Musical Director, Romulus Franceschini; Technical Director, Peter Flynn; Press, Elizabeth Roten;

COMPANY

Henry Smith, Michael Rivera, Johanna Albrecht, Michele Rebaud, Sebastian Ellison, Ellen Parks, Kris Varjan

PROGRAM

"LA BAS" (conception and direction, Henry Smith; assistant to the director, Michael Rivera; Music, Romulus Franceschini; Lighting, Peter Flynn; Costumes; Bosha & Johnson)

EDEN'S EXPRESSWAY
June 17–20, 1976 (4 performances)

FRANCES ALENIKOFF DANCE THEATER COMPANY

Artistic Director-Choreographer, Frances Alenikoff; Lighting Design-Production Manager, Ben Dolphin; Stage Manager, Laurie Stichman; Musician-Composer, Carole Weber

COMPANY

Frances Alenikoff	Olgalyn Jolly
Art Berger	Dalienne Majors
Kenneth Boys	Myrna Packer
Kenneth Fischer	Lynne Weber

PROGRAM: "Fingers" (Carole Weber, Frances Alenikoff), "Fresh Water-Earth Jar" (Noel DaCosta/Jacques Coursil, Alenikoff), "I Don't Want to Kiss Your Mouth of Salt" (Argentinian Tangoes, Alenikoff), "The One of No Way" (Fragments from "The Tablets" by Armand Schwerner, Alenikoff), "Duad" (Weber, Alenikoff), "Sign Language & Hieroglyphs" (Weber, Alenikoff)

AMERICAN THEATRE LABORATORY
June 17–20, 1976 (4 performances)
Dance Theater Workshop presents:

JUDITH SCOTT DANCE THEATER

Director-Choreographer, Judith Scott; Lighting Design, Edward I. Byers; Stage Manager, Kate Elliott

COMPANY

Suzanne Castelli
Tracy Flanagan
Jill Jacobson
Irene Kassow
Bernadette McCarthy
Cindy Pollack
Judith Scott

PROGRAM: *Premiere* of "Rosarium" (David Van Tieghem, Judith Scott; Myth, Laura Simms; Sculpture, Richard F. Van Tieghem; Photography and Slides, Janet Goto, Judith Scott)

**Left: Judith Scott, Jill Jacobson,
Suzanne Castelli in "Rosarium"**

THEATER OF ST. CLEMENT'S
June 17–20, 1976 (4 performances)
The Valerie Bettis Theatre/Dance Company presents:

ECHOES OF SPOONRIVER

Adapted, Choreographed and Directed by Valerie Bettis; Music, Francis Thorne; Set and Costumes, Vittorio Capecce; Lighting Design, Blu Lambert; Assistant to Miss Bettis, Carol Walter; Stage Managers, John Sillings, Elizabeth Greenberg, Pam Roth-Shoemaker; Production Assistants, Anne Smith, Leah Shahmoon; Press, Cindy Rebello

COMPANY

John Darrell Black
Gaynelle Clay
Laura Delano
Sara Dillon
Gary Filsinger
Peri Frost
Donna Gabel

Elizabeth Lage
Carole Ann Lewis
Charles Maggiore
Wendy Osserman
Curt Ralston
Jack Scalici
Michael Walker

**Elizabeth Lage, Donna Gabel
in "Echoes of Spoon River"**
(Ron Reagan Photo)

THERESA L. KAUFMANN AUDITORIUM
June 17–20, 1976 (4 performances)

MATTEO ETHNOAMERICAN DANCE THEATER

Artistic Director-Choreographer, Matteo; Associate Director, Carola Goya; Assistant to Matteo, Carolyn Deats; Costume Director, Carola Goya; Stage Manager, Robin Schraft; Sound, Robert Walker; Manager, Mark Jones

COMPANY

Matteo
Terry Yorysh
Carolyn Deats
Homer Garza

Deborah Novotny
Judith Landon
Sandra Fernandez
Robert Chiarelli

Guest Artist: Sahomi Tachibana

PROGRAM: "Pwe," "Ts'ing P'ing T'iao," "Seraglio Story," "Havdalah Bukharian," "Ho O Puka," "A Hilo Au," "Courtship Dance," "Okame to Gombei," "Aiya Bushi," "Juraku Mai," "Ocho," "Devotional Song," "Ganesha-Shiva Stuti," "Jethimala," "Slokam," "Natanam Adinar," "Tamasha"

Matteo EthnoAmerican Dance Theater

TRYNTJE SHAPLI
and RACHEL LAMPERT

with Stuart Hodes, Holly Harbinger, Alfredo Gonzales, Michael Aitchison, Laurie McKirahan, Andrea Stark, Michael Aike, Ellen Ducker, Mitzi Maxwell, Colette Bischer, and Sergio Cervetti, (pianist).

PROGRAM: "Oddysey before Brunch" (four songs by Cole Porter, Lampert), "Issue" (Ivanovici, Lampert), "Again" (Bach, Shapli; mask by Theodora Skipitares), "Corridor Sonata" (Schubert, Shapli; costume by Phoebe Neville), "Thaw" (Bach, Shapli), "Brahms Variations on A Theme By Handel" (Lampert)

**Left: Rachel Lampert Dancers
in "Issue"** *(Ron Reagan Photo)*

THEATRE OF THE RIVERSIDE CHURCH
June 23–30, 1976 (9 performances)
American Dance Foundation presents:

U. S. TERPSICHORE

Artistic Directors, Barbara Fallis, Richard Thomas; Artistic Consultant, Royes Fernandez; Lighting Design-Stage Manager, William C. Westervelt; Assistant Stage Manager, Pamela Schug; Company Coordinator, Jacqueline Maskey; Technical Assistant, Rob Brenner; Festival Coordinator, James Van Abbema; Pianist, Barbara Kamhi

COMPANY

Bronwyn Thomas, Sean Lavery, Marissa Benetsky, Manuel Gomez, Christina Foisie, Michael DeLorenzo, Millard Hurley, Alice Avolio, Raymond Kurshals, Senior Artists Dick Andros, David Vaughan

Ann Arnoult, Bernadette Bleuzen, Alicia Enterline, Darcy Evans, Ina Golden, Janis Mandrus, Virginia Parks, Leslie Rubinstein, Ellyn Rosenthal, Colette Ross, Sallie Stadlen, Gino Karczewski, Patrick McCord, Andrew Needhammer, Daniel Pelzig, Michael Puleo, Richard Thorne, Joseph Towey

REPERTOIRE

"Les Sylphides" (Chopin, after Fokine), "Valse-Fantaisie" (Glinka, Balanchine/Victoria Simon), "Black Swan Pas de Deux" (Tchaikovsky, Petipa), "Graduation Ball" (Strauss, Lichine/Tatiana Riabouchinska), "Giselle" (Adam, Dolin after Coralli), "Caprice" (Stravinsky, Daniel Levans), "Grand Pas from La Bayadere Act II" (Minkus, Petipa/Kaleria Fedicheva), "Swan Lake Act I" (Tchaikovsky, Ivanov/Petipa), "Canciones Amatorias" (Granados, Levans), "Pas de Deux from Le Corsaire" (Drigo, Petipa/Marilyn Burr), "Stars and Stripes Pas de Deux" (Sousa, Balanchine/Victoria Simon), and *World Premieres* of "Italian Concerto" (Bach, Daniel Levans; Costumes, Stanley Simmons) on Saturday June 26, 1976 "A Winter's Waltz" (Emil Waldteufel, American Dancing School Traditional) on Sunday, June 27, 1976.

**David Vaughan, Dick Andros
in "Graduation Ball" (U.S. Terpsichore)**

Gudde Dancers in "Beethoven's 32 Variations"
(Ron Reagan Photo)

MARYMOUNT MANHATTAN THEATRE
June 24–28, 1976 (5 performances)

GUDDE DANCERS

Artistic Director-Choreographer, Lynda Gudde; Dancers: Lynda Gudde, Tanya Cimonetti, Silvia De La Rosa, Shelley Pressley, Linda Torrey

PROGRAM

"Introibo ad altare Dei" (Collage, Gudde), "Beethoven's 32 Variations on an Original Theme in C Minor" (Beethoven, Gudde), "Wide Southern Country" (Country, Gudde) (No other details available)

HENRY STREET SETTLEMENT PLAYHOUSE
June 25–27, 1976 (3 performances)
Henry Street Settlement Arts for Living presents:

FRANK ASHLEY DANCE COMPANY

Artistic Director-Choreographer, Frank Ashley; Managing Director, Delos R. Smith; Company Manager, Francine Dobranski; Lighting Design, George Greczylo; Stage Manager, Tony Leto; Rehearsal Assistant, Carole Simpson; Technical Director, C. Richard Mills; Press, Harry Zlokower, Howard Rubenstein Associates; Executive Director, Bertram Beck; Associate, Atkins Preston; Director Arts for Living, Mark Tilley

COMPANY

Frank Ashley	Jan Hazell
Carole Simpson	Hope Sogawa
Wendy McDade	Bernard Riddick
Sylvia Rincon	Jamil Garland

PROGRAM: "Rock Steady Suite" (White/Franklin/Ross/Withers, Ashley), "Vakako" (Herbie Hancock, Ashley), "The Game" (Gheorghe Zamfir, Ashley), "Garvey" (Burundi/Blackbyrds/Weather Report/John Coltrane/Burning Spear, Ashley), and *PREMIERE* of "Threshold of a Hope" (Michael Torres, Frank Ashley)
December 10–12, 1976 (3 performances)
PROGRAM: "Threshold of a Hope," "Garvey," and *PREMIERES* of "Time of Day" (Lucas Mason, Frank Ashley), "Dirty Blues" (Brownie McGhee/Sonny Terry/Memphis Slim/Levester Carter/Bo Diddley, Ashley)

BIJOU THEATRE
Saturday, June 26, 1976

BERNICE JOHNSON DANCE COMPANY

Executive Director, Bernice Johnson; Artistic Director, Michelle Simmons; Lighting Design, Jan Kroeve, Leah Randolph; Business Manager, Bud Johnson

COMPANY

Kendall Bean, Vanessa Benton, Margo Blake, Lorna Gray, Kevin Jeff, Audrey Lawrence, Terry Mason, Valerie Pettiford, Eric Sawyer, Crystal Smith, Rodney Smith, Earleen Sealy, Carolyn Vance, and drummers David Copper, Bud Johnson, Karim Braithwaite, Clifford Tyler
PROGRAM: "Ember" (Isaac Hayes, Winston DeWitt Hemsley), "Linear" (The Counts, Michael Peters), and *Premieres* of "Take My Hand" (Mahalia Jackson, Company), "Haqaiba" (Drums, Lee Thompson) "Hatchett's" (Atlantic Disco Band, Frank Hatchett), "A Space in Love" (Claus Ogerman/Bill Evans, Michele Simmons), "A Nature's Warmth" (Drums, Johnson), "Essence" (Nina Simone/Zulema/Roberta Flack/Nikki Giovanni, Martial Roumain/Leah Randolph)

Eiko and Kóma in "White Dance"
Above: Thomas Holt in "White Rabbit"

76

AMERICAN MODERN DANCE THEATRE
July 1–5, 1976 (5 performances)

PROGRAM

"White Rabbit from Afterhours in Wonderland" (Jefferson Airplane) choreographed and danced by Thomas Holt; "Improvexx" (Oliveros/Jan Hammer, George Stevenson) danced by Fred Cantaloupe, Billy Josefs, Doreen O'Connor, Sandra Rios, Audrey Taitt, Cynthia Yee; "A New Discovery" (Khachaturian) choreographed and danced by George Stevenson; "Green Moon Paradise" (Jan Hammer, Sandra Rios) danced by Sandra Rios, Billy Josefs; "Adoration of the Earth" (Stravinsky, George Stevenson) danced by Fred Cantaloupe, Billy Josefs, Reginald Browning, Doreen O'Connor, Diane Roye, Sandra Rios, Audrey Taitt, Cynthia Yee; "Second Avenue Scrapbook" (Laura Nyro) choreographed and danced by Laura Nyro; "Moods" (Roberta Flack) choreographed and danced by Diane Roye; "Masquerade" (Leon Russell) choreographed and danced by Sandra Rios and Cynthia Yee; "Gospel Suite" (George Stevenson) danced by Audrey Taitt, George Stevenson, Thomas Holt, Reginald Browning

THE PERFORMING GARAGE
July 7–11, 1976 (5 performances)
Dance Theater Workshop presents:

EIKO & KOMA
in
WHITE DANCE

based on Japanese poem "A Moth," choreographed and performed by Eiko and Koma

Top: Sylvia Rincon, Frank Ashley, Carole Simpson
in "Garvey" *(Vince Orgera Photo)* Below: Bernice
Johnson Dance Company in "Essence" *(Ron Reagan Photo)*

BICENTENNIAL DANCE FESTIVAL

Administrative Director, Nanette Bearden; Financial Director, Isidore Dresdner; Artistic Director, Edith Stephen; Production Manager, Hank Frazier; Festival Photographer, Ron Reagan; Stage Manager, Peter Xanthos; Electrician, D. Victor; Props, Chris Shelton

COMPANIES

ALL AMERICAN MOVIN' MUSCLE
Seamus Murphy, Artistic Director-Choreographer and Steven Williams, Hugo Bregman, Justis Skae, Hugh Vernon, Seamus Murphy

ALONSO CASTRO DANCE THEATRE
Alonso Castro, Artistic Director-Choreographer; Sally Small, Lighting Designer; Bill Ortzbach, Costumes; Ina Kahn, Company Manager; Sergio Vincencio, Assistant to Mr. Castro; Company: A.O. Forduna, Helen Breasted, Martin Feldman, Jeannette Hardie, Shirley Hardie, Clifton Jones, Alonso Castro, Kim Sullivan, Martha Gonsalves

ARGYR LEKAS and her SPANISH DANCE COMPANY
Argyr Lekas, Artistic Director-Choreographer; Isidore Dresdner, Company Manager; Lighting Designer, Jan Kroeze; Enrique Areaga, Luis Rodriguez, Costumes; Ruth Dresdner, Program Coordinator; Alexandera Lekas, Wardrobe Mistress; Ramos De Vigil, Maria Constancia, Luis Liciaga, Cecila Torres, Carolina Leon, La Rubia, Dancers; Ramon De Los Reyes, Special Guest Star; Paco Alonso, Guest Artist; Paco Juanas, Guitarist; Domingo Alvarado, Flamenco Singer

BALLET CLASSICS
Marian Horosko, Artistic Director-Choreographer; Dancers: Anthony Bassae, Richard Larcada, Marian Horosko; Michael Purri, Lighting Designer.

BERNICE JOHNSON DANCE COMPANY
Bernice Johnson, Director; Dancers: Audrey Lawrence, Kendall Bean, Carolyn Vance, Earlene Sealy, Valerie Pettiford, Allison Manson, Eric Sawyer, Crystal Smith, Kevin Jeff, Vanessa Benton, Phillip Wright, Terence Mason

BI-CENTENNIAL BALLET and BALLET WORKSHOP
Imogen S. Wheeler, Director; Dancers: Cynthia Penn, Dara Burrows, Archer Clark, Susan Gaylord, Grace Horonian, Laura Lidral, Stephanie Lyon, Sara Rothrock, JoAnna Sopio, Madeleine Watson, Vivian Wheeler, Kevin Montgomery, Alexander Bennett

CHAMBER DANCE GROUP
Nanette Bearden, Director; Dancers: Toni Ann Gardela, Christopher Corry, John Bates, James Roberts, Shelly Gunderer, Sheila Nowosadko, Justis Skae, Marilyn Marchiella

CHARLES MOORE
Dances of Africa interpreted by Mr. Moore

EDITH STEPHEN DANCE COMPANY
Edith Stephen, Artistic Director-Choreographer; Ralph M. Thomas, Assistant Director; Barbara Davis, Arts Administrator; Barbara Hollister, Demetria Daniels, Press; Michael Purri, Lighting Designer; Michelle Bodden, Michael Allen, Administrative Assistants; James Gayles, Design Consultant; Robert M. Gewald, Inc., Management; Dancers: Edith Stephen, Ralph M. Thomas, Paula Odellas, Sydney Lynn Haupert, Joan Liptak, Michael Bucher

ELEO POMARE DANCE COMPANY
Eleo Pomare, Artistic Director-Choreographer-Costumes; Dancers: Jennifer Barry, Robin Becker, Sara Snow Bogard, Bill Chaison, Joe Johnson, Patricia Jones, John Juhl, Strody Meekins, Rick Kealohi Ornellas, Larry Schiffer, Rosalie Tracey, Rebecca West, Mina Yoo, and Eleo Pomare; Virgil D. Akins, General Manager; Robert Tadlock, Assistant Manager; Jennifer Barry, Bill Chaison, Dance Captains; Ben Dolphin, Lighting; Shirley Herz, Press; Sheldon Soffer Management, Inc.

JUDITH JANUS
Judith Janus, Dancer-Choreographer; Sally Small, Lighting.

KINETIC ENERGY
Gordon Fladger, Administrative Director; Kevin Austin Hunt, Artistic Director; Dancers: Allison Williams, George Bellinger Jr., Wanda Dryer, Darryl Tribble, Robin Greene, Louis Williams, Daryl Richardson, Morris Johnson, Jr., Phenecia Folkes, Eartha Robinson; Ron Reagan, Company Photographer

LAURA VELDHUIS DANCE COMPANY
Laura Veldhuis, Artistic Director-Choreographer; Dancers: Lee Michaelson, Julia Gale, Cynthia Breidenback, Paul Kessman, Bruce Weitzmon, Laura Veldhuis; Joop Veldhuis, Technical Director

SHEILA ROHAN and WILLIAM SCOTT
Both dancers courtesy of The Dance Theatre of Harlem

Top Right: Eleo Pomare Dance Company
Below: Bicentennial Ballet
(Ron Reagan Photos)

Laura Veldhuis Dance Company
Above: Judith Janus
(Ron Reagan Photos)

PROGRAMS

Wednesday-Thursday, July 7–8, 1976
ALL AMERICAN MOVIN' MUSCLE: *PREMIERES* OF
"Drill," "Bicentennial Suite," "Flowers For My Father," (Tape
Collages, Seamus Murphy)
 Friday, July 9, 1976
GALA BENEFIT for Lincoln Center Library of the Performing
Arts
CHAMBER DANCE GROUP: "Baroque" (15th Century music,
Marvin Gordon)
JUDITH JANUS: "Introduction" from "Celebration" (Bach,
Janus), "Grasshopper" from "Bugs, or, How to Smell with the
Knees, Taste with the Feet, and Wear a Skeleton on the Outside"
(Amadeo Roldan, Janus)
BICENTENNIAL BALLET: "Coppelia Pas de Deux, Act III"
(Delibes, St. Leon). *N.Y. PREMIERE* of "Storm" (Tim Wengerd)
ARGYR LEKAS SPANISH DANCE COMPANY: "Sunday In
Seville" (Kelly, A. de Cordoba/Argyr Lekas), "La Vida Breve
Dance No. 1" (De Falla, A. de Cordoba)
SHEILA ROHAN and WILLIAM SCOTT: "Gimme Somethin'
Real" (Ashford, Scott)
ALL AMERICAN MOVIN' MUSCLE: "Bicentennial Suite"
EDITH STEPHEN DANCE COMPANY: "Peacock" (Switched-
on Bach, Stephen)
CHARLES MOORE: "Sacred Forest Dance" (adapted by Moore)
ALONSO CASTRO DANCE THEATRE: "N.Y. 110th Street"
(Tito Puente, Marvin Gordon)
KINETIC ENERGY: "Kaleidescopes" (Herbie Hancock, Kevin
Austen Hunt)
 Saturday, July 10, 1976
BALLET CLASSICS: "A Dream That Was Never Meant To Be"
(silent, Marian Horosko/based on a 1909 movie)
BICENTENNIAL BALLET-BALLET WORKSHOP: "Biljane"
(traditional Macedonian music, staged by Imogen S. Wheeler),
"Storm" (choreography, Tim Wengerd), *U.S. PREMIERE* of
"Death And The Maiden" (Schubert, Alexander Bennett after An-
dre Howard), "Coppelia Pas De Deux, Act III" (Delibes, St. Leon)
CHAMBER DANCE GROUP: "Baroque" (15th Century Music,
Marvin Gordon), "Journey" (Marvin Gordon)

BERNICE JOHNSON DANCE COMPANY: "Essence" (Tape
collage, Marshall Roumain/Leah Randolph), "Thankful" (Black-
birds, Michelle Simmons), "Ember" (Isaac Hayes, W. De Witt
Hemsley)
 Sunday, July 11, 1976
ARGYR LEKAS and her SPANISH DANCE COMPANY:
"Zapadeado" (Paco Juanas, Ramon de los Reyes), "Panaderos" (a
17th Century dance), "La Vida Breve, Dance No. 1" (De Fila,
Antonio De Cordoba), "Cana" (Paco Juanas/Domingo Alvarado,
Ramon De Los Reyes), "Caracoles" (Juanas/Alvarado, Lekas),
"Allegrias De Ramon" (Gypsy Rhythm, Ramon De Los Reyes),
"Tambourin-Jota" (Lekas), "Pinturas Flamencas" and *PREMIERE*
of "Domingo En Sevilla" (Kelly, De Cordoba/Lekas)
 Wednesday-Saturday, July 14–17, 1976
ELEO POMARE DANCE COMPANY: "Transplant" (Pointer
Sisters/Graham Central Station, Pomare), "Las Desenamoradas"
(John Coltrane, Pomare), " 'Nother Shade of Blue" (Traditional/-
Roberta Flack/Laura Nyro/Judy Collins, Pomare), "Narcissus Ris-
ing" (Collage by Michael E. Levy from music of the Blues Project,
Pomare), "Climb" (Kelemen, Pomare), revivals of "Hex" (Partch,
Pomare), "Gin-Woman-Distress" (Bessie Smith, Pomare),
WORLD PREMIERES of "The Queen's Chamber" (Bartok,
Pomare; costumes by Judy Dearing), "Sextet" (Bach, Pomare; cos-
tumes by Judy Dearing), "Tetramain" (Subotnick, Pomare), "Home
Suite Home" (Lukas Foss, Pomare)
 Sunday (matinee), July 18, 1976
BALLET CLASSICS: "Dead Swan," "Dream of a Love That Can
Never Be," "She Gave Him Her Key" (all choreography by Marian
Horosko)
CHAMBER DANCE GROUP: "Baroque," "Haiku" (classical
Japanese and Tibetan music, Marvin Gordon), "Journey" (Pen-
dereski, Gordon), "N.Y. 110th Street"
 Sunday (evening), July 18, 1976
KINETIC ENERGY: "Rituals of Eerie" (Mahavishnu Orchestra,
Kevin Austin Hunt), "I'm His Lady" (Melba Moore, George Bellin-
ger, Jr.), "Jesus, Is This America?" (Stevie Wonder/Marvin Gaye,
Company), "Press'In" (Grover Washington, Jr., Hunt), "Love and/
or Happiness" (Roberta Flack/Barbra Streisand/LaBelle, Hunt),
"Kaleidescopes" (Herbie Hancock, Hunt), and *WORLD PRE-
MIERE* of "Throsh" (choreography by the Company)

78 Top Right: All American Movin' Muscle in
"Bicentennial Suite" Below: Charles Moore
in "Sacred Forest Dance" *(Ron Reagan Photos)*

Kinetic Energy in "Kaleidescopes" Above: Bernice
Johnson Dance Company *(Ron Reagan Photos)*

BIJOU THEATRE

Wednesday-Thursday, July 21–22, 1976
ALL AMERICAN MOVIN' MUSCLE: "Drill," "Flowers For My Father," "Bicentennial Suite," and *N.Y. PREMIERE* of "And The Fallen Petals" (Chow Wen-Chung, Seamus Murphy)
ALONSO CASTRO DANCE THEATRE: "Vignettes of Carmina Burana," "Concerto #5" (Bach, Castro), "Threshold" (Irwin Bazelon, Castro)
LAURA VELDHUIS DANCE COMPANY: "Walk Softly" (Stan Kenton, Veldhuis), "Miles From Nowhere" (Cat Stevens, Veldhuis), "Those Who Came To Build" (Gustav Mahler, Veldhuis), "Grief" (Benjamin Britten, Veldhuis), and *WORLD PREMIERE* of "Those Who Loved The Land And Sky First" (Dr. Louis W. Ballard, Veldhuis).

Friday-Saturday, July 23–24, 1976
ALL AMERICAN MOVIN' MUSCLE: "Drill," "Flowers For My Father," "Bicentennial Suite," "And The Fallen Petals"
ALONSO CASTRO DANCE THEATRE: "Journey" (E. Bloch, Castro), "N.Y. 110th Street," "Transitions For A Mime Poem by Owa" (Irwin Bazaleon, Castro; directed by Thomas Martin Brimm), "Psalm" (F. Handel, Castro)
JUDITH JANUS: "Celebration, Introduction and Opening," "Mantis and Grasshopper/Motorcycle from 'Bugs, or How to Smell with the Knees, Taste with the Feet, and Wear a Skeleton on the Outside' " ("Mantis" music by William Russell and Lou Harrison; "Grasshopper/Motorcycle" music by Amadeo Roldan)

Sunday (matinee and evening) July 25, 1976
EDITH STEPHEN DANCE COMPANY: "Nostalgia Revisited" (Satie/Debussy, Stephen), "Pique '76" (Manu Dibango, Ralph M. Thomas), "Dream of the Wild Horse" (Jacque Lasri, Stephen; film by B.C. De Daimant), "The Peacock" (Switched-On Bach, Stephen), "This Tender Thread" (The Big Apple, Thomas/Stephen), "Spaces Indescribable" (Francois Bayles, Stephen; poems by Storm De Hirsch)

537 BROADWAY

Friday & Saturday, July 9 & 10, 1976 (4 performances)

CAMEL

A solo by Ann Darby, a solo by Elizabeth Streb, and a duet by Ann Darby and Elizabeth Streb

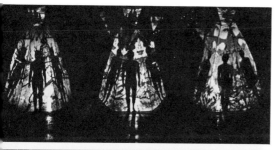

Nikolais Dance Theatre in "Styx"
(Greenfield Photo) **Above: "Triad"**
(Schaaf Photo)

Alonso Castro Dance Company
(Ron Reagan Photo)

Argyr Lekas (C) in "La Vida Breve" *(Ron Reagan Photo)*

BEACON THEATRE

Opened Tuesday, August 3, 1976.*
Kazuko Hillyer presents:

NIKOLAIS DANCE THEATRE

Direction, Choreography, Sound Score, Costume and Lighting Design by Alwin Nikolais; Costume Director, Frank Garcia; Assistants, William Davis, Gus Pollek, Andrew Rudin

COMPANY

Lisbeth Bagnold	Chris Reisner
Suzanne McDermaid	Jessica Sayre
Jude Morgan	Karen Sing
Gerald Otte	James Teeters
Carlo Pellegrini	Joe Zina

REPERTOIRE: "Temple," "Duet from Somniloquy," "Triple Duet from Grotto," "Tensile Involvement from Masks, Props and Mobiles," "Noumenon from Masks, Props and Mobiles," "Group Dance from Sanctum," "Trio from Vaudeville of the Elements," "Foreplay"
WORLD PREMIERES: "Styx" on Tuesday, August 3, 1976, and "Triad" on Wednesday, August 4, 1976.

Company Manager: Kriss Schaffer
Press: Eileen Penn
Stage Manager: Ronald M. Bundt

* Closed August 15, 1976 after limited engagement of 13 performances.

MARYMOUNT MANHATTAN THEATRE
September 8–12, 1976*

JERRY AMES TAP DANCE COMPANY

Director-Choreographer, Jerry Ames; Pianist, Jack Urbont; Lighting Design, Ben Dolphin; Production Manager, Eugene McDougle; Sound, Gregory Parisek; Stage Manager, Olga Kuvish

COMPANY

Jerry Ames   Cinda Mast
Kathy Burke   David Finch
Gary McKay   Sunny Summers

PROGRAM: "The Tapists," "Happy Tap," "Slip and Slide," "Mood Espagnol," "Waltz Time," "Swing Time," "An American Irish Jig," "Sound Footing," "Improvisation," "Bistro," "Elegante," "Maid of Rhythm," "Softly," "Steppin' Out"
* Returned for 4 additional performances Dec. 9–12, 1976.

AMERICAN THEATRE LABORATORY
September 17–19, 1976 (4 performances)
Dance Theater Workshop presents:

MARIKO SANJO

with Jim McConnell, Martha Roth, Michael Schwartz, Fran Spector
PROGRAM: "Voices" (Collage, Sanjo), "Jomon" (Toko Takemitsu, Sanjo), "Bird" (Casals, Sanjo)

Jerry Ames   **Mariko Sanjo**
          (K. Togashi Photo)

GERSHWIN THEATRE
September 17–19, 1976 (4 performances)
Guest Artists Series/Dance presents:

PASCHAL GUZMAN/DOWNTOWN BALLET

Artistic Director-Choreographer, Paschal Guzman; Executive Director, Robert Shuster; Lighting Design, Mallary Perry; Costumes, John Dransfield; Wardrobe Mistress, Brunhilda Montenora; Production Assistants, Mercedes Lois, Brunhilda Montenora, Jeannette Munoz, Irmgard Mahler-Welch

COMPANY

Gerald Banks, Cynthia Breindenbach, Machiko Cho, Giovanni Cotto, Jane Gallagher, Paschal Guzman, Phoebe Meyers, Howard Pitterson, Jacqueline Reed, Chris Roesel, Beth Rosenbluth, Della Weinheimer, Mercedes Lois (Guest Artist), and Keith Cooper, Ester Montenora, Felipe Rose
SPECIAL GUEST ARTISTS: Yoko Morishita and Tetsutaro Shimizu (American Premiere) dancing "Grand Pas de Deux from Don Quixote" (Minkus, Petipa) on Friday, September 17, 1976.

PROGRAM

"Banjo" (American Folk, Guzman), "Our Song" (Gladys Knight, Guzman), "Waltz of the Flowers" (Tchaikovsky, Guzman) and *PREMIERES* of "Dance a Dance" (Beethoven, Guzman), "From House of Bondage to Soul and Rock" (Granville Lee, Guzman), "Julia de Burgos" (Collage, Guzman)

AMERICAN THEATRE LABORATORY
September 24–26, 1976 (3 performances)
Dance Theater Workshop presents:

CONCERT DANCE COMPANY

Artistic Director, Barbara Lazarus Kauff; Manager, Joel Press; Assistant Manager, Kathryn Daniels; Lighting, Beverly Emmons Gombosi; Stage Manager, Sylvia Yoshioka; Press, Louise Lillienfeld; Costumes, Susan Smith White, Kathryn Quick Spingler

COMPANY

Ann Asnes   Faith Pettit
Peggy Brightman   James Plumb
Kathryn Daniels   Roger Tolle
Patrick Hayden   Deborah Wolf

PROGRAM: "For Betty" (Vivaldi, Bill Evans), "Cartouche" (Purcell, Phoebe Neville), "Pilobolus" (Jon Appleton, Moses Pendleton/Jonathon Wolken/Pilobolus Dance Theatre), "Day on Earth" (Aaron Copland, Doris Humphrey), "Hard Times" (Deseret String Band, Bill Evans), "Headquarters" (Collage, Art Bauman)

Concert Dance Company in "Hard Times"
80   **Above: Paschal Guzman in "Our Song"**
    (Steve Turi Photo)

MANHATTAN COLLEGE OF MUSIC
September 29-October 3, 1976 (4 performances)

UTAH REPERTORY DANCE THEATRE

Lighting Designer-Production Manager, M. Kay Barrell; General Manager, Bruce A. Beers; Company Manager, Dana Bowen; Designer-Costumer, Marina Harris; Stage Managers, Gary Justesen, Steve P. Smith; Tour Manager, Carolyn Wood

COMPANY

Ellen Bromberg	Ruth Jean Post
Michael Kelly Bruce	Ron Rubey
R. McAllister Burrows	Thom Scalise
Kay Clark	Linda C. Smith
Martin Kravitz	Karen Steele
John Malashock	Lynne Wimmer

REPERTOIRE: "Nocturne" (Moondog, Donald McKayle), "Lost and Old Rivers" (Brahms, Lynne Wimmer), "Between Me and Other People There Is Always a Table and A Few Empty Chairs" (Burt Alcantara, Jennifer Muller), "A Piece for Evan" (Linda C. Smith), "Synapse" (Songs of the Humpback Whale, Karen Steele), "There Is a Time" (Dello Joio, Limon/Jennifer Scanlon), "My Brother's Keeper" (Hal Cannon/Chris Montague, Wimmer), "Session" (Lar Lubovitch)

Karen Steele, Michael Kelly Bruce, Kay Clark, Ron Rubey in "Session" *(Doug Bernstein Photo)*

THE LOFT
September 30 - October 3, 1976 (4 performances)*
Circum-Arts Foundation, Inc. presents:

GALE ORMISTON DANCE COMPANY

Richard Biles
Gale Ormiston
Luise Wykell

in "Sequitur" with choreography, costumes, sound score, and decor by Gale Ormiston

 Repeated Dec. 18–22, 1976 (5 performances) and April 22 -May 1, 1977 (6 performances)

Luise Wykell, Gale Ormiston, Richard Biles in "Sequitur" *(Gale Ormiston Photo)*

NEW YORK UNIVERSITY THEATRE
September 30 - October 2, 1976 (4 performances)
Kazuko Hillyer presents:

YASS HAKOSHIMA MIME THEATRE

Assistant, Renate Boue; Technical Director, Charles Miller; Lighting Design, Donna Stiles; Choreography, Sound and Lighting arrangement by Yass Hakoshima

PROGRAM

"Fisherman," "Illusion," "Ecdysis" (Mayuzumi), "Trap," "Labyrinth" (Stockhausen), "Laughter," "Thinking" (Ussachevsky), "Surgeon" (Sala), "Vision of 'Ego' " (Cowell/Mayuzumi), "Puppet," "Eagle"

MERCE CUNNINGHAM STUDIO
October 1–3, 1976 (3 performances)

SATORU SHIMAZAKI
AND DANCERS

in *Premiere* of "Out of the Blue" choreographed by Satoru Shimazaki; Lighting, Jon Garness; Costumes, Jacki Apple; with dancers Barbara Finney Berkey, Diane Duncan, Nancy Hall, Susanne Hunter, Steven Keith, Susan Peters, Susan Tamlyn, Robbie Tessler, Satoru Shimazaki; "First Section: Get" (Composed and recorded by Thom Edlun), "Second Section: Take It" (Composed and recorded by Thom Edlun), "Last Section" "Catch" (Composed and recorded by Richard Cahn)

The second half of the program consisted of "Geki-Sei" (John Watts, Shimazaki), "Work in Progress" (Shimazaki), "Child Is Father to Man" (Shimazaki)

Satoru Shimazaki Dancers in "Out of the Blue" *(Lois Greenfield Photo)* **Above: Yass Hakoshima in "Labyrinth"** *(Serge Maljkovicz Photo)*

Hannah Kahn, Dalienne Majors
(Laura Pettibone Photo)

Ballet Folklorico de Mexico
(also above)

DANCE UPTOWN
Seventeenth Series

Director, Janet Soares; Designer and Coordinator, Jennifer Herrick; Stage Managers, Sylvia Yoshioka, Elaine Smith; Sound, Mark Seiden, Press, Rosa Vega

BARNARD GYMNASIUM
October 7–9, 1976 (3 performances)

PROGRAM

GARY MASTERS DANCE COMPANY: Sam Harris, Jay Todd, Cindy Anderson, Amanda Kreglow, Nadine Vuillemain, and Naomi Brunswick, Mary Lisa Burns, Rachel Cohen, Katherine Cunningham, Nina Hennessey, Joyce de Moose, Donna Nicholas, Emily Pease, Ann Wigglesworth dancing "Quest" (Norma Dalby, Gary Masters)
ZE'EVA COHEN SOLO DANCE REPERTORY performing *NY Premiere* of "Listen II" (George Crumb, Cohen) danced by Ze'eva Cohen
CONCERT DANCE COMPANY: Faith Pettit, Deborah Wolf, Roger Tolle, Ann Asnes, Patrick Hayden performing "Five Songs in August" (Stanley Sussman, Bill Evans)
October 14–16, 1977 (3 performances)
DANCERS' EXCHANGE: Kathy Colihan, Jane Comfort, Eva de Kievet, David Lusby, David Malamut, Nancy Mapother, Garry Reigenborn, John Schnieder dancing the *Premiere* of "Catch" (Charlie Morrow, David Lusby; Costumes, Eva de Kievet)
HANNAH KAHN/DALIENNE MAJORS AND DANCERS: Carol Hess, Peter Healey, Kate Johnson dancing "Duet" (Mitchell Korn, Hannah Kahn)
RUDY PEREZ DANCE THEATRE: Leslie Koval, Harry Streep III, Katherine Liepe, Karen Goodman performing the *Premiere* of "Rally" (Tape, Rudy Perez) with Christina Bernat, Victoria Berning, Terry Dillin, Natalie Elman, Nicole Fautaux, Naomi Frank, Rise Gerber, Sally Hechinger, Erica Kapuler, Suzanne Konowitz, Charles Krause, Sally Levine, Lee Madinger, Daniel McCuster, Anne McHugh, Michael Molthen, Allison Monsor, Diane Peepas, Stephen Prutting, Jenny Rosairo, Kay Rosenberg, David Schulberg, Amy Schwartzman, Jill Shaffer, Jamie Shapiro, Gabrielle Tomchinsky, Hara Trambert, Jann-Meri Trambert, Cindy Trombley, Joan Wan, Mary Catherine Ward, Celeste Williams

FELT FORUM
October 7–9, 1976 (4 performances)
Hurok in association with Madison Square Garden Productions presents:

BALLET FOLKLORICO DE MEXICO

General Director-Choreographer, Amalia Hernandez; Dance Coordinator, Jose Villanueva; Settings and Costume Designer, Guillermo Barclay; Lighting, Gilbert V. Hemsley, Jr.; Wardrobe, Carlotta Hernandez, Mario Sosa; Dance Coordinator, Simon Semenoff; Sound, Sherman Steadman; Wardrobe Supervisor, Deborah Musgrove

CORPS DE BALLET

Susana Barrera, Maria del Carmen Cardenas, Martha Flores, Rosa Gallardo, Elsa Maria Garcia, Leticia Gonzalez, Angeles Gutierrez, Mercedes Loza, Haydee Maldonado, Alma Rosa Martinez, Teresa Minguet, Concepcion Morales, Eva Morales, Aida Polanco, Eva Rodriguez, Nestor Castelan, Emilio Ceron, Francisco Cruz, Alfredo Espinoza, Jose Manuel Esquivel, Mario Garcia, Rodolfo Hernandez, Guillermo Pensado, Carlos Rios, David Rodriguez, Pedro Rodriguez, Antonio Rodulfo, Manuel Romano, Jaime Roura, Jose Santacruz, Jose Villasenor, and singers Ofelia Gaona, Carolina Hadda

PROGRAM

"Los Matachines," "Zacatecas," "Fiesta in Tlacotalpan," "Los Totonacas," "La Boda de Jesusita en Chihuahua," "Danza de Venado" (Deer Dance), "Jalisco"

Company Manager: Wally Adams
Press: Norman Lombino
Stage Managers: Jose Autulio, David Thurow

THE GLINES
October 7 - November 14, 1976 (20 performances)

ALL AMERICAN MOVIN' MUSCLE

Artistic Director-Choreographer, Seamus Murphy; dancers, John Dickerson, Pamela DeSio, Garth Miano, Louis Solino, Jack Walsh, performing "Bicentennial Suite," "Busstop," "Dudes," "Flowers for My Father," "Forsaken," "Jack's Dream," "Intergalactic Space Theatre"

ZALKIND AND BURKE

in "Stories You Might Have Heard" choreographed and performed by Debra Zalkind and Cameron Burke

MARIAN HOROSKO COMPANY

Marian Horosko (Choreographer-Dancer) with Richard Larcada, Jack Walsh, Frank Crapanzano performing "The Movie Company"

AMERICAN THEATRE LABORATORY
October 7-10, 1976 (4 performances)
Harry's Foundation and Dance Theater Workshop present:

HARRY

All works by Senta Driver; Lighting Design, Robin Kronstadt; Stage Managers, Tina Charney; Staff Assistants, Jack Perez, Mary DeQuette, Lynn Hoogenboom

COMPANY
Senta Driver
Michaele Sallade
Timothy Knowles
Charles Lee Redman Trio

PROGRAM: "Second Generation" (Henry Purcell), "Matters of Fact," "Music for This Occasion" (Jim Burton/Hank Williams), "Piece D'Occasion" (Jim Burton), "Board Fade Except" (Thomas Skelton), "Suite from Gallery" (John Fahey/Patsy Cline), "In Which a Position is Taken, and Some Dance" (Gilbert & Sullivan/Terrill Jory)

Zalkind and Burke
Below: Marian Horosko in "Movie Company"
(Ron Reagan Photos)

AMERICAN THEATRE LABORATORY
October 14-17, 1976 (5 performances)
Dance Theater Workshop presents:

MARCUS SCHULKIND DANCE COMPANY

Artistic Director-Choreographer, Marcus Schulkind; Co-Artistic Director, Elisa Monte; General Manager, Charles Moody; Lighting Design, Tina Charney; Stage Manager, Rosemary Cunningham; Costumes, Elisa Monte

COMPANY
Marcus Schulkind

Gloria Chu	Sharon Filone
Keiko Takeya	Christine Wright
Randal Harris	Lonne Moretton

PROGRAM: (all choreography by Marcus Schulkind) "Lambent" (Beethoven), "Ladies' Night Out" (Beatles), "Onus" (Crumb), "God's Pieces" (Randy Newman), "Affettuoso" (Telemann), "A Piece of Bach" (Bach/Bussoni)

EISNER & LUBIN AUDITORIUM
Thursday, October 14, 1976 (1 performance)
The Loeb Student Center of NYU presents:

WENDY OSSERMAN DANCE COMPANY

Andrea Borak	John Proto
Thomas Lague	Jeffrey Strum
Judy Lasko	Wendy Osserman

Musicians: Ann Bass, Lloyd McNeill

PROGRAM: "Flight In/Flight Out" (Leo Kotke. Wendy Osserman), "Breakfast" (Ann Bass, Osserman), "Me Strong, Me Scared" (Lloyd McNeill, Osserman), "Cycles" (Balinese gamelan, Tibetan bells, Osserman), "Double Entendre" (Stanley Clarke, John Proto/Wendy Osserman), "Dream Animal" (McNeill, Pink Floyd)

John Proto, Wendy Osserman *(Barnet Silver Photo)*
Above: Marcus Schulkind Dance Company in
"A Piece of Bach"

ELIOT FELD BALLET

Artistic Director-Choreographer, Eliot Feld; Administrator, Cora Cahan; Company Pianists, Gladys Celeste Mercader, Peter Longiaru; Lighting Design, Thomas Skelton; Wardrobe Master, Kristina Kaiser; Sound, Roger Jay

COMPANY

Aturo Azito, Helen Douglas, Mona Eigh, Eliot Feld, Richard Gilmore, Michaela Hughes, Cynthia Irion, Charles Kennedy, Edmund LaFosse, Remus Marcu, Linda Miller, Gregory Mitchell, George Montalbano, Mark Morris, Jennifer Palo, Mary Randolph, Shirley Reevie, Christine Sarry, Jeff Satinoff, Paul Stewart, Gwynn Taylor GUEST ARTISTS: Birgit Keil, Vladimir Klos

REPERTOIRE

"At Midnight" (Mahler, Feld), "The Consort" (Dowland/Neusidler/Others/Arranged by Michael Jaffe, Feld), "Cortege Parisien" (Chabrier, Feld), "Excursions" (Barber, Feld), "The Gods Amused" (Debussy, Feld), "Harbinger" (Prokofiev, Feld), "Intermezzo" (Brahms, Feld), "The Real McCoy" (Gershwin, Feld), "Tzaddik" (Copland, Feld), *Company Premieres* of "A Poem Forgotten" (Wallingford Riegger, Eliot Feld), "A Soldier's Tale" (Stravinsky, Feld), "Waves" (Laurie Spiegel, Kathryn Posin), and *WORLD PREMIERE* of "Impromptu" (Albert Roussel, Eliot Feld; Costumes, Willa Kim; Scenery, Ming Cho Lee; Lighting, Thomas Skelton) danced by Birgit Keil on Wednesday, October 20, 1976.

Press: Merle Debuskey, Susan L. Schulman, Fred Hoot
Stage Managers: John H. Paull III, Bruce Goldstein, Zack Arkontaky

* Closed Nov. 20, 1976 after limited engagement of 38 performances.

Birgit Keil in "Impromptu" *(Lois Greenfield Photo)* **Top: Richard Gilmore, Eliot Feld, John Sowinski in "Tzaddik"** *(Tom Victor Photo)* **Left Center: Eliot Feld Ballet in "Excursions"** *(Migdoll Photo)*

CAROL CONWAY DANCE COMPANY

Director-Choreographer, Carol Conway; Lighting Design, Paul Butler; Stage Manager, Djuna Moran; General Manager, Will Ansorge; Costumes and Sets, James Pelletier, Raya

COMPANY

Carol Conway

June Anderson	Sandra Sheridan
Will Ansorge	Craig Sloane
Molissa Fenley	Brian Webb

REPERTOIRE: "Product of the Sides" (Sergio Cervetti, Carol Conway), "Red Right Returning" (Cervetti, Conway), "In the Center of the Night" (Linda Thomas, Brian Webb), "Duelle" (Cervetti, Conway), "Together Passing" (Cervetti, Conway), and *Premieres* of "Cat Court" (Bach, Brian Webb), and "Bagging at the Bottom" (Cervetti, Conway)

SHANGO-HAITIAN COMPANY

"Sacrifice to Damballa" (directed, choreographed, and designed by Arnold Elie, assisted by Albert P. Louigene and Jose Suares) danced by Gislaine D'Janvier, Aline Jules, Esther Pulliam, Carolyn Clemans, Raymande Gabriel, Jeanne Hunt, Alescandra Stavraw, Arnold Elie, Arnold Vixama, Claude Similus, Albert Tierre, Serya Chalatan, Kenel Archer, Kharlo Chatelain; songs by Myriam Dorisme; music: "Congo" (Salvi Gislame-Arnolar), "Arraignee" (Salis Kenel), "Djouba" (Graup), "Banda" (Solis Louis Celestin), "Ceremonie" (Graup), performed by drums: Anathan Charles, Catilus Lageurre, Bruce Hubland, Louis Celestin; flute: Luc Richard; lights by Michael Traummell

Shango-Haitian Company in "Sacrifice to Damballa" *(Ron Reagan Photo)*

KAUFMANN CONCERT HALL
Saturday, October 30, 1976

THE RETURN OF LOIS BEWLEY

World Premiere of one-woman dance concert by Lois Bewley performing "Concerto Grosso" (Corelli), "Emily Jane," "Quatro Tonadillos" (Granados), "Quartet No. 3 for Strings and Electronic Tape" (Leon Kirchner), "Short Shorts" (Scott Joplin), "Sally Mae" (No other details available)

AMERICAN THEATRE LABORATORY
November 3–7, 1976 (5 performances)
Dance Theater Workshop presents:

RUDY PEREZ IN 'SOLO'
with Company

Artistic Director-Choreographer, Rudy Perez; Company Manager, Sandra Fowlkes; Stage Manager, Kenneth F. Merkel; Production Assistants, Jane Barrell, Rick Ladson, Peter Rietz; Lighting Design, Kenneth F. Merkel

COMPANY

Leslie Koval   Katherine Liepe
Harry Streep III   Karen Goodman
with Naomi Frank, Sally Hechinger, Carol Kennedy, Suzanne Konowitz, Charles Krause, Hope Mauzerall, Daniel McCusker, Kay Rosenberg, David Schulberg, Amy Schwartzman, Jill Shaffer, Jamie Shapiro

REPERTOIRE

"Running Board for a Narrative" (Arranged, Perez), "Rally" (Arranged, Perez), "System" (Arranged, Perez), "Take Your Alligator with You" (Perez), "Countdown" (Songs of the Auvergne, Perez), "Update" (Noah Creshevsky, Perez), "Coverage" (Arranged, Perez)

Top Right: Lois Bewley
(Henry Wolf Photo)
Below: Rudy Perez in "System"
(Johan Elbers Photo)

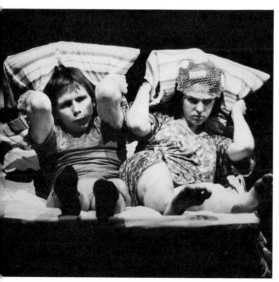

Cameron Burke, Debra Zalkind
(Ron Reagan Photo)

BIJOU THEATRE
Wednesday & Thursday, November 3 & 4, 1976 (2 performances)
Adkind presents:

DEBRA ZALKIND/CAMERON BURKE
in
"Stories You Might Have Heard"

with DENII SNAPP and ROLANDO JORIFF; Staged and Choreographed by Debra Zalkind and Cameron Burke; Lighting, Ron Bundt; Costumes, Evan Williams, Debra Zalkind, Cameron Burke; Stage Manager, Vicki Margules; Press-Photography, Ron Reagan

PROGRAM

"The Streetcleaner's Saga" (Bach/Traditional/Smokey Robinson/Percy Sledge), "The Sweepstake" (Henry Purcell/Dory Previn/Bach/Elton John), "It Happened One Night and then it happened again ... " (Porter/Gershwin /Schwartz/Humpheld), "Denii Sings the Blues" (Denii Snapp, Burke/Zalkind), "Send in the Clowns" (Sondheim/Snapp)

WASHINGTON SQUARE METHODIST CHURCH
November 4–6, 1976 (3 performances)

DANCES BY DORIS GINSBERG AND
RANDOLYN ZINN

PROGRAM: "Chapter Nine" (Chopin) choreographed and performed by Randolyn Zinn; Pianist, James Irsay; Lighting, Lynn Gutter; "Deepmouthed Figure" (Sounds from the Kabuki, Doris Ginsberg) performed by Art Berger; "I Am a Fanatic" (Rodriego, Zinn; Poem, Peter L. Wilson) performed by Laurie McKirahan, Stuart Smith, Randolyn Zinn; "Broken Flight; In Ink" (Vivaldi) choreographed and performed by Doris Ginsberg; "Memory Fades, Flowers Die" (Oregon, Ginsberg) performed by Mickie Geller, Doris Ginsberg, Laurie McKirahan, Kathy Robens, Randolyn Zinn

APPLEBY STUDIO THEATRE
November 4–6, 1976 (3 performances)

DANCES BY APPLEBY

COMPANY: Craig Brashear, Agnes Denis, Claudia Isaac, Martha Karess, Rachel List
PROGRAM: "Bestiary" (Debussy/Subotnik, Claudia Isaac), "Overspill" (Martha Karess), and *Premieres* of "Voice" (Carol Weber, Rebecca Kelly), "Thirst" (Hovhaness, Claudia Isaac), and "American Landscape" (Bill Kleinsmith/Linda Thomas, Rebecca Kelly)

COOPER UNION GREAT HALL
Friday, November 6, 1976*
Performing Arts Foundation presents:

PHILIPPINE DANCE COMPANY OF NEW YORK

Artistic Director-Choreographer, Ronnie Alejandro; Executive Director, Bruna P. Seril; Technical Director, Chuck Golden; Stage Manager, Lee Horsman; Producer, Herman Rottenberg

COMPANY

Ronnie Alejandro, Christy Canonizado, Rodgee Cao, Joy Coronel, Bennie Felix, Kristin Jackson, Nancy Latuja, Lett Llagas, Neneng Llagas, Maxie Luna, Ramon de Luna, Don Marasigan, Bubut Montenegro, Menchie Obligacion, Nelma Obligacion, Jun Pascual, Kathy Serio, Eddie Sese, Cecile Sicangco, Vicky Tiangco, Rosemarie Valdes, Vicky Valdes

PROGRAM

DIWANG FILIPINO: THE FILIPINO SOUL IN DANCE: "Bailes de Ayer Suite" (Spanish-influenced dances), "Sarimanok Suite" (Muslim dances of the South), "Taga-Bundok Suite" (Tribal dances from the Mountains), "Sa Kabukiran Suite" (Rustic Festive Dances)
* This program repeated April 2, 1977 at American Museum of Natural History Auditorium

AMERICAN MODERN DANCE THEATRE
November 9-15, 1976 (8 performances)

GEORGE STEVENSON DANCE COMPANY

GEORGE STEVENSON DANCE COMPANY: Jay Geils, Deena Hoffman, Doreen O'Connor, George Stevenson

THOMAS HOLT DANCE ENSEMBLE

THOMAS HOLT DANCE ENSEMBLE: Thomas Holt, Lucinda Gehrke, JoAnne Kuhn, Ann Moser, Kelly Roth, Carol Elsner, David McComb, Nobert DuBois, Elaine Frezza

PROGRAM

"Greek Myth" (Toshiro Mayazumi, George Stevenson), "Duet for Summer" (Lee Holdridge, Thomas Holt), "Computer Date" (Collage, George Stevenson), "Arienata" (Vivaldi, Thomas Holt), "Metamorphosis" (George Stevenson), "Pas de Deux Pourune" (Faure, Deena Hoffman), "Westward" (Thomas Holt)

DANCERS STUDIO
Tuesday, November 9, 1976

DANCERS

Artistic Director, Dennis Wayne; COMPANY: Buddy Balough, Miguel Campaneria, Donna Cowen, James Dunne, Kenneth Hughes, Linda Kuchera, Deirdre Myles, Christine O'Neal, Lawrence Rhodes, Marilee Stiles, Nancy Thuesen, Dennis Wayne.
PROGRAM: "New Work" (Beethoven, Marcus Schulkind), "Song of the Wayfarer" (Mahler, Maurice Bejart), "Pavan" (Faure, Norman Walker), "Of Us Two" (Lutoslawksi, Cliff Keuter), "Prussian Officer" (Bartok, Norman Walker), "New Work" (Shostakovitch, Francois Szony)

Top Right: Martha Karess, Rebecca Kelly in "Overspill" *(Caroline Fabricant Photo)* Below: Philippine Dance Company *(Ely Pascual Photo)*

Nancy Thuesen, Dennis Wayne, also above *(Ron Reagan Photo)*

THE LOFT
November 11–14, 1976 (4 performances)
Circum-Arts Foundation presents:

LUISE WYKELL DANCE CONCERT

Choreography, Luise Wykell; Lighting Design, Gale Ormiston; Costume Design, Luise Wykell; Technical Director, Norman Ader
DANCERS: Luise Wykell, Gale Ormiston, Rosemary Newton, Valerie Farias, Richard Biles
PROGRAM: "Pardon Me, But Haven't We. . . ." (Collage, Wykell), "Cervidae" (Marcello, Wykell), "Reciprocity" (Monk, Wykell), "Maillol, We Salute You!" (Purcell), "Palette" (Arranged, Wykell)

MERCE CUNNINGHAM DANCE STUDIO
Saturday & Sunday, November 13 & 14, 1976 (2 performances)
The Experimental Intermedia Foundation presents:

ELAINE SUMMERS DANCE AND FILM COMPANY

PROGRAM: "Solitary Geography" (Pierre Ruiz, Elaine Summers) a *Premiere* danced by Matt Turney, "Times Four" (David Gordon) danced by Edward Bhartonn, Gail Donnenfeld, Deborah Glazer, David Schulberg, "Energy Changes" (Philip Corner, Elaine Summers) danced by Michelle Berne, Edward Bhartonn, Tedrian Chizik, Roberta Escamilla, Alexandra Ogsbury, Tim Shelton

TOWN HALL
Wednesday, November 17, 1976 (1 performance)
Interludes presents:

GUS GIORDANO JAZZ DANCE COMPANY

Director-Choreographer, Gus Giordano; Dance Coordinator, Lea Darwin; Manager, Libby Beyer; Associate Director, Clarence Teeters

COMPANY
Gus Giordano

Clarence Teeters	Jeffrey Mildenstein
Julie Walder	Kim Darwin
Meribeth Kisner	Jim Kolb

PROGRAM: "Judy" (Judy Garland, Giordano), "Solar Wind" (Pointer Sisters, Earnest Morgan), "The Rehearsal" (Stevens, Giordano), "Holy Hoppin' Hallelujah" (Gold/Udell, Giordano)

AMERICAN THEATRE LABORATORY
November 18-21, 1976 (4 performances)
Dance Theater Workshop presents:

ROSALIND NEWMAN & DANCERS

Choreography, Rosalind Newman; Lighting Design-Stage Manager, Tina Charney

DANCERS

Richard Alston, Tom Borek, Jean Churchill, Kate Johnson, Clarice Marshall, Rosalind Newman, Idelle Packer, Karen Shields, Elizabeth Streb, Mark Taylor, Debra Wanner

PROGRAM

"Third Watch" (Latin Mass, Rosalind Newman), "Flakes" (Steve Drews, Newman) "Topaz" (Stravinsky/Ravel, Newman), and *NY Premiere* of "Moorings" (Folk Music of USSR and Poland, Tom Borek/Rosalind Newman)

CONSTRUCTION COMPANY STUDIO
Friday & Saturday, November 19 & 20 (2 performances)

FREE ASSOCIATION

A dance theatre improvisational group consisting of dancers Michele Gordon, Jack Guidone, Sandra Goodman, Barbara Mueller, Sidney Miller, Margaret Ramsay, and musicians Robert Hallahan, Dee Kohanna

Top Right: Gale Ormiston, Richard Biles in "Reciprocity"
(Norman Ader Photo) **Below: Gus Giordano Jazz Dance Co.**
(EPS Studio Photo)

Free Association   Above: Rosalind Newman and Dancers in "Topaz" *(Johan Elbers Photo)* **87**

THE KITCHEN
November 19-21, 1976 (3 performances

SYLVIA WHITMAN

with Jeff Aron, Lynne Morrison, Carol Parkinson performing "Clear View (One Place at a Time)" choreographed by Sylvia Whitman in 8 parts: "Introducing the Andrade Family," "Pole Vault," "Fans" (Terry Riley), "Cigar," "Ironing," "My brother rehearsing for the funeral of Father Mayer in 1951," "With a tree," "Green Line"

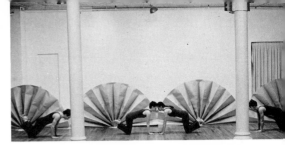

COLDEN CENTER FOR THE PERFORMING ARTS
Saturday, November 20, 1976
The Colden Center for the Performing Arts presents:

METROPOLITAN OPERA BALLET ENSEMBLE

Artistic Director, Norbert Vesak; Associate to Artistic Director, Robert-Glay LaRose; Pianist, Irving Owen; Executive Director, Anthony A. Bliss; Manager, Jane Hermann; Administrator, Audrey Keane; Production Manager, James Nomikos

COMPANY

Patricia Heyes, Naomi Marritt, Diana Levy, Suzanne Laurence, Ellen Rievman, Eugenia Hoeflin, Anthony Santiago, Marc Verzatt, Pauline Andrey, Jack Hertzog, William Breedlove, Judith Thelen, Vicki Fisera, Marcus Bugler, Lucia Sciorsci, Alastair Munro

PROGRAM

"Pas de Quatre" (Pugni, Dolin/Lester), "Pas de Trois from La Ventana" (Lumbye, Bournonville), "Le Carnaval" (Schumann, Fokine/Vesak/LaRose, "Belong" (Norbert Vesak), "Rich Man's Frug" from "Sweet Charity" (Coleman, Fosse/Eddie Gasper)

INTERARTS STUDIO
Saturday, November 20, 1976.

DANCES BY SUE BARNES/JUDY KONOPACKI/WENDY OSSERMAN

with Andrea Borak, Thomas Lague, Judy Lasko, John Proto, Jeffery Strum
PROGRAM: "Me Strong, Me Scared" (Lloyd McNeill, Wendy Osserman), "Double Entendre" (Stanley Clarke, Wendy Osserman), "Still Me" (Walter Carlos, Wendy Osserman), "Solo for an Interrupted Afternoon" (Collage, Sue Barnes), "Etherealities" (Collage, Judy Konopacki), "Triumph" (Sue Barnes)

TERRA FIRMA STUDIOTHEATRE
Saturday & Sunday, November 20 & 21, 1976 (2 performances)
Terra-Synergy Inc. presents:

CATCH A FALLING STAR

a chamber concert for two dancers and three musicians—choreographed by Katherine Liepe with music by Charley Gerard. Performed by dancers Katherine Liepe and Felice Dalgin, and musicians Charley Gerard, Amy Cohen, Bonnie Robiczek

WARD-NASSE GALLERY
November 22–24, 1976 (3 performances)
Richard Biles Dance Company presents:

THE PALE

Choreography, Richard Biles; Sound Score, Eddie Gomez, Jeremy Steig; Costumes, Props, Lighting Design, Richard Biles; Stage Manager, Phillip Weiner

COMPANY

Richard Biles	Geoffrey Hood
Georgia Connor	Marjorie Myles
Jane Durbin	Sharon Spanner
Donna Evans	Peggy Vogt

Richard Biles, Donna Evans, Jane Drubin in "The Pale" *(Norman Ader Photo)* **Above: Katherine Liepe** *(Gary Azon Photo)*

Top: Sylvia Whitman and dancers *(Babette Mangolte Photo)*
Below: Pauline Andrey, Anthony Santiago in "Le Carnaval" *(J. Heffernan Photo)*

HENRY STREET SETTLEMENT PLAYHOUSE
November 26-December 5, 1976 (7 performances)
Tina Ramirez presents:

BALLET HISPANICO OF NEW YORK

Artistic Director, Tina Ramirez; Ballet Mistress, Lolita San Miguel; Stage Manager-Lighting Ronald M. Bundt; Production Assistants, Alfredo Rico, Tyrone Sanders, David Ticotin; Wardrobe Director, Bill Blackwell; Administrators, Natsu Ifill, Josephine Irvine; Company Manager, Marush

COMPANY

Valerie Contreras	Ramon Galindo
Judith Reyes	Marcial Gonzalez
Sandra Rivera	Antonio Iglesias
Alicia Roque	Lorenzo Maldonado
Nancy Ticotin	Roy Rodriguez

PROGRAM: "Fiesta en Vera Cruz" (J. Palbo Moncayo, Jose Coronado), "Deer Dance" (Yaqui Indian Music, Jose Coronado), "Sedalia" (Scott Joplin, Lois Bewley), "Games" (Traditional, Donald McKayle), and *WORLD PREMIERE* of "Danse Creole" (Franz Casius, Geoffrey Holder; Costumes, Geoffrey Holder; Lighting, Ronald M. Bundt)

JAPAN HOUSE/WALLACE AUDITORIUM
Monday, November 29, 1976
The Japan Society presents:

MARIKO SANJO

Director-Choreographer, Mariko Sanjo; Lighting Design, Mitsuo Kano; Set and Costumes, Naoco Kumasaka, Mitsuo Kano, Mariko Sanjo

COMPANY

Mariko Sanjo	Fran Spector
Junko Kikuchi	John DeMarco
Eri Majima	Jim McConnell
Martha Roth	John Parton

PROGRAM: "Sarabande," "Song without Words," "Generations," "Bird"

Lorenzo Maldonado, Sandra Rivera in "Danse Creole"
(Tom Caravaglia Photo) **Above: Martha Roth, Jim McConnell in "Song without Words"** *(Togashi Photo)*

Ramon Galindo in "Deer Dance"
(Tom Caravaglia Photo)

AMERICAN THEATRE LABORATORY
December 2-5, 1976 (4 performances)
Dance Theater Workshop presents:

DANCES BY DEBORAH JOWITT & ELINA MOONEY

Lighting, Nicholas Wolff Lyndon; Stage Manager, Tina Charney; Production Assistant, Jean Rasenberger

PROGRAM

"Water Pieces" (Deborah Jowitt) danced by Lee Olsen, Idelle Packer, Dana Roth, Evan Williams, Debra Zalkind, and Robbie Nadas, Mahala Tillinghast; "Figure" (Subotnick, Elina Mooney; Costumes, Theodora Yoshikami) danced by Carla Maxwell, Luly Santangelo; "Community" (Jowitt) danced by Marc Beckerman, Lee Olsen, Idelle Packer, Dana Roth, Evan Williams, Debra Zalkind; and *Premiere* of "Moment" (Bach, Mooney; Costumes, John Dayger) danced by Joan Finkelstein, Ellen Jacob, Deborah Jowitt, Rachel Lampert, Luly Santangelo

FELT FORUM
December 3-5, 1976 (4 performances)
Mel Howard in association with Madison Square Garden Productions presents:

BALLET NACIONAL FESTIVALES DE ESPANA

Director General, Juan Maria Bourio; Assistant Director, Jesus Manjon; Technical Director, Francisco Caballero; Sound, Eduardo Sousa; Costumer, Angel Ramos Rodriguez; Ballet Mistress, Aurora Pons; Artistic Representative, Jose Hernandez Galian

COMPANY

Aurora Pons, Maria del Sol, Mario La Vega, Juan Manuel, Angel Arocha, Ana Gonzalez, Angela del Moral, Rosa Lugo, Mary Carmen Villena, Concha Cerezo, Maria Pia, Esperanza Piera, Tommy Tellez, Luisa Ortiz, Mercedes Fuertes, Rosa Alvarez, Lupe Gomez, Felipe Sanchez, Felix Granados, Manolo Segura, Pedro Lara, Antonio Salas, Rafael Torres, Antonio Gavilan, Lario Diaz, Miguel Corpas, Curro Landa, Clemente Gimenez, singers Miguel de Alonso, Juan Jose, guitarist Jose Maria Molero

PROGRAM

"Bolero" (Ravel, Jose Granero), "Por Mirabras" (Popular, Mario La Vega), "Alegrias" (Popular, Traditional), "Bulerias" (Popular, Jose Granero), "En La Alhambra" (Tomas Breton, Mario La Vega), "El Chaleco Blanco" (Jimenez, Alberto Lorca), "Intermedio de Goyescas" (Granados, Lorca), "Zapateado" (Breton, Lorca), "La Boda de Luis Alonso" (Jimenez, Lorca), "El Sombrero de Tres Pico" (de Falla, Mario La Vega), "Bolero" (Lorozabal, Lorca), "Pavana" (Nieto, Lorca), "Danza de Escuela Espanola" (de Falla, Aurora Pons), "Jota de la Dolores" (Breton, Lorca)

MARY ANTHONY DANCE STUDIO
December 4-19, 1976 (6 performances)

A RENAISSANCE TAPESTRY

Choreography, Gwendolyn Bye; Music, Michael White; Poetry Readings, Ralph Capan; Costumes, Laura Butcher, Gwendolyn Bye; Sound-Lighting Design, Stefan R. Capan; Artistic Director, Mary Anthony

COMPANY

Gwendolyn Bye
Timothy Brown
Jim Boone
Leigh Crawford

Kenny Gardner
Linda Hayes
Cliff Shulman
Gayle Tannenbaum

BIJOU THEATRE
Sunday & Monday, December 5 & 6, 1976 (2 performances)

YOU AND THE LADIES

Director, John Parks; Press, Zita D. Allen; Lighting Designer-Stage Manager, Sandy Ross; Technical Assistant, Martha Gardner

PROGRAM

"Hex" (Harry Partch, Eleo Pomare) danced by Diana Ramos; "Every Mother's Child" (Hubert Lawa/Vera Hall/Roberta Flack, Shawneequa Baker-Scott) danced by Ms. Baker-Scott and Dyane Harvey; "Nubian Lady" (Yusef Lateef, John Parks) danced by Estelle Spurlock; "A Free Thing" (Gwendolyn Nelson-Fleming) choreographed and performed by Dianne McIntyre; "Bittersweet" (Aretha Franklin) choreographed and danced by Shawneequa Baker-Scott; "Roots" (Collage, Pomare) danced by Dyane Harvey; *Premieres* of "Sophisticated Lady" (Natalie Cole, Parks) danced by Frances Morgan, Lois Hayes, Shirley Black-Brown; "Good Morning Heartache" (Natalie Cole, Parks) danced by Frances Morgan; "Get Away" (Earth Wind and Fire, Parks) danced by F. Morgan, L. Hayes, S. Black-Brown, Jan Hazell, Djenaba Obena Gyinaba

Top Right: "A Renaissance Tapestry"
Below: Dyanne Harvey in "Roots"
(Ron Reagan Photo)

JAPAN HOUSE/WALLACE AUDITORIUM
Monday, December 6, 1976 (1 performance)
Japan Society presents:

SATORU SHIMAZAKI AND DANCERS

Susanne Hunter, Nancy Hall, Steven Keith, Juliet Neidish, Susan Tamlyn, Susan Peters, Barbara Finney Berkey, Robbie Tessler dancing "Out of the Blue" (John Watts/Thom Edlun/Richard Kahn, Satoru Shimazaki), "Geki-Sei," "Work in Progress," "Child is Father to Man" (David Smadbeck, Shimazaki), and *Premiere* of "They Clasp in Time" (Jeff Talman, Shimazaki; Pianist, Robert Max Braham; Lighting Design, Jon Garness)

ROUNDABOUT STAGE ONE
December 7,-19, 1976 (16 performances)
Roundabout Theatre presents:

THE SPIRIT OF DENISHAWN

Staged by Klarna Pinska; Artistic Supervisor, Joyce Trisler; Lighting, Chenault Spence; Costumes, Pearl Wheeler; Produced in cooperation with the New Dance Group Studio (Harry Rubenstein, Executive Director); Pianist, John Colman; Stage Manager, Douglas Drew

COMPANY

THE JOYCE TRISLER DANSCOMPANY: Elaine Anderson, Miguel Antonio, Jacqulyn Buglisi, Nancy Colahan, Ralph Farrington, Don Foreman, Maggy Gorrill, Anne-Marie Hackett, Kate Johnson, Laurie Kaplan, Clif de Raita

PROGRAM

"Techniques of Denishawn," "Music Visualizations:" "Second Arabesque" (Debussy, Ruth St. Denis/Doris Humphrey), "Dance in Space" (Chaminade, Klarna Pinska after Humphrey), "Brahms Waltzes" (Brahms, St. Denis), "Liebstraum" (Liszt, St. Denis), "Bach" (Bach, Ted Shawn), "Sonata Pathetique" (Beethoven, St. Denis/Humphrey), "Orientalia:", "Nautch" (Cadman, St. Denis), "Gnossienne" (Satie, Shawn), "Red & Gold Sari (Stoughton, St. Denis), "Spear Dance Japonesque" (Horst, Shawn), "Soaring" (Shumann, St. Denis/Humphrey)

Steven Keith, Satoru Shimazaki
in "Out of the Blue" *(Lois Greenfield Photo)*

TEARS STUDIO
December 10-12, 1976 (3 performances)

PHOEBE NEVILLE DANCE COMPANY

Artistic Director-Choreographer, Phoebe Neville; Lighting Design, Nicholas Wolff Lyndon; Company Manager, Kaylynn Sullivan

COMPANY

Phoebe Neville
John Dayger
Marleen Pennison
Tryntje Shapli

PROGRAM: "Tigris" (Carol Weber, Phoebe Neville), "Oran" (Traditional, Phoebe Neville)

CARNEGIE RECITAL HALL
Saturday, December 11, 1976 (1 performance)
Chhandas (Rhythm) presents:

RITHA DEVI

in "Nrityollas: Ecstacy of Dance": Prayer, Patha-Pallavi, Nritya-Madhuri, Draupadi, Shiva-Keerthanam, Patim Dehi, Ambapali

WASHINGTON SQUARE UNITED METHODIST CHURCH
Sunday, December 12, 1976 (1 performance)
Washington Square United Methodist Church presents:

THOMAS HOLT DANCE ENSEMBLE

Thomas Holt, Ann Moser, Carol Elsner, Lucinda Gehrke, Kelly Roth, Norbert DuBois, Allan Seward, Elaine Frezza, performing "Arienata" (Vivaldi, Thomas Holt), "Duet for Summer" (Holdridge, Holt), "In Autumn to Romp" (Bartok, Holt), "The Conception of the Nativity" (Handel, Holt), "Westward" (Rodrigo/Serendipity Singers/New Christy Minstrels/Woods/Holtzman, Thomas Holt)

Cliff Keuter Dance Company in "Interlude"
(Ron Reagan Photo) **Top: (L) Phoebe Neville,**
John Dayger in "Oran" *(Philip Hipwell Photo)*
(R) Bhaskar, Carolyn Kay *(Ron Reagan Photo)*

MARYMOUNT THEATRE
Tuesday, December 14, 1976

DANCE GALA '78

BHASKAR: Dances of India: "Natanam Adinar," "Naga Nirthan," "Surya Nirtham;" performed by Bhaskar and Carolyn Kay; costumes, Candace Gay Hibbard, Douglas Meeks.

CLIFF KEUTER DANCE COMPANY: "Interlude," (tape collage, Keuter) performed by Michael Tipton, John Dayger, Joan Finkelstein; "Tetrad" (tape collage, Keuter) performed by Susan Whelan, Karla Wolfangle, John Dayger, Ernest Pagnano; costumes and set, A. Christina Giannini.

STARS OF AMERICAN BALLET: "Flower Festival" (Eduard Helsted, Bournonville) performed by Phyllis Papa and Lawrence Hunt.

CLAUDE KIPNIS MIME THEATRE: "Main Street" (Kipnis) performed by Kipnis, "Eine Kleine Nachtmusik" (Mozart, Kipnis) performed by Lunne Jassem, Jay Nateele, Jon Ruddle, Judi Ann Coles, Michael Piatowski, Cindy Benson, Claude Kipnis

AMERICAN MODERN DANCE THEATRE
December 15-20, 1976 (7 performances)

PROGRAM

"In Autumn to Romp" (Bartok, Thomas Holt) danced by Norbert DuBois, Thomas Holt, Allan Seward; "Reflections" (Mozart, Denna Hoffman), "Excerpt from Easter Oratorio" (Tom Rice, George Stevenson), "Second Avenue Scrapbook" (Laura Nyro, Thomas Holt) danced by Carol Elsner, Thomas Holt, JoAnne Kuhn, Ann Moser, Nina Williams, Allan Seward; "A Christmas Gift" (Traditional, Stevenson); "Jewish Dances" (Denna Hoffman), "The Conception of the Nativity" (Handel, Thomas Holt) danced by the company

Claude Kipnis Mime Theatre Above: Lawrence
Hunt, Phyllis Papa in "Flower Festival"
(Ron Reagan Photos)

SHEPARD GREAT HALL
Thursday & Friday, December 16 & 17, 1976 (2 performances)
The Leonard Davis Center for the Performing Arts presents:

SANASARDO DANCE COMPANY

Artistic Director-Choreographer, Paul Sanasardo; Stage Manager, Judy Kayser; Associate Director, Diane Germaine; Executive Director, William Weaver; Lighting Design, Karen de Francis

COMPANY

Diane Germaine, Joan Lombardi, Janet Panetta, Michele Rebeaud, Anne-Marie Hackett, Elyssa Paternoster, Robin Shimel, Jeri McAndrews, Bert Terborgh, Douglas Nielsen, Harry Laird, Jose Meier, Alex Dolcemascolo

PROGRAM: "A Consort of Dancers" (Watson, Sanasardo), "Shadows" (Satie/Scarlatti/Bach, Sanasardo), "Metallics" (Cowell/Badings, Sanasardo), "The Path" (Drews, Sanasardo), and *NY PREMIERE* of "Abandoned Prayer" (Tomaso Albinoni, Paul Sanasardo)

AMERICAN THEATRE LABORATORY
December 16–19, 1976 (4 performances)
Dance Theater Workshop (David R. White, Executive Director) presents:

CHOREO-MUTATION

Artistic Directors-Choreographers, Shirley Rushing, Thomas Pinnock, Noel Hall; Lighting Design-Stage Manager, Tina Charney; Board Members, Cliff Lashley, Sydney Hibbert; Technical Director, Paul Harkins; Costumes, Ede, Nantambu, Thomas Pinnock

COMPANY

Thomas Pinnock, Shirley Rushing, Noel Hall, Melvada Hughes, Mickey Davidson, Fatisha, Cleveland James, Pierre Barreau, Ibikunle, Ajayi, Gregory Adetobi Jackson, Rhema Yetunde Pinnock

REPERTOIRE

"Creature" (Herbie Hancock/Bennie Maupin, Shirley Rushing), "Consummation" (Gladys Knight/Nina Simone, Noel Hall), "Fetish" (Miles Davis, Rushing), "From the Soul" (Aretha Franklin, Rushing), "Feline Feelings" (Aretha Franklin, Hall), "Hosanna" (Shirley Caesar, Rushing), "Insights to a New Work" (Thomas Pinnock/Burning Spear, Thomas Pinnock), "J. C. on Broadway" (Taj Mahal, Rushing), "Joy" (Edwin Hawkins Singers/ War, Hall), "Salute to the Islands" (Traditional, Hall), "Tenement Rhythms" (Bob Marley and the Wailers/Traditional Rasta/ Eric Gayle, Thomas Pinnock)

Top Right: Diane Germaine, Michele Rebeaud, Sara Singleton, Paul Sanasardo in "Shadows"
Below: Shirley Rushing and Choreo-Mutation in "Insights" *(Bill Hilton Photo)*

JUILLIARD THEATER
Friday, December 17, 1976
The Juilliard School (Peter Mennin, President) presents:

JUILLIARD PHILHARMONIA
JUILLIARD DANCE ENSEMBLE

Conductor, Victoria Bond; Choreography, Hector Zaraspe after Antonio; Assistant, Gloria Marina; Costumes, Rosario Galan; Lighting Design-Production Supervisor, Joseph Pacitti; Set Supervisor, Robert Yodice; Costume Supervisor, Kristina Watson; Makeup, Dianne Burak

COMPANY

Victoria Vergara, Offer Sachs, Stephen Pier, Julie Berndt, Ayala Rimon, Anthony Balcena, Benjamin Greenberg, Walter Kennedy, Keith Martin, Joseph Rich, Thea Barnes, Pamela Condon, Deborah Dawson, Ellen Field, Audrey Jansen, Marc Lind, Lisa Miller, Marie Molander, Beatrice Neuwirth, Judy Sebert, Leith Symington, Irene Tsukada, Jill Wagoner, Kathryn Woglow, Jane Carrington, Teresa Coker, Yveline Cottez, Elizabeth Harris, Jane Maloney

PROGRAM

"Scheherazade Op. 35" (Rimsky-Korsakov), "Second Suite from The Three-Cornered Hat" (De Falla), "El Amor Brujo" (De Falla)

WASHINGTON SQUARE METHODIST CHURCH
December 17–19, 1976 (3 performances)
Impulses Company and Dance Theater Workshop present:

CHRISTMAS IMPULSES

Director-Choreographer-Dancer, Margaret Beals; Lighting Design, Edward M. Greenberg; Musicians, Janaki, Michael Rodwinds, Badal Roy, Gwendolyn Watson; Guest Artists, Ann Bass, Bill Conway, Sandy Gregg, Arnie Lawrence, Mike Richmond

Juilliard Dance Ensemble in "El Amor Brujo"
(Peter Schaaf Photo)

92

JULIE MALONEY DANCE COMPANY

Artistic Director-Choreographer, Julie Maloney; Stage Manager, Joanne Leone Corris; Lighting Design, Andy Tron; Sound-Tapes, Lou DiLiberto

COMPANY

Joanne Edelmann   William Shepard
Rebecca Kelly   Scott Volk
Julie Maloney   Paul Wilson

PROGRAM: (all choreography by Julie Maloney) "Unison" (Handel/Pachelbel), "Conversation" (Donald Erb), "Hat Strut" (Perigeo), and *PREMIERES* of "A Clown" (John Cage, Julie Maloney; Costumes, Joanne Leone Corris) danced by Paul Wilson and Scott Volk, "Liquid Heartbeat" (Lou Grassi, Julie Maloney; Poem by Anne Sexton, read by Maruta Friedler; Costumes, Chris Lindahl, Martha Roth) danced by the company

LIBRARY & MUSEUM OF PERFORMING ARTS
Friday, October 15, 1976

VIJA VETRA
in
"Dances of India"

TERRA FIRMA
Tuesday & Wednesday, December 21 & 22, 1976 (2 performances)

PROGRAM

"Duet for Three" (Rose Auslander) danced by Rose Auslander, Rick Moore, Roselle Warshaw; "Garbo Waltz" (John Field) choreographed and danced by Marian Sarach; "13 Ways of Looking at a Blackbird" (Boris Blacher, Marian Sarach) danced by Yvonne Marcus, Robin Silver, Roselle Warshaw; "Reverie" (Liszt, Warshaw) danced by Rose Auslander, Rick Moore, Roselle Warshaw; "The Tale Itself" (Brahms) choreographed and danced by Marian Sarach; "Gazelles on My Doorstep" (Webern) choreographed and danced by Rose Auslander; "Space to Fill" (Joni Mitchell) choreographed and danced by Roselle Warshaw; "Honeydew" (Lost Highway Band/Progressive Bluegrassers, Auslander) danced by Rose Auslander, Rick Moore (No photos available)

NYU LOEB STUDENT CENTER
January 5–7, 1977
NYU Program Board Performing Arts Committee presents:

DANCES

Lighting Designer-Stage Manager, Mike Soluri; Lighting Technician, Kevin Molloy; Sound Technician, Aaron Lightman

PROGRAM

PARTITA (Georg Philipp Telemann, Claudia Gitelman; Costumes, Frank Garcia) danced by Wendy Ansley, Paul Cohen-Myers, Jon Friedman, Terry Kaelber, Tom Kanthak, Jenise Parris, Patricia Payne, Dale Thompson
HOMAGE TO MAHLER (Gustaf Mahler, Hanya Holm; Costumes, Frank Garcia) danced by Claudia Gitelman, Terry Kaelber
SUNDY DANCES (Paul Petersky, Claudia Gitelman) danced by Candice Christakos, Claudia Gitelman, Patricia Payne, Dorian Petri, Dale Thompson
SOLO (Stanley Walden, Alice Teirstein) danced by Art Bridgman, Michael Cichetti, Anita Feldman, Olgalyn Jolly, Madeleine Perrone
INSIDE SAM (Gerald Otte, Claudia Gitelman) danced by Jeffrey Fox, Patrick Ragland
FOX TROT (Richard Einhorn, Alice Teirstein) danced by Bruce Block, Kathy Kramer, Rick Ornellas, Marta Renzi

WHITMAN HALL/BROOKLYN CENTER FOR PERFORMING ARTS
Saturday, January 8, 1977

SUZANNE FARRELL
PETER MARTINS

with Bart Cook, and other dancers from NYC Ballet: Victoria Bromberg, Judith Fugate, Kathleen Haigney, Heather Watts, Daniel Duell, Gerard Ebitz, Jay Jolley, Ulrik Trojaborg
PROGRAM: "Allegro Brillante" (Tchaikovsky, Balanchine), "Songs of Innocence, Songs of Experience" (Schubert, Richard Tanner), "In G Major" (Ravel, Robbins), "Tarantella" (Gottschalk, Balanchine), "Reflection" (Faure, Robert Weiss), "Who Cares?" (Gershwin, Balanchine), "Calcium Night Light" (Ives, Tanner/Martins), "Agon Pas de Deux" (Stravinsky, Balanchine), "Pas de Deux" (Tchaikovsky, Balanchine)

Suzanne Farrell, Peter Martins
Top Right: Julie Maloney Dance Company
Below: Vija Vetra

BROADWAY DANCE FESTIVAL

January 10–31, 1977
(12 companies, 13 performances)

Administrative Director, Nanette Bearden; Artistic Director, Edith Stephen; Press, June Kelly; Production Manager, Hank Frazier; Lighting Design, Jack Ranson; Technical Director, Leo Johnson; Festival Photographer, Ron Reagan; Stage Manager, Peter Xanthos

Ron Reagan Photos

Chamber Dance Group in "Raymonda Variations"
Above: Bicentennial Ballet in "Carnaval"

BIJOU THEATRE
Wednesday & Thursday, January 12 & 13, 1977
JERRY AMES TAP DANCE COMPANY
Directed and Choreographed by Jerry Ames; with Kathy Burke, Randy Skinner, Gary McKay, Sunny Summers, Jerry Ames, Nancy Lee Lewis, performing "The Tapists," "Happy Tap," "Slip and Slide," "Sound Footing," "Mood Espagnol," "Waltz Times," "Swing Time," "An American Irish Jig," "Bistro," "Elegante," "Maid of Rhythm," "Softly," "Stepping Out"
NEUBERT BALLET COMPANY
Directed and Choreographed by Christine Neubert; Scenery and Designs, Paul Jordan; Costumes, Ramsey and Trutti Gasparinetti; Music, Audiomontage by Christine Neubert. Names of company not submitted; performing "Into Ballet," "Fair Ladies of Mantua," "Excerpts from 'Little Rats of the Paris Opera,' " "The Girl with the Enamel Eyes" (Delibes, Alexander Bennett/Christine Neubert), Grand Finale

Friday, January 14, 1977*
LINDA DIAMOND & COMPANY
Choreography, Linda Diamond; Lighting Design-Press, Richard Gottlieb; Costumes, Joe Bigelow; Musical Director, Jonathan Kramer; Stage Manager, Orland Richardson

COMPANY

Linda Diamond, Richard Hall, Doris Pasteleur, Becky Perces, Stephen Underwood, Gail Waterman

PROGRAM

"Soupir" (Tiberio Nascimento/Robert Armes, Diamond), "A Propos" (Collage/William Lord, Diamond), and *PREMIERES* of "Shadoflash" (Jonathan Kramer, Diamond), "Renascence" (Kramer, Diamond), "Lean-Two" (Kramer, Diamond), "A Tribute to Calder" (Harry Partch, Diamond)
* Program repeated on Saturday, January 29, 1977.

Sunday, January 16, 1977
KINETIC ENERGY COMPANY
Artistic Director-Choreographer, Kevin Austin Hunt; No other details available.

BIJOU THEATRE
Friday, January 21, 1976.
BICENTENNIAL BALLET & BALLET WORKSHOP
Director-Choreographer, Imogen Stooke Wheeler; Lighting Design, Jennie Ball; Stage Manager, Mark Burrows

COMPANY

Seth Kaufman, Jay Jolly, Sarah Rothrock, Holly Graves, Gregory Fawkes, Phillip Crawford, Susan Gaylord, Barnaby Ruhe, Laura Gates, Vivian Wheeler, Dara Burrows, Cynthia Penn, Ina Sorens, Sharon Blamer, Erika Naginski, Sarah Rothrock

PROGRAM

"Nocturne" (Rossini/Britten, Imogen Wheeler), "Romeo and Juliet" (Prokofiev, Alexander Bennett), "Storm" (Choreography, Tim Wengerd), "Carnaval" (Schumann, Fokine)

Saturday, January 22, 1977
JOAN MILLER AND THE DANCE PLAYERS
Director-Choreographer, Joan Miller; Lighting Design, Jack Ranson; Guest Artists, Gwendolyn Watson, Ruth Ann Lief; Production Assistant, James Nichols; Video Engineer, Carol Indianer; Administrative Assistant, Margaret Hanks; Rehearsal Director, Sylvia Rincon; Production Coordinator, Pamela Greene; Production Assistant, Allan Seward

COMPANY

Donlin Freeman, Pamela Greene, Theresa Kim, Bernard Riddick, Sylvia Rincon, Allan Seward, William Fleet, Jr. (musician)

PROGRAM

"Escapades" (Gwendolyn Watson, Joan Miller), "Soundscape," " 'Nother Shade of Blue" (Traditional/Roberta Flack/Judy Collins/Laura Nyro, Eleo Pomare), "Offspring Sprung" (Watson, Miller), "Improv" (Watson, Miller), "Mix" (Roebuck Staples/David Coffee/Billy Preston/Watson, Miller),

Sunday Matinee, January 23, 1977
CHAMBER DANCE GROUP
Monica Diaz, Shelley Gunderson, John Romanosky, Kenneth Frett, Victor Lucas, Roberto Garcia, Sheila Nowosadko performing "Raymonda Variations" (Glazounov, Marian Horosko), "Journey" (Pendereschi, Marvin Gordon), "Rooftop" (John Lewis, Marvin Gordon)

**Top Left: Neubert Ballet in "Fair Ladies
of Mantua" Below: Linda Diamond, Stephen
Underwood in "Lean-Two"**

BIJOU THEATRE

JUDITH JANUS with TONY SMALL
performing "Excerpts from Celebration" (Bach, Janus), "Bugs, or How to Smell with the Knees, Taste with the Feet, and Wear a Skeleton on the Outside" (Selected, Janus)

THE UNIQUE DANCERS
Joachim La Habana, Deena Hoffman, Ivan Torres, Reginald Browning, Jim Lloyd performing "Reflections" (Mozart, Deena Hoffman), "Outer Space Duel" (Sal Soul Orchestra/Tony Janik, Joachim La Habana)

Sunday Evening, January 23, 1977

ARGYR LEKAS & SPANISH DANCE COMPANY
Staged and Supervised by Argyr Lekas; Lighting Design, Michael Purri; Stage Manager, Hank Frazier; Press, June Kelly; Wardrobe Mistress, Alexandra Lekas

COMPANY

Daniel De Cordoba, Albaro Tena, Luis Liciaga, John Bate, Larry Vine, Vera Lekas, Cecilia Torres, Maria Constancia, Lina Leon, Paco Juanas (guitarist), Domingo Alvarado (Flamenco singer), "Ramon De Los Reyes" (Special Guest Star)

PROGRAM

"Domingo en Sevilla" (Kelly, Antonio De Cordoba/Argyr Lekas), "Zapadeado" (Traditional, Ramon De Los Reyes), "Nobleza Espanola" (Choreography by Marvin Gordon), "Vida Breve" (De Falla, De Cordoba), "Tarantos" (Ramon De Los Reyes), "Caracoles" (Argyr Lekas), "Allegrias de Ramon," "Tambourin-Jotas" (Argyr Lekas), "Pinturas Flamencas"

Monday, January 24, 1977

GALA BENEFIT PROGRAM
BICENTENNIAL BALLET COMPANY (Seth Kaufman, Jay Jolly, Sarah Rothrock, Holly Graves, Gregory Fawkes, Phillip Crawford, Susan Gaylord, Barnaby Ruhe, Laura Gates, Vivian Wheeler, Susan Gaylord, Dara Burrows, Phillip Crawford, Seth Kaufman, Greg Fawkes) dancing "Carnival" (Schumann, Fokine)
EDITH STEPHEN DANCE COLLECTION (Carol Baxter, Andrew Jamietti, Paula Odellas, Ralph M. Thomas) dancing "Love in Different Colors" (Michael Dreyfuss, Edith Stephen)
JUDITH JANUS dancing "Spider" from "Bugs Suite" which she choreographed
ARGYR LEKAS SPANISH DANCE COMPANY (Daniel De Cordoba, Albaro Tena, Vera Lekas, Cecilia Torres, Maria Constancia, Lina Leon) dancing "Domingo en Seville" and "Vida Breve" both choreographed by Antonio De Cordoba
JUNE LEWIS AND COMPANY (Judith Leifer, Howard Normann, Deborah Lessen, Barbara Mateer, Martin Morgainsky, Claude Assante, Pat Russell, Ruth Mandel) dancing "A Killing Frost" (Paul Spong, June Lewis)
CHAMBER DANCE GROUP (Marian Sarach, Shelley Gunderson, Kenneth Frett) dancing "Garbo Waltz" (John Field, Marian Sarach) and "Rooftop" (John Lewis, Marvin Gordon)
UNIQUE DANCERS (Joachim La Habana, Deena Hoffman, Ivan Torres, Reginald Browning, Jim Lloyd) dancing "Outer Space Duel" (Sal Soul Orchestra, Joachim La Habana)

Friday & Saturday, January 28 & 29, 1977

DANCE JUNE LEWIS AND COMPANY
Director-Choreographer, June Lewis; Lighting, Gerald Rothman, Robert Litt; Stage Manager, Cindy S. Tennenbaum; Costumes, Alice Pegran, Janet Mooney, Gela Baum; Sound Tapes, Frank Angel, Paul Spong; Technical Director, Leo Johnson

COMPANY

Judith Leifer, Howard Hormann, Deborah Lessen, Barbara Mateer, Martin Morginsky, Claude Assante, Pat Russell, Ruth Mandel

REPERTOIRE

"Spring Is the Well" (Stuart Isacoff, June Lewis), "The Unknown Gate" (Paul Spong, Lewis), "If I Am I" (Spong, Lewis), "A Killing Frost" (Giuffre, Lewis)

Monday, January 31, 1977

THE RON DAVIS DANCERS IN CONCERT
(No details available)

(Ron Reagan Photos)

Top Right: Judith Janus in "Bugs" June Lewis Co. in "A Killing Frost" Below: Unique Dancers in "Outer Space Duel"

**Ron Davis Dancers in "Love Duet"
Above: Edith Stephen Co. in
"The Peacock"**

95

January 15, 22, 29, 1977 (3 performances)

DANCES FOR THREE SATURDAYS

January 15, 1977
"Ice-Cascades" (Mozart) choreographed and danced by Judy Kono-packi; "Triumph" (Jazz/Waves/Jazz) choreographed and danced by Sue Barnes; "Shimmy Sh-ush Suite" (Sounds, Sheila Sobel) danced by Cindy Kanewischer, Jane Regan, Sheila Sobel, Patricia Usakowska, Viva Beck, Sharon Sakai; "Love Doesn't Work in America" (David Bowie) choreographed and danced by Sue Barnes; "Moving Road Song" (Selected, Sheila Sobel) danced by MWC Dance Company.
January 22 & 29, 1977
MWC DANCE COMPANY: Sheila Sobel, Jane Regan, Sharon Sakai, Viva Beck, Katia Noyes, Cindy Kanewischer, Corinne Sarian, Patricia Usakowska dancing "Moving Road Song" (John Cage/Crucifixus/Phantom Gondolier/George Crum/Snake Charmer/Paskastani, Sheila Sobel; Costumes, Jane Regan; "Shimmy Sh-ush Suite" (Sounds/Betty Carter Religious Music/Meade Lux Lewis, Sobel), "Dark Star" (Greatful Dead, Patricia Usakowska), "Clothing" (Sharon J. Sakai, Sobel)

WARD-NASSE GALLERY
Wednesday & Thursday, January 19 & 20, 1977 (2 performances)

PICTURES OFF THE WALL

Choreography, Patrice Evans, Helen Kent, Jody Oberfelder; Lighting Design, Craig Evans; Stage Manager, Jeffrey Eichenwald; Press, Dianne Markham

PROGRAM

"All Overall the Place" (Keith Marks, Jody Oberfelder; Costumes, Jody Oberfelder) performed by Mark Esposito, Jody Oberfelder; "Lunar Lullaby" (Craig Evans, Patrice Evans; Costume, Patrice Evans, Craig Evans) danced by Patrice Evans; "Before Time" (Earl Packard, Patrice Evans) performed by Steven Iannacone, Helen Kent, Jody Oberfelder, Earl Packard; "Frondescene" (Paul McCandless, Helen Kent; Costume, Frank Garcia) danced by Helen Kent; "Undercurrent" (Rob Esposito, Pamela Francis/Jody Oberfelder) danced by Pamela Francis and Jody Oberfelder; "Vessel" (Collin Walcott/Bennie Maupin, Helen Kent; Costumes, Anne McLeod) danced by Patrice Evans, Helen Kent

Top Right: Sue Barnes in "Love Doesn't Work in America" Below: MWC Dance Company in "Movin' Road Song"
(Barnet Silver Photo)

AMERICAN THEATRE LABORATORY
January 20–23, 1977 (5 performances)
Dance Theater Workshop presents:

JOSE CORONADO AND DANCERS

Lighting Designer-Stage Manager, Tina Charney; Assistant Technical Director, Paul Harkins; General Assistants, Angela Caponigro, Sue Henle

COMPANY

Vincent Angelis, Cameron Basden, Kathy Brenner, Jose Coronado, Ann Foley, Linda Gelinas, German Hernandez, Ralph Hewitt, Joselyn Lorenz, Ricardo Mercado, Nancy Mikota, Eileen Mooney, Meg Anne Potter

PROGRAM

"Danses Sacree et Profane" (Debussy), "O Beautiful Dreamer" (Ives), "Mujeres" (Handel), "# or 4 Minor Pieces" (Satie), "La Cita" (Villalobos), "Danza Mexicana #1: The Postcard" (Moncaya)

CONSTRUCTION COMPANY DANCE STUDIO
Saturday, January 22, 1977 (1 performance)
Theater Dance Associates presents:

DANCES OF JUDITH

All works choreographed and danced by Judith Ackerman; Lighting Design, Ted Cosbey; Sound, John Beaulieu; Stage Manager, Anne Leong

PROGRAM

"Reflections on Israel" (John Beaulieu), "Deja Vu" (John Beaulieu), "Judith's Voices" (Beaulieu), "Older" (Beaulieu)

Judith Ackerman

CARNEGIE HALL
Saturday & Sunday, January 22, 23, 1977 (2 performances)
Hurok presents:

RAJKO HUNGARIAN GYPSY ORCHESTRA AND DANCERS

General Manager, Pal Szigeti; Artistic Director-Choreographer, Tibor Somogyi; Artistic Manager, Janos Matyas; Conductor, Bela Berki

PROGRAM

Introduction, "Csardas-Rhapsody," "Dances from Kalotaszeg," "Csardas," "Tidy Kate" "Shepherd Dances," "Hungarian Rhapsody No. 14," "Gypsy Wedding," "Old Hungarian Dances," "Gypsy Fantasy," "Old Serenade," "Bottle Dance," "Bachelor Dance," "Gypsy Songs," "The Lark," "Gypsy Spoon Dance"

CLOUDCHAMBER
Monday, Januray 24, 1977
Minxco presents:

MAO'S INSANE SON

Choreography, Margot Colbert; Script, R. J. Colbert; Music, Carol Henry, Luis Elmore; Costumes, Pamela Pardi; performed by Margot Colbert, Marina Valenti, Amy Wallin, Pamela Pardi; and excerpt from "Medicine Show" performed by Jim Barbosa, Barbara Vann, Chris Brandt
(No photos available)

Rajko Hungarian Gypsy Dancers

MARYMOUNT MANHATTAN THEATRE
January 27–30, 1977 (4 performances)

NIMBUS
A Dance Theatre Company

Artistic Directors, Jack Moore, Erin Martin; Lighting Design, Jon D. Andreadakis; Set Design, Justin Mattison; Costumes, Jack Moore, Elaine Massas, Erin Martin, Davidson Lloyd; Stage Managers, Kenneth F. Merkel, Art Bridgman; Choreographers Assistant, Regina Larkin; Technical Assistants, John Griffin, Drew Hoag, Rene Sanfiorenzo; Press, Debra Stone, Phillip Moser

COMPANY

Jack Moore, Erin Martin, Georgiana Holmes, Davidson Lloyd, Art Bridgman, Michael Cichetti, Holly Harbinger, Olgalyn Jolly, David Malamut

REPERTOIRE

"Four Netsukes" (Evelyn DeBoeck, Jack Moore), "le clue" (Erin Martin/Davidson Lloyd), "Downstairs" (Harvey Ray/Frank Luther, Georgiana Holmes), "Nightshade" (DeBoeck, Moore), "Raspberry Jam" (Don Ellis, Erin Martin) PREMIERES: "Area" (Michael Colina, Georgiana Holmes) danced by Holly Harbinger, Georgiana Holmes, Olgalyn Jolly, Erin Martin; "Cold Frame" (Music, Choreography, Direction, Jack Moore) performed by Erin Martin, Davidson Lloyd, Art Bridgman, Olgalyn Jolly, David Malamut

Nimbus: (from top) Art Bridgman, Erin Martin, Davidson Lloyd, Jack Moore, Georgiana Holmes, Michael Cichetti, David Malamut, Olgalyn Jolly, Holly Harbinger *(Mariette Pathy Allen Photo)*

LARRY RICHARDSON'S DANCE GALLERY
January 27–30, 1977 (4 performances)
Dance Theatre Workship presents:

RICHARD BULL DANCE THEATRE

Director-Choreographer, Richard Bull; Assistant Director, Cynthia Novack; Production Manager-Lighting Design, Lance Olson; Costume Coordinator, Cynthia Novack; Original Music, Richard Bull, Lou Grassi, Duvid Smering

COMPANY

Anne Ackerman, Richard Bull, Rosanne Buters, Anne Coltre, Lisbeth Davidow, Joyce Dolan, Peentz Dubble, Kathy Duncan, Lou Grassi, Robin Hertlein, Michael Immerman, Betsy Keenan, Kathy Kramer, Brenda Maloy, Cynthia Novack, Judith Penski, Rosie Polsky, Charles Seltzer, Duvid Smering, Diana Tanzosh, Lois Welk, Ted Williams, Arnie Zane

PROGRAM: "Visions" (Keith Jarrett, Bull), "The Cosmic Egg" (Bull/Smering), "The Barn Dance" (Grassi/Smering, Bull), "Jesus' Blood" (Gavin Bryars, Bull)

Richard Bull Dance Theatre
(Johan Elbers Photo)

HARLEM PERFORMANCE CENTER

Monday, January 31, 1977 (1 performance)
Harlem Cultural Council (Geanie Faulkner, Executive Director; Emory Taylor, Producing Director) present:

CHOREO-MUTATION

COMPANY: Thomas Pinnock, Shirley Rushing, Noel Hall, Melvada Hughes, Fatisha, Cleveland James, Joe Nicholson-Ajayi, Gregory Adetobi Jackson, Rhema Yetunde Pinnock
PROGRAM: "Speng and Spar" (Thomas Pinnock), "Fetish" (Miles Davis, Shirley Rushing), "Consummation" (Gladys Knight/ Nina Simone, Noel Hall), Fatisha, "Creature" (Herbie Hancock, Rushing), "Salute to the Islands" (Noel Hall)

ALVIN AILEY REPERTORY WORKSHOP

COMPANY: Joe Avegado, Marsha Clark, Ronni Favors, Paul Grey, Merle E. Holloman, Keith McDaniels, Steve Mones, Clayton Palmer, Coco Pelaez, Quincella Swyningan, Mina Yoo, Josiah Young
PROGRAM: "Myth" (Stravinsky, Alvin Ailey), "Baby Child Born" (Valerie Simpson, Gary Ellis Frazier), "Afro-Eurasian Eclipse" (Duke Ellington, Raymond Sawyer)

TOWN HALL

Wednesday, February 2, 1977 (1 performance)
Interludes presents:

EMILY FRANKEL

dancing "Childsplay" (Britten/Variations on a Theme of Frank Bridge, Emily Frankel), and "Haunted Moments" (Sound effects, Emily Frankel)

Top Right: Alvin Ailey Dance Ensemble
(Ron Reagan Photo)
Below: Emily Frankel in "Childsplay"
(Gustavo Photo)

JAPAN HOUSE/WALLACE AUDITORIUM

Thursday, February 3, 1977

GALA BENEFIT FOR THE PERFORMING ARTS PROGRAM

Prima Ballerina YOKO MORISHITA and Premier Danseur TETSUTARO SHIMIZU of the Matsuyama Ballet Company of Tokyo with Guest Artist David Starobin, guitarist; Lighting Design, Mary Ann Moore

PROGRAM

"Grand Pas de Deux from Le Corsaire" (Drigo), "Duet from The Red Warrior Tunic" (Hiroshi Oguri, Mikiko Matsuyama/Yoshiaki Tonozaki), "Adagio from the Grand Pas de Deux of Don Quixote" (Minkus)
David Starobin played "Gavota-Choro" and "Schottish-Choro" from "Suite Populaire Bresiliencne" (Heiter Villa-Lobos), and "Looking for Claudio" (Barbara Kolb)

NEW YORK UNIVERSITY THEATRE

February 3–5, 1977 (3 performances)
The Departments of Dance and Dance Education present:

PEOPLE/DOROTHY VISLOCKY DANCE THEATRE

Director-Choreographer, Dorothy Vislocky; Musical Consultant, Robert Ellis Dunn; Lighting Design, Robert Rosentel; Costumes, Lucy Lucerna, Margaret Hoeffel; Tapes, John Devers; Stage Managers, Robert Rosentel, Dona Brady, Michael Richardson; Company Managers, Shannon Connell, Barbara Fraser

COMPANY

Dorothy Vislocky

Shannon Connell	Frances Lucerna
Jana Feinman	Barbara Mahler
Barbara Fraser	Frances Park
Margaret Hoeffel	David Schulberg
Chuck Krause	Ilana Snyder;

PROGRAM: "Ellis Island" (Vislocky), "Prisms of Time" "Celebration" (Vislocky), and *Premiere* of "Ballad for Anne" (Czechoslovakia and Rumanian) danced by Frances Lucerna, Barbara Mahler, Jana Feinman
Repeated for two additional performances (April 13–14, 1977) at Lehman College Studio

Frances Lucerna in "Ballad for Anne"
(Frank Gimpaya Photo)

Left Center: Tetsutaro Shimizu, Yoko Morishita in "Le Corsaire Pas de Deux" *(Ron Reagan Photo)*

AMERICAN THEATRE LABORATORY
February 3–6, 1977 (4 performances)

3 OF DIAMOND'S

Choreography, Matthew Diamond; Lighting Design, Edward M. Greenberg; Costumes and Sets, Gretchen Warren; Music composed by Laurie Spiegel, Mitchell Korn; Press, Herb Striesfield

COMPANY
Matthew Diamond

Daniel Lewis   Merle Salsberg
Jennifer Clark   Frans Vervenne
Carol-Rae Kraus   Barry Smith

PROGRAM: "Dead Heat", "Escalante," "Understudy"

THEATER OF THE OPEN EYE
Friday & Saturday, February 4 & 5, 1977 (2 performances)

RITHA DEVI

in Three Traditions of Hindu Temple-Dance:Kuchipudi, Bharatha Natyam, Mahari Nritya

541 BROADWAY
February 4 - 6, 1977 (4 performances)

MAD MEG DANCE COMPANY

Artistic Director-Choreographer, Marta Renzi; Costumes, Mary Trev Warren, David Freelander

COMPANY: Marta Renzi, Jude Cassidy, Ken Pierce, Mary Trev Warren, Anita Feldman, John Bernd

PROGRAM: "Attic Suite" (Bach), "Your Move," "Rain" (Ed Billows)

Matthew Diamond

BIJOU THEATRE
Saturday & Sunday, February 5 & 6, 1977 (2 performances)

BERNICE JOHNSON DANCE COMPANY

Executive Director, Bernice Johnson; Artistic Directors, Michelle Simmons, Michael Peters; Business Manager, Bud Johnson; Lighting Design, Jan Kroeye, Leah Randolph

COMPANY

Margo Blake, Charles Epps, Kevin Jeff, Audrey Lawrence, Ronald McKay, Frances Morgan, Valarie Pettiford, Earleen Sealy, Crystal Smith, Rodney Smith, Carolyn Vance, Phillip Wright, Lorna Gray, Tatrina Hofler, drummers Chief Bey, David Copper, Maurice James, Karim Braithwaite, Clifford Tyler
GUEST ARTIST: Shirley Black-Brown

PROGRAM

"Sands of Time" (Morgana King, Michelle Simmons), "Night Birds" (Patrice Rushen, Peters), "Bembe" (drums, Lee Thompson), "Take My Hand" (Jackson, Work Shop), "Essence" (Simone/ Zulema/Flack/Giovanni, Martial Roumain/Leah Randolph), "Linear" (The Counts, Michael Peters), and *Premieres* of "Reminis" (Stevie Wonder, Shirley Black-Brown), "Who Are the Good Guys?" (Diana Ross/Bee Gees/Ashford & Simpson/Kool and the Gang/Elton John, Michael Peters), "Return to Greatness" drums, Chuck Davis), "Bitter Tears" (Laura Nyro, Carolyn Vance), "Someone to Lean On" (J.C. White Singers, Kevin Jeff), "Thankful" (Black Birds, Michelle Simmons)

Bernice Johnson Dance Co. in "Who Are the Good Guys?"
(Ron Reagan Photo) **Above: Ritha Devi** *(Vinanti Sarkar Photo)*

BEACON THEATRE
Opened Tuesday, February 8, 1977.*
Kazuko Hillyer presents:

MURRAY LOUIS DANCE COMPANY
NIKOLAIS DANCE THEATRE

MURRAY LOUIS DANCE COMPANY: Murray Louis (Artistic Director-Choreographer), Micheal Ballard, William Holahan, Helen Kent, Dianne Markham, Anne McLeod, Jerry Pearson, Sara Pearson, Robert Small
REPERTOIRE: "Revue" (8 Divertissments choreographed by Murray Louis: "Go Six opening dance," "Solo from Journal," "Duets I & II from Cleopatra" (*U.S. Premiere*), "Solo from Landscapes," "Gold Trio from Hoopla," "Bach Suite opening dance," "Junk Dances duet"), "Proximities" (Brahms, Louis), "Porcelain Dialogues" (Tchaikovsky, Louis), "Continuum" (Corky Siegel Blues Band/Alwin Nikolais, Louis), "Glances" (Dave Brubeck, Louis), "Geometrics" (Alwin Nikolais, Louis), "Scheherezade" (Rimsky-Korsakov/Alwin Nikolais/Free Life Communication, Louis), "Index"
WORLD PREMIERES: on Tuesday, Feb. 8, 1977 "Ceremony" (Andrew Rudin, Murray Louis) danced by the company; on Wednesday, February 16, 1977 "Deja Vu" (Laure/Tarrega/Lauro/-Scarlatti/ Albeniz) choreographed and performed by Murray Louis
NIKOLAIS DANCE THEATRE: Lisbeth Bagnold, Suzanne McDermaid, Jude Morgan, Gerald Otte, Carlo Pellegrini, Chris Reisner, Jessica Sayre, Karen Sing, James Teeters, Joe Zina; Artistic Director-Choreographer-Composer-Designer, Alwin Nikolais
REPERTOIRE: "Group Dance from Sanctum," "Triad," "Temple," "Foreplay, "Styx," "Tower"
WORLD PREMIERES: on Wednesday Feb. 9, 1977 "Guignol (Dummy Dances)," and on Friday, Feb. 11, 1977 "Arporisms"
* Closed March 6, 1977 after limited engagement of 31 performances.

Photos by Caravaglia, Greenfield, Elbers, Markatos, Agor

"Porcelain Dialogues"
Top: Murray Louis in "Hoopla"

"Proximities"
Above: "Index"

MURRAY LOUIS DANCE COMPANY

"Styx" Above: "Sanctum"
Top: "Guignol (Dummy Dances)"
also below

"Triad" Above: "Foreplay"
Top and Below: "Arporisms" 101
NIKOLAIS DANCE THEATRE

AMERICAN THEATRE LABORATORY
February 10 - 13, 1977 (5 performances)
Dance Theater Workshop presents:

Dancers
(on view in two parts)

Directed and Choreographed by Grethe Holby; Lighting Design, Sally Locke; Sound, Peter Anderson; Design, Franco Colavecchia; Performance and Texts for Sound Tracks by Carol Asmann, Angela Cocchini, Kathy Duncan, Pat Graf, Claudia Isaac, Martha Karess, Debra Jo Levine, Alison Ozer, Karen Peterson, Joan Sabba

AMERICAN MODERN DANCE THEATRE
February 11- 14, 1977 (4 performances)

THOMAS HOLT DANCE ENSEMBLE

Norbert DuBois, Carol Elsner, Elaine Frezza, Thomas Holt, JoAnne Kuhn, Ann Moser, Kelly Roth

PROGRAM

"Points in a Crystal" (Milton Babbitt, Robert Diaz) danced by Robert Diaz and Patricia Payne; "Pas de Deux for Old Friends" (Satie, Felice Lesser) dancec by Felice Lesser and Thomas Holt; *Premiere* of "Concrete and Country" (Porter/ Roy Rogers, Kelly Roth) danced by Elaine Frezza, JoAnne Kuhn, Kelly Roth, Allen Seward; "Why Don't I Quit" (Halim El-Dabh, Patricia Payne), "Bola!" (Scott Joplin, Robert Diaz); *Premiere* of "The Ambitious" (Beethoven, Ann Moser) danced by Nancy Mikota, David McComb, Thomas Holt; *Premiere* of "Ishiland" (Pharoh Saunders/Walter Murphy/Norbert DuBois) danced by the company; "Westward" (Collage, Thomas Holt) danced by the company.

CUNNINGHAM STUDIO
Tuesday & Wednesday, February 15 & 16, 1977 (2 performances)

SARA RUDNER
DANCING 33 DANCES

(No other details available)

Karen Peterson, Allison Ozer in "Dancers on View"
(Phillip Jones Photo)

AMERICAN THEATRE LABORATORY
February 17-27, 1977 (8 performances)
Dance Theater Workshop presents:

SOLOMONS COMPANY/DANCE

Artistic Director-Choreographer, Gus Solomons, Jr.; Lighting Design, Ruis Wortendyke; Stage Manager, Ruis Wortendyke; Manager, Phillip Moser

COMPANY

Gus Solomons, Jr.	Katherine Gallagher
Jack Apffel	Nanna Nilson
Ruedi Brack	Judith Ren-Lay
Donald Byrd	Carl Thomsen

PROGRAM: "Statements of Nameless Root I (Observations)", *NY Premiere* of "Ad Hoc Transit," *World Premieres* of "All But One" and "Boogie"

PACE UNIVERSITY SCHIMMEL CENTER
Friday, February 18, 1977 (1 performance)

CINCINNATI BALLET COMPANY

Executive Artistic Director, David McLain; Assistant Artistic Director, David Blackburn; Music Director, Carmon DeLeone; Resident Designer, Jay Depenbrock

COMPANY

Paula Davis, Diane Edwards, Colleen Giesting, Melissa Hale, Renee Hallman, Janice James, Karen Karibo, Patricia Kelly, Sheila McAulay, Patricia Rozow, Alyce Taylor, Katherine Turner, Pam Willingham, John Ashton, Ian Barrett, David Blackburn, Michael Bradshaw, Richard Earley, Michael McClelland, John Nelson, Kevin Ward, Lynn Ferszt, Kay Thompson, Suzanne Haas, Jane Henry, Debra Kelly, Margo Krody, Margarita Martinez, Renee Powers, Patrick Hinson, Eric Johnston GUEST ARTISTS: Odetta and Gospel Choir of Newburgh, directed by Ronald R. Sutherland

PROGRAM

"Pas de Dix" (Glazounov, Franklin/Petipa), "The Beloved" (Hamilton, Truitte/Horton), "Guernica" (DeLeone, Truitte/Horton), "With Timbrel and Dance, Praise His Name" (DeLeone, Truitte)

Jack Apffel, Judith Ren-Lay, Nanna Nilson
in "Boogie" *(Lois Greenfield Photo)* **Above: Sara Rudner**

THE KITCHEN
Saturday & Sunday, February 19 & 20, 1977 (4 performances)
Experimental Intermedia Foundation presents:

WINDOWS IN THE KITCHEN

by Elaine Summers Dance and Film Company; Choreography, Elaine Summers; Music composed and played by Sam Rivers; Technical Director, Paula Court; Assistant, Howard Brookner; Administrator, George Ashley

PROGRAM

"Images on the Wooster Street Wall," "Windows" danced by Matt Turney, "Solitary Geography" danced by Matt Turney; "Geography for One or More" danced by Barbara Berger, Gail Donnenfeld, Deborah Glaser, Shirley Mischer, Alfredo Godot Pinheiro, Joan Sabba, David Schulberg, Gail Waterman, Matt Turney, "City Corners"

CUNNINGHAM STUDIO
Saturday & Sunday, February 19 & 20, 1977 (2 performances)

NIDUS

Created by Jan Wodynski; Poem, Lawrence Ferlinghetti; Costumes, Jan Wodynski; Score-Lighting and Set Design, Mike Wodynski; Sound, Judith Lipka; Manager, Stephen Harris Miller

Performed by Jan Wodynski and Mike Wodynski

ALICE TULLY HALL
Thursday, February 24, 1977 (1 performance)
The Performing Arts Program of the Asia Society presents:

YAMINI KRISHNAMURTI

dancing "Alarippu," "Varnam (Saamiyai)," "Navarasa Slokam," "Tillana," "Krishna Sabdam," "Manduka Sabdam"

Matt Turney (center) in "Windows in the Kitchen"
(Paula Court Photo)

Yamini Krishnamurti

SHEPARD GREAT HALL
Thursday & Friday, February 24 & 25, 1977
The Leonard Davis Center for the Performing Arts presents:

MARIKO SANJO

PROGRAM: "Take 33," "Breeze," "Generations," "Bird," "Song without Words," "Generations"

DANCE GALLERY
February 24–March 30, 1977 (16 performances)
The Larry Richardson Dance Foundation presents:

LARRY RICHARDSON
AND DANCE COMPANY

Artistic Director-Choreographer, Larry Richardson; Administrative Director, J. Antony Siciliano; Lighting Design, William Otterson

COMPANY

Larry Richardson	Wendy Stein
Cameron Burke	Karen Lashinsky
Glenn Ferrugiari	Faye Fujisaki Mar
Gene French	Alison Ozer
Myra Hushansky	Liz Rosner
Julie Lachow	Hideaki Ryo

Guest Artist: Hugh Lynch

REPERTOIRE: "The Heart's Rialto" (Debussy/Bertoncini, Richardson), "Kin" (Bach/Buxtehude/Schutz/Xenakis, Richardson), and *World Premiere* of "Earth" (Moussorgsky, Richardson; Costumes, Zoe; Masks, Tom Pitzpatrick) danced by the company on March 3, 1977

Jan and Mike Wodynski in "Nidus" *(Chuck Saaf Photo)*
Above: Larry Richardson in "The Heart's Rialto"
(Ted Yaple Photo)

103

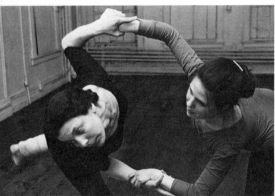

AMERICAN THEATRE LABORATORY
March 2–6, 1977 (6 performances)
Dance Theater Workshop presents:

DANNY WILLIAMS GROSSMAN AND DANCE COMPANY

Director-Choreographer, Danny Williams Grossman; Costumes, Lighting, Stage Manager, Peter Anderson; Production Assistants, Paul Harkins, Kate Elliott

COMPANY

Eric Bobrow, Skip Carter, Janet Danforth, Danny Grossman, Judith Hendin, Mitchell Kirsch, Richard Lambertson, Dindi Lidge, Jan Messer, Greg Parks, Nancy Reichley, Marty Sprague, Julie Strandberg, Dale Woodland

PROGRAM

"Couples" (Terry Riley, Danny Williams Grossman), "Inching" (Mbira music of Zimbabwe/Dumisani Abraham Maraire, Grossman), "Back Dance" (Traditional West African, Grossman), "Fratelli" (Milhaud, Grossman), "Triptych" (Milhaud, Grossman), "Curious Schools of Theatrical Dancing Part I" (Couperin, Grossman), "National Spirit" (Marches and Anthems, Grossman), "Higher" (Ray Charles, Grossman)

BYRD HOFFMAN SPACE
March 4 & 5, 12 & 13, 1977 (4 performances)

DIALOGUES WITH A SINGLE PERFORMER

choreographed and performed by Tannis Hugill: "Hands," "Psalter," and "Without Interlude"

135 WEST 14th STREET
Friday, March 4, 1977

ROBERT YOHN SOLO PROGRAM

"Fall Down in Brown November" (Darrell Crim, Robert Yohn), "Three Centuries Apart" (Vaughan Williams, Richard Ploch), "Cruciform" (Debussy, Yohn), "Silent Passing Through" (Debussy, Ploch), "Temperance Songs" (Rescue Songs, Yohn)

537 BROADWAY
Friday & Saturday, March 4 & 5, 1977 (2 performances)
Dance Theater Workshop presents:

SOLOS/DUETS

PROGRAM: "Solo" (Ish Bicknell, Ann Darby) danced by Elizabeth Streb, "Duet" choreographed and performed by Ann Darby and Elizabeth Streb, "Solo" (Vera Lynn, Elizabeth Streb) danced by Ann Darby, "Duet II" (Katherine Hafemeister) choreographed and danced by Elizabeth Streb and Ann Darby

SUN OCK LEE STUDIO
March 4–12, 1977 (4 performances)
Sun Ock Lee presents Paul Wilson's:

THEATREDANCE ASYLUM

Artistic Director-Choreographer, Paul Wilson; General Manager, Dennis Haines; Production Manager, Doris Fountain; Lighting Design, Marshall Spiller; Sound, Lou DiLiberto; Stage Manager, Doris Fountain; Sets, Scott Volk, Gerrard Little; Costumes, Gerrard Little

COMPANY

Barry Barychko
Joanne Edelmann
Doris Ginsberg
Laurie McKirahan
Randolyn Zinn

Joe Schwarz
William Shepard
Stuart Smith
Scott Volk

PROGRAM: "Vigil" (Collage, Laurie McKirahan), "I Am a Fanatic" (Rodriego, Randolyn Zinn), "Dancing on a Grave" (Joe Schwarz, Paul Wilson), and Premieres of "Kinks" (Keith Jarrett, Paul Wilson), "Secrets" (Charles Ives, Paul Wilson)

TheatreDance Asylum in "Secrets" (Ron Reagan Photo)
Above: Elizabeth Streb, Ann Darby

Top Left: Danny Williams Grossman Dance Company (Andrew Oxenham Photo) Below: Robert Yohn in "Fall Down in Brown November" (Ian Anderson Photo)

AMERICAN MUSEUM OF NATURAL HISTORY
Sunday, March 6, 1977

ALVIN AILEY REPERTORY ENSEMBLE

Artistic Adviser, Alvin Ailey; Artistic Director, Sylvia Waters; Executive Director, Edward Lander; Dancers: Marsha Clark, Josiah Young, Joe Alegado, Lonne Moretton, Ronni Favors, Mina Yoo, Steve Mones, Keith McDaniel

PROGRAM: "Deep South Suite" (Duke Ellington, Dianne McIntyre), "Still Life" (Duke Ellington, Cristyne Lawson), "Night Creature" (Duke Ellington, Ailey).

CUNNINGHAM STUDIO
Sunday, March 6, 1977 (2 performances)

Peggy Stern Jazz Duo
Sara Rudner and Wendy Rogers

performing "November Duets/Molly's Suite" (Stern, Rudner)

AMERICAN MUSEUM OF NATURAL HISTORY
Sunday, March 13, 1977 (1 performance)
The Performing Arts Program of the Asia Society presents:

PONGSAN MASKED DANCE-DRAMA OF KOREA

COMPANY: Kim Son-bong, Yang So-un, Kim Ki-su, So Sin-won, Yun Ok, Chang Yong-il, Chong Chae-ch'on, Kim Chong-yop, Cho Un-yong, Ch'oe Chang-ju, Lee Kil-son, Lee Mi-won

PROGRAM
"Ceremonial Opening by the Four Young Monks," "Eight Buddhist Monks," "Dance and Songs by Sadang and Kosa," "Old Priest's Dance," "The Prodigal," "The Lion Dance," "The Shoe-seller," "The Noblemen and Their Servant," "The Old Couple," "Ritual for the Dead"

THE OPEN EYE
March 16 - 23, 1977 (4 performances)

OP ODYSSEY

Conceived and Realized by Doris Chase; Kinetic Sculpture-Synthesized Film, Doris Chase; Lighting Design, George Gracey; Choreography, Valerie Hammer; Music, Robert Mahaffay; Poetry, Diane Wakoski; Spoken by Gloria Tropp

DANCERS

Nancy Cohen
Valerie Hammer
Jonathan Hollander

AMERICAN THEATRE LABORATORY
March 17 -20, 1977 (4 performances)
Dance Theater Workshop presents:

HANNAH KAHN/DALIENNE MAJORS & DANCERS
with Mitchell Korn Ensemble

Co-Artistic Directors and Choreographers, Hannah Kahn, Dalienne Majors; Lighting Designer-Stage Manager, Edward M. Greenberg

COMPANY

Hannah Kahn
Michael Blue Aiken
Jessica Fogel
Douglas Hamby
Peter Healey

Dalienne Majors
Carol Hess
Kate Johnson
Catherine Sullivan
Teri Weksler

REPERTOIRE: "Aviary Pulse" (Mitchell Korn, Hannah Kahn), "Domesticated" (Korn, Kahn), "Kvugng: The Viking I Lander" (Korn, Dalienne Majors), "Trilogy" (Dylan, Majors), "Catches from a Strand" (Collage, Jessica Fogel), "Mating" (Korn, Kahn)

Kate Johnson in "Aviary Pulse" *(Manza Photo)* **Above: Op Odyssey** *(Lois Greenfield Photo)* **Center: Pongsan Masked Dance Drama** *(Ron Reagan Photo)*

Top Left: Alvin Ailey Repertory Ensemble *(Ron Reagan Photo)* **Below: Wendy Rogers, Sara Rudner** *(Lois Greenfield Photo)*

Jennifer Muller and The Works

QUEENS THEATRE IN THE PARK
March 17 - 20, 1977 (4 performances)
Playwrights Horizons presents:

JENNIFER MULLER
AND THE WORKS

Artistic Director-Choreographer, Jennifer Muller; Music Director, Burt Alcantara; Lighting Design, Richard Nelson; Stage Manager, John Luckacovic; Wardrobe, Cynthia Demand

THE WORKS

Jennifer Clark	Carol-rae Kraus
Jennifer Muller	Angeline Wolf
Matthew Diamond	Jean-Marie Marion
Christopher Pilafian	John Preston

PROGRAM: "Beach" (Burt Alcantara, Jennifer Muller), "Biography" (Alcantara, Muller), "Speeds" (Alcantara, Muller)

CAMI HALL
Friday, March 18, 1977 (1 performance)

TONY WHITE

In his one-man concert of modern jazz tap dancing

CUNNINGHAM STUDIO
Friday & Saturday, March 18 & 19, 1977 (2 performances)

SOLOMONS COMPANY/DANCE

Artistic Director-Choreographer, Gus Solomons, Jr.; Lighting Design-Stage Manager, Ruis Woertendyke; Costumes, Eva Tsug; Manager, Phillip Moser; Artistic Coordinator, Nora Larke

COMPANY

Gus Solomons, Jr.	Donald Byrd
Nanna Nilson	Jack Apffel
Ruedi Brack	Carl Thomsen
Katherine Gallagher	Judith Ren-Lay

PROGRAM: *World Premiere* of "Bone Jam" (Mio Morales, Gus Solomons, Jr.)

Gus Solomons, Jr.
(Lois Greenfield Photo)

BIJOU THEATRE
Saturday, March 19, 1977

EDITH STEPHEN DANCE
CONNECTION

Artistic Director, Edith Stephen; Assistant Director, Ralph M. Thomas; Arts Administrator, Christine Beckert; Administrative Associate, Barbara Davis; Administrative Assistants, Awilda Tirado, Judy Kramer, Peggy Benitz; Business Administrator, Joanne Nesbitt; Design Consultant, James Gayles; Lighting Designer, Michael Purri; Photographer, Ron Reagan; All Costumes by Edith Stephen unless noted; Management, Robert M. Gewald Management, Inc.

COMPANY

Edith Stephen, Ralph M. Thomas, Carol Baxter, Reginald Browning, Andrew Jannetti, Paula Odellas

PROGRAM

"Love In Different Colors" (M. Dreyfuss, Stephen; film, R. Schneider), "Dream of the Wild Horse" (Jacques Lasri, Stephen; film, B. C. De Daimant), "The Peacock" (Switched-On Bach, Stephen), "Spaces Indescribable" (F. Bayles, Stephen; environmental sculpture, C. Bunch), and *PREMIERE* of "Not So Amazing Graces" (Debussy, Stephen; costumes by Barbara Davis)

(Ron Reagan Photo)

**Edith Stephen Dance Connection
in "The Peacock"**

SACHIYO ITO & COMPANY

Choreography, Sachiyo Ito; Lighting Design, Robert Rosenthal; Stage Manager, Stephen Riley; Musical Transcription and Direction, Dan Erkkila.

COMPANY

Sachiyo Ito

Teresa Richards	Cherel Winette
Leslie Watanabe	Dan Erkkila
Teiji Ito	John Genke

PROGRAM: "Devil Dance" (Traditional), "White Heron Maiden" (Kabuki), "Ayako-Mai" (Traditional), "Folk Song from Akita" (Traditional), "Interlude" (Michio Miyagi, Ito), "The Night" (Dan Erkkila, Ito)

Top Left: Sachiyo Ito and Company
(Nicholas Murrer Photo)

BAYANIHAN
PHILIPPINE DANCE COMPANY

President, Helena Z. Benitez; Executive Director, Leticia Perez de Guzman; Press, Lourdes B. Guillermo; Performing Arts Director, Lucrecia R. Kasilag; Choreographer-Dance Director, Lucrecia Reyes Urtula; Company Director-Costume Director, Isabel A. Santos; Artistic Director, Jose Lardizabal; Technical Director, Raymond Salvacion; Production Manager, William J. Mullaney; Press, Herbert H. Breslin, Marvin Jenkins

COMPANY

Glenna Aquino, Leila Atienza, Mercedes Aves, Purissima Helena Benitez, Florian Capistrano, Susanna Asuncion Dizon, Isabel Espina, Theresa Feliciano, Rosella Grajo, Eleanor Mescallado, Beverly Mijares, Norieta Montecillo, Angelina Morales, Marijo Palencia, Judith Paragas, Mercedes Vibar, Cecille Villacorta, Mareeya Yuhico, Angelito Alanes, Melvin Colona, Enrico Cruz, Aristeo David, Orlando Eijansantos, Emmanuel Ilarina, Jose Mandanas, Hernani Pengson, Reynaldo Raymundo, Rodolfo Soriano, Carlos Tadefa, Melito Valecruz, and Rolando Delfino, Leo Ona, Jesus Tan, Crescencio Ventura, Reynaldo Yco

PROGRAM

"The Thunder and the Fire," "The Plains of Mindanao," "Luzon - The Mountains," "Tacon y Punta," "The Many-Colored Vinta," "People under the Sun"

Bayanihan Philippine Dance Company

ZE'EVA COHEN
Solo Dance Repertory

Guest Artist, Helen Katz; Lighting Design-Production Manager, Edward I. Byers; Stage Manager, Tina Charney, Assistant Stage Manager, Kate Elliott

PROGRAM

"Three Landscapes" (Alan Hovhaness/John Cage/Ali Akbar Khan, Cohen), "Countdown" (Songs of the Auvergne, Rudy Perez), "Listen II" (George Crumb, Cohen), "32 Variations in C Minor" (Beethoven, James Waring; Pianist, Helen Katz) performed by Ze'eva Cohen

Ze'eva Cohen in "The One of No Way"
(Jack Mitchell Photo)

182 DUANE STREET
Friday & Saturday, March 25 & 26, 1977 (2 performances)

CHIP SHOT

Choreographed and Performed by Karen Bernard with Freddi Berg and Marjorie Katz; Production Assistants, Jim Colby, Steve Elliott, Mary Louise Sibley

PROGRAM

"Minus Plus Minus," "Foam Rubber," "Skating," "Me Laughing, London 1972" (David Tremlett), "Burlap Bags"

THEATER OF THE OPEN EYE
Sunday, March 27, 1977

LINEA DANCE COMPANY

Director-Choreographer, Yvonne D. Hicks; Music Director, Randall Hicks; Technical Director, Michael Purri; Lighting Design, Douglas Drew
COMPANY: Robert Beck, Anne Berry, Carolyn Churchill, Eric Clopper, Gina Fisher, Elke Hauser, Frederic Hood, Tambra Isenogle, Yvonne Lee, Wendy Oliver, Ellen Pundyk, Deborah Stone
PROGRAM "Suite in D" (Bach, Hicks), "Eroica Second Movement" (Beethoven, Hicks), "Pas de Deux" (Prokofiev, Hicks), "Three Illusions" (Satie, Hicks), "Brahms/Handel Variations" (Brahms, Hicks)

83 EAST FOURTH STREET
March 30 - April 24, 1977 (20 performances)
The Rubenstein Theater Foundation presents:

ORGAN

Conceived and Directed by Ken Rubenstein; Choreographic Assistant, Fae Rubenstein; Production Manager-Technical Supervisor, Rene Sanfiorenzo; Production Assistant, Bernard Lias; Press, Roz Rubenstein; Technical Assistant, Fred Griem

Performed by Cristobal Carambo and Ellyce Stillwater

AMERICAN MODERN DANCE THEATRE
April 1 - 4, 1977 (4 performances)

THOMAS HOLT DANCE ENSEMBLE

Thomas Holt, Norbert DuBois, Carol Elsner, Elaine Frezza, Joanne Kuhn, Ann Moser, Kelly Roth, Allan Seward, Nina Williams

PROGRAM

"Duet for Summer" (Holdridge, Holt), "In Autumn to Romp" (Bartok, Holt), "Second Avenue Scrapbook" (Nyro, Holt), "Afterhours in Wonderland" (Collage, Holt)

MARYMOUNT MANHATTAN THEATRE
April 1 - 3, 1977 (3 performances)

MARIANO PARRA SPANISH DANCE COMPANY

with Mariano Parra (Director-Choreographer), Jerane Michel, Ines Parra, Mariana Parra, Lillian Ramirez, Emilio Prados (Guitarist), Luis Vargas (singer), Daniel Waite (pianist)

PROGRAM

"Sequidillas" (Albeniz), "Triana" (Albeniz), "Estampa de Alegrias" (Traditional), "Impresiones" (Mompou), "Jota Valenciana" (Traditional), "Romanza Gitana" (Traditional), "Zapateado" (Sarasate), "Sequiriyas" (Traditional), "Playeras" (Granados), "Tablao Flamenco" (Traditional)

Top Right: Marjorie Katz, Freddi Berg in "Chip Shot"
(Miriam Shapiro Photo) **Below: Tambra Isenogle, Angel**
108 Casteleiro in "Brahms/Handel Variations"

Thomas Holt Dance Ensemble in "Second Avenue Scrapbook" *(Gerry Goodstein Photo)* **Above: Ellyce Stillwater, Cristobal Carambo in "Organ"**

LARRY RICHARDSON'S DANCE GALLERY
April 1 - 4, 1977 (4 performances)

JUDY PADOW DANCE COMPANY

Director-Choreography, Judy Padow; Costumes, Diana Rolls; Sound, Albee Gordon, Jocko Marcellino; Lighting Design, Tom Cathcart

COMPANY

Judy Padow
Cynthia Hedstrom
Eric Hess
Mary Overlie
Danny Tai

PROGRAM: (All choreography by Judy Padow) "Jamming," "The Drift," "The Snake Dance," "Panorama" "Cameo" (Bela Bartok), "Ensemble"

THE NEW SCHOOL STUDIO C-1
April 1 - May 13, 1977 (12 performances)

LAURA FOREMAN DANCE THEATRE
in
"Heirlooms"

Original Sound Score by John Watts; Choreography by Laura Foreman; Lighting Design, Cheryl Thacker; Costumes, Sharon Weaver; Stage Manager, Martha Ellen; Special Effect, John Watts; Sound, Hank O'Neal
Performed by Roxanne Bartush, Satoru Shimazaki, Laura Foreman

The program was repeated for 8 additional performances (May 21–29, 1977) at the Vorpal Gallery.

PACE SCHIMMEL CENTER
April 7–10, 1977 (4 performances)
Saracen Foundation for Dance presents:

RAYMOND JOHNSON DANCE COMPANY

Janice Birnbaum
Barbara deMardt
David Hochoy
Raymond Johnson
David Lee
Linda Lippencott
Fern Zand

REPERTOIRE: "Scintilla" (Gottschalk, James Waring), "Feathers" (Mozart, Waring), "Landmark" (Byrds/Sam the Sham/Ohio Express, Johnson) and *Premieres* of "Sugar Cane" (Joplin/Scott/Jansen, Raymond Johnson), "Chamber" (George Rochberg, Johnson), "Threshold" (Rochberg, Johnson), "Corridor" (Rochberg, Johnson), "As the World Turns Out" (Chopin, Johnson), "Wolfman" (Ron Roxbury, Johnson)

CUNNINGHAM STUDIO
Friday & Saturday, April 8 & 9, 1977 (2 performances)
Dance Theater Workshop presents:

NEW YORK CHAMBER DANCE GROUP

Artistic Director-Choreographer, Richard Bull; Lighting Design-Production Manager, Lance Olson; Assistant Director, Cynthia Novack; Sound, Duvid Smering; Costume Coordinator, Cynthia Novack

COMPANY

Richard Bull
Peentz Dubble
Robin Hertlein
Betsy Keenan
Cynthia Novack
Duvid Smering

PROGRAM: "The Counting Dance" (Richard Bull), "Ambiance" (Nonesuch, Bull), "Deja Vu" (Popular Songs, Cynthia Novack), "Jesus' Blood" (Govin Bryors, Richard Bull)

Top Right: Danny Tai, Judy Padow in "Cameo"
(Babette Mangolte Photo)

Raymond Johnson Dance Company *(Ron Reagan Photo)*
Above: Satoru Shimazaki, Roxanne Bartush in
"Heirlooms" *(Lois Greenfield Photo)*

ROUNDABOUT STAGE ONE
April 11-16, 1977 (7 performances)
The Roundabout Theatre Company and Louis Falco Dance Company present:

LOUIS FALCO DANCE COMPANY

Artistic Director-Choreographer, Louis Falco; Associate Director, Juan Antonio; Artistic Adviser, William Katz; Lighting Design, Richard Nelson; Stage Manager, David Rosenberg

COMPANY

Louis Falco   Juan Antonio
Ranko Yokoyama   John Cwiakala
Tony Constantine   Lisa Nalven
Jane Lowe   Bill Gornel

REPERTOIRE: "Hero" (Badal Roy/Radha Shottam/Frank Tusa, Louis Falco), "The Sleepers" (Louis Falco), "Champagne" (Big Band Collage, Falco), "B-Mine" (Keith Jarrett, Juan Antonio), "Two Penny Portrait" (Burt Alcantara, Falco), "Caviar" (Robert Cole, Falco)

KAUFMANN CONCERT HALL
April 13-17, 1977 (5 performances)
The 92nd Street YM-YWHA presents:

PEARL LANG & DANCE COMPANY

COMPANY: Pearl Lang, Lar Roberson, Barry Smith, Richard Arbach, Jerome Sarnat, Larry Damien Stevens, Erica Drew, Judith Garay, Eva Grubler, Alicia Henley, Clifford Schulman

REPERTOIRE

"Lamentations of Jeremiah" (Serfiu Natia, Pearl Lang), "Prologue from The Possessed," "A Seder Night" (Panderecki, Lang), "Shira" (Hovhaness, Lang), "Piece for Brass" (Alvin Ettler, Lang), "Prairie Steps" (Copland, Lang), and *Premieres* of "Roundelays" (Carl Philipp Emanuel Bach, Pearl Lang), "I Never Saw Another Butterfly," and "Kaddish" (Lazar Weiner, Pearl Lang) (No other details available)

Pearl Lang and Company in "Prairie Steps" *(Ron Reagan Photo)* Above: Louis Falco Company in "Caviar"

AMERICAN THEATRE LABORATORY
April 14-24, 1977 (8 performances)
Dance Theater Workshop presents:

MARGARET BEALS
in concert

with Guest Artists Brooke Myers, Gwendolyn Watson and Arnie Lawrence; Choreographed and performed by Margaret Beals; Lighting Design-Stage Manager, Edward M. Greenberg; Production Assistant, Kate Elliott

REPERTOIRE

"Love Is a. . . ." a theatre production with dance based on the poetry of Carl Sandberg, Edna St. Vincent Millay and Sylvia Plath: "Prologue" (Sandburg), "Renascence" (Millay), "Working Girls" (Sandburg), "The Other" (Plath), and "Epilogue" (Sandburg), "Free Duet" (an improvisation), "Movement Monologues," "Contentment" (Arnie Lawrence)

SUN OCK LEE STUDIO THEATRE
April 15-16, 22-23, 1977 (4 performances)

SUN OCK LEE DANCE COMPANY

Artistic Director-Choreographer, Sun Ock Lee; Lighting Design, Marshall S. Spiller; Manager, Paul B. Berkowsky; Technical Assistants, Marc Martin, Suk in Park

REPERTOIRE

"Puri Temple" (Dagar) choreographed and danced by Uttra Coorlawala; "Chair Piece" (Bob Moses) choreographed and danced by Gary Davis; "Choon Hyang" (Mme. Kim So Kee, Sun Ock Lee), "Kinks" (Keith Jarrett, Paul Wilson) danced by Paul Wilson, Joanne Edelmann; "Kum Moo" (Seing Kang Lee & Co.), "Mirror" (Ravel, Sun Ock Lee) danced by Sun Ock Lee, Muna Tsen, Uttra Coorlawala, and *Premiere* of "Karma" (Edith Piaf, Sun Ock Lee) danced by Ms. Lee, Judy Dearing, Gary Davis, Paul Wilson

Sun Ock Lee in "Love and Farewell" *(John Chang McCurdy Photo)* Above: Margaret Beals, Brooke Myers *(Ron Reagan Photo)*

110

ROUNDABOUT STAGE ONE
April 19–23, 1977 (6 performances)
Roundabout Theatre and Jose Limon Dance Foundation present the thirtieth anniversary season of:

JOSE LIMON DANCE COMPANY

Artistic Director, Ruth Currier; Assistant Artistic Director, Carla Maxwell; Lighting Design, Eugene Lowery; Production and Stage Manager, John Toland; Costume Supervisor, Allen Munch; Costumer, Herbert Binzer; Technical Director, Paul Lindsay Butler; Press, Tom Kerrigan

COMPANY

Mark Ammerman, Ginga Carmany, Bill Cratty, Robyn Cutler, Ken Ganado, William Hansen, Ryland Jordan, Carla Maxwell, Lane Sayles, Jennifer Scanlon, Holly Schiffer, Tonia Shimin, Luis Solino, Risa Steinberg, Clifton Thompson, Nina Watt, and GUEST ARTISTS Gary Chryst, Clay Taliaferro

REPERTOIRE

"Ritmo Jondo" (Carlos Surinach, Doris Humphrey/Lucy Venable), "Landscapes" (Alvin Walker, Murray Louis), "Cassandra" (Aaron Copland, Pauline Koner), "Psalm" (Eugene Lester, Jose Limon/Carla Maxwell), "The Green Table" (Cohen, Jooss), "Phantasmagoria" (Berg/Ives, Currier), "Choreographic Offering" (Bach, Limon): "Air for the G String" (Bach, Humphrey/Stodelle), "Two Ecstacies" (Humphrey/Stodelle), "The Shakers" (Traditional, Humphrey), "The Emperor Jones" (Dello Joio, Limon), "The Winged" (Johnson, Limon)

Bhaskar, Carolyn Kay
(Lyn Hutchinson Photo)

Ballet Hispanico of New York
(Carleton Sarver Photo)

Jose Limon Company in "Ritmo Jondo"
(Martha Swope Photo)

TOWN HALL
Wednesday, April 20, 1977 (1 performance)
Interludes presents:

BHASKAR— DANCES OF INDIA
with
Carolyn Kay
Candace Hibbard

Producer, Marilyn Egol; Choreography, Bhaskar; Costumes, Candace Hibbard; Lighting, Ronald Kantor

PROGRAM

"Nathan Adinar," "Thilana," "Lasya," "Maya," "Thala Nirtham," "Naga Nirtham," "Surya Nirtham"

ANTHOLOGY FILM ARCHIVES
Friday & Saturday, April 22 & 23, 1977 (2 performances)
Elaine Summer Dance and Film Company presents:

TOWN HOUSE

A work in progress; Text collaged from writings of Oscar Wilde; Suggested by Robert Dunn; Choreography, Elaine Summers. Dancers: Michelle Berne, Roberta Escamilla-Garrison, Shirley Mischer, Alexandra Ogsbury, David Schulberg, Timothy Shelton, George Ashley

GERSHWIN THEATRE
April 22–24, 1977 (3 performances)
Guest Artist Series/Dance presents:

BALLET HISPANICO OF NEW YORK

Artistic Director, Tina Ramirez; Ballet Mistress, Lolita San Miguel; Stage Manager, Michael Smart; Production Assistant, Tyrone Sanders; Wardrobe Director, Bill Blackwell; Executive Director, Natsu Ifill; Company Manager, Marush

COMPANY

Valerie Contreras, Judith Reyes, Sandra Rivera, Maria Rodriguez, Alicia Roque, Carmen Sauce, Ramon Galindo, Alfredo Gonzales, Marcial Gonzalez, Lorenzo Maldonado, Roy Rodriguez, and Martina Ebey

PROGRAM

"La Boda de Luis Alonso" (Gimenez, Paco Fernandez), "Fiesta en Vera Cruz" (Moncayo, Coronado), "Echoes of Spain" (Albeniz/Temptations/Mandrill, Louis Johnson), "Portrait of Carmen" (Bizet/Shchedrin, Tina Ramirez), "Danse Creole" (Casius, Holder)

DIPLOMAT HOTEL
Wednesday, April 17 & Thursday, May 5, 1977

VIOLA FARBER DANCE COMPANY

Artistic Director-Choreographer, Viola Farber; Composer, Alvin Lucier; Stage Manager, Lewis Mead; Company Manager, Cheryl Wall

COMPANY
Viola Farber

Jumay Chu
Larry Clark
Willi Feuer
June Finch

Anne Koren
Susan Matheke
Ande Peck
Jeff Slayton

PROGRAM: "Dinosaur Parts" (David Tudor, Viola Farber), and *World Premiere* of "Lead Us Not into Penn Station" (Viola Farber; Costumes, A. Christina Giannini; Lighting, Beverly Emmons) On Thursday, April 28, and Wednesday, May 4, 1977 the program consisted of "Motorcycle/Boat" (Alvin Lucier, Farber), and *NY Premiere* of "Sunday Afternoon" (Alvin Lucier, Viola Farber; Costumes, Remy Charlip)

HENRY STREET PLAYHOUSE
April 23–24, 1977 (3 performances)
Henry Street Settlement Arts for Living presents:

FRANK ASHLEY DANCE COMPANY

Artistic Director-Choreographer, Frank Ashley; Managing Director, Delos R. Smith; Company Manager, Francine Dobranski; Lighting George Greczylo; Stage Manager, Tony Leto; Rehearsal Assistant, Carole Simpson

COMPANY

Frank Ashley, Carole Simpson, Wendy McDade, Sylvia Rincon, Hope Sogawa (on leave), Michelle Beteta, Naomi Mindlin, Bernard Riddick, Jamil Garland, Henry Daniel, Luis Manuel

PROGRAM

"Time of Day" (Lucas Mason, Frank Ashley), "Manipulation" (Max Roach/Herbie Hancock Sextant, Frank Ashley), *Premieres* of "Things Fall Apart" (Bela Bartok, Frank Ashley; Costumes, Barbara Maccarone), "Dirty Blues" (Brownie McGhee & Sonny Terry/Memphis Slim/Levester Carter/Bo Diddley, Frank Ashley)

LARRY RICHARDSON'S DANCE GALLERY
April 28–30, 1977 (3 performances)
Ron Lovingood presents:

BRUCE PACOT AND DANCE COMPANY

Artistic Director-Choreographer, Bruce Pacot; Manager, Ron Lovingood; Lighting Design, Rick Claflin, Gary Greer

COMPANY

Bruce Pacot
John DeWees
Judith DeJean
Sally Edelstein

Ellen Ducker
Wendy Lai
Nancy Mapother
Kenneth Tosti

PROGRAM: "Premonition" (Traditional Irish Folk/Prokofiev, Bruce Pacot), "Parting Dances" (Eliot Carter, Pacot), "Delusion of the Fury" (Harry Partch, Pacot), "Back on Back" (Martinu, Pacot) On Saturday, April 9, 1977 Mr. Pacot, Ellen Ducker and John DeWees danced two performances of "Premonition" in the lobby of the South Tower of the World Trade Center.

DIPLOMAT HOTEL
Tuesday, May 3, 1977 (1 performance)

DOUGLAS DUNN/LAZY MADGE

An Ongoing Choreographic Project by Douglas Dunn with Ellen Webb, Daniel Press, Dana Roth, Diane Frank, Michael Bloom, Ruth Albert, Douglas Dunn, Jennifer Mascall, David Woodberry

Douglas Dunn, Jennifer Mascall *(Nathaniel Tileston Photo)* **Above: Bruce Pacot, John DeWees, Ellen Ducker in "Premonition"** *(Picture This Photo)*

Top Left: Viola Farber Dance Company *(Johan Elbers Photo)* **Below: Frank Ashley Company in "Dirty Blues"**

Judith Phelps, Pamela Smith,
Kathryn Kollar, Alexandra Nelson (kneeling)

WASHINGTON SQUARE CHURCH
April 29–May 8, 1977 (6 performances)

WINDOWPANE JOURNEY

A dance in four sections choreographed by Susan Rankin; Set, Susan Rankin, David Craft; Lighting Design, Bob McAndrew; Tape, Lee Townsend; Adviser, Jim Eaves; Technical Crew, David Craft, Joseph Cicarell, July Den, Alex DiVincenti, Raoul L'Hote

PROGRAM

"The Titanic" performed by Linda Reeder, Susan Rankin, Viva Joyce Beck, Sarah Johnson; "Mob" (Terence Mann) with Anton Bluman, John Wells, Jamie Stiller, Sarah Johnson, Susan Rankin; "Glutton" performed by Anton Bluman, Susan Rankin, John Wells; "Fairy Tales and Cobwebs" danced by Susan Rankin

Mariano Parra, Jerane Michel

WARD-NASSE GALLERY
May 5–8, 1977 (8 performances)

MARIAN SARACH DANCE COMPANY

Don Comras, Mark French, Yvonne Marcus, Marian Sarach, Robin Silver, Roselle Warshaw, Ed Wojcik dancing "Spring Bionics" (M. Steven Brooks, Marian Sarach; Visuals, Pat Zukas)

Presented May 11 & 12, 1977 for 2 additional performances at Theater of the Open Eye.

CUNNINGHAM STUDIO
Friday & Saturday, April 29 & 30, 1977 (2 performances)
Dance Theater Workshop presents:

KATHRYN KOLLAR & COMPANY

Artistic Director-Choreographer, Kathryn Kollar; Lighting Design, John Fisher; Costumes, Judith Phelps

COMPANY

Kathryn Kollar
Alexandra Nelson
Judith Phelps
Pamela Smith

PROGRAM: "Tropos" (Walter Carlos, Kollar), "Puck 'n' High Heels" (Lee Walkup, Kollar), "Probe" (Collage, Kollar), "When They Dress Like That, They're Just Asking for Trouble" (Lee Walkup, Kollar)

Susan Rankin

GRAMERCY ARTS THEATRE
Sunday May 1, 1977 (1 performance)
Spanish Theatre Repertory Company (Gilberto Zaldivar, Producer) presents:

MARIANO PARRA SPANISH DANCE COMPANY

with Mariano Parra (Director-Choreographer), Jerane Michel, Ines Parra, Mariana Parra, Lillian Ramirez, Luis Vargas (singer), Daniel Waite (pianist), Reynaldo Rincon (guitarist)

PROGRAM

"Las Mujeres de Cadiz" (Traditional), "Soleares" (Traditional), "Impressiones" (Mompou), "Zapateado" (Sarasate), "Leyenda" (Albeniz), "Tablao Flamenco" (Traditional)

Marian Sarach
(Ron Reagan Photo)

DANCES FOR SATURDAYS

"Dances for Women" (Rossini, Sue Barnes) danced by Sue Barnes, Eve Salzman; "Untitled" (Collage) choreographed and danced by Judy Konopacki; "Triumph" (Various, Sue Barnes); "Meeting at 16 and 40" (Collage, Susanne Hunter) danced by Susanne Hunter, Steven Keith; "Etherealities" (Collage, Judy Konopacki), "Movement for the Spaces Inbetween" (Charles Madden, Sue Barnes) danced by Sue Barnes, Eve Salzman

LARRY RICHARDSON'S DANCE GALLERY
Saturday & Sunday, May 7 & 8, 1977 (3 performances)

BRUCE KING DANCE COMPANY

Artistic Director-Choreographer, Bruce King; Lighting Design, William Otterson; Stage Manager, Michael Forcade; Management, Frances Schram

COMPANY
Bruce King
Dawn Da Costa
Karen Berley

PROGRAM: (All choreography by Bruce King) "Bamboo" (Lou Harrison), "Omens and Departures" (Edgar Varese), "Swarm" (Antonio Soler), "Vigil" (Charles Ives), "General Booth Enters into Heaven" (Ives), "After Guernica" (Morris Knight), "Leaves" (William Penn), and *NY PREMIERE* of "Autumn" (Charles Ives, Bruce King)

Bruce King

JUILLIARD DANCE ENSEMBLE

Director, Martha Hill; Production Supervisor, Joseph Pacitti; Stage Manager, D. Alessandro Bravo; Costume Supervisor, Kristina Watson; Makeup Supervisor, Carolyn Haas; Sound, William Haviland; Administrative Assistant, Mary Chudick; Costumes, Robert Yodick; Lighting, Peter M. Ehrhardt

COMPANY

Yael Barash, Naomi Browar, Teresa Coker, Carolann Cortese, Yveline Cottez, Thelma Drayton, Betsy Fisher, Nancy Hill, Barbara Hoon, Audrey Jansen, Mare Lind, VV Matsuoka, Madeline Ribbing-Messihi, Andrea Morris, Val Ondes, Maria O'Neill, Judith Otter, Ayala Rimon, Elizabeth Sung, Jill Wagoner, Kathryn Woglom, Nan Friedman
Anthony Balcena, Henry Daniel, Benjamin Greenberg, Neil Greenberg, Walter Kennedy, Russell Lome, V. Keith Martin, Ohad Naharin, Morris Perry, Stephen Pier, Joseph Rich, Offer Sachs, Jack Waters, and the Juilliard Chorus (Abraham Kaplan, Conductor) and Juilliard Chamber Ensemble (Stephen Colvin, Conductor)

PROGRAM

"Missa Brevis" (Zoltan Kodaly, Jose Limon/Daniel Lewis), "Rooms" (Kenyon Hopkins, Anna Sokolow), and *PREMIERES* of "Concerto" (Bach, Kazuko Hirabayashi), "The Holy Place" (Ernest Block, Anna Sokolow), "Rounds" (Teo Macero, Kazuko Hirabayashi)

Juilliard Dance Ensemble in "Missa Brevis"
(Jane Rady Photo)

I NEVER SAW ANOTHER BUTTERFLY

A theatre/dance piece choreographed by Wendy Osserman; Songs, Peter Schlosser; Lighting Design, Andy Tron; Costumes, Jackie Robinson; Piano, Woody Regan; Bass, Jared Bernstein; Assistant to Ms. Osserman, Davida Wittman; Press, Elaine Shipman

COMPANY

Andrea Borak   Wendy Osserman
Thomas Lague   Andreas Perris
Judy Lasko   Jeffrey Strum
Musicians and Singers: Alice Rosengard, John Taylor, Alan Fleisig, Dirk Fitzpatrick, Kevin Brown
Performed in two parts and fifteen scenes.

"I Never Saw Another Butterfly"
(Barnet Silver Photo)

AN EVENING OF DANCES

"Greeting—Plain and Simple" (Purcell/Stefan Wolpe) choreographed and danced by Sarah Ford; "Sympathetic Vibrations" (Stephen Goldberg, Alice Teirstein) danced by Alice Teirstein and Art Bridgman; "Escape from Rooms" (Hopkins, Sokolow) danced by Sarah Ford; "Spring Bionics" (Marian Sarach) danced by Don Comras, Mark French, Yvonne Marcus, Marian Sarach, Robin Silver, Rosell Warshaw, Ed Wojcik; *Premiere* of "Celebration" (Bach, Judith Janus) danced by Judith Janus, Bambi Anderson, Maureen Miller, Marianne Schultz, Curtis Gooden, Alice Teirstein

LARRY RICHARDSON'S DANCE GALLERY
May 11–14, 1977 (4 performances)
Bruce Michael-Neil Fleckman Associates presents:

RUSH DANCE COMPANY

Director-Choreographer, Patrice M. Regnier; Lighting Design, Charles Fields; Stage Manager, Christopher Adler; Costume Consultant, Barbara Brown

COMPANY

Patrice M. Regnier   Jane Hedal
Cornelius Fisher-Credo   Russell Lome

PROGRAM: "Don't Look Back" (Diane Ponzio, Patrice M. Regnier), "Peer" (Traditional, Regnier), "Bernard: A Portrait, First Movement" (Bill Evans/Benny Goodman, Regnier), "Second Movement" (Joseph Blunt, Regnier)
(No photos available)

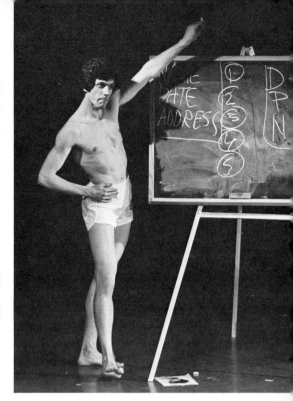

Paul Wilson in "Show 'n' Tell"
(Ron Reagan Photo)

AMERICAN THEATRE LABORATORY
May 12–15, 1977 (4 performances)
Dance Theater Workshop presents:

JULIE MALONEY & PAUL WILSON

Lighting Design, George Titus; Sound Technician, Lou DiLiberto; Stage Manager, Joanne Leone Corris; Production Coordinator, Kate Elliott; Technical Director, Paul Harkins

PROGRAM

"Show 'n' Tell" (A conflict instigated by Paul Wilson with Kathy Eaton after Frances Witkowski); "A Clown" (John Cage, Julie Maloney) danced by Scott Volk, Paul Wilson; *Premieres* of "Spaghetti I" (Dvorak) choreographed and danced by Julie Maloney; "Drifting" (Keith Jarrett) choreographed and danced by Paul Wilson; "Spaghetti II" (Dvorak) choreographed and danced by Julie Maloney

ANTHOLOGY FILM ARCHIVES
May 13–15, 1977 (3 performances)
Anthology Film Archives presents:

VIDEODANCE BY AMY GREENFIELD

PROGRAM: "Dialogue for Cameraman & Dancer" danced by Amy Greenfield; "Fragments: Nat/Glass" danced by Ben Dolphin; "Advent" danced by Amy Greenfield; "Dervish" danced by Amy Greenfield; "Work-in-Progress" danced by Amy Greenfield and Ben Dolphin; "Dirt" danced by Amy Greenfield; "Transport" danced by Amy Greenfield and Lee Vogt; "One-O-One" danced by Douglas Dunn; "Encounter" danced by Rima Wolff and Amy Greenfield; "Element" danced by Amy Greenfield; "Nine Variations on a Dance Theme" by Hilary Harris, danced by Bettie DeJong; "Thanatopsis" by Ed Emshwiller, danced by Becky Arnold; "Study In Choreography for Camera" by Maya Deren, danced by Talley Beatty

Amy Greenfield *(John Budde Photo)* **Above: Art Bridgman, Alice Tierstein in "Sympathetic Vibrations"** *(Ron Reagan Photo)*

FELT FORUM
Saturday & Sunday, May 14 & 15, 1977 (3 performances)
Madison Square Garden Productions presents:

GEORGIAN DANCERS OF ISRAEL

Founder-Artistic Director-Choreographer, Ilia Namtalashvili, and a company of 50 dancers, singers and musicians in traditional Jewish dances and music in the Soviet-Georgian tradition, making their U.S. debut. (No other details available)

THEATRE OF THE OPEN EYE
Tuesday & Wednesday, May 17 & 18, 1977 (2 performances)

AN EVENING WITH THREE CHOREOGRAPHERS

PROGRAM: "Interiors" in three parts: "Oeuf" (Henry Cowell), "Woman" (Javanese Gamelan), "Ghost" (Shakuhachi) all choreographed and danced by Muna Tseng; Mask and Costumes, Eric Bass, Sun Ock Lee; "The Wanderings of a Good Soul" conceived, choreographed, taped, designed, and performed by Ari Darom and Tamar Rogoff

Renni Greenberg, Kiyo Machida, Karen Bean in "Waterplay" Above: Georgian Dancers of Israel

ST. PETER'S EPISCOPAL CHURCH
May 19–21, 1977 (3 performances)

DANCES BY ERICA MEYERS

Choreography, Erica Meyers; Music, Axel Gros; Lighting Design, Nancy Golladay

COMPANY

Karen Bean	Erica Meyers
Renni Greenberg	Julio Acosta
Kiyo Machida	Axel Gros

PROGRAM: "Waterplay," "Reunion," "Bringin' in the May"

AMERICAN THEATRE LABORATORY
May 19–22, 1977 (4 performances)
Dance Theater Workshop presents:

TWO OF A FASHION
Candice Christakos
Gael Stepanek

PROGRAM: "Downtown Blues" (Jim Kweskin's Jug Band; Gael Stepanek) danced by Janis Brenner, Bill Kirkpatrick, Gael Stepanek, Richard Thorne; "Madrigal" (Thomas Dillow, Candice Christakos) danced by German Bacaicoa and Candice Christakos; "Portrait of Three" (Mozart/Average White Band/Sound Effects, Gael Stepanek) danced by Gael Stepanek, Janis Brenner, Candice Christakos; "Distractions" (Candice Christakos/Thomas Dillow, Christakos) danced by Candice Christakos, Kathy Colihan, Laura Crown, Dorian Petri, Sandra Seymour; "Voyage sans Title: Untitled Voyage" (Satie/Rossini/Sound Effects, Gael Stepanek) danced by Janis Brenner, Candice Christakos, Bill Kirkpatrick, Lonne Moretton, Gael Stepanek, Richard Thorne

Bill Kirkpatrick, Gael Stepanek in "Untitled Voyage"
(Ron Reagan Photo)

CHILDREN'S DANCE THEATRE

COMPANY

Michelle Ferguson, Lara Lippman, Rebecca Wolfe, Kerri Barriero, Daphne Latham, Michael Ferguson, Carla Murphy, Gabrielle Marzone, Giuliana Santini, Josh Rogoff, Gillian Dey, Gian Paolo Santini, Meghan Samitz, Ross Snyder, Gabrielle Votano, and Gloria Kosowski (Director)

PROGRAM

YOUNG DANCERS ALOFT: "Synopsis '76" (Tape Collage/ Gershwin, Kosowski; film by Paul Rosenberg; slides by Dennis Maier), "Skirt Dance" (Taj Mahal, Kosowski), "Playground Athletes" (none, Kosowski/students), "Night Fantasies-Rag Recipes" (Vivaldi/Joni Mitchell, Santini/Kosowski/Latham), "Garden Suite" (Neil Diamond, Kosowski)

QUEENS THEATRE IN THE PARK
May 26–29, 1977

PEARL LANG
AND DANCE COMPANY

Artistic Director-Choreographer, Pearl Lang; General Manager, David Donadio; Production Manager, Jeffrey Schissler; Stage Manager, Paul Mathiesen; Rehearsal Directors, Ellen Tittler, Ahuva Anbary; Sheldon Soffer Management, Inc.; Lighting Design, Jeffrey Schissler, Ken Billington.

COMPANY

Debra Zalkind, Erica Drew, Wendy McDade, Judith Garay, Bettze McCoy, Larry Damien Stevens, Jerome Sarnat, Richard Arbach, Oded Kafri, Frank Colardo, Philip Grosser, Alicia Henley, Eva Grubler, Clifford Shulman, Lar Roberson, soloist, and Pearl Lang

PROGRAM

"Roundelays" (Carl Phillipp Emanuel, Lang), "I Never Saw Another Butterfly" (Henry Cowell/Igor Stravinsky/Irving Srul Glick, Lang), "Shira" (A. Hovhaness, Lang)

ARENA STUDIO
May 26–June 25, 1977 (20 performances)
The Multigravitational Aerodance Group presents:

HOMAGE TO PICASSO

Artistic Director-Choreographer, Stephanie Evanitsky; Music, Richard Hayman; Costumes, Nils Eklund

COMPANY

Stephanie Evanitsky
Suellen Epstein
Kay Gainer
Arthur-George Hurray
Donald Porteous
Barbara Salz
Bronya Weinberg

TERRA FIRMA STUDIO
Friday & Saturday, May 27 & 28, 1977. (2 performances)

OIBRE EALAIN

(translated from Gaelic: *work of art*) Director-Choreographer, Deirdre Glasheen; Costumes, Suzinina Rottblat; Films, Lisa Rinzler, Michael Glasheen; Lighting Design, Lauren Angheld

COMPANY

David Basque   Donna Masalgo
Deirdre Glasheen   Kirstin Moore

PROGRAM: "Crossings" (Deirdre Glasheen), "Film" (Lisa Rinzler, Glasheen), "American Beauties" (Kristin Moore), "Outlist" (Deirdre Glasheen)

Pearl Lang Company in "I Never Saw Another Butterfly"
Above: Children's Dance Theatre *(Ron Reagan Photos)*

Oibre Ealain *(Mariano Pastor Photo)* **Above: Members of Multigravitational Aerodance Group in "Homage to Picasso"** *(Robert Fiala Photo)* **117**

ANNUAL SUMMER DANCE FESTIVALS OF 1976

AMERICAN DANCE FESTIVAL
New London, Connecticut
June 28–August 7, 1976
Twenty-ninth Year

Director, Charles L. Reinhart; Dean, Martha Myers; Administrators, Mary Jane Ingram, Lisa Booth, Joya Granbery Hoyt; Coordinator, Jay P. Parikh; Press, Nigel Redden, Anne P. Kearns; Project Directors, Merrill Brockway, Deborah Jowitt, Linni Silberman, Sheldon Soffer, Walter Nicks, Robin Baker, Martha Myers; Technical Director, Benjamin Howe

Monday, June 28, 1976
BILL EVANS performing "Allemande and Gigue" (Bach, Evans), "Harold" (Joplin, after Spider Kedelsky), "Hard Times" (Deseret String Band, Evans), "Song in August" (Sussman, Evans), "Opus Jazz Loves Bach" (Bach, Mattox), "Lyric Suite" (Berg, Sokolow), "The Five O'Clock Whistle and What's Your Story, Morning Glory?" (Glenn Miller, Evans), "Tin-Tal" (Misra, Evans)

Tuesday, June 29, 1976
ANNABELLE GAMSON performing "Dances by Isadora Duncan," "Dances by Mary Wigman," "Dances by Annabelle Gamson."

Friday & Saturday, July 2 & 3, 1976
PAULINE KONER DANCE CONSORT (Georgiana Holmes, Deborah Pratt, Karen Shields, Martha Curtis, Tamara Grose, Michael Freed, Harry Grose, George White) dancing "Concertino" (Pergolesi, Koner), "Cassandra" (Copland, Koner), "Solitary Songs" (Berio, Koner), and *World Premiere* of "A Time of Crickets"

Thursday, July 8, 1976
CHUCK DAVIS DANCE COMPANY (Marilyn Banks, Onika Bgemon, Chuck Davis, Normadien Gibson, Diarrah Sule, Juanita Tyler, Charles Wynn) performing "Dyembe and Chant," Molu Yamee," "Konkoba," "Shakares," "Yarabi," "Boot Dance," "Kalimba," "Sea Ritual"

Friday & Saturday, July 9 & 10, 1976
METROPOLITAN OPERA BALLET ENSEMBLE (Lucia Sciorsci, Eugenia Hoeflin, Jack Hertzog, Pauline Andrey, Skiles Fairlie, Naomi Marritt, Anthony Santiago, William Breedlove, Vicki Fisera, Marcus Bugler, Ellen Rievman, Marc Verzatt; Artistic Director, Norbert Vesak) dancing "Die Fledermaus Variations" (Strauss, Vesak), "Once for the Birth of...." (Rachmaninoff, Vesak), "Le Carnaval" (Schumann, Fokine), "Belong" (Syrinx, Vesak), "Rich Man's Frug" (Coleman, Fosse)

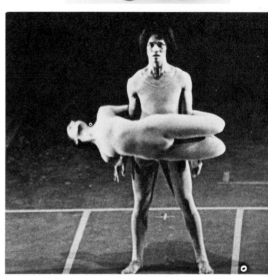

Ellen Rievman, Marcus Bugler in "Belong"
(J. Heffernan Photo) **Top Right: Bill Evans**

Members of Pauline Koner Dance Company
Above: Chuck Davis

118

AMERICAN DANCE FESTIVAL

Wednesday, July 14, 1976
KIRK NUROCK AND NATURAL SOUND with Shelley Hirsch, Claire Picher, Skip LaPlante, Greg Alper, performing "Rhythm Chant Prelude," "Track," "Om Sea and Balkan Counterpoint," "Audience Oratorio Part II"

Friday & Saturday, July 16 & 17, 1976
NIKOLAIS DANCE THEATRE (Lisbeth Bagnold, Bill Groves, Suzanne McDermaid, Gerald Otte, Carlo Pellegrini, Chris Reisner, Jessica Sayre, Karen Sing, James Teeters, Joe Zina) performing "Temple," "Duet from Somniloquy," "Triple Duet from Grotto," "Tensile Involvement from Masks, Props and Mobiles," "Tribe"

Sunday & Monday, July 18 & 19, 1976
MABOU MINES (Susan Kampe, Jessica Nelson, Suzanne White, Deborah Ann Cali, Candace Allyn, Kim Haflich, Carol Eggers, Terry O'Reilly, Rose Montano, Lesley Farlow, Becka Reed, Greg Mehrten, Ruth Maleczech, Linda Wolfe, Bill Raymond, Fred Neumann, Clove Galilee) performing "22 Cuts from the Red Horse Animation," "Soundtrack from the Shaggy Dog Animation"

Thursday, Friday, Saturday, July 22–24, 1976
BELLA LEWITZKY DANCE COMPANY (Loretta Livingston, Iris Pell, Nora Reynolds, Sean Greene, Kurt Weinheimer, Robert Hughes, David Caley, Kim Richardson, Amy Ernst, Serena Richardson) dancing "Greening" (Copland, Lewitzky), "Ceremony for Three" (Rhodes, Lewitzky), "Spaces Between (Marcus, Lewitzky), "Five" (Lifchitz, Lewitzky), "On the Brink of Time" (Subotnick, Lewitzky)

Thursday, July 29, 1976
BILL EVANS DANCE COMPANY (Ann Asnes, Jim Coleman, Regina DeCrosse, Bill Evans, Gregg Lizenbery, Kathleen McClintock, Joanne Mendl Shaw, Shirley Wiegman) dancing "End of the Trail" (Bill Monroe/Montana Slim, Evans), "The Dallas Blues" (Bessie Smith, Evans), "The Legacy" (Shapero, Evans), "Take the 'A' Train" (Glenn Miller, Evans), "Bach Dances" (Bach, Evans), "Hard Times" (Deseret String Band, Evans)

Sunday, August 1, 1976
GUTHRIE-ROTANTE DANCE COMPANY (choreographed and directed by Ted Rotante and Nora Guthrie) performing "Field," "Brick," "The Five Boons of Life"

Friday & Saturday, August 6 & 7, 1976
NANCY MEEHAN DANCE COMPANY (Risa Friedman, Trude Link, George Macaluso, Nancy Meehan, Mary Spalding, Dean Theodorakis, Eli Pollack, Wendy Shifrin) performing "Live Dragon" (Moryl, Meehan), "Threading the Wave" (Hovda, Meehan)

MURRAY LOUIS DANCE COMPANY (Michael Ballard, Richard Hiasma, Helen Kent, Dianne Markham, Anne McLeod, Jerry Pearson, Sara Pearson, Robert Small) dancing the *World Premiere* of "Glances" (Brubeck, Louis)

Nora Guthrie, Ted Rotante
Top Right: Mabou Mines

Members of Bella Lewitzky Dance Company in "Spaces Between" Above: Nancy Meehan
(Lois Greenfield Photo)

119

DANCE FESTIVAL/THE MALL
New York, N. Y.
July 9–August 15, 1976

Sponsored by Clark Center for the Performing Arts and the City University Graduate Center; Director, Louise Roberts; Administrative Director, Joan Chanin; Production Coordinator, Technical Assistance Group; Lighting Design, Craig Miller; Stage Managers, James Harrison, Jim Irwin; Technical Director, Gordon Link; Design Consultant, Steve Duffy; Press, Howard Atlee, Clarence Allsopp, Becky Flora

July 9, 10, 11, 1976 (3 performances)
NEW CHOREOGRAPHERS CONCERT: "Striation" (Bartok) choreographed and danced by Ron Paul; "Sonata in G Major" (Schubert, Devon Wall) danced by Carole Staewen and J. Edward Sydow; "Clara's Lament" (Schumann) choreographed and danced by Patty Shenker; "Aubade" (Penderecki, Fred Mathews) performed by Colette Bischer, Mark Ammerman; "Sextet Foranna" (Copland, Susan Dibble) danced by Susan Dibble, Glenn Ferrugiari, Alan Good, Meralee Guhl, John Hadden, Paul Thompson; "Amalgam" (Don Salmon/Susan Deaver, Cathryn Williams) danced by Kathyanne Guy; "Everybody Works/All Beasts Count" (Jesse Fuller/Linda Berry/Arnie Zane) choreographed and danced by Bill T. Jones; "Piece D'Occasion" (Jim Burton, Senta Driver) performed by Michaele Sallade, Timothy Knowles, Senta Driver; "Coretta" (Nina Simone/Martin Luther King, Jr., Carole Kariamu Welsh) danced by Frances Hare, Yvonne James, Baynell Sherrod, Carole Kariamu Welsh

July 14–18, 1976
FRED BENJAMIN DANCE COMPANY: Karen Burke, Marilyn Banks, Cheryl Bell, Brenda Braxton, Alfred Gallman, Donald Griffith, Linda James, Ronald McKay, Mark Rubin, Fred Benjamin (Director-Choreographer), and Guest Artists Michele Simmons and Winston DeWitt Hemsley, performing "Mountain High" (Ashford-/Simpson, Benjamin), "Ceremony" (Collage, Benjamin), "Ember" (Issac Hayes, Winston DeWitt Hemsley), "From the Mountain of the Moon" (Weather Report/Herbie Hancock/Earth, Wind and Fire, Benjamin), "Beauty Is Skin Deep ... Ugly Is to the Bone" (Quincy Jones/Headhunters/Natalie Cole, Talley Beatty; *World Premiere*) "Love's Requiem" (George Harrison, Benjamin), "The Sands of Time" (Morgana King, Michele Simmons), "Facts and Pain" (Contemporary, Benjamin), "Travels, Just Outside the House" (Deadato/Alice Coltrane/Carlos Santana/Yusef Lateef, Benjamin), "Parallel Lines (Hubert Laws/War, Benjamin)

July 21, 22, 23, 1976
CHARLES MOORE DANCES AND DRUMS OF AFRICA: Charles Moore, Ella Thompson Moore, Carmen Benitez, Reggie Brown, Ramona Candy, Elliott Gillette, Cassandra Ford, David Pace, Audrey Hubbard, Jaspar Prince, Sharon Miles, Serge Rene, Donna Williams, and drummers Chief Bey, Louis Celestin, Albert Louis-Jean, performing "Moon Dance", "Fast Agbekor," "Three Spirits," "Awassa Astrige," "Siychi," "Spear Dance," "Tokai," "Souvenir d'Haiti."

July 24–25, 28–29, 1976 (4 performances)
KEI TAKEI'S MOVING EARTH: Amy Berkman, Richmond Johnstone, Regine Kunzle, John de Marco, Elsi Miranda, John Parton, Maldwyn Pate, Joan Schwartz, Kei Takei, Laurie Uprichard, Howard Vichinsky performing "Light Part 4" (Lloyd Ritter, Takei), "Lunch" (Takei), "Light Part 7: Diary of the Field" (Maldwyn Pate/Lloyd Ritter, Takei)

July 30, 31, August 1, 1976
OTIS SALLID NEW ART ENSEMBLE: Kamal Abdullah, Shawneequa Baker-Scott, Clyde Barret, Shirley Black Brown, Richard Barclift, Gina Chew, Eulaula, Dyane Harvey, Deidre Lovelle, Judy Mercer, Frances Morgan, Daryl Richardson, Otis Sallid, Eric Sawyer, Phillip Wright, dancing "Heat Is On" (Isley Brothers, Sallid), "Disco-Lady" (Johnny Taylor, Sallid), "Persechetti" (Persechetti, Sallid), "Big Band" (Hank Crawford, Sallid), "Bach" (Villa Lobos, Sallid), "Every Mother's Child" (Hubert Laws/Roberta Flack, Shawneequa Baker-Scott), "Love Songs" (Coltrane/Hathaway/-Wonder/Withers/Hopkins/Sallid, Sallid)

August 4–8, 1976 (5 performances)
THEATRE DANCE COLLECTION: Rodney Griffin, Diana Haight, Don Lopez, Cynthia Riffle, Audrey Ross, Lynn Simonson, Peter Sommen, Lynne Taylor, Jaclyn Villamil dancing "Clean Sheets" (Callipes, Rodney Griffin), "Ballad of the False Lady" (Traditional, Emily Frankel), "Legacy" (Steven Cagen, Lynne Taylor), "Diary" (Judith Lander, Lynne Taylor), "Spy" (Lynne Taylor/-Judith Lander), "My Father" (Judy Collins, Jaclynn Villamil), "Rialto" (George Gershwin, Rodney Griffin)

August 13, 14, 15, 1976
LOUIS JOHNSON DANCE THEATRE: Clyde Barrett, Muriel Burwell, Leroy Cowen, Michael Goring, Syrina Irving, Kashka, Arnold Kingsbury, Lavern Howell-Reed, Phoebe Redmond dancing "Moods Three" (Vivaldi/Prokofiev/Isley Brothers, Louis Johnson), "Lament" (Villa-Lobos, Johnson), "When Malindy Sings" (Contemporary/Classical, Johnson)

Fred Benjamin Dance Co. in "Pretty Is Skin Deep ..."
(Nathaniel Tileston Photo)

Top: Charles and Ella Thompson Moore
Below: Clyde Barrett, Dyanne Harvey
in "Disco Lady" Bottom: Theatre Dance
Collection in "Clean Sheets"
(Nathaniel Tileston Photos)

JACOB'S PILLOW DANCE FESTIVAL

Lee, Massachusetts
June 29–August 21, 1976
Forty-fourth Season

Founder, Ted Shawn (1891–1972); Director, Norman Walker; Comptroller, Grace Badorek; Press, Donald Westwood; Music Director, Jess Meeker; Technical Directors, David M. Chapman, Randy Klein; Wardrobe Mistress, Pauline Juillerat; Production Assistants, Barbara Barr, James Mertz, Doug Nakamoto, Norton Owen, Howard Sonenklar, Brenda Steady

June 29-July 3, 1976
ROYAL DANISH BALLET SOLOISTS: Frank Andersen, Ib Andersen, Dianna Bjorn, Annemarie Dybdal, Niels Kehlet, Eva Kolborg, Hans Jacob Kolgaard, Anne Marie Vessel dancing "Etudes" (Ludvig Smith, Bournonville), "Pas de Deux from the Kermess in Bruges" (Paulli, Bournonville/Brenaa/Flindt), "Pas de Trois from The Conservatory" (Paulli, Bournonville/Brenaa), "Balabile from Napoli Act I" (Paulli, Bournonville/Brenaa/Ralov), "The Chairs" (Charles Koecklin, Peter-Paul Zwartjes), "Pas de Six and Tarantella from Napoli Act III" (Helsted/Paulli, Bournonville/Brenaa/Ralov), "Pas de Deux from Flower Festival in Genzano" (Paulli, Bournonville/Brenaa),

July 6-10, 1976
JACOB'S PILLOW DANCERS: Michael Dean, Horacio Cifuentes, Douglas Nakamoto, Wesley Robinson, Charles Sheek, Mark Townes dancing "Polonaise" (McDowell, Ted Shawn/Norman Walker)
JOYCE TRISLER DANSCOMPANY: Nancy Colahan, Elaine Anderson, Anne-Marie Hackett, Jacqulyn Buglisi, Clif de Raita, Don Foreman, Miguel Antonio dancing "Four against the Gods" (Stravinsky, Trisler), "Butterfly" (Subotnick, Rael Lamb)
ANNABELLE GAMSON dancing recreated works by Isadora Duncan: "Water Study" (Schubert), "Five Waltzes" (Brahms), "Dance of the Furies" (Gluck), "Etude" (Sciabin), and "Valse Brilliante" (Chopin)
SUZANNE FARRELL and PETER MARTINS dancing "Pas de Deux from Agon" (Stravinsky, Balanchine), and "Tchaikovsky Pas de Deux" (Tchaikovsky, Balanchine)

July 13-17, 1976
MARIA ALBA SPANISH DANCE COMPANY: Maria Alba, Manuel Arenas, Ana Maria Cristina, Melina Montoya, Carlota Santana, Teodoro Felipe, Guillermo Rios, Simon Serrano, Roberto Lorca, Luis Rivera dancing "Danzas Fantasticas" (Turina), "Intermezzo" (Granados), "Farruca," "Tarantos," "Zapateado," "Asturias" (Albeniz), "Aires de Andalucia," and *World Premieres* of "Ritmos Flamencos" and "Reflecciones" (Turina/Albeniz, Manuel Arenas/Maria Alba)

July 20-24, 1976
NIKOLAIS DANCE THEATRE: Lisbeth Bagnold, Suzanne McDermaid, Jude Morgan, Gerald Otte, Carol Pellegrini, Chris Reisner, Jessica Sayre, Karen Sing, James Teeters, Jo Zina dancing "Group Dance from Sanctum," "Trio from Vaudeville of the Elements," "Noumenon from Masks, Props and Mobiles," "Tensile Involvement from Masks, Props and Mobiles," "Tribe," "Temple," "Duet from Somniloquy," "Triple Duet from Grotto," "Foreplay," "Cross-Fade," "Scenario"

Annabelle Gamson Top Right: Frank Andersen
Below: Joyce Trisler Danscompany
(Lois Greenfield Photo)

Maria Alba Spanish Dance Company
(Jack Mitchell Photo)

121

JACOB'S PILLOW DANCE FESTIVAL

July 27–31, 1976
CHARLES MOORE dancing "Awassa Astrige," "Spear Dance," "Sacred Forest Dance"
HELEN DOUGLAS and BURTON TAYLOR dancing "Pas de Deux from Swan Lake Act II" (Tchaikovsky, Ivanov/Petipa), and "Grand Pas de Deux from The Nutcracker" (Tchaikovsky, Ivanov)
EMILY FRANKEL dancing "The Four Seasons" (Vivaldi, Frankel)
JACOB'S PILLOW DANCERS: Regina Larkin, Terese Capucilli, Carol Parker, Mary Ann Neu, Roberta Mathes, Cathy McCann, Alice Gill, Kim Jurrius, Nancy Lushington dancing "Songs" (Tadiuz Baird, Norman Walker)

August 3–7, 1976
MILWAUKEE BALLET COMPANY: Leslie McBeth, Maxine Lampert, Nanette DiLorenzo, Margaret McLaughlin, Steven Lockser, Lee Larkin, Lydia Morales, John Davis, Kathryn Moriarty, Mark Diamond, Madalene Baenen, Elizabeth Corbett, Donald Rottinghaus, Kristin Johnson, Richard Rock, Mulie Marszalkowski, Angela House, Carl Swanson, with Guest Artist Ted Kivitt dancing "Points and Counterpoints" (Beethoven, Marjorie Mussman), "Le Corsaire Pas de Deux" (Drigo, Nureyev) performed by Leslie McBeth and Ted Kivitt, "Daughters of Mourning" (Frank Martin, Jean Paul Comelin), "Diversions" (Britten, Comelin), "Partita" (Bach, Comelin), "A Cocktail Party" (Poulenc, Mussman), "Sonata a Tre" (Albinoni, Comelin), "Paquita" (Minkus, Petipa/-Comelin)

JACOB'S PILLOW DANCE FESTIVAL
August 10–14, 1976

CLAUDE KIPNIS MIME THEATRE: Claude Kipnis, Michael Piatkowski, Jon Ruddle, Jay Natelle, Lynne Jassem, Judi Ann Coles, Cindy Benson, performing "Main Street," "Pictures at an Exhibition" (Moussorgsky/Ravel, Kipnis)
TEODORO MORCA, GISELA, ISABEL MORCA, WILLIAM CARTER, GARY HAYES in "Flamenco in Concert": "La Vida Breve" (de Falla, Antonia de Cordoba), "Bach Trilogy" (Bach, Teodoro Morca), "Danze Molinero" (de Falla, Manolo Vargas), "Asturias" (Albeniz, Tarriba), "Adagio, Concierto de Aranjuez" (Rodrigo, Vargas/de Cordoba), "Homage a Carmen Amaya" (Romeras, T. Morca)

August 17–21, 1976
LAWRENCE RHODES and DENNIS WAYNE dancing "The Prussian Officer" (Bartok, Norman Walker)
BOB BOWYER and JO-ANN BRUGGEMANN dancing "Menuetto" (Mozart, Bowyer), "Teen Angels" (Elton John, Bowyer), and *Premieres* of "A Best Friend" (Marion McPartland, Bowyer), and "Travelin' On" (Glenn Miller, Bowyer)
JACOB'S PILLOW DANCERS in *Premieres* of "Prelude to a Summer's Evening" (Ravel, Norman Walker), and "Echoes from the Tempest" (George Crumb, Norman Walker) danced by Anita Brockie, Deborah Donaldson, Jennifer Donaldson, Karen Fraction, Kathryn Holt, Cathy McCann, Brenda Steady, Kathleen Wimpress, William Arroyo, Horacio Cifuentes, Wesley Robinson, Mark Townes, Stephen Driscoll, Wesley Robinson, Regina Larkin, Carol Parker, Alice Grill, James Lepore, Clement Sheek, Douglas Nakamoto, Michael Deane, Norton Owen, Cathy McCann, Kim Jurrius, Nancy Lushington, Mary Ann Neu, Barbara Barr, Terese Capucilli, Roberta Mathes, Sheryl Mirsky, Bruce Ballinger, James Mertz, William Soleau, Howard Sonenklar, Mark Sovocool, Chris Webster

122
Helen Douglas   Isabel Morca
Top Right: Emily Frankel Below:
Claude Kipnis Mime Theatre

Bob Bowyer, Jo-Ann Bruggemann
Above: Teodoro Morca

NEW YORK DANCE FESTIVAL

ELACORTE THEATRE, CENTRAL PARK
NEW YORK, NEW YORK
September 3–13, 1976

Presented by Joseph Papp; Administrator, TAG Foundation Ltd.,
ghting Designer, Thomas Skelton; Associate Producer, Bernard
rsten; Production Supervisor, Jason Steven Cohen; Press Repre-
tative, Merle Debuskey, Susan Schulman; Associate Lighting De-
ner, Louis Guthman; Stage Managers, Robert Kellogg, Rosemary
nningham; Technical Director, Darrell Ziegler; Assistant to Mr.
elton, Tim Snyder

PROGRAMS

Friday & Saturday, September 3–4, 1976
ON REDLICH DANCE COMPANY: Jennifer Donohue, Irene
genheimer, Barbara Roan, Billy Siegenfeld, Don Redlich dancing
races" (Traditional American Folk Music, Redlich)

ARGARET BEALS AND THE IMPULSES COMPANY:
argaret Beals, Dance; Edward M. Greenberg, Light; Janaki,
ice; Michael Rod, Wind Instruments; Badal Roy, Tabla; Gwen-
yn Watson, Cello; "Improvisation for Dancer and Musicians"

RMEN de LAVALLADE performing *NEW YORK PRE-
IERE* of "Les Chansons De Bilitis" (Debussy/Twelve poems by
rre Louys, de Lavallade; Lighting, Carol Waaser; Costumes,
offrey Holder)

R LUBOVITCH DANCE COMPANY: Susan Weber, Rob
sserer, Mari Ono, Gerri Houlihan, Aaron Osborne, Charles Mar-
, Laura Gates, Christine Wright, Harry Laird, Lar Lubovitch
cing *NEW YORK PREMIERE* of "Les Noces" (Stravinsky,
bovitch; Lighting, Craig Miller; Costume Design, Lubovitch)

unday (afternoon), September 5, 1976
IE PHILIPPINE DANCE COMPANY performing "Sulyap"
aditional, Reynaldo G. Alejandro)

RRY performing "The Star Game" (Senta Driver)

ALTER NICKS DANCE THEATRE WORKSHOP: J. Vernon
yd, Troy C. Jackson, Emilio Lastarria, David Lee, Deidre Lovell,
ndetta Mathea, Elisabeth Thompson, Jack Walsh dancing
ORLD PREMIERE* "Roots Revisited" (Santana: "Solo Con Sal-
/Wayne Shorter: "Reflection"/The Voices of East Harlem:
oving, A Street Scene,"/Sonny Terry and Brownie McGee:
ooting Blues, A Rural Breakdown," Walter Nicks; Costumes,
tti, Maria Contessa, Bernard Johnson; Stage Manager, Erik Hart;
hersal Director, Walter Raines)

unday (evening) & Tuesday, September 5 & 7, 1976
RRY: Michaele Sallade, Timothy Knowles, Senta Driver danc-
and Music performed by the Charles Lee Redman Trio (Jim
rton, Jon Deak, Ed Friedman) "Piece D'Occasion" (Jim Burton/
h Country Helium, Driver)

AHID SOFIAN with musicians Charles "Chick" Ganemian,
nan Yeginsoy, Mohamed El-Akkad, John Vartan, Robert Marsh-
, Steve Knight performing *WORLD PREMIERE* "Raqs
rqi" (Traditional Middle Eastern, Sofian)

W YORK DANCE THEATRE: Elaine Bauer, Pamela Mitch-
Deirdre Myles, Judith Shoaff, Alexandra Williams, David
wn, James Dunne, Mark Johnson, Robert Maiorano, Darryl
binson dancing *WORLD PREMIERE* "Romanzen" (Brahms,
nk Ohman)

ARL LANG AND DANCE COMPANY: Pearl Lang, Susan
Lain, Alice Coughlin, Erica Drew, Barry Smith, Larry Smith,
ndy Mc Dade dancing "Prairie Steps" (Copland, Lang; Lighting,
n Billington; Costumes, A. Christina Giannini)

I TAKEI'S MOVING EARTH: John De Marco, Maldwyn
e, Kei Takei dancing "Light Part 5" (Marcus Parsons III, Takei)

ALTER NICKS DANCE THEATRE WORSHOP dancing
oots Revisited"

Ron Reagan Photos

Top: (L) Don Redlich Dance Co. in "Traces"
(R) Carmen de Lavallade in "Les Chansons
de Bilitis" Below: Margaret Beals and
the Impulses Co.

N.Y. Dance Theatre in "Romanzen"
Above: Walter Nicks Dance Theatre
Workshop in "Roots Revisited"

123

NEW YORK DANCE FESTIVAL

Wednesday & Thursday, September 8–9, 1976
NANCY MEEHAN DANCE COMPANY: Risa Friedman, Trude Link, George Macaluso, Nancy Meehan, Wendy Shifrin, Mary Spalding, Dean Theodorakis, dancers, with Jon Deak, Michael Trentacosti, musicians, performing "Split Rock" (Deak, Meehan; Lighting, Jon Knudsen)

NALA NAJAN performing *NEW YORK PREMIERE* "Krishna Ni Begane Baro" (Vyasaraya, improvisation), "Pushpanjali" (Traditional)

BURTON TAYLOR and ANNA ARAGNO dancing "Le Corsair"

LINDA TARNAY DANCE COMPANY: John Stuart Dewees, Alfredo Gonzales, Holly Harbinger, Rachel Harms, Cynthia May, Tryntje Shapli, Linda Tarnay dancing "Ocean" (Sergio Cervetti, Tarnay)

DANNY WILLIAMS GROSSMAN DANCE COMPANY: Judith Hendin and Danny Williams Grossman performing "Higher" (Ray Charles, Grossman)

MARIA BENITEZ' ESTAMPA FLAMENCA dancing *WORLD PREMIERE* "Tribute to Garcia Lorca" (Pavon/Tribute to Benitez; Costumes, Traditional; Lighting and Narrator, Cecilio Benitez; Guitarist-Guest Artist, Rene Heredia; Singer, Miguel Galvez)

Friday & Saturday, September 10–11, 1976
THEATRE DANCE COLLECTION: Lynne Taylor, Don Lopez, dancers, and Judith Lander, composer-pianist performing "Diary" (Lander, Taylor)

PHOEBE NEVILLE DANCE COMPANY: John Dayger, Toby Towson, Anthony La Giglia, Phoebe Neville, Marleen Pennison, Tryntje Shapli dancing "Cartouche" (Henry Purcell, Neville)

THE OHIO BALLET: Ann Corrado, Carol Thwaite, Ronald Earley, Marc Ozanich performing "Summer NIght" (Chopin, Heinz Poll)

THE FRED BENJAMIN DANCE COMPANY: Karen Burke, Cheryl Bell, Brenda Braxton, Alfred Gallman, Gregory Hinton, Linda James, Ronald Mc Kay, Mark Rubin, Marilyn Banks, Fred Benjamin dancing "Pretty Is Skin Deep . . . Ugly Is To The Bone" (Natalie Cole/Quincy Jones/Headhunters/War, Talley Beatty)

MARIA ALBA AND LUIS RIVERA dancing "Intermezzo" (Granados, Rivera), "Volver A Siempre (Cana)" (Guillermo Rios, guitar/ Simon Serrano, singer, choreography: Robert Lorca), "Aires Andaluces (Romeras)" (Rios/Serrano/Jose Antonio, Antonio), "Encuentro En La Noche (Seguiriyas)" (Rios/Serrano, Rivera); Lighting, Edward Effron

THE PAULINE KONER DANCE CONSORT: Martha Curtis, Michael Freed, George White, Harry Grose, Tamara Grose, Deborah Pratt, Karen Shields, James Voisine, Georgiana Holmes dancing *NEW YORK PREMIERE* "A Time of Crickets" (Michael Colina, Koner)

Sunday (matinee), September 12, 1976
MARIA ALBA and LUIS RIVERA: Traditional Flamenco

HARRY performing "The STAR GAME"

THE FRED BENJAMIN DANCE COMPANY dancing "Pretty Is Skin Deep . . . Ugly Is To The Bone"

Sunday & Monday, September 12–13, 1976
MS. (Sara) RUDNER, (Deni) BANK, (Francesca) BARTOCCINI, (Wendy) ROGERS dancing *WORLD PREMIERE* "Wendy's Solution" (choreography, Rudner)

DYANE HARVEY dancing "Roots" (American Folk Music/Billie Holiday/Nikki Giovanni, Eleo Pomare)

CLIFF KEUTER DANCE COMPANY: John Dayger, Ernest Pagnano, Michael Tipton, Cliff Keuter performing "The Murder of George Keuter" (Keuter Tape collage and choreography; Set design, Walter Noble)

LAWRENCE RHODES AND NAOMI SORKIN dancing *WORLD PREMIERE* "Andante Cantabile" (Georges Enescu, Paul Sanasardo)

RACHEL LAMPERT and DANCERS: Holly Harbinger, Alfredo Gonzales, Rachel Lampert dancing "Issue" (Ivanovici, arranged by Sergio Cervetti; Lampert)

JENNIFER MULLER & THE WORKS: Jennifer Clark, Carol-rae Kraus, Jennifer Muller, Angeline Wolf, Matthew Diamond, Christopher Pilafian, John Preston dancing "Speeds" (Burt Alcantara, Muller; Lighting Richard Nelson)

Jennifer Muller & the Works in "Speed"
Above: Pauline Koner Dance Consort in
"A Time of Crickets" *(Ron Reagan Photos)*

124

Top Left: Linda Tarnay Dance Co. in "Ocean"
Below: Fred Benjamin Dance Co. Center Left:
Phoebe Neville Dance Co. in "Cartouche"
(Ron Reagan Photos)

THE YARD
Chilmark, Massachusetts
June 28 - August 29, 1976

Director, Patricia N. Woolner; Production Manager, Hal Lemmerman; General Manager, Donald Moore; Press, Mary Beth Dooley; Production Assistants, Bart Hipp, Susan Goldsmith, Skip Peterson; Lighting Design, Hal Lemmerman; Technical Consultant, Mike Wodynski; Stage Manager, David Malamut

Thursday & Friday, July 29 & 30, 1976
Three Premieres: "Progressions" (Choreography, Miguel Angel Diaz) danced by Karen Gober; "Solo" (choreographed by Alice Teirstein) danced by Arthur Bridgman, Michael Cichetti, Anita Feldman, Olgalyn Jolly, Madeleine Perrone, musicians Troy Tyson, Dennis Warren; "le clue" a tragicomic dance-play in four parts with entré acts by Erin Martin and Davidson Lloyd; Choreography, Erin Martin; performed by Arthur Bridgman, Michael Cichetti, Anita Feldman, Karen Gober, Olgalyn Jolly, Madeleine Perrone

Thursday & Friday, August 26 & 27, 1976
Four Premieres: "Area" (Michael Colina, Georgiana Holmes) danced by Karen Gober, Georgiana Holmes, Holly Harbinger, Olgalyn Jolly, Erin Martin; "Eternal Spring" (Dinu Ghezzo, Patricia N. Woolner) danced by Madeleine Perrone, Michael Cichetti, Arthur Bridgman, Jan Wodynski; "Volley" (Zen Flute, David Malamut) danced by Michael Cichetti, Anita Feldman, Karen Gober Holly Harbinger, Olgalyn Jolly, Madeleine Perrone

Right: Michael Cichetti, Anita Feldman in "Volley"
Top: Madeleine Perrone in "Eternal Spring"

Madeleine Perrone, Michael Cichetti, Arthur Bridgman, Olgalyn Jolly, Karen Gober, Anita Feldman in "le clue"

REGIONAL AND PROFESSIONAL DANCE COMPANIES

(Failure to meet deadline necessitated several omissions)

ALBERTA CONTEMPORARY DANCE THEATRE

Edmonton, Alberta, Canada

Artistic Directors, Jacqueline Ogg, Charlene Tarver; Assistant Artistic Director, Sherrie Waggener; Managing Director, Ronald Holgerson; Costumes-Taping, Wendy Albrecht; Lighting, Gary Critchley; Guest Choreographer, Ernst Eder; Guest Designers, Sean Wagar, Charles Hilton, Pat Galbraith, Bruce Bentz, Jasper von Meerheimb, Allan MacInnis

COMPANY

Janie Achtemichuk, Cathy Cahoon, Valerie Moore, Sherrie Waggener, Donald Burnett, Gordon Duchaine, Kelly Rude, Ronald Holgerson, and apprentices Bente Friemel, Margund van Huystee, Lynn Schwabe GUEST ARTISTS: Carol Eder, Ernst Eder, Ann Hildenbrand, Laura Nichols, Marina Shepherd, Natalie Wilson

REPERTOIRE

"Islands of Infinity" (Paul Horn, Charlene Tarver), and *Premieres* of "City Mo(u)rning" (Michal Oldfield, Ronald Holgerson), "Overlay" (Loggins/Messina, Sherrie Waggener), "Journey" (Stockhausen/Syrinx, Waggener), "Ancient Aires & Dances: A Celebration" (Ottorino Respighi, Jacqueline Ogg), "And.... the Third Day" (Dionne/Bregent, Ernst Eder), "Portrait" (Ravel, Waggener), "Girl in a Chair" (silent, Waggener), "Deja Vue" (Bruce Cockburn, Don Burnett)

Right: Valerie Moore, Cathy Cahoon in "Overlay"
Above: Don Burnett in "Islands of Infinity"
(Alberta Contemporary Dance Theatre)

Atlantic Dance Company

ATLANTIC DANCE COMPANY

New Smyrna Beach, Florida

Artistic Director-Choreographer, Jean Tepsic; Associate Directors, Mary W. Hall, Marjorie Tepsic; Technical Directors, Renee Clift, Andrew Baker

COMPANY

PRINCIPALS: Jean Tepsic, Elizabeth Elmquist, Sarah Timberlake, Jennifer York, Lynne Meyers
CORPS: Karen Anderson, Tina Drellos, Carol Fuquay, Pat Griffin, Margi Kosmas, Terri Martin, Kathryn Pieters, Darlene Yurgalewicz, Dan Casale, Michael Caruso, Mirek Korbut

REPERTOIRE

(All choreography by Jean Tepsic) "Peter and the Wolf" (Prokofiev), "Renaissance Dances" (Traditional), "Courant" (Haydn), "4 X 6" (K. C. and the Sunshine Band), "Sleeping Beauty Divertissements" (Tchaikovsky, after Petipa), "Magnetic Rag" (Joplin), "Tabakaryaska" (Traditional/Mahler), "Pepperland" (Martin), and *PREMIERES* of "Kouros" (McCosh, Tepsic), "The Reconstruction of the Battle of Lexington and Concord" (Collage, Tepsic), "Emmie" (Nyron, Tepsic), "J. B. U." (McCosh, Tepsic)

ATLANTA BALLET
Atlanta, Georgia

Founder-Consultant, Dorothy Alexander; Artistic Director, Robert Barnett; Ballet Mistress, Merrilee Smith; Assistant Director, Tom Pazik; Directors of Chamber Company, Mannie Rowe, Joanne Lee; General Manager, Charles Fischl; Associate Manager, Sally Way; Business Manager, Dan Sedgwick; Administrative Coordinator, Linda C. Fischl; Conductor, John Head; Choreographers, Robert Barnett, Todd Bolender, Norbert Vesak, Tom Pazik, Ginger Prince Hall, Conrad Ludlow, Saeko Ichinohe; Costumes, Tom Pazik, Daniel Lomax; Lighting, Pat Simmons, Charles Fischl, Lee Betts; Sets, Leo Meyer, Richard Gullickson, Louis Maza; Company Manager, Lee Betts; Stage Manager Bill Esterby

COMPANY

Ann Burton, Maniya Barredo, Pennie Abel, Victoria Cabrera, Merry Clark, Darrell Cooper, Kathryn McBeth, Ronnie Jones, Andrew Kuharsky, Caron Osborn, Kathy Bliss Rhodus, Rose Barile, Jeffrey Stuart, Pam Tylor, Candace Allen, Beverly Barwick, Lori Black, Gil Boggs, Suzie Bramblett, Kristi Brininger, Patrick Brown, Becky Bryan, Nanette Clem, Lisa Davison, Lorenne Fey, Mitch Flanders, Debby Goldberg, Fran Gould, Mary Gould, Julie Gresham, Sarah Harrell, Judi Harrison, Kandy Hodges, Lisa Hudson, Diane Johnson, James Lee, Mary Ann Lupton, Suzanne MacIntyre, Patti Pirkle, Linda Pretz, Elise Rawson, Caroline Spears, Elaine Wadsworth, Leslie Weiner, Mary Davison, Joan Dvorscak, Peggy Howard, Celeste Jabczenski, Eliza Jennings, Katrina Wells, Lisa Riggs, **GUEST ARTIST** Burton Taylor

REPERTOIRE

"Lumenesque" (Saint-Saens, Barnett), "Peasant Dances" (Adam, Barnett), "Peter and the Wolf" (Prokofiev, Pazik), "Black Swan Pas de Deux" (Tchaikovsky, Cranko), "Circles" (Berio, Ichinohe), "Cry without a Sound" (Brel/Hollander, Pazik), "Rococo in White" (Mozart, Zompakos), "Still Point" (Debussy, Bolender), "Heloise and Abelard" (Suk, Ratcliff), "Gift to Be Simple" (Traditional, Vesak), "Concierto de Aranjuez" (Rodrigo, Barnett), "Lifeline" (Husa, Hall), "Pas de Trois" (Minkus, Balanchine), "Song of Life" (Suk, Noble), "Valse" (Strauss/Gungle, Barnett), "Glinkadances" (Glinka, Barnett), "Counterform" (Fifter, Myers), "Just Two" (Varese, Hall), "Wedding Pas de Deux from Raymonda" (Glazounov, after Petipa), "Waltz Pas de Deux" (Nikode, Barnett), "Don Quixote Pas de Deux" (Minkus, Traditional), "Flower Festival in Genzano" (Helsted, Bournonville), "Giselle" (Adam, Blair), "Nutcracker" (Tchaikovsky, Balanchine), "Serenade" (Tchaikovsky, Balanchine), "Good Morrow" (Mahler, Vesak), "Great Scott" (Joplin, Pazik), "No Sunrise Finds Us" (Albanoni, Pazik), "Wautre Vignettes" (Britten, Barnett), and *PREMIERES* of "L'Histoire du soldat" (Stravinsky, Ludlow), "Pas de Quatre" (Pugni, Dolin), "Scherzo" (Litolff, Pazik), "Tzigne" (Budashkin, Pazik)

(Melanie Thompson Photos)

Right: "Great Scott"
Top: "Still Point"

"Lifeline"

"Still Point"

AUSTIN BALLET THEATRE

Austin, Texas

Artistic Director-Choreographer, Stanley Hall; Director, Judy Thompson; Sets, Rick Adams, Kathleen Gee, Steve Parks; Costumes, Marguerite Wright, Kathleen Gee, Eugenia Prann; Lights, Mark Loeffler; Sound, Lee Thompson; Stage Manager, Cappy White; Wardrobe, Mary Alice Ziegler, Elizabeth Cameron; Press, Eva Larson, Betty Adams, Linda Anderson, Kate Bergquist

COMPANY

Lisa Frantz, Shelley Schleier, Lisa Smith, Sandra Storm, Judy Thompson, Mary Claire Ziegler, Douglas Becker, Steven Brule, Clint Fisher, James Haile, William Haile, George Stallings, Gina Adams, Suzanne Blanchard, Sheila Darilek, Julie Ellis, Angela Erck, Adriana Guajardo, Debra Hardy, Norma Hawkins, Alicia Howard, Arletta Howard, Lea Johnson, Eve Larson, Lynda Lindsay, Kris Lindstrom, Pam Lindstrom, Michie Magyar, Robin Spear, Suzanne Stern, Rosemary Thomas, Lucia Uhl, Roberto Adams, Clark Johnston, Dave Larson, Kenny Larson, Len Ripley, Terry Startzel, Rocker Verastique, Doug Wilburn

REPERTOIRE

(All choreography by Stanley Hall) "Napoli Pas de Trois" (Panelli/-Helsted/Gade), "Vespre Siciliennes" (Verdi), "Flickers, American Ethnic Dances," "Tchaikovsky Suite" (Tchaikovsky), "Le Combat" (Khachaturian), "Tregonell" (Jerry Goldsmith/Ussachevsky), "Gemini" (Massenet)
PREMIERES: (choreographed by Stanley Hall) "Carmina Burana" (Orff), "Grieg Concerto" (Grieg), "Gaiete Parisienne" (Offenbach), "Belle Galathee" (Suppe), "Parody of Isms," "Episodes" (Suk), "Introduction to a Company" (Chopin/Tchaikovsky)

(Ron Dorsey Photos)

Austin Ballet Theatre in "Parody of Isms"
and above in "Gaiete Parisienne"

Carol Hageman in "The Nutcracker"
(Ballet Binghamton)

BALLET BINGHAMTON

Binghamton, N. Y.

Artistic Director, Joan Kunsch; Assistant Director, Carol Hageman; Administrative Adviser, Laura B. Martin; Artistic Adviser, Juli Nunlist; Principal Choreographers, Joan Kunsch, Carol Hageman; Sets and Lighting, Richard Dyman; Wardrobe, Cathy Jo Williams; Stage Manager, Charles Kiessling; Press, Terri Shea, Peg Tallet

COMPANY

Heidi Crocker, Aviva Gans, Julie Haber, Carol Hageman, Demaris Hollembeak, Nancy Pasquariello, Debbie Payne, Kate Ragan, Joyce Salls, Sandy Schoeps, Caroline Skinger, Rachel Sterling, Sarah Teuchtler, Lauren Thornblad, Adriana Warner, Thomas Dyno, Arthur Goldweit
GUEST ARTISTS: Christina Bernal, Laurence Matthews, and Wilkes-Barre Ballet Theatre Company

REPERTOIRE

(All choreography by Joan Kunsch) "CantaNeruda" (Palbo Neruda), "Five Spanish Dances" (Moritz Moszkowski), "Grand Tarantelle" (Louis Gottschalk), "Variations from the Nutcracker" (Tchaikovsky)
PREMIERES: "Old Testament Suite" (Bela Bartok, Carol Hageman/Aviva Gans/Demaris Hollembeak), "The Creation" (Poems of James Weldon Johnson, Demaris Hollembeak)

BALLET DES JEUNES
Philadelphia, Pennsylvania
Merchantville, N. J.

Artistic Directress-Choreographer, Ursula Melita; Choreographers, Ruth Skaller, Carmencita Lopez, Andrea Handler; Stage Director, George Landers; Wardrobe Mistress, Sherry Bazell; Pianist, Irene Andrews; Wig Mistress, Lolly Schussler; Press, Katie Tambussi, Jeannie O'Hara

COMPANY

Cindy Alberts, Myra Bazell, Wendy Bendyna, Ann Marie Bright, Kathleen Bright, Claudia Collings, Maria DeRosa, Amelia DeRosa, Joy Edelman, Andrea Elsner, Kim Forlini, Betsy Fox, Karen Elliott, Kathy Fuzer, Amanda Gamel, Terry Howell, Marina Iossifides, Sally Jackson, Sarah Jones, Shelley Gregory, Caroline Krakower, Dianne Landers, Ginny Magee, Kathy Miller, Marylin Morris, Connie O'Hara, Debbi O'Hara, Gina Papatto, Linda Pfrommer, Beth Peterson, Wendy Puchalski, Jackie Reisman, Amy Orloff, Lisa Robbins, Holly Ruckdeschel, Carol Rubin, Debbie Saldana, Karen Schussler, Donna Tambussi, Renee Vekkos, Douglas Vlaskamp, Kristine Vlaskamp, Evelyn Wang, Lisa Weinstein, Amy Wilen, Anita Zypilli, Michael Polotowicz

REPERTOIRE

"Sorcerer's Apprentice" (Dukas), "Snow Queen" (Mayer), "Three Cornered Hat" (DeFalla), "Hoe Down" (Copland), "Search for Spring," "Shostakovich, "Suite of Spanish Dances" (Folk), "Slavonic Dances" (Dvorak), "The Beauty of Dance and the Joy of Dance" (Chopin), "Serenard" (Mozart), "Hello World" (Mayer), "Exhibition of Degas Paintings" (Chopin), "Romanian Rhapsody" (Enesco), and *PREMIERE* of "Glimpses of Art, 1776–1976" (Ronald Brown, Ursula Melita)

Ballet Des Jeunes

Molly Lynch, David Panaieff, also above
with Ballet Pacifica members in "Coppelia"

BALLET PACIFICA
Laguna Beach, California

Founder-Artistic Director-Choreographer, Lila Zali; General Director, Douglas Reeve; Artistic Adviser, Michel Panaieff; Press, Sally Reeve; Technical Director, Carl W. Callaway; Ballet Mistress, Kathy Jo Kahn; Coordinator, Elizabeth Townsend; Choreographers, Dick Ford, Kathy Jo Kahn, Carrie Kneubuhl, Victor Moreno, Leona Norman, Michel Panaieff, Norbert Vesak; Sets, Tania Barton, Ann Gordon; Costumes, Tania Barton, Lila Zali; Lights, David Challis, Todd Elvins, Darci Linke

COMPANY

PRINCIPALS: Randy Barnett, Louis Carver, Roger Faubel, Louise Frazer, Carrie Kneubuhl, Molly Lynch, Paul Maure, Victor Moreno, David Panaieff, Lisa Robertson, Kristi Stephens, Sam Velasquez

SOLOISTS: Charles Colgan, Jennifer Engle, Kathy Jo Kahn, Robert Petel, Billie Pulliam, Sandra Rasmussen, Belinda Smith, Glenn Smith, Cynthia Tosh

CORPS: Allison Bryant, Corinne Calamaro, Rika Creed, Andrea Daywalt, Shawn Daywalt, Heidi Edgren, Eve Henderson, Briana Line, Lori McCoy, Gail Melfi, Laurie Miller, Laurie Mittman, Christine Rasmussen, Gary-John Rasmussen, Julie Renfro, Caroline Sutherland, Nancy Sutton, John Tally, Tricia Toliver, Arabella Wibberley

GUEST ARTIST: Judith Aaen

REPERTOIRE

"Coppelia" (Delibes, Panaieff), "Festival of Nations" (Compiled, Zali), "Aurora's Wedding" (Tchaikovsky, Zali after Petipa), "Ballet Portraits, 18th Century" (Corelli, Zali), "Carnival Tutu" (Milhaud, Ford), "Danse Classique" (Glinka, Panaieff), "La Danse et la Musique" (Chopin, Panaieff), "Le Corsaire Pas de Deux" (Drigo, Panaieff after Petipa), "Paquita" (Minkus, Moreno), "Nutcracker" (Tchaikovsky, Zali), "Illusion" (Ravel, Kahn), "Encounter near Venus" (Russell/Wibberley, Zali), "Stone Flower" (Prokofiev, Zali), "Snow White and the Seven Dwarfs" (Compiled, Kneubuhl), "The Dove Descending" (Stravinsky, Kahn), "The Courtly Dances" (Britten, Kahn), "Black Swan Pas de Deux" (Tchaikovsky, Ivanov), "Golden Moments of Ballet" (Compiled, Norman), "Don Quixote Pas de Deux" (Minkus, after Celli), "Cinderella" (Prokofiev, Zali)
Sally Reeve Photos

BALLET ROYAL
Winter Park, Florida

Artistic Director-Choreographer, Edith Royal; Assistant Director, Carol Willson; Associate Director, Jackie Everidge; Technical Director-Business Manager, Bill Royal; Design and Wardrobe, Phyllis Watson

COMPANY

Elizabeth Alicea, Muffett Baker, William Bartlett, Kenneth Braso, Kim Bruce, Cindy Bryant, Bettina Buckley, Harriet Cherry, Susie Ellis, Neill Foshee, DeeDee Fouts, Robin Grant, Maura Hayes, Terri Hearn, Tana Kaiser, Carol Ann Karas, Sahun Lewis, Pennisu Mance, Clint Nolle, Luis Perez, Anita Phillips, Deanna Pitman, Brian Price, Karen Rader, Lynne Rader, Mike Ragan, Cindy Ratcliffe, Cindy Rossetto, Shelly Segrest, Lisa Siegfried, Dena Snider, Vel Thomas, Trisha Will, Judy Wisniewski

REPERTOIRE

"Birdland Fable" (Schoen, Royal), "The Village" (Bertha Egnos, Ron Daniels), and *PREMIERES* of "Coppelia" (Delibes, Edith Royal), "Daphnis and Chloe" (Ravel, Thomas Armour), "The Abdication" (Carol Willson), "Three Dances" (Jim Weisberg, Dermot Burke), "Verdi" (Verdi, Royal)

Ballet Royal
in "The Village"

BALLET TACOMA
Tacoma, Washington

Director-Choreographer, Jan Collum; Ballet Mistress, Frankie Ramey; Costumes, Judy Loiland; Sound, Kearney; Sets and Lighting, Paul VanGiffin; Guest Choreographer, Robert Rodham

COMPANY

David Hitchcock, Jomarie Carlson, Valli Hale, Hunter Hale, Patti Shippy, Lorna Newton, Robyn Jones, Linnea Norby, Lynn Jacobson, Marnie Palmquist, Debbie Griffin, Kate Foley, Lysle Wilhelmi, Jean Laudadio, Michelle Erwin, Nancy Pitzen, Cindy Herr, Kally Felkor, Theresa Reardemphl, Mitch Hale, Robert Griffin, Debbie Ramsey

REPERTOIRE

ALL PREMIERES: "Rhapsody Tsigane" (Jan Collum), "Scarlatti Now" (Scarlatti, Collum), "Ginko" (Albinoni, Robert Radham), "Parting of the Son" (Lawrence Ebert, Hunter Hale)

Right Center: Ballet Tacoma

BALLET WESTERN RESERVE
Youngstown, Ohio

Director-Choreographer, Michael Falotico; Conductors, Franz Bibo, C. Watson, Tony Leonardi, Donald Byo; Sets, Robert Elden, Richard Gullicksen, Galen Elser; Costumes, Robert Elden, Georgann Sherwood, Bruce Mac, Roberta Johnson, Russ Moore, Priscilla Taylor; Lighting, Kenneth Lowther; Stage Manager, Galen Elser; Press, Friedman Associates, Donna Ellers; Business Manager, Catherine McPhee; Executive Producer, Youngstown Ballet Guild

COMPANY

Nancy Tiberio, Lenore Pershing, Beth Rollinson, Robert Tupper, Martin Andrews, Edward Patuto, Steven Nagel, Suzanne Swan, Cathy Amendolara, Lisa Devine, Laura Anderson, Elizabeth Dory, Marisa Manolukas, Gina Gangale, Holly Weibel
GUEST ARTISTS: Diana Byer, Martin Fredman, Leigh Hudacek, Rachel List, Matthew Nash

REPERTOIRE

"Giselle Act II" (Adam, Edward Myers), "Nutcracker" (Tchaikovsky, Falotico), "The Witching" (R. Moffatt, Falotico), "La Creation du Monde" (Milhaud, Martin Andrews), "Sonata" (Bondon, Falotico), "A Charm of Lullabies" (Britten, Georgann Sherwood), "Grand Faux Pas de Deux" (Lanchbery, Falotico), "Romeo and Juliet Balcony Scene" (Prokofiev, Falotico), "Side Show" (Abramson, Falotico), "Tancredi and Clorinda" (Monteverdi, Rachel List), "Navarra" (Minkus, Falotico), "A La Vivaldi" (Vivaldi, Falotico), "Masque" (Sessions, Falotico), "Emily" (Della Joio, Falotico), "TKO" (Michael Mears)
PREMIERES: "Le Sacre du Printemps" (Stravinsky, Falotico), "Soldier's Tale" (Stravinsky, Falotico), "Pierrot Lunaire" (Schonberg, Falotico), "Opera Jazz" (Ellington/Garbin, Falotico), "Deux Valses" (Glazounov, Falotico)

Ballet Western Reserve

BALLET WEST

Salt Lake City, Utah

Artistic Directors-Choreographers, Willam F. Christensen, Bruce Marks; Ballet Mistress, Sondra Sugai; Assistant Ballet Misstress, Tenley Taylor; General Manager, Robert G. Bradford; Company Manager, Steven H. Horton; Press, Toni R. Carter, Stanley Knoles; Stage Managers, David K. Barber, Greg Geilmann; Lighting, Greg Geilmann; Costume Mistresses, Carlie Shurtliff, Linda Stasco; Special Advisers, Mattlyn Gavers, Bene Arnold, Toni Lander; Musical Director, Ronald Mead Horton; Principal Conductor, Ardean Watts

COMPANY

Bruce Caldwell, Vivien Cockburn, Suzanne Erlon, Christopher Fair, Corey Farris, Charles Fuller, Linda Gudmundson, Frank Hay, John Hiatt, Carey Homme, Tauna Hunter, Diane Jenkins, Keith Kimmel, Karen Kuhn, Sharee Lane, Mark Lanham, Leonore Maez, Victoria Morgan, Elizabeth Nesi, Michael Onstad, Leigh Provancha, Carole Ann Ramme, Catherine Scott, Anita Siegel, Derryl Yeager, Cynthis Young

REPERTOIRE

"Giselle" (Adam, after Coralli) "The Nutcracker" (Tchaikovsky, Willam F. Christensen), "Octet" (Stravinsky, Christensen), "N.R.A." (Collage, Robert Gladstein)
PREMIERES: "Punch and Judy" (LeRoy J. Robertson, Derryl Yeager), "Songs of the Valley" (Aaron Copland, Bruce Marks), "Woman Remembered" (James Prigmore, Willam F. Christensen), "Dichterliebe: A Poet's Love" (Robert Schumann, Bruce Marks; Text, Heinrich Heine), "Don Quixote" (Isaac Albeniz/Manuel de Falla, Bruce Marks)

"Carmina Burana" Above: "Quintet"
Top: Bruce Caldwell, Leigh Provancha, Carey Homme, Anita Siegel in "Dichterliebe" *(L. Reece Photos)*

Top: "Don Quixote de la Mancha"
Below: "The Nutcracker"

131

BECKY ARNOLD AND THE DANCING MACHINE

Boston, Massachusetts

Artistic Director-Choreographer, Becky Arnold

COMPANY

Dorsey Yearley
Judy Cohen
Jackie Melnick
Kathy Immerman
Guest Artists: Linda Rabhan, Susan Brown

REPERTOIRE: "Journey to Within" (Santana, Arnold), "Discovery" (David Sanborn, Jay Norman), "Fats Dancing" (Fats Waller, Arnold), "Dancing Machine" (Jackson Five, Arnold), "Flight Time" (Donald Byrd, Arnold), and *PREMIERE* of "Dear Duke" (Duke Ellington, Becky Arnold)

Left: Becky Arnold

BELLA LEWITZKY DANCE COMPANY

Los Angeles, California

Artistic Director-Choreographer, Bella Lewitzky; Costume and Light Designs, Darlene Neel; Music Director, Larry Attaway; Company Manager, Darlene Neel; Production Manager, Stewart Christie; Electronics, Scott Duncan; Press, Rosalind Jarrett

COMPANY

Bella Lewitzky

Sean Greene	Robert Hughes
Iris Pell	David Caley
Loretta Livingston	Serena Richardson
Nora Reynolds	Amy Ernst
Kurt Weinheimer	Jennifer Hubbert

REPERTOIRE: (All choreography by Bella Lewitzky) "V.C.O." (Larry Attaway), "Spaces Between " (Cara Bradbury Marcus), "Five" (Max Lifchitz), "Game Plan," "Bella and Brindle" (Reginald Smith-Brindle), "Ceremony for Three" (Marcus), "Kinaesonata" (Alberto Ginastera), "Pietas" (Marcus), "On the Brink of Time" (Morton Subotnick), "Orrenda" (Marcus), "Trio for Saki" (Anton Dvorak)
PREMIERES: "Greening" (Aaron Copland, Bella Lewitzky) on July 23, 1976, "Inscape" (Mel Powell, Bella Lewitzky) on Dec. 21, 1976.

Dan Esgro, Amy Ernst Photos

"Inscape" also above and left

BOSTON BALLET
Boston, Massachusetts

Founder-Artistic Director, E. Virginia Williams; Executive Director, Ruth G. Harrington; General Manager, Robert V. Brickell; Regiseusse, Ellen O'Reilly; Ballet Masters, James Capp, Sydney Leonard, Lorenzo Monreal; Resident Choreographers, Ron Cunningham, Lorenzo Monreal; Conductors, Arthur Fiedler, Michel Sasson; Lighting Design, Thomas Skelton, Richard Nelson, Toni Goldin; Production Manager, Aloysius Petrucelli

COMPANY

PRINCIPALS: Elaine Bauer, Anamarie Sarazin, Edra Toth, Laura Young, David Brown, Tony Catanzaro, Ron Cunningham, Woytek Lowski, Augustus Van Heerden, Anthony Williams
SOLOISTS: David Drummond, Mark Johnson, Larry Robertson
CORPS: Durine Alinouq, Katheryn Anderson, Linda Bass, Carinne Binda, Kaethe Devlin, Belinda Holt, Debra Mili, Stephanie Moy, Pamela Royal, Judith Shoaff, Rachel Whitman, Alexandra Williams, Leslie Woodies, Clyde Nantais, Kennet Oberly, James Reardon, Thomas Richards, Darryl Robinson, Victor Wesley

REPERTOIRE

"Serenade" (Tchaikovsky, Balanchine), "Prodigal Son" (Prokofiev, Balanchine), "Scotch Symphony" (Mendelsohn, Balanchine), "Cinderella" (Prokofiev, Ron Cunningham), "The Nutcracker" (Tchaikovsky, after Ivanov-Petipa), "Incident at Blackbriar" (William Sleator, Cunningham), "Hamlet" (Shostakovich, Lorenzo Monreal), "Fanfare" (Britten, Jerome Robbins), "Flowering into New Battles" (Yamash'Ta, Martha Armstrong-Grey), "Goat Dance" (Iranian and Greek Folk, Ze'eva Cohen), "Classical Symphony" (Prokofiev, Monreal), full-length "Sleeping Beauty" (Tchaikovsky, E. Virginia Williams/Lorenzo Monreal), "Rodeo" (Copland, Agnes deMille), "Fall River Legend" (Gould, deMille), "Death and the Maiden" (Schubert, deMille), *PREMIERE* of "Logger's Clog" (David Baker, Agnes deMille)

Top: Anamarie Sarazin, Tony Catanzaro in "Flowering into New Battles" Below Edra Toth, Augustus Van Heerden in "Sleeping Beauty" *(Abe Epstein Photos)*

Woytek Lowski, Laura Young in "Sleeping Beauty"
Above: Lorenzo Monreal, Elaine Bauer in "Hamlet"

"Graduation Ball"
(Birmingham Ballet)

BIRMINGHAM BALLET
Birmingham, Alabama

Artistic Director-Choreographer, Alfonso Figueroa; General Manager, Norman Israel; Ballet Mistress, Gaenor Grange, Rehearsal Mistresses, Mimi Ransley, Janet Moran; Wardrobe, Miguel Romero; Stage Manager, Dan Wiseman; Press, Chuck Auton

COMPANY

PRINCIPALS: Janet Moran, Marylou Hume, Alfonso Figueroa, James Lewis, Donnie Miller
CORPS: Cynthia Church, Rio Cordy, Lisa Gholson, Marsha Hooks, Randall Penn, Mimi Ransley, Therese Hooks, Kathy Townsend, Joseph Towey

REPERTOIRE

"Ives Pas de Deux" (Ives, Figueroa), "Remember When?" (Traditional, Figueroa), "Terpsichoros" (Mozart, Figueroa), "Primus" (Gassman, Figueroa), "Spring Waters" (Rachmaninoff, Messerer) "Corsaire Pas de Deux" (Minkus, Monreal after Petipa), "Autumn Dialogues" (Barber, Walker), "Graduation Ball" (Strauss, Lichine) "Changes" (Brahms, Figueroa), "Peter and the Wolf" (Prokofiev Kurkjian)
PREMIERES: "Visions Fugitives" (Prokofiev, Figueroa), "First Symphony" (Ives, Figueroa), "The Seasons: Part II of Remember When?" (Hotel, Figueroa)

BLACK DANCE WORKSHOP
Buffalo, N. Y.

Artistic Director-Choreographer, Carole Kariamu Welsh; Artistic Adviser, Pearl Reynolds; Lighting Design-Stage Manager, Steve Porter; Press, Glendora Johnson

COMPANY

Carole Kariamu Welsh
Frances Hare
Yvonne James
Gaynell Sherrod
Christina Young

REPERTOIRE: "Coretta" (Hal Frazier/Chambers Brothers/Martin Luther King/Nina Simone, Carole Kariamu Welsh), "Contemporary Blues" (LaBell/Gladys Knight/Nina Simone, Welsh) "Gestures" (Hubert Laws/Aretha Franklin, Welsh), "Journey North" (Slaves/Simone/Redding/Dakota Staton/Chambers Brothers, Welsh), "Prophecy and Prayer" (Billy Paul/Stevie Wonder/Yusef Lateef, Welsh), "Slave Suite" (Yusef Lateef/Odetta Welsh),
PREMIERES: "Flowers" (Shinichi Yuize/Yotsuo Koyama Cherry Blossom Ensemble, Welsh), "Pastime Paradise" (Stevi Wonder, Welsh), "Samba" (Emile Latimer/Traditional, Pearl Reynolds), "Syvilla Suite" (Emile Latimer, Pearl Reynolds), "Children Suite" (Peter, Paul & Mary/Bill Withers/"Lost Man"/"The Wiz" Welsh)

Frances Hare, Yvonne James, Gaynell Sherrod,
Carol Kariamu Welsh in "Coretta"
(Buffalo Black Dance Workshop)
(Nathaniel Tileston Photo)

CHARLESTON BALLET COMPANY
Charleston, South Carolina

Directors-Choreographers, Don Cantwell, Robert Ivey

COMPANY

Christine Cantwell, Gina Farrar, Jan Fisher, Kathleen Gianaris Louise Hall, Ann Bacot Igoe, Cathy Myers, Ann Marie Osborne Lisa Perea, Anita Lane, Evelyn Johnson, Geormine Stanyard, Patricia Strang, Tamalyn Watkins, Susan Slider, David North, Steve Phlegar, Warren Chavous, Bill Struhs, Lee Brunner, Debbie Wolfe Valerie Kipnis

REPERTOIRE

"The Nutcracker" (Tchaikovsky, Don Cantwell/Robert Ivey after Petipa), "The Little Mermaid" (Ravel, Cantwell), "The Kimono" (Toshiro Mayuzumi/Frank Martin, Ivey), "Street Games" (Shostakovich, Ivey)
PREMIERES: "Allegro for Five" (Haydn, Cantwell), "Jazzic" (Tchaikovsky/Chopin/Walter Murphy, Ivey), "Pastorale" (Beethoven, Ivey)

Charleston Ballet Company
(Bill Buggel Photo)

CINCINNATI BALLET COMPANY

Cincinnati, Ohio

Executive Artistic Director, David McLain; General Manager, R. Dean Amos; Assistant Artistic Director, David Blackburn; Music Director, Carmon DeLeone; Resident Designer-Production Coordinator, Jay Depenbrock; Costumes, Annie Peacock Warner; Company Manager, Patricia C. Losey; Press, Salley Dunker; Program Coordinator, Michael Rozow; Wardrobe, Mildred Benzing; Stage Manager, Vicki West Zimmerman; Rehearsal Assistant, Claudia Rudolf; Pianist, John Iden.

COMPANY

Paula Davis, Diane Edwards, Colleen Giesting, Melissa Hale, Renee Hallman, Janice James, Karen Karibo, Patricia Kelly, Carol Krajacic, Sheila McAulay, Patricia Rozow, Alyce Taylor, Katherine Turner, Pan Willingham, John Ashton, Ian Barrett, David Blackburn, Michael Bradshaw, Richard Earley, Michael McClelland, John Nelson, Kevin Ward, Lynn Ferszt, Kay Thompson, Suzanne Haas, Jane Henry, Debra Kelly, Margo Krody, Margarita Martinez, Renee Powers, James Exum, Patrick Minson, Eric Johnston

REPERTOIRE

"Aubade" (Poulenc, Sabline), "The Beloved" (Hamilton, Truitte/ Norton), "Concerto" (Poulenc, McLain), "Concerto Barocco" (Bach, Balanchine), "Dear Friends and Gentle Hearts" (Foster/ Proto, Saddler), "Dedication to Jose Clemente Orozco" (Klaus, Truitte/Norton), "Divertissement Classique" (Burgmuller, Jasinski), "Face of Violence" (Norton/DeLeone, Horton/Truitte/ DeLavallade), "Firebird" (Stravinsky, Jasinski/Larkin), "Frevo" (DeLeone, Truitte/Horton), "Guernica" (DeLeone, Truitte), "Guitar Concerto" (Castelnuovo/Tedesco, McLain), "Le Combat" (DeBanfield, Dollar), "Night Soliloquies" (Barlow/Rogers/Hanson, McLain), "Nutcracker" (Tchaikovsky, Franklin/Jasinski/Larkin), "Pas de Dix" (Glazounov, Franklin), "Pas de Quatre" (Pugni, Dolin/Markova), "Serenade" (Tchaikovsky, Balanchine), "Winter's Traces" (Verdi, McLain), "With Timbrel and Dance Praise His Name" (DeLeone, Truitte)

Sandy Underwood Photos

Patrick Henson in "Peter and the Wolf"
Above: John Nelson, Janice James in "Swan Lake"
Top: "Swan Lake"

Top: Melissa Hale in "Swan Lake"

135

CHARLESTON BALLET

Charleston, West Virginia

Director-Choreographer, Andre Van Damme; Stage Director, Tony Seralrio; Lighting Director, William Lutman; President, Arnold C. Burke; Costumes, Maggy Van Damme; Sets, Kozak

COMPANY

Jennifer Britton
Kim Pauley
Julianne Kemp
Cookie Sloman

Nor Brunschwyler
Monique Jordan
Lisa Sadd
Brenda Taylor

REPERTOIRE: *Premieres* of "Carmina Burana" (Carl Orff, Andre Van Damme), "La Fille Mal Gardee" (Ferdinand Herold arranged by John Lanchbery, Andre Van Damme)

Gayle Chambliss Photo

Charleston Ballet

Barbara Boyle, Christopher Tabor
in "Suite Caracteristique"

CLEVELAND BALLET

Cleveland, Ohio

Artistic Director-Choreographer, Ian Horvath; Associate Director-Choreographer, Dennis Nahat; General Manager, Gerald Ketelaar; Ballet Master, Charles Nicoll; Ballet Mistress, Pamela Pribisco; Costumes, Ginger Shane, Toodie Wittmer; Lighting, Jennifer Tipton; Business Manager, Helen Horvath; Press, Robert Noll; Stage Manager, Michael D. Gibson; Production Supervisor, Russell O. Wulff; Music Director; Dwight Oltman; Associate Music Director, Boris Halip

COMPANY

Barbara Boyle, Mary-Beth Cabana, Margaret Carlson, Kay Eichmann, Michael Gleason, Cynthia Graham, Ian Horvath, Leigh Ann Hudacek, Jeff Jones, Geoffrey Kimbrough, Dennis Nahat, Pamela Pribisco, Veronica Soliz, Naomi Sorkin, Christopher Tabor
APPRENTICES: Eddie Barger, James Fatta, Alice Holloway, Joseph Konicki, John Lucas, Patrick Nalty, Lisa Powell, Regan Quick, Lisa Villarini, Kim Von Brandenstein

REPERTOIRE

COMPANY PREMIERES: "Things Our Fathers Loved" (Ives, Nahat), "US" (American Traditional, Horvath/Nahat), "Some Times" (Ogerman, Nahat), "Three Virgins and a Devil" (Respighi, deMille), "Laura's Women" (Nyro, Horvath), "Grand Pas de Dix" (Glazounov, Nahat), "Ontogeny" (Husa, Nahat)
WORLD PREMIERES: "Suite Caracteristique" (Tchaikovsky, Dennis Nahat), "In Concert" (Verdi, Gounoud/Nahat), "Contra Concerti" (Vivaldi, Nahat)

Dennis Nahat, Ian Horvath in "Things Our Fathers Loved" Above: Pamela Pribisco, Ian Horvath in "US"

(Louis Peres Photos)

COLORADO CONCERT BALLET
Denver, Colorado

Artistic Directors-Choreographers, Lillian Covillo, Freidann Parker; Company Coordinator, Erica Nicholson; Ballet Mistress, Laura Walker; Wardrobe, Argia Martelon; Press, Dede Nieto, Kathy Hammond Nelson; Design, Henry E. Lowenstein, Bruce Jackson, Jr.; Stage Manager, Andrew Cady

COMPANY

Laura Beth Walker, Kathleen Hammond Nelson, Dede Nieto, Sue Spencer, Larry Pech, Jeff Woodman, Raul Valdez, Christina Martelon, Mark Ream, Stephen Moore, Carol Lepthien, Julie Kane, Desbah Organick, Joyce Schuyler, Karen Jaszkowiak, Stephen Nye, Hank Mercer, Cynthia Elsey, Julie Lorenzo, James Bruce, Rachel Conover, Ken Miller, Carmen McKinney, Paulette Niehoff, Douglas Martelson, and members of Covillo-Parker Schools of Ballet

REPERTOIRE

"Nutcracker," "Symphony of Psalms," "Facade," "Dance the Four Winds"

Laura Beth Walker
(Colorado Concert Ballet)

CONCERT BALLET OF VIRGINIA
Richmond, Virginia

Director, Robert Watkins; Assistant Director, Scott Boyer; General Manager, Byron D. Spargo; Ballet Mistresses, Carolyn Pillow Mayhew, Nan Rennie; Technical Director, de Veaux Riddick; Wardrobe, Erline Eason, Donna Campbell; Sound-Tapes, Robert Carson; President, Mrs. Thomas C. Rennie; Sets and Decor, Scott Boyer, Larry Brown, Betty Dapper, de Veaux Riddick, Robert Watkins; Lighting, Randy Mercer, de Veaux Riddick

COMPANY

PRINCIPALS: Renee Basso, Scott Boyer, Carolyn Pillow Mayhew, Karen Moore, Nan Rennie
SOLOISTS: Kenneth Alkire, Sharon Daley, Susan Eason, Leslie Lieser, Kim McCue, Diane Simmons, Gwendy Spargo, Vanessa Watson
CORPS: Mark Blackwell, Charles Campbell, Debbie Cibo, Michelle Clarke, Carol Cunningham, Lynn Cunningham, Terry Daley, Rhonda Everett, Martha Gatewood, Briar Harris, David Holicky, Chris Holland, Laura Jones, Rolfe Joyner, Connie Lipford, Don Lucas, Randy Mercer, Dennis Parrish, Beth Rutherford, Jim Sanders, Tamara Shelton, Cindy Tune, Camia Tyler, Kim Barefoot, Kim Blaska, Katherine Brown, Tracey Campbell, Jerry Cibo, Lisa Cibo, Kelly Davis, Anne Angels, Lawrence Garnett, Valerie Garnett, Connie Hall, Kim Hall, Mary Suzanne Handy, Kathy Hansen, Tim Keen, Kari Keen, Alice Kirby, Kim Longest, Krista McCue, Mary Beth Meacham, Carol Moran, Leslee Oberg, Diane Quimby, Patti Parker, Sam Rapp, Jackie Reardon, Michele Schalow, Mathew Smith, Deidre Smith, Sara Smith, Leslie Spargo, Chad Taylor, Todd Taylor, Ned Theakston, Christopher Tyler, Cathie Walsh

REPERTOIRE

"Nutcracker" (Tchaikovsky, after Petipa/Ivanov), "Afternoon on the Grande Jatte" (Poulenc, Carolyn Pillow Mayhew), "Homage to Leonor Fini" (Debussy, Mayhew), and *PREMIERES* of "Degas" (Gounod, Elaine Bass Draucker), "The Last Spring" (Grieg, Mayhew), "American Saturday Night" (Fiedler, Draucker), "Ode for the Fourth of July" (Rowley, Draucker), "If You Knew Sousa" (Sousa, Draucker), "Symphonic Variations" (Franck, Nan Rennie), "The Engulfed Cathedral" (Debussy, Mayhew), "Litany" (Barber, Rennie), "Lehar Waltzes" (Lehar, Karen Moore), "Babes in Toyland" (Herbert, Renee Basso), "Many Moods of Christmas" (Traditional Carols, Mayhew), "Winter Celebrations" (Frackenpohl, Basso), "Harp Concerto" (Boieldieu, Rennie), "Walk to the Paradise Garden" (Delius, Basso), "Pachebel Kanon" (Pachebel, Rennie), "Swan Lake Act II" (Tchaikovsky, after Ivanov/Petipa), "OrganSymphony" (Saint Saens, Rennie), "Agnus Dei" (Bizet, Rennie), "Rhosymedre" (Williams, Rennie)

Carolyn Pillow Mayhew, Scott Boyer in "The Engulfed Cathedral" Above: Nan Rennie, Scott Boyer in "The Nutcracker" (Concert Ballet of Virginia)

137

CONNECTICUT VALLEY REGIONAL BALLET

Hartford, Connecticut

Artistic Director-Choreographer, Marguerite de Anguera; Co-Director, Dorothy Silverherz; Adviser, Michael Arnaud; Honorary Director, Leon Danielian

COMPANY

(Names not submitted)

REPERTOIRE: "Coppelia" (Delibes, de Anguera), "Les Patineurs" (Meyerbeer, Fernand Nault), "Degas Fantasy" (Pugni, de Anguera), "Melodies" (Rachmaninoff, de Anguera), "Salle de Ballet" (de Anguera)

"Salle de Ballet"
(Connecticut Valley Regional Ballet)

DALLAS BALLET

Dallas, Texas

Artistic Directors, George Skibine, Marjorie Tallchief; General Manager, John Bedford; Costume Mistress, Sara McClellan; Ballet Mistress, Elaine Comsudi; Resident Choreographer, George Skibine; Guest Choreographers, James Clouser, Kenneth Johnson, Eugene Tanner; Conductors, Anshel Brusilow, Mischa Seminitsky, James Rives Jones; Costume Designs, J. Bowden, Claudia Fisher, Sonja Zarek, Sara McClellan, Peter J. Hall, Rolf Gerard, Tracey Colvill, Thom Coates; Sets, David Gibson, Peter J. Hall, Rolf Gerard; Lighting Design, David Gibson, Charles Suggs, Jr.; Sound, B. W. Griffith, Jr.; Stage Managers, Stuart Hale, Jerry Dawson, Randy White; Press, Judy Bonner Amps

COMPANY

Kevin Brown, Donald Dadey, Angela Hagedorn, Kirt Hathaway, Cyndi Jones, Samuel McManus, Marcella Shannon, Sarah Smith, DeAnne Tomlinson, Karen Travis, Edward Tuell, and Susan Camille Guenther, Cathy Hanson, Cheryl Hartung, Lisa Owen
GUEST ARTISTS: Suzanne Farrell, Peter Martins, Patricia McBride, Jean-Pierre Bonnefous, Kay Mazzo, Jacques d'Amboise

REPERTOIRE

"A Shape of Light" (Arthur Foote, Stuart Hodes), "Tarantella Americana" (Gottschalk, George Skibine), "Combat" (de Banfield, William Dollar), "Gaite Parisienne" (Offenbach, Skibine), "Firebird" (Stravinsky, Skibine), "Nutcracker Suite" (Tchaikovsky, Skibine after Petipa), "Romeo and Juliet" (Tchaikovsky, Skibine), "Pas de Trois" (Minkus, Petipa), "Pas de Quatre" (Pugni, Anton Dolin), "Raymonda Variations" (Glazounov, Eugene Tanner), "Merry Widow" (Lehar, Ruth Page), and *PREMIERE* of "Surprise Symphony" (Joseph Haydn, James Clouser) on September 5, 1976.

Kevin Brown, Karen Travis in "Romeo and Juliet"
Above: "A Shape of Light" Left: "Tarantella Americana"

DANCE THEATRE OF HARLEM
New York, N.Y.

Directors, Arthur Mitchell, Karel Shook; Conductor, Tania Leon; Technical Director/Lighting Design, Gary Fails; Costumes, Zelda Wynn; Assistant Musical Director, David Gagne; Ballet Master, William Scott; Ballet Mistress, Gayle McKinney; Wardrobe Master, Lawrence Taylor; Coordinators, Herbert Smith, Lorenzo James; Company Manager, Robert Frissell; Press, Lorenzo James; Stage Managers, Gary Fails, Richard Gonsalves

COMPANY

Lydia Abarca, Karen Brown, M. Elena Carter, Stephanie Dabney, Brenda Garrett, Yvonne Hall, Virginia Johnson, Susan Lovelle, Gayle McKinney, Melva Murray-White, Sheila Rohan, Karen Wright, Roman Brooks, Homer Bryant, Ronald Perry, Paul Russell, Allen Sampson, Samuel Smalls, Keith Saunders, William Scott, Eddie Shellman, Mel Tomlinson, Derek Williams, Joseph Wyatt

REPERTOIRE

"Fete Noire" (Shostakovich, Arthur Mitchell), "Forces of Rhythm" (Traditional/Contemporary, Louis Johnson), "Holberg Suite" (Grieg, Mitchell), "Le Corsaire Pas de Deux" (Drigo, Karel Shook), "Every Now and Then" (Quincy Jones, William Scott), "Biosfera" (Marlos Nobre, Mitchell), "Dougla" (Geoffrey Holder, Holder), "Rhythmetron" (Nobre, Mitchell), "Allegro Brillante" (Tchaikovsky, George Balanchine), "Bugaku" (Mayuzumi, Balanchine), "Concerto Barocco" (Bach, Balanchine), "Caravansarai" (Santana, Talley Beatty), "Agon" (Stravinsky, Balanchine), "Don Quixote Pas de Deux" (Minkus, Shook), "Design for Strings" (Tchaikovsky, John Taras), "Afternoon of a Faun" (Debussy, Jerome Robbins), "The Beloved" (Hamilton, James Truitte/Lester Norton), "The Combat" (deBanfield, William Dollar). "Carmen" (Bizet, Ruth Page), "Manifestations" (Primous Fountain III, Mitchell), "Concerto" (Mendelssohn, Dollar), "Romeo and Juliet Pas de Deux" (Prokofiev, Gabriella Taub-Dervish)

Susan Lovelle, Homer Bryant, Mel Tomlinson in "Manifestations" Top: Virginia Johnson in "Forces of Rhythm" *(Martha Swope Photo)*

DAYTON BALLET COMPANY
Dayton, Ohio

Founder-Artistic Director-Choreographer, Josephine Schwarz; Associate Directors, Jon Rodriguez, Bess Saylor; Costumes, Barbara Trick, Jon Rodriguez, Hermene Schwarz; Set and Lighting Design-Technical Director, John Rensel; Set Designer, Linda Carmichael; Wardrobe Mistress, Barbara Trick

COMPANY

Steven Lee Baldwin, Beth Berdes, Cynthia Bowden, Summer Cast, Gregory Clough, Elena Comendador, Candice Decaire, Judith Denman, DeAnn Duteil, Amy Eifert, Sermin Ercan, Gigi Gardner, Ron Hollenkamp, Mary Louise Hubler, Daniel Jamison, Stewart Jarrett, Jane Kleinmann, Susan Koenigsberg, Peter Means, Tanya Mesenzeff, Lynne Moon, Jeff Nelson, Shellie Nielsen, Kelly Olson, Meggin Rose, Camille Ross, Beth Saidel, Theresa Schmidt, Melissa Lynne Swartz, Elizabeth Tierney, Lisa Valeri, Ann Vandevander, Karen Welch, James Wert, Alison Willis

REPERTOIRE

"Papillons" (Schumann, Schwarz), "Pas de Quatre" (Pugni, Stapp), "Tarantella" (Gottschalk, Balanchine), "Dance Overture" (Creston, Schwarz), "Archaic Fragments" (Haines, Schwarz), "Concertino" (Pergolesi, Koner), "Vivaldiana" (Vivaldi, Rodriguez), "The Sovereign Pays Court" (Pachelbel, Saylor), "Periphrastic" (Denisov, Saylor), "Concerto Barocco" (Bach, Balanchine), "Flower Festival Pas de Deux" (Helsted, Bournonville), "Anya's Journey" (Shostakovich, Saylor) "Pas de Trois" (Tchaikovsky, Rodriguez), "Celebrations" (Vivaldi, Yuriko), "Grand Pas Espagnol" (Minkus, Rodriguez), "Homage to Georg Friderich" (Handel, Rodriguez), "There Are No Roses in My Garden" (Penderecki, Rodriguez), "Willoughby" (Prokofiev, Rodriguez), "Encore '75" (Santana, Saylor/Ross/Gribler/Duell), "Moving On" (Winter, Saylor), "Soft and Gentle Poems" (Schubert, Rodriguez), "Billy the Kid" (Copland, Loring), "Cinderella" (Prokofiev, Rodriguez), "To Albinoni" (Albinoni, Saylor), "Nutcracker" (Tchaikovsky, Rodriguez), "Fliessende Tanschrifte" (Hindemith, Saylor), "Trio" (Ibert, Rodham) *PREMIERES:* "Symphony" (Goldmark, Rodriguez), "Duet" (Prokofiev, Saylor), "L'Air" (J. B. Loeillet, Saylor)

Judith Denman in "Tarantella" (Dayton Civic Ballet) *Walt Kleine Photo* **139**

DALLAS METROPOLITAN BALLET
Dallas, Texas

Artistic Directors-Choreographers, Ann Etgen, Bill Atkinson; Technical Director, Jeannine Stegin; Costumes, Ellarose Sullivan, Sue Rozelle; Sets, Peter Wolfe, Bob Maize; President, Pat Baker, Jr.

COMPANY
Christy Dunham, Trudi Perrin, Jane Scichili, Suzanne Wagner, Cynda Potter, Mitzi Smith, Vicki Butler, Cynthia Norton, Michael Stammer, Rusty Simmons, Brad Moranz, Jerry Kelly, Cecil Fulfer, Edward Morgan, Ralph Bernie Brown, Richard Condon, Stephen Crenshaw, John Klineline, Billy Stephens, Mark Lamadue, Amy Andrews, Dede Barfield, Kaye Dalton, Cindy Flippo, Andrea Hines, Kendal Happy, Tracey King, Debbie Marston, Susan Scobie, Andrea Scoggin, Tracie Bruce
GUEST ARTISTS: Fernando Bujones, Marianna Tcherkassky

REPERTOIRE
"Rags" (Joplin, Etgen-Atkinson), "Suite for Fun" (Shostakovitch, Etgen-Atkinson), "Coppelia Act II" (Delibes, Robert Lunnon-Dorcen tempest), "Christina's World" (Collage, Norbert Vesak), "La Valse" (Ravel, Marc Wilde), "Peter and the Wolf" (Prokofiev, Richard and Christina Munro), "Cinderella Pas de Deux" (Prokofiev, Etgen-Atkinson)

Jane Scichili, Ralph Bernie Brown, Christy Dunham, Michael Stammer, Suzanne Wagner, Rusty Simmons in "Suite for Fun" (Dallas Metropolitan Ballet)

DELTA FESTIVAL BALLET
Metairie, Louisiana

Artistic Directors, Joseph Giacobbe, Maria J. Giacobbe; Lighting Design-Stage Manager, Karen Greenberg; Technical Director, David Gano; Costume Design, Frank Bennett; Sound, Henry Campo; President, Rose Magri; Ballet Mistress, Gayle Parmalee; Pianist, Julia Adams; Makeup, Joe Marion

COMPANY
Suzann Derby, Lisa Everett, Kelly Fortier, Gwen Delle Giacobbe, Nancy Herron, Mary Ann Louviere, Tammie Magri, Bonnie McCormack, Gretchen Newburger, Denise Oustalet, Kathryn Philpot-Hill, Denise Pons, Mary Shuppert, Deborah Simkin, Laurie Volny, Louise Zollinger, Francisco Alecha, Alfonso Hildalgo, Cutting Jahncke, Ozzie Laporte, Tom Quintini, Michael Taormina, David Wedemeyer
GUEST ARTISTS: Edward Villella, Anna Aragno, Fernando Bujones, Wilfride Piollet, Rochelle Zide, Jerel Hilding

REPERTOIRE
"Sleeping Beauty" (Tchaikovsky, Fiorella Keane after Petipa), "Polovtsian Dances" (Borodin, Richard and Christina Munro after Fokine), "Gym Dandy" (Prokofiev, Ann Etgen/Bill Atkinson), "Capriccio" (Mendelssohn, Richard Englund), "Pas de Quatre" (Pugni, Andra Corvino after Dolin), "Pas de Trois from Swan Lake" (Tchaikovsky, Petipa), "Memento" (Bizet, Orejudos), "Saddles and Sashes" (Copland, Joseph Giacobbe), and Premiere of "Three Benedictions" (Samuel Barber, Dom Orejudos)

DELAWARE REGIONAL BALLET
Dover, Delaware

Artistic Director-Choreographer, John Wilkins; Ballet Mistress, Beth Riggi; Costumes Designer, Bunkie Meyer

COMPANY
Mary Lou Brumer, Renee Breault, Cheryl Lawrence, Cathy Metzner, Denise Mathewson, Shelly Miller, Diana Snare, Julia Snare, Lyn Brown, Liz Fels, Raymond McKee, Karen McNatt, Cecilia Houseman, Mike Shortell, Jimmy Caccamo, Bill Comer, Don Mathewson
GUEST ARTISTS: Allan Douglas, Merilee Hodgins, Cherie Noble

REPERTOIRE
"The Nutcracker" (Tchaikovsky, John Wilkins after Petipa), and Premieres of "Le Carnaval" (Schumann, Wilkins), "Release" (Poulenc, Beth Reggi), "Solstice" (Michel Blavet, Helen Wilkins), "The Poet" (Bartok, John Wilkins), "Clover and Sal" (Joplin, Cherie Noble/Bill Comer)

Left Center: Cheryl Laurence, Raymond McKee in "Le Carnaval"

Martine Van Hamel, Clark Tippett and Delta Festival Ballet in "Sleeping Beauty"
(David Sandberg Photo)

DISCOVERY DANCE GROUP
Houston, Texas

Director-Choreographer, Camille Long Hill; Associate Director, Pam Stockman; Stage Manager, Jerry Springborn

COMPANY

Valentine Boving, Kathleen Buck, Bill Henry, Bonnie McMillian, Martha Owen, Kathleen Thompson, Jeff Smith, Pam Stockman, and Sara Whitaker, Ranson Fullinwider, Galyn Baylis, Donna Caldwell, Maureen Callahan, Karen Schneider, Debbie Schiro, Christine Sullivan

REPERTOIRE

"Triangle" (E. Bernstein, Camille Long Hill), "The Jazz Bit" (Hill), "Sea Visions" (Garson, Hill), "A Time Remembered" (Ravel, Ron Sequoio), "Nocturne" (Lateef, Hill), "Four Faces of Love" (Fanidi, Hill), "Prelude" (Villa-Lobos, Sequoio), "Dance for Six" (Barron, Hill), "Etude" (Mauriat, Hill), "I of Me" (Mingus, Hill), "Being Beginning" (Horn, Lynn Reynolds), "Sunless Sea" (Mancini/Grusin/Amron/Floyd/Lewis/Khatchaturian, Martha B. Owen) *PREMIERES:* "Interlude" (Vivaldi, Camille Long Hill), "Hear No, Speak No, See No Evil" (Johnson and Shorter, Hill)

Discovery Dance Group
in "The Jazz Bit"

Patti Sawyer, Christopher Wilson
(Elizabeth City Ballet)

ELMIRA-CORNING BALLET
Elmira, N. Y.

Founder-Artistic Director-Choreographer, Mme. Halina; Conductors, Fritz Wallenburg, David Einfeld, Theodore Hollenbach; Technical Director-Set Design, Floyd Lutomski; Costumes, Donna Jump; Stage Manager, Lauren Trescott; Press, Mary Smith; President, Carlton LeTourneau

COMPANY

Ilona Lutomski, Marilyn Schmarder, Mark Smith, Jeanine Clate, Karen Minch, Mary Ellen Hagy, Cathy Curran, John Luther, Luke Smith, Sally Updyke, Gay-Lin Horton, Debby Carroll, Wavalyn Aronson, Jackie Mekes, Joann Russen, Lindsay O'Connor, Lorreine Gile, Mandy Noretti, Deirdre Power, Carolyn Lee, Robyn Hart, Jenniffer Campbell, Jerry L. Jump, Jackie Weideman, Joyce Zehr, Cathy Joseph
GUEST ARTISTS: Michael Falotico, Val Deakin, Rachel List, Georgann Falotico, Jane Freeman

REPERTOIRE

"Peter and the Wolf" (Prokofiev, Val Deakin), "Memories Then" (Arranged, Mme. Halina), "Cirque" (Shostakovich, Halina), "Carnival of Animals" (St. Leon, Deakin), "Stars and Stripes" (Sousa, Halina), "Gaieties" (Joplin, Falotico), "A La Carte" (Arranged, Halina), "Excerpts from La Fille Mal Gardee" (Lanchbery, Halina), "Jazz" (Dubby, Deakin)

ELIZABETH CITY BALLET
Elizabeth City, N. C.

Directors-Choreographers, Gene Hammett, Susan Borre, Patti Sawyer; Lighting Design, George Schneider

COMPANY

Patti Sawyer, Signe Albertson, Kathy Sawyer, Mark Croston, Christopher Wilson, Kelli Hammonds, Patrick Cline, Laura Buckley, Sandra Barth, Allison Jackson, Lori Jo Chappell, Beth Zins, Kristie Eadie, Shannon Houtz, Barbara Gilbert, Melissa Kaufman, Katherine Sweeney, Beth McLees, Meredith Johnson, Christina Lawless, Mary Ellen Lawless, Carolyn Bynum, Christy Waters, Rosalind Spence, Laura Bowden, Stacy Cox, Carrie Daneker, Janice Talley, Maria Trent, Camille Daniels, Chris Davis, Jenny Zins, Barbara Symons, Tina Ethridge, Lisa Walker, Marga Massey, Claire Moncla, Jeanna Marshall, Granette Trent, Cindy Ownley, Julie White, Tina Cox, Tonya Little, Kristin Ocmuzzio
GUEST ARTISTS: Denise Hernandez, Michael Webster, Joan Taso, Erin Sabater, Lee Thompson, Maria Tenbraak, Sandy Blocker, Michael Barriskill, Terri Tompkins
REPERTOIRE: "Ecole de Ballet" (Offenbach, Patti Sawyer/Susan Borree/Gene Hammett/Glenn White)

Ilona Lutomski
(Elmira-Corning Ballet)

"Parson Weems and the Cherry Tree"
(Erick Hawkins Dance Company)

ERICK HAWKINS DANCE COMPANY
New York, N.Y.

COMPANY

Erick Hawkins (Director-Choreographer), Nada Diachenko, Natalie Richman, Cathy Ward, Alan Lynes, John Wiatt, Kevin Tobiason, Kristin Peterson, Cori Terry, Judy Davis, Cynthia Reynolds

REPERTOIRE

"Parson Weems and the Cherry Tree" (Virgil Thomson), "Plains Daybreak" (Alan Hovhaness), "Ah Oh" (Lucia Dlugoszewski), "Classic Kite Tails" (David Diamond), "Hurrah!" (Virgil Thomson), "Meditation on Orpheus" (Alan Hovhaness), "Death Is the Hunter" (Wallingford Riegger), "Dawn Dazzled Door" (Toru Takemitsu), "New England" (William Schuman)

EMPIRE STATE BALLET THEATRE
Buffalo, N. Y.

Artistic Director-Choreographer, Barbara Striegel; Associate Directors, Thomas Banasiak, Maryanne Scully, John Osborne; Sets and Costumes, Carolyn Pulk, Barbara Striegel

COMPANY

Michelle Becker, Moira Murphy, Carolyn Pulk, Lisa Mast, Jean Bacon, Vicki Bogacki, Maryanne Scully, Sonya Ross, Susan Lafferty, Margaret Heather, Maria Messina, Dianne Marra, Susan Scully, Thomas Banasiak

REPERTOIRE

"Coppelia" (Delibes, Striegel), "Pas de Quatre" (Pugni, Perrot/ Striegel), "Tchaikovsky Concerto #1" (Tchaikovsky, Striegel), "Sleeping Beauty" (Tchaikovsky, Striegel), "The Nutcracker" (Tchaikovsky, Striegel), "Firebird" (Stravinsky, Striegel), "Petrouchka" (Stravinsky, Striegel)
PREMIERES: "Le Corsaire" (Drigo, Striegel), "Gaite Parisienne" (Offenbach, Striegel)

FIRST CHAMBER DANCE COMPANY
Seattle, Washington

Artistic Director, Charles Bennett; Executive Administrator, Harriet Cavalli; Ballet Master, Perry Brunson; Costume Designs/ Wardrobe Master, Alan Madsen; Stage Manager, Frank Simons; Technical Director, Richard Weil

COMPANY

Charles Bennett	Flemming Halby
Rita Agnese	Douglas Hevenor
Frank Bays	Alexis Hoff
Sara de Luis	Donna Silva

GUEST ARTISTS: Teodoro Morca, Raymond Bussey, Marlene Jones

REPERTOIRE

"Take 7 - Roll 'Em" (Miscellaneous, Charles Bennett), "Leyenda" (Albeniz, Teodoro Morca), "Le Corsaire Pas de Deuz" (Drigo, Bennett/Perrot), "Suite Espanola" (Albeniz/Bach/deFalla, Morca), "The Moor's Pavane" (Purcell, Limon), "Don Quixote" (Minkus, Bennett), "Aire y Gracia" (Bach, Bennett/Petipa), "Assorted Rags" (Joplin, Raymond Bussey), "Albinoni Adagio" (Albinoni, Bennett), "La Chasse" (Massenet/Anonymous, Lotte Goslar), "Les Sylphides" (Chopin, Fokine/Bennett), "La Petenera" (Traditional, Vargas), "Nagare" (Traditional, Bennett), "Flower Festival Pas de Deux" (Helsted, Bournonville/Bennett), "By Candlelight" (Buffy St. Marie/Traditional, Bennett)
PREMIERES: "A Curtain Raiser" (Donizetti, Bennett), "El Albaicin" (Albeniz, Jose Granero), "Black Swan Pas de Deux" (Tchaikovsky, Bennett after Petipa/Ivanov), "Anima/Animus" (Mahler, Bennett), "Raymonda Pas de Deux" (Glazounov, Bennett), "Cenogenesis" (Diodato, Raymond Bussey)

First Chamber Dance Company
(Bob Peterson Photo)

Right Center: Michelle Becker, Thomas Banasiak in "Le Corsaire"
(Empire State Ballet Theatre)
Thomas Banasiak Photo

Suzanne Spanton, Jinkey Gleaton, Teil Rey
in "Toy Symphony" (Florida Ballet Theatre)

FLORIDA BALLET THEATRE
Tampa, Florida

Chairman Artistic Board, Richard Rader; Assistant Chairman, Betty Lee Ray; Choreographer in Residence, Frank Rey; Ballet Mistress, Charlotte Addington; Chairman Executive Board, Jean Taylor; Stage Manager, A. C. Spanton, Jr.

COMPANY

Julie Beronda, Sheri Brockmeier, Jinkey Gleaton, Teil Rey, Cathy Smith, Suzanne Spanton, Cathy Wood, Valerie Clevenger, Lona Coonradt, Mary Frances ·Leto, Josette Manougian, Jackie Page, Jama Cooley, Beth Dretzka, Carolina Ficarrotta, Jennifer Jones, Denise Mohr, Michele Prado, Margareth Spencer, Peggy Taylor, Jennifer Woehlk

REPERTOIRE

"Zelda" (Gershwin, Rey), "Swan Lake Act III" (Tchaikovsky, Martin-Viscount after Petipa/Ivanov), "Gloria de Misa Criolla" (Ramirez, Rey), "Leroy Anderson/Christmas Tribute" (Anderson, Rey)
PREMIERES: "A Gentle Thing" (Couperin, Rey), "Oft Times" (Gregorian Chants, Rey), "Toy Symphony" (Reinecke/Taylor, Rey), "When Violets Roared" (Joplin, Rey)

GEORGIA DANCE THEATRE COMPANY
Augusta, Georgia

Artistic Director-Choreographer, Frankie Levy; Ballet Mistress, Bebe Graham; Manager, Ann-Toni Estroff; Costume Design, Randa Yvel, Ann-Toni Estroff, Keith Cowling, Claude Astin; Technical Director, Steve Walpert; Lighting Design, Steve Walpert, Frankie Levy, Ann-Toni Estroff; Sound, Bernard Chambers; Press, Frankie Levy, Nelson Danish, Ann-Toni Estroff

COMPANY

Bebe Graham, Dede Shiver, Tina Hagler, Ann Marie Schweers, Martha Teets, Ann Lum, Charlene Linder, Christine Mareska, Lynn Barrett, Velvie Ketch
GUEST ARTISTS: Violette Verdy, Edward Villella, Allegra Kent, Bonnie Mathis, Dennis Wayne, Frank Ohman, Nolan T'Sani, Linda Yourth, Polly Shelton, Susan Hendl, Patricia McBride, Helgi Tomasson

REPERTOIRE

"The Little Match Girl," "Holy, Hopping Hallelujah" (Geld/Udell, Giordano), "Chopin Today" (Chopin, Levy), "Garden Dances" (Chopin, Levy), "Dansas Espanol" (Moszkowski, Levy), "Grand Esprit" (Bach, Levy), "Pas de Quatre" (Pugni, Levy), "et mors" (Saint-Saens, Levy), "Summer Song" (Mozart, Levy), and *PREMIERES* of "Fantasy" (Scriabin, Levy), "Accolada" (Verdi, Holden), "Il Gardellino" (Vivaldi, Levy)

Ann-Marie Schweers, Tina Hagler, Andrea Lum
in "Grand Esprit" (Georgia Dance Theatre Co.)
(Ann-Toni Estroff Photo)

Lynn Rempalski in "Magazine"
(Gloria Newman Dance Theatre)

GLORIA NEWMAN DANCE THEATRE
Orange, California

Artistic Director-Choreographer, Gloria Newman; General Manager, Charles M. Schoenberg; Company Manager, Lenita Kellstrand; Production Manager, Penny Leavitt; Technical Director, Stan Lanich; Stage Manager, Tom Grond

COMPANY

Jo Ella Lewis, Lynn Rempalski, Barbara Dobkin, Wanda Lee Evans, Gladys Kares, Sandra Puerta, Lynn Rabin, Arthur Mikaelian, Dennis Holderman, Alvin Mayes, Larry Ham, Louis Gillombardo

REPERTOIRE

"Tromperie" (Bowles, Newman), "Parentheses" (Elizabeth Keen), "Orbits" (Bazelon, Newman), "Magazine" (Newman), "Of Winds and Time" (Lou Harrison, Newman), "Games" (Traditional, McKayle), "Rooms" (Hopkins, Sokolow)
PREMIERES: "Interstice" (Aminadav Aloni, Gloria Newman), "Come Bid to the Piper's Calling" (Aminadav Aloni, Gloria Newman)

143

HAMPTON ROADS CIVIC BALLET

Hampton, Virginia

Directors, Edgerton B. Evans, Muriel Shelley Evans; Stage Manager-Designer, Duff Kliewer; Costumes, Frances Goodwin, Linda Harville; Sound, D. Earl White; Ballet Mistress, Lisa Shaw

COMPANY

SENIOR MEMBERS: Teresa Adams, Kathryn Blevins, Mary Guy, Deborah Harrison, Kathy Johnson, Mary Leath, Karen Peters, Sidney Sale, Anne Stafford, Jill Spielberger, Cathy Welsh, Joanna Walberg, Jane White, Lisa Shaw, Ron Braswell
APPRENTICE COMPANY: Susan Cooper, Loree Ferguson, Sharon Goodwin, Wendy Gibson, Kim Kuop, Bella Kar, Andrea Kostoff
GUEST ARTISTS: Leigh Catlett, Ken Pierce

REPERTOIRE

"The Nutcracker" (Tchaikovsky, Ivanov/Petipa), "Swan Lake" (Tchaikovsky, Ivanov/Petipa), "The Process" (Rousell, Lisa Shaw), "Valses Nobles et Sentimentales" (Ravel, Muriel Shelley Evans), "Chanson Triste" (Tchaikovsky, Muriel Shelley Evans), "Pavan" (Ravel, Edgerton B. Evans), "The Wind and the Sun" (Beethoven, Muriel Shelley Evans)

**Joanna Walberg, Ron Braswell
in "The Process" (Hampton Roads Civic Ballet)**
Linda Kliewer Photo

HARTFORD BALLET

Hartford, Connecticut

Artistic Director-Choreographer, Michael Uthoff; Managing Director, Ellsworth Davis; Ballet Master, Truman Finney; Press, Pamela Lang; Company Manager, Jack Anderson; Stage Manager, Jerry Kelch; Technical Director, Mark Anson; Guest Conductor, Robert Cole; Guest Set and Costume Designer, Charles Tomlinson; Costumer, Mary Wolfson

COMPANY

Robert Buntzen, Kristen Corman, John DeVilliers, Truman Finney, Jeffrey Giese, Thomas Giroir, Judith Gosnell, Karen Kelly, Linda Marx, Clover Mathis, Cynthia McCollum, Joan Merrill, Roland Roux, John Simone, Jeanne Tears, Michael Uthoff

REPERTOIRE

"Antumalal" (Ginastera, Uthoff), "Arcady" (Debussy, Sebastian), "Aves Mirabiles" (Foss, Uthoff), "Brahms Variations" (Brahms, Uthoff), "Cantata" (Ginastera, Uthoff), "Duo" (Clark, Uthoff), "La Malinche" (Lloyd, Limon), "Leggieros" (Beethoven, Goslar), "Little Improvisations" (Schumann, Tudor), "Nutcracker" (Tchaikovsky, Uthoff/Lynn), "Primavera" (Rossini, Uthoff), "Windsong" (Elgar, Uthoff)
PREMIERES: "Grand Pas de Dix" (Glazounov, Nahat), "Mir Ken Gehargnet Veren" (Strauss, Uthoff), "Tom Dula" (Welling/Walach, Uthoff), "Unstill Life" (Mahler, Uthoff)

**Center: (L) Truman Finney, Jeanne Tears
in "Grand Pas de Dix" (R) "Leggieros"**
(Siegfried Halus Photos)

HARTFORD BALLET CHAMBER ENSEMBLE

Hartford, Connecticut

Artistic Directors, Michael Uthoff, Enid Lynn; Managing Director: Ellsworth Davis; Press, Pamela Lang; Ballet Mistress, Robyne Watkin; Stage Manager, Tom Hunter; Costumers, Mary Wolfson, Sara Covalt

COMPANY

Ruthanne Belotti, David Curwen, Deborah Evens, Elizabeth Fisk, Karen Fleming, Robert Kowalski, Addison Hoffman, Martha Purl, Bradford Roth, Jeffrey Schweizer, Lynn Short, Cynthia Vermillion, Susan Wolfson

REPERTOIRE

"American Portrait" (Compiled, Lynn), "Concerto Grosso" (Vivaldi, Uthoff), "Dusk" (Satie, Uthoff), "La Malinche" (Lloyd, Limon), "Leggieros" (Beethoven, Goslar), "Little Improvisations" (Schumann, Tudor), "Marosszek Dances" (Kodaly, Uthoff), "Nutcracker Dances" (Tchaikovsky, Uthoff/Lynn), "Peter and the Wolf" (Prokofiev, Uthoff)
PREMIERES: "Echoplex" (Bolling, Barker), "Taking Shape" (Kotke/Beck, Roth)

Bradford Roth, Elizabeth Fisk, David Curwen in "La Malinche" (Hartford Ballet Chamber Ensemble)

HOUSTON BALLET

Houston, Texas

Artistic Director-Choreographer, Ben Stevenson; Ballet Master, Hiller Huhn; Conductor, Charles Rosekrans; Stage Manager, William A. Banks; Company Manager, Stephanie Sormane; Administrative Director, Mary K. Bailey; Press, Rowland Bachman

COMPANY

Soili Arvola, Leo Ahonen, Andrea Vodehnal, Deidre Grohgan, Mary Margaret Holt, Suzanne Longley, Rosemary Miles, Janie Parker, Whit Haworth, Dorio Perez
CORPS: Michael Bjerknes, Thomas Boyd, Gloria Brisbin, Steven Cook, Gloria de Santo, Jean Doornbos, Jory Hancock, Jennifer Holmes, Meghan Hurley, Michael Job, Melissa Lowe, Pamela Mitchell, William Pizzuto, Kurt Putzig, Kristine Richmond, John Rozelle, Adrian James
GUEST ARTISTS: Merle Park, Imre Dosza

REPERTOIRE

"Cinderella" (Prokofiev, Ben Stevenson), "Graduation Ball" (Strauss, Lichine), "Eaters of Darkness" (Britten, Gore), "Courante" (Bach, Stevenson), "Harlequinade" (Drigo, Stevenson), "The Nutcracker" (Tchaikovsky, Stevenson), "Caliban" (St. Elmo's Fire, James Clouser), "Bartok Concerto" (Bartok, Stevenson), "Raymonda Act III" (Glazounov, Petipa), "Concerto Barocco" (Bach, Balanchine), "Three Preludes" (Rachmaninoff, Stevenson), "Pi R Square" (Varese, Lois Bewley), "Corsaire Pas de Deux" (Drigo, Petipa)
PREMIERES: "Ramifications" (Ligeti/Purcell, Rudi van Dantzig), "Im Abendrot" (Richard Strauss, Ben Stevenson), "You Can't Tell by Looking" (Tchaikovsky, James Clouser)

Jory Hancock in "Caliban" Above: Soili Arvola, Whit Haworth in "Cinderella" Right: "Cinderella" (Houston Ballet)

IDEA COMPANY
Santa Monica, California

Director-Choreographer, Claudia Chapline; Musical Director, Panotraguis; Filmmaker, Miklos Gyulai; Designers, Elizabeth M. Kuder, J. Scott; Technical Consultant, Robert Grauch

COMPANY

Claudia Chapline	John Sutherland
Gillian Warren	Judith Hill
Harold Schwarm	Lyn DelliQuadri
Holly Rosenwald	Sandra Migliaccio

REPERTOIRE

(All premieres, and all choreography by Claudia Chapline) "Trip the Light" (Panotraguis), "The Stories" (Panotraguis), "Potatoes" (Panotraguis), "Aqua Light" (Panotraguis), "Mandala" (Panotraguis), "Leonard Ellis Plays the Santa Monica Auditorium" (Leonard Ellis), "Mars Landing" (Panotraguis), "Preamble" (Panotraguis), "Frankenstein and Tinkerbell" (James Talmadge, Claudia Chapline/Harold Schwarm), "Square Dance" (Traditional), "Orbit" (Panotraguis)

Top Left: Idea Company in "Square Dances"
(Lyn Smith Photo)

INDIANA DANCE THEATRE
South Bend, Indiana

Artistic Director, Marie Buczkowski; Choreographer, Ciretta Coty; Lighting and Staging, Judy Fields; President, Cleor Kelsch; Press, Dorothy Hawkins

COMPANY

Lisa Kelsch, Ginger Flowers, Ross McDowell, Julie Morrical, Meredith Hawkins, Margaret Gleason (names of corps not submitted)

REPERTOIRE

"Passport Europe" (Khachaturian/Glinka/Maksymowicz, Ciretta Coty/Marie Buczkowsky) in four acts

Indiana Dance Theatre

ITHACA DANCEMAKERS
Ithaca, N.Y.

Artistic Directors-Choreographers, Saga Ambegaokar, Barbara Dickinson, Janice Kovar, Petty Lawler; Business Manager, Sorrel Fisher; Stage Manager, Rosemary Harms; Company Manager, Randy Cash; Lighting Design, Bill Owen, Andy Tron

COMPANY

Karen Bell
Barbara Dickinson
Alix Keast
Janice Kovar
Peggy Lawler
Saga Ambegaokar

GUEST ARTISTS: Jane Desmond, Kristin Draudt, Kenneth Fischer, Wendy Jones, Tony Ndogo, Clifford Schulman, Stephen Buck, Bruce Lieberman

REPERTOIRE

"Lento" (Dvorak, Janice Kovar), "Venus in Capricorn" (Zen Meditation, Kovar), "Ritual" (Tantric Rituals, Kovar), and *PREMIERES* of "Second Thoughts" (Linda Fisher, Barbara Dickinson), "I'm Beginning to See the Light" (Duke Ellington, Barbara Dickinson), "Little Pieces" (Bartok, Peggy Lawler), "Moss" (Elton John, Saga Ambegaokar), "Just Passin Thru" (Gershwin, Kovar), "White Water" (David Borden, Jane Desmond)

Ben Guthrie Photo

**Ithaca Dancemakers
in "Lento"**

JAN VAN DYKE & DANCERS
Washington, D.C.

Artistic Director-Choreographer, Jan Van Dyke; Lighting Design-Technical Director, Jack Halstead; Costume Designer, Terri Hume Prell; Company Manager, Susan Kaller; Press, Patricia Mochel

COMPANY
Jan Van Dyke
Elly Canterbury
Virginia Freeman
Jean Jones
Susan Marilyn Sachs
Rebecca Slifkin

REPERTOIRE: "Waltz" (Strauss), "Big Show" (Sousa), "Ceremony I" (Leo Sayer/Dave Courtney/Hank Williams), "Ceremony II with roses" (Pachelbel/Rolling Stones), "The Stronger"(Diane Frank/Boulez, Virginia Freeman), "Paradise Castle" (Berlin/Crumb), "Ella" (Sylvia Fine)
PREMIERES: "Silence" (Jan Van Dyke), "Elly's Dance" (Paul Desmond, Jan Van Dyke), "Origami" (Sally Nash), "The Story of Twilight, the deep glow legend of crystal, the tale of fantastic enchantment, the evensong of shimmering dawn" (Albinoni/Foss/-Vivaldi, Jan Van Dyke)

**Jan Van Dyke (R) and dancers in
"Ceremony II with roses"**
(Curt Collins Photo)

JAZZ DANCE THEATRE
University Park, Pennsylvania

Director-Choreographer, Jean Sabatine; Assistants to Director, Audrey Tischler, William Morgan; Stage Managers, Caron Buinis, Cathie Crust; Costumer, Tracy Sherritt; Lighting Design, Pam Chestek; Administrative Director, John R. Bayless; Press, Michael B. Elkins

COMPANY
Mary Lou Belli, Susan Belli, Michael Bologna, Anna Davis, Aida Dequick, Jeff French, Terry Garlick, Deborah Girasek, Dennis Gersten, Belinda Hart, Sandra Hebbon, David Hodge, Martha Kent, Joseph Kubala, Ross Lehman, Debbie LeMire, Thomas O'Leary, Vance Ormes, Bill Rohe, James Alan Smith, Curt Whipple

REPERTOIRE
(All choreography by Jean Sabatine) "Impressions of the Blues" (Yusef Lateef), "Angles of Impact" (Robert Prince), "Family Tree" (CCS/Chubby Checker/Glenn Miller/The Platters/Others), "Moves and Interactions" (Prince), "The Affair" (Gil Evans), "Loneliness" (Herbie Mann/Yusef Lateef/Gil Evans/Stan Getz), "Anne Boleyn" (Rick Wakeman), "Black Despair on a White Stage" (Booker T. and the M.G.'s/Gil Evans/Leonard Bernstein), "Trilogy" (Grover Washington, Jr./Bob James), "Chances" (Washington), "Njamba" (Olatungi), "Nameless Hour" (Miles Davis/ Billy Colbham/Duke Ellington) (no photos submitted)

**Jazz Dance Theatre
in "Angles of Impact"**

KUNI DANCE THEATRE COMPANY
Los Angeles, California

Artistic Director-Choreographer, Masami Kuni; Choreographers, Linda Wojcik, Paul Edwards; Music, Isao Tomita, Masami Kuni; Lighting, Saburo Ohba, Larry Wiemer, Fred Sutton, Jerry McColgan; Costumes, Henrietta Soloff, Becky Wiemer; Performance Directors, Henrietta Soloff, Paul Edwards

COMPANY
Linda Wojcik, Tomiyo Nagahashi, Miriam Tait, Stephanie Romeo, Becky Wiemer, Valerie Sied, Jeanette Triomphe, Paul Edwards, Joyce Shrode, Aki Ishimi, Miriam Tait
GUEST ARTISTS: Chie Murata, Judy Jarvis

REPERTOIRE
"Terra Incognito," "The Sea," "Song of Chain," and *Premiere* of "Vision" (Masami Kuni)

**Kuni Dance Theatre Company
in "Vivion"**

LES GRANDS BALLETS CANADIENS

Montreal, Quebec, Canada

Founder-Director, Ludmilla Chiriaeff; Artistic Director, Brian Macdonald; General Manager, Colin McIntyre; Resident Choreographer, Fernand Nault; Ballet Mistress, Linda Stearns; Repetiteur-Production Assistant, Daniel Jackson; Lighting Design, Nicholas Cernovitch; Musical Director, Vladimir Jelinek; Resident Teacher, William Griffith; Press, Gilles Morel, John Burgess; Company Manager, Evelyn Dubois; Company Coordinator, Leslie-May Downs; Pianist, Jeanne d'Arc Lemieux; Wardrobe, Nicole Martinet; Scenery, Claude Berthiaume, Michael Hagen

COMPANY

Annette av Paul, James Bates, Alexandre Belin, Christiane Berardelli, Denise Biggi, Susan Bodie, Lucien Bordeianu, Richard Bouchard, Karen Brown, Michael Brown, Nicole Brunet, Cathy Buchanan, Jerilyn Dana, Louise Dore, Beatrice Dujardin, David Graniero, Edward Hillyer, Peter Toth-Horgosi, Manon Hotte, Sylvie Kinel-Chevalier, David La Hay, Deanne Lay, Maurice Lemay Peter Locke, Lucie Martineau, Yvan Michaud, Michele Morin, Myriam Moutillet, Gwendolyn Murphy, Harry Paterson, Kevin Peterman, Reva Pincusoff, Jean-Hugues Rochette, Christina Rottinghaus Dwight Shelton, Aaron Shields, John Stanzel, Jacques St.Cyr, Sonia Vartanian, Ann Waite, Vincent Warren, Wendy Wright, and **GUEST ARTIST** Lawrence Rhodes

REPERTOIRE

"Tournament" (Baroque Traditional, Brian Macdonald), "Concerto Barocco" (Bach, Balanchine), "Lines and Points" (Pierre Mercure, Macdonald/Brydon Paige), "Bawdy Variations" (Zez Confrey, Macdonald), "Swan Lake Act II" (Tchaikovsky, Ivanov/Petipa), "Carmina Burana" (Orff, Fernand Nault), "The Nutcracker" (Tchaikovsky, Nault), "Diabelli Variations" (Beethoven, Macdonald), "Time out of Mind" (Paul Creston, Macdonald), PREMIERES: "Concerto" (Bach, Lavergue Meyer), "Feelings" (Alain Stivell, Alexandre Belin), "The Attic" (John Williams, Renald Rabu), "Silent Episode" (Anton Webern, Lavergne Meyer), "Four Working Songs" (Carlos Miranda, Judith Marcuse)

Right: "Carmina Burana" Above: John Stanzel and company in "Tam Ti Delam" Top: "Tommy"

Alexandre Belin, Sylvie Kinal-Chevalier in "Romeo and Juliet"

Sonia Vartanian, David La Hay in "Swan Lake"

148

LOS ANGELES BALLET

Los Angeles, California

Artistic Director-Choreographer, John Clifford; General Manager, Newman E, Wait III; Ballet Mistress, Nancy Robinson; Principal Teacher, Irina Kosmovska; Music Director, Clyde Allen; Scenic Design, Philip Gilliam; Lighting Design, Christiaan Wagener; Costumes, Ardeth Haddow; Administrative Assistants, John Mitchell, Melanie Cotton, Frances Dorfman

COMPANY

April Anderson, Martha Ashley, Ellen Bauer, John Clifford, Nancy Davis, Stephen Eads, Charles Flemmer, John Fogarty, Richard Fritz, Elizabeth Hall, Colette Jeschke, Jarnette Jones, Johnna Kirkland, James Lane, Jana Malloy, Juliana Mathewson, Mark McLaughlin, Kolleen McQuillen, Risa Oganesoff, Reid Olson, David Rodriguez, Polly Shelton, Evette Voss, Lesli Wiesner

REPERTOIRE

(all choreography by John Clifford except where noted) "Afternoon of a Faun" (Debussy), "Allegro Brillante" (Tchaikovsky, Balanchine), "American in Paris" (Gershwin), "Bartok Concerto 3" (Bartok), "Brandenburg Concerto" (Bach), "Cinderella" (Prokofiev), "Concerto Barocco" (Bach, Balanchine), "Concerto in F" (Gershwin), "Concerto Grosso" (Vivaldi), "Dumbarton Oaks" (Stravinsky), "Dvorak Serenade" (Dvorak), "Entropia" (de Falla, Robinson), "Fantasies" (Vaughan Williams), "Firebird" (Stravinsky), "Four Seasons" (Verdi), "I Got Rhythm" (Gershwin), "Introduction and Allegro" (Ravel), "Ivesiana" (Ives, Balanchine), "Corsaire Pas de Deux" (Drigo, Petipa), "Les Aimants" (Debussy), "Lullaby" (Gershwin), "Mother Goose" (Ravel), "Pas de Dix" (Glazounov, Balanchine), "Pas de Quatre" (Pugni, Dolin), "Pastoral" (Bloch, Zall) "Pavane" (Faure), "Poeme Electronique" (Varese), "Prokofiev Violin Concerto" (Prokofiev), "Rachmaninoff Suite" (Rachmaninoff), "Raymonda Variations" (Glazounov, Balanchine), "Rhapsody in Blue" (Gershwin), "Red Back Book" (Joplin), "Serenade in A" (Stravinsky), "Sitar Concerto" (Shankar), "Sonata" (Debussy), "Stravinsky Piano Concerto" (Stravinsky), "Symphony" (Saint-Saens), "Tarantella" (Gottschalk, Balanchine), "Terpsichore Dances" (Praetorius), "Tchaikovsky Pas de Deux" (Tchaikovsky, Balanchine), "Three Preludes" (Gershwin), "Zolotoye Concerto" (Shostakovich), and *Premiere* of "Mahler" (Mahler, John Clifford)

Photos by Linda Simon, Ted Petit, Kevyne Baar

Right Center: "Symphony" Top: Johnna Kirkland, John Clifford in "Pas de Dix"

Kolleen McQuillen, Lesli Wiesner, Johnna Kirkland, Risa Oganesoff in "Oas de Quatre"

"Brandenburg Concerto"

149

LOUIS JOHNSON DANCE THEATRE
Washington, D.C.

Artistic Director-Choreographer, Louis Johnson; Costume Designer, Quay Truitt; Lighting Design, Ron Truitt; Stage Manager, Clinton Jackson; Manager, Ivy C. Booking

COMPANY

Muriel Burell, Lyndell Davis, Syrena Irving, Laverne Reed, Phoebie Redmond, Michael Goring, Kashka, Arnold Kingsbury, Tom Kelly

REPERTOIRE

"The Ball" (Maison Williams, Louis Johnson), "Moods Three" (Vivaldi/Prokofiev/ Isley Brothers, Johnson), "No Outlet" (Rachmaninoff, Johnson), "Lament" (Villa Lobos, Johnson), "Malindy" (Contemporary/Classic, Johnson)

Top Left: Burnie Gibson, David Cameron
in "Rite" (Louis Johnson Dance Theatre)

MACON BALLET GUILD
Macon, Georgia

Artistic Director-Choreographer, Gladys Lasky; Lighting Design, Charles O'Kelley; Stage Manager, T. M. Northington; Press, Elizabeth Drinnon

COMPANY

Leslie Bowen, Kathy Padgett-Lewis, Jean Ference, Cathy Hess, Cathy Willis-Sheffield, Melissa Garrette, Edith Newton, Karen Hinson, Claire Davis
CORPS: Misses Barulsen, Freant, Jones, Sheffield, Sreeran, Tamayo, Coggins, McKelvey, Rogers, Kay, Lanford, Newton, Schwartz, Brown, Sessions, Becker, Wrigley, Wise, Andrews, Hortman, Basch, Brown, Azzi, Schlosburg

REPERTOIRE

"The Nutcracker" (Tchaikovsky, Gladys Lasky after Petipa), "Les Sylphides" (Chopin, Fokine), "Dances from Napoli" (Gade/Helsted/Paulli, Bournonville), and *Premieres* of "Albinoni" (Albinoni, Sergiu Stefanschi), "Bach on the Koto" (Bach, Kathy Padgett-Lewis)

Macon Ballet Guild in "The Nutcracker"

Erick Hodges, Greta Owens, Kevin Tolson, Minna
Keller, Renee Oliver in "I-71"

MARYLAND DANCE THEATER
College Park, Maryland

Artistic Director, Larry Warren; Artistic Adviser, Dorothy Madden; Rehearsal Director, Anne Warren; Technical Director, Joseph Jennings; Stage Manager, Mary Mitchell; Tour Director, Gwen Olexik

COMPANY

David Capps, Erick Hodges, Minna Keller, Renee Oliver, Greta Owens, Allyson Paul, Helen Pelton, Trudy Solomon, Kevin Tolson, Anne Warren, Dorothy Yowaiski
GUEST ARTIST: Jan Van Dyke

REPERTOIRE

"For Betty" (Vivaldi, Bill Evans), "Widow's Walk" (Miriam Brunner, Dorothy Madden), "Earthrush" (Airto, Diane Baumgartner), "Errands" (The Ventures/Beethoven, Art Bauman), "Nightflight" (Kraftwerk, Diane Baumgartner), "I-71" (Dmitri Kabalevsky, Vera Blaine), and *Premiere* of "Dance in Red" (Lou Harrison, Anne Warren)

MATTI LASCOE DANCE THEATRE COMPANY

Santa Ana, California

Artistic Director-Choreographer, Matti Lascoe; Executive Director, Jerry Lascoe; Directors, Anita Grossman, Sonya Newberg, Ray Lamoureaux

COMPANY

Sandy Asay, Robert Ruiz, Lou Dewey, Jeff Burbage, Cari Johnson, Kathy Harbin, Virginia Bryant

REPERTOIRE

(All choreography by Matti Lascoe)
"Fourth/Street" (Keith Jarrett), "Zero—Lot Line" (Morton Subotnick), "Skylights" (Steve Reich), "Ellipsis" (none), "fiveforoctoberfive" (Darius Milhaud), "The Great American Marble" (Keith Jarrett), "This Body Belongs to Me" (Robin Frederick)

Sandy Asay, Robert Ruiz in "Fourth/Street"
(Tim Menneally Photo)

MEMPHIS BALLET COMPANY

Memphis, Tennessee

Artistic Director-Choreographer, Michael Tevlin; Associate Director, Judy Tevlin; Conductor, Vincent deFrank; Costume Designs, Minta Dietrich

COMPANY

Nancy Turpin, Michael Tevlin, Judy Tevlin, Lydia Faiers, and Tina Cimino, Carol Dietrich, Elizabeth Govan, Kirby Hade, Rebecca Harkness, Naomi Hashimoto, Jan Heatherly, Susan Hollis, Leslie Howard, Lisa Kallaher, Dorothy Shrein, Jeanette Sisk, Katie Smythe, Brenda Street, Tom Titone, Melva Howard, Diedre Hade, Audrey Thompson, Karen Turner
GUEST ARTISTS: Karen Kain, Frank Augustyn, Nicholas Humphrey, Kenneth Melville

REPERTOIRE

"Airs de Ballet" (Gretry, J. Tevlin), "La Favorita" (Donizetta, Cecchetti), "Pas de Deux from Flower Festival" (Helsted, Bournonville), "La Mort de L'Amour" (Delibes/Arbeau/Gervaise, M. Tevlin), "Village Festival Quadrille" (Foster, M. Tevlin), "Tchaikovsky Suite" (Tchaikovsky, Kenneth Melville), "Pas de Quatre" (Pugni, Dolin), "Bluebird Pas de Deux" (Tchaikovsky, Nureyev after Petipa), "Peasant Dances" (Bartok, M. Tevlin), "The Nutcracker" (Tchaikovsky, M. Tevlin)

"Peasant Dances"
(Memphis Ballet)

METROPOLITAN BALLET COMPANY OF MARYLAND

Bethesda, Maryland

Director-Choreographer, Charles Dickson; Assistant Director-Choreographer, Alan Woodard; Stage Manager-Lighting Designer, Joan Arhelger; Costumes, Katherine Larson; Wardrobe Mistress, Gladys Fuller

COMPANY

PRINCIPALS: Cathy Caplin, Michael Kessler
SOLOISTS AND CORPS DE BALLET: Deborah Byrd, Elizabeth Chastka, Kim Conley, Elaine Heubusch, Jana Klavik, Amanda McKerrow, Mary Miller, Monica O'Neal, Georgina Slavoff, Nancy Szabo, Gregory Fisher, James Mundell, Michael Tracy, Daniel West, Susan Beiter, Robin Carrigan, Marla Eist, Virginia Inglese, Naomi Itscoitz, Laurie MacIntyre, Haruko Minato, Kay Tidman, Janice Waldron

REPERTOIRE

"Snow Maiden" (Tchaikovsky, Dickson/Woodard), "Sylvia" (Delibes, Dickson/Woodard), "Sestetto" (Marcello, Dickson), "Ballet Romantique" (Helsted, Woodard), "Britten Variations" (Britten, Woodard), "Death of Actaeon" (Poulenc, Dickson), "Anticipation" (Glazounov, Dickson), "Balletese" (Glazounov, Dickson), and *Premieres* of "La Peri" (Dukas, Dickson), "Summer Evening" (Dvorak, Woodard)

Metropolitan Ballet of Maryland

151

METROPOLITAN BALLET OF ST. LOUIS

St. Louis, Missouri

Founder-Artistic Director-Choreographer, Nathalie LeVine; Associate Director-Choreographer, Gary Hubler; President, Richard Halbert; Lighting, Jim Renner; Stage Manager, Bernie Corn; Costumes, Alice Gavin; Press, Judy Halbert; Wardrobe, Diane Duckworth, Sella Koblick

COMPANY

Marianne Bellinger, Cindy Butler, Paul Cavin, Lisa Dellinger, Dina Duckworth, Elizabeth Eckart, Janet Ferguson, Kim Gavin, Laura Halbert, Patricia Kelsten, Karen Kemp, Melinda Koblick, Nikki LeVine, Angela Liao, Gus Licare, Valerie Ratts, Mary Lou Sinnott, Laurie Stream, Marvin Sunnenschein, Kathleen Sutton, Karen Van Meter, Christy Wencker, Leigh Ann Wencker
Ellen Barry, Joy Clayton, Halli Cohn, Amy Eckart, Tracy Gavin, Elizabeth Guller, Dana Kahn, Marnie Kleinfeld, Dawn Lease, Vivienne Lee, Denise Lee, Beth McDonald, Laura Michaels, Beth Miller, Lee Platt, Nina Platt, Susan Rowe, Kristina Schwarz
Theresa Bell, Becky Brady, Lauren Cohn, Rica Cuenca, Suzanne Ertzgaard, Blair Gensamer, Denise Lee, Anne Rosenthal, Melissa Silverman, Katy Wilson, Julia Wollrab, Mary Zucchero
GUEST ARTISTS: Gary Hubler, Mark Krupinski, John Dement

REPERTOIRE

"The Nutcracker" (Tchaikovsky, Hubler/LeVine/Mendolia), "Swan Lake Act II" (Tchaikovsky, Valerie Miller/Elizabeth Rutherford after Petipa), "Pas de Quatre" (Pugni, Dolin), "Back to Bach" (Bach, Hubler), "Rag" (Joplin, Levin), "Games" (Gould, Tulchinsky), "Love Set" (Britten, LeVine), "Trilogy on Love" (Mardin, Londe), "Salute" (Sousa, Hubler), "Foyer de la Danse" (Schumann, LeVine), "The Skaters" (Meyerbeer, LeVine), "Consumer's Guide" (TV Commercials, Londe)
PREMIERES: "Dances for Six" (Satie, Hubler/LeVine), "Slavonic Dances" (Dvorak, Landovsky), "Malt Shop Hop" (Selected, Krupinski), "The Seasons" (Glazounov, LeVine), "Missouri River Portraits" (Traditional Folk, Mayer), "Salute" (Sousa, Hubler)

Ted Kivitt (L) and Miami Ballet
in "Prince Igor"
Left Center: Dina Duckworth and Gary Hubler with
Metropolitan Ballet of St. Louis in "Swan Lake"

MIAMI BALLET

Miami, Florida

Artistic Director-Choreographer, Thomas Armour; Co-Directors, Robert Pike, Renee Zintgraff, Martha Mahr; Conductor, Bruce Steeg; Sets and Costumes, Robert Pike, Allan Madsen, Barbara Buguski, Jacqueline Kegeles, Jo-Dee Mercurio; Lighting Design, Richard Mix; Stage Manager, Demetrio Menendez

COMPANY

Barbara Abbott, Susie Caswell, Maritza Diaz-Silveira, Diane Dismuke, Susie Garcia, Lynne Lardizabal, Margarita Martinez, Maritza Moreno, Adelaida Muniz, Tracy Poulter, Kate Prahl, Ana Marta Sala, Sheleva Schill, Julie Smith, Karen Smith, Phyllis Vasquez, Cathy Wilson, Paula Donelan, Charlotte Fenlon, Sheri Franzen, Helen Frost, Susan Willig, Roy Dunan
GUEST ARTISTS: Merle Park, Helgi Tomasson

REPERTOIRE

"The Nutcracker" (Tchaikovsky, Magda Aunon), "Paquita" (Minkus, Jean Paul Comelin after Petipa), and *Premieres* of "Verdiana" (Verdi, Thomas Armour), and "Sonata" (Leclair, Robert Pike)

MID-HUDSON BALLET COMPANY

Poughkeepsie, N.Y.

Artistic Directors-Choreographers, Estelle & Alfonso; President, Joseph V. Towers; Set Designers, Lloyd Waldon, Ruth Waldon; Costumes, Olive Pearson; Company Manager, Shirley Sedore; Stage Manager, Robert McCord; Production Manager, Annette Woodard; Ballet Mistress, Karen Cassetta

COMPANY

Barbara Brinckerhoff, Karen Cassetta, Sharon Moore, Carol Schreiber, Michele Schreiber, Jan Silkworth, Betty Jean Theysohn, Tracey Vita, Mary Chris Wall, Taryn Noel Weinlein, Misha McDonald, Phil Lenkowksy

REPERTOIRE

(All choreography by Estelle & Alfonso except where noted) "Melange" (Horowitz/DeVorzon/Romanis), "Let Freedom Ring" (Public Doman), "The American Bride" (Gilbert & Sullivan), "The Big Country" (J. Moross), "Origins in Geometric Progressions" (Peter Sinfield), "Little Drummer Boy" (Simeon/Onorati/Davis), "Sonata No. 3" (Grieg, Alexander Dube), "Festival Flashback" (Rutanen/Sullivan, Benny Reehl/Denise Reehl)

Mid-Hudson Ballet Company

MILWAUKEE BALLET COMPANY
Milwaukee, Wisconsin

Artistic Director-Choreographer, Jean Paul Comelin; Associate Director, Marjorie Mussman; Managing Director, Charles Ray McCallum; Music Director, Daniel Forlano; Company Manager, Randall J. Voit; Costume Designer, Ann Marie Marszalkowski; Lighting Design, Richard Graham; Wardrobe, Mary Belle Potter, Jan Sprecher; Stage Manager, Walter Schoen; Technical Director, Edward Buck; Audio, James Birder; Press, Billie Cohen; Pianists, Melinda Leimgruber, Pat Bishop, Mary Host, Tim Dirksen

COMPANY

Madalene Baenen, Cher Carnell, Elizabeth Corbett, John Henry Davis, Mark Diamond, Nanette DiLorenzo, Ann England, Katherine Frey, Angela House, Kristin Johnson, Maxine Lampert, Stephen Lockser, Julie Marszalkowski, Leslie McBeth, Margaret McLaughlin, Lydia Morales, Kathryn Moriarty, Richard Rock, Donald Rottinghaus, Raymond Serrano, Diane Stapp, Carl Swanson

REPERTOIRE

"Caribbean Fire Dance" (Coltrane, Mark Diamond), "A Cocktail Party" (Poulenc, Marjorie Mussman), "Le Corsaire Pas de Deux" (Drigo, Rudolf Nureyev), "Daughters of Mourning" (Martin, Comelin), "Diversions" (Britten, Comelin), "Don Quixote Pas de Deux" (Nimkus, Mikhail Oboukof), "Fantasie" (Faure, Comelin), "Farewell" (Strauss, Comelin), "Idylle Pas de Deux" (Hertel, Comelin), "Nutcracker Act II" (Tchaikovsky, Comelin/Ivanov), "Paquita" (Minkus, Comelin/Petipa), "Partita" (Bach, Comelin), "Points and Counterpoints" (Beethoven, Mussman), "Raymonda Pas de Dix" (Glazounov, Balanchine/Petipa), "Solo: A Portrait" (Ravel, Jorge Samaniego), "Sonata a Tre" (Albinoni, Comelin), "A Song for Jose" (Bach, Mussman), "Textures" (Toru Takemitsu, Comelin), "Three Greek Dances" (Skalakotas, Diamond), "Trio" (Ibert: Robert Rodham)
PREMIERES: "Daphnis and Chloe" (Ravel, Comelin), "Friends" (Michel Colombier, Comelin), "Handel Suite" (Handel, Mussman), "Three Episodes" (Leos Janacek, Mussman)

Martha Swope Photos

"Diversions"

Leslie McBeth, Raymond Serrano (also above) with Milwaukee Ballet in "Daphnis and Chloe"

MISSISSIPPI COAST BALLET
Gulfport, Mississippi

Artistic Director-Choreographer, Delia Weddington Stewart; Conductor, James Shannon; Choreographers, Hazle White, Merrily Carter; Stage Manager-Lighting Design, Bennie W. Stewart

COMPANY

PRINCIPALS: Delia Stewart, Hazle White, Molly Johnson, Jill Wilson, Mark Hamilton, Stanley Kinberger, Merrily Carter, Cheryl Dawson
SOLOISTS: Barbara Titler, Debbie Wolff, Patsy Williams, Julie Stewart, Ellen Booth, Rebecca Fountain, Michele Thigpin
GUEST ARTIST: Christina Backstrom

REPERTOIRE

"Relache" (Satie, Stewart), "I Know My Love" (Folk, Bruce Wells), "Spirituals" (Gould, White/Carter/Stewart), and *Premieres* of "Meditations unto Motion" (White/Wells/Stewart), "Dance to the Duke" (Ellington, Merrily Carter)

Jill Wilson and Mississippi Ballet in "Relache"

MINNESOTA DANCE THEATRE
Minneapolis, Minnesota

Artistic Director-Choreographer, Loyce Houlton; Balletmaster, Larry Hayden; Repetiteurs, David Voss, Siri Kommedahl; Acting General Manager, James Neumann; Press, Diane Fridley; Production Coordinator, John Linnerson; Costumiere, Lynne Steincamp; Costume Designer, Judith Cooper; Stage Manager, Blaine Marcou; Lighting Design, Jan MacDonald

COMPANY

Robert Alwine, Cynthia Carlson, Cathy Fox, Cheryl Gomes, Marianne Greven, Michael Hackett, Peter Hauschild, Lise Houlton, Stephanie Karr, Sandra Machala, Glen Martin, Toni Pierce, Andrew Rist, Alyson Swenson, Joseph Teague, Andrew Thompson, Susan Thompson, Mark Townes

REPERTOIRE

(All choreography by Loyce Houlton except where noted) "Ancient Air" (George Crumb), "Carmina Burana" (Orff), "Circles" (Stravinsky), "Le Corsaire" (Drigo), "Collage" (Frank Martin), "Earthsong" (Copland), "Encounters" (Hans Werner Henze), "Giselle Pas de Deux" (Adam), "Kaleidoscope" (et al), "Knoxville: Summer of 1915" (Barber), "La Malinche" (Norman Lloyd), "Paquita Pas de Trois" (Minkus), "Pas de Quatre" (Pugni, Dolin), "Riders of the Earth Together" (Krzysztof Penderecki, Tai Koons), "Seedless Stonemoons" (Crumb), "Slaughter on Tenth Avenue" (Richard Rodgers), "Twisted Tree" (Michel Tippet), "293.6" (Webern), "Wingborne" (Dvorak), "Yellow Variations" (Vivaldi)
PREMIERES: "Essays of Night" (Hans Werner Henze, Loyce Houlton), "Treacles" (Leonard Bernstein, Loyce Houlton/Larry Hayden/David Voss), "Song of the Earth" (Gustav Mahler, Loyce Houlton), "Incidents" (Louis Ballard, Loyce Houlton)

Joe Giannetti, Myron Papiz Photos

Right: "Ancient Air" Above: "Knoxville: Summer of 1915"

Lise Houlton, Andrew Thompson in "Wingborne"

"Song of the Earth"
Above: "Mythical Hunters"

NANCY HAUSER DANCE COMPANY

Minneapolis, Minnesota

Artistic Director-Choreographer, Nancy Hauser; Co-Artistic Director, Heidi H. Jasmin; Technical Director, Paul Scharfenberger; Press, Jan G. Wiezorek, Chyrll Weimar; Staff Coordinator, Janette Guterson; Costumes, Martha Keys, Bev Sonen, Jan Atridge

COMPANY

Heidi H. Jasmin
Jim Kelly
Merile Halley
Gary L. Lund
Penny Burr-Pinson
Steve Potts
Marilyn Scher
Bev Sonen
GUEST ARTISTS: Irene Feigenheimer, Shirley Mordine, Jeff Duncan

REPERTOIRE

"Abstract" (Brubeck, Hauser), "Beginnings" (Collage, Hauser), "Partapartita" (Bach, Hauser), "Recherche" (Stravinsky, Hauser), "Temporary Site" (Kimmel, Farber), "Moose Lake" (Collage, Cunningham), "In a Garden" (Collage, Redlich), "Proximities" (Brahams, Louis), "Ceremonial" (Kimmel, Jasmin), "Dal-A-Bye" (Kimmel, Jasmin), "Richter's Ball" (Kimmel, Jasmin), "Crel" (Tilley, Lund), "En Passant & Other Maneuvers" (Handel, Wray), "Open End" (Tilley, Potts), "Patterns from Beaumont" (Satie, Sonen), "Countenance" (Lund), "Chromylium" (Buchen, Jasmin), "Excess Baggage" (Potts), and *PREMIERES* of "A Celebration" (Ellington, Hauser), and "Dream Cycle" (Hauser, Hauser)

Merile Halley, Marilyn Scher, Bev Sonen
(Nancy Hauser Dance Company)

NANCY SPANIER DANCE THEATRE

Boulder, Colorado

Artistic Director-Choreographer, Nancy Spanier; Technical Direction-Lighting Design, Debora Stoll; Art Director, Ken Iwamasa; Costume Designs, David Busse; Company Manager, Thomas Hast

COMPANY

Nancy Spanier
Paul Oertel
Emily Wadhams
Jane Franklin
Thomas Evans
Terry Freedman

REPERTOIRE: (All choreography by Nancy Spanier except where noted) "Glass Camellias" (Pink Floyd), "Time Wounds All Heals" (Collage), "Abundance" (Bach), and *PREMIERES* of "Show on Earth" (Mozart/Tribal Music/Nitzsche, Spanier), "I'll Take Romance" (Collage, Spanier), "Scenes" (Strauss/Chopin/D. H. Lawrence, Spanier), "earthreach" (Norgaard, Wadhams)

Nancy Spanier Dance Theatre
in "Abundance"

NEW REFLECTIONS DANCE THEATRE

Charlotte, N. C.

Artistic Directors-Choreographers, Gerda Zimmermann, Mary Ann Mee; Set and Costume Designs, Rogert Croghan

COMPANY

Rebecca Burns, Roy Cosper, Mary Ann Mee, Hardin Minor, Beth Pochynock, Pamela Sofras, Debbie Tyndall, Stacy Williams, Rosemary Wyman, Gerda Zimmermann
APPRENTICES: Cheryl Card, Esther Conner, Susannah Hewson, Antonia Mills, Jim Rivers, Vickie Plott, Terry Watson

REPERTOIRE

"Luna Park" (Perrey/Kingsley, Gerda Zimmermann), "Lot's Wife" (Thomas Turner, Zimmermann), "Brahms Waltzes" (Brahms, Charles Weidman), "Arachne" (Turner, Zimmermann), "Do It" (Collage, Raymond Johnson), "Mary, Clyde & Eddie" (Ives, Kista Tucker), and *PREMIERES* of "Earthbound Glow" (Olatunji, Zimmermann), "Sibyls" (Donald Martin, Pamela Sofras), "Reflections of a City" (Collage, Hardin Minor), "Phases" (Barbara Webster, Mary Ann Mee), "Charlotte Ruby" (Howard R. Winokuer, Kista Tucker), "Crawfish Queen" (Ives, Sofras), "A Choice" (Raymond Scott, Zimmermann)

New Reflections Dance Theatre in "Luna Park"
(John Daughtry Photo)

New Jersey Dance Theatre Guild
in "The Nutcracker"

NEW JERSEY DANCE THEATRE GUILD

Edison, N. J.

Artistic Director-Choreographer, Alfredo Corvino; Ballet Mistress-Choreographer, Andra Corvino; Ballet Chairman, Patricia McCusker; Business Director, Helen Bechtold; Administration and Production Consultant, Yvette Cohen; President, Gertrude Weinberg; Costumes, Gail Rae, Marcella Corvino; Sets, Norman Cohen; Stage Managers, Verne Fowler, Jackie Lynn

COMPANY

Judy Bolanowski, Nancy Butchko, Eileen Byrne, Ruth Capaldo, Gina DeBenedetto, Cecily Douglas, Melanie Geigel, Diane Gressing, Melody Kiegel, Dawn Lore, Michelle Massa, Claire Miller, Mary Beth Nollstadt, Rosemary Sabovick, Patricia Scarangello, Judy Schaefer, Carol Schneider, Janice Sorrentino, Elizabeth Stewart, Mary Stoltenberg, Debbie Strauss, Leslie Strauss
GUEST ARTISTS: Joyce Cuoco, Jeff Satinoff, Mercie John Hinton, Jr., Jay Todd, Jay Seaman, Dean Badolato, Bruce Weitzman, Joseph Fernandez
REPERTOIRE: "The Nutcracker" (Tchaikovsky, Corvino after Ivanov)

NORFOLK BALLET

Norfolk, Virginia

Directors, Gene Hammett, Teresa Martinez; Choreographers, Patricia Sorrell, Glen White; Ballet Mistress, Suzie Boree; Stage Manager-Sets, John Senter; Sets, Warren Richardson; Costumes, Peggy Jones; Costumes-Design, Angelina Martinez; Wardrobe, Maudeanne Barriskill; Press, Carole Hernandez

COMPANY

PRINCIPALS: Stacie Caddell, Loretta Dodd, Donna Sheppard, Steve Pasco, Michael Webster, Sandra Falder
SOLOISTS: Alexis Brown, Kim Fielding, Mark Croston, Tom Luna, Lee Thompson, Lori Buckley, Denise Hernandez, Ana Maria Martinez, Sherri Foshee, Beth Richardson, Catharine Anne Smith, Joan Tsao, Terri Thompkins, Debbie Vastano, Michael Barriskill, Joanne Berson, Janis Paiva
CORPS: Dolores Cloud, Judith Faulkner, Maria Griffith, Jody Lynn Guard, Caroline O'Brien, Daphne Singleton, Anne Elizabeth Todd, Clary Washington, Miriam Washington, Lisa Buckley, Maureen Gordon, Shelly Gough, Alice Lorraine Haworth, Robin Lawhorne, Marie Miller, Crystal Deanna Powell, Sharon Prosser, Jeanie Rula, Erin Sabater, Kathleen Sawyer, Stefanie Stecker, Alexis Brown, Virginia Caroline Gage, Sandra Lynn Flader, Melissa Hoffer, Laura Keller, Lynn Owen, Sharon Sanchez, Tracy D. Smith, Ginny Thumm, Ami Tsao
GUEST ARTISTS: Ralph Hewitt, Gregory E. Pope, Lorraine Graves

REPERTOIRE

"Bayadere" (Minkus, Petipa), "Paquita" (Minkus, Petipa), "Spring Waters" (Rachmaninoff, Asaf Messer), "Tchaikovsky Pas de Deux" (Tchaikovsky, Balanchine), "Don Quixote Pas de Deux" (Minkus, Petipa), and *Premieres* of "Life Rhythms" (Bette Midler/Stevie Wonder/Elton John, Nina Werness), "Snowhite" (Bergmueller, Gene Hammett/Glenn White), "Broadway Gypsies" (Marvin Hamlisch, Glenn White/Gene Hammett)

Donna Sheppard, Michael Webster and Norfolk Ballet in "Paquita" *(Danny Hager Photo)*

NORTH CAROLINA DANCE THEATRE

Winston-Salem, N. C.

Artistic Director, Robert Lindgren; General Manager, Stan Ward

COMPANY

Principals Svea Eklof and Michel Rahn with 15 dancers (names not submitted)

REPERTOIRE

"A Time of Windbells" (Collage, Norbert Vesak), "Adagio for Ten and Two" (Barber, Richard Gibson), "Bach: Brandenburg Three" (Bach, Charles Czarny), "Changes" (Honegger, Carlos Carvajal) "Fugitive Visions" (Prokofiev, Job Sanders), "The Grey Goose of Silence" (Ann Mortifee, Vesak), "Myth" (Stravinsky, Alvin Ailey) "Nocturnal Sun" (Michael Colina, Richard Kuch), "Raymonda" (Glazounov, Balanchine/Danilova), "Reflections" (Brahms, Sanders), "Symphony Thirteen" (Haydn, Duncan Noble), "Virginia Sampler" (Leo Smit, Valerie Bettis), "Wedding Cake" (Saint-Saens Sanders)

North Carolina Dance Theatre in "Soleriana"

OBERLIN DANCE COLLECTIVE
San Francisco, California

Trustees, Brenda Way, Kimi Okada, Doug Winter; Composer, Doug Skinner; Lighting Designer-Technical Director, Bill Chetel; Choreographers, Brenda Way, Kimi Okada, Pam Quinn, Margot Crosman, Doug Skinner, Marc Smith

COMPANY

Brenda Way, Kimi Okada, Pam Quinn, Margot Crosman, Doug Skinner, Mercy Sidbury, Eric Barsness, Katie Nelson, Marc Smith, and Guest Artists: Bill Irwin, Michael O'Connor

REPERTOIRE

"Format V" (Brenda Way), "Time and Again" (Kimi Okada), "Hit or Miss" (Kimi Okada), "Hide Hide the Cow's Outside" (Doug Skinner), and *Premieres* of "Ladies in Waiting" (Brenda Way), "Madcap Repose" (John Mizelle, Margot Crosman), "Two Step" (Pam Quinn), "Hitch Hike" (Marc Smith), "Circa" (Bill Irwin), "Joseph Knowles" (Doug Skinner), "Red Shoes" (Doug Skinner, Collective)

Top Left: Oberlin Dance Collective
(Doug Winter Photo)

OHIO STATE UNIVERSITY DANCE COMPANY
Columbus, Ohio

Director-Choreographer, Vera Blaine; Company Assistant, Douglas Cummings; Lighting Designer, Louis Guthman; Guest Choreographer, Kenneth Rinker

COMPANY

Mary Jane Allen, Barbara Boyd, Timothy Buckley, Douglas Cummings, Karen Gober, Marilyn Jones, Robin Klingensmith, Ida LaPenta, Irene Meltzer, Jon Mensinger, Claire Porter, Mary Richter, Nancy Scotfort, Sheryl Sedlacek, Nancy Stoner, Randy Thomas, Marcia Trees, Rachelle Weinstein, Jayne Wood

REPERTOIRE

"A Gift of Wings" (Vivaldi, Rosalind Pierson), "Configurations" (Britten, Pierson), "Tracks" (Tom MacDonald/Collage, Vera Blaine), and *Premieres* of "Fallin In" (Sergio Cervetti, Kenneth Rinker), "Nine Lollipops" (NY Jazz Repertory Co., Sheldon Ossosky), "Conversations" (Harry Fleetwood/Eugeniusz Rudnik, Claire Porter), "Transit" (John Cage, Karen Gober)

Doug Cummings, Karen Gober, Claire Porter, Tim Buckley in "Tracks"
(Ohio State University Dance Company)

OLYMPIA BALLET
Olympia, Washington

Artistic Director-Choreographer, Virginia Woods; Conductor, Brian Olendorf; Music Director, Ken Olendorf; Art Director, Ray Gilliland; Stage Manager, Chuck Foster; President, Carole Shoop

COMPANY

Debbi Haverlock, Debi Campbell, Kathy Minnitti, Nancy Isely, Sue Foster, Kendra Olendorf, Krystal Shoop, Michiko Yamane, Kathy Coniff, Dan Heitzmann, Eric Foster, Fred Knittle, Pam Zielin, Tammy Stehr, Lisa Kipp, Valerie Pennell, Joel Crothers, Andrea Lightburne, Diana Columbus

REPERTOIRE

"The Nutcracker" (Tchaikovsky, Woods), "Frankie and Johnny" (Gershwin, Woods), "Entrance to Hades" (Hindemith, Woods), "We Believe in Music" (Popular, Woods), "The Night before Christmas" (Traditional, Woods), and *Premieres* of "The Dig" (Olendorf, Woods), "The Legend of Manatu" (Villa-Lobos/Chavez, Woods)

Krystal Shoop, Nancy Isely, Debbi Haverlock
in "Legend of Manatu"
(Olympia Ballet)

157

ONE PLUS ONE
Champaign, Illinois

Artistic Director-Choreographer, Patricia Hruby; Music Director, David Onderdonk; Lighting Design-Technical Director, Carl Banfi; Management Consultant, Mark Ludke

COMPANY

Patricia Hruby
David Onderdonk

REPERTOIRE: "In the Beginning," "A Detail from Birds" (Vivaldi), "Discontents" (Dennis Kita), "Match" (Delibes), "Album" and *Premiere* of "And They're Still Married ..." (James Staley)

David Onderdonk, Patricia Hruby

Sam Weber, Rosine Bena in "Vinesa"
(Peninsula Ballet Theatre)

PENINSULA BALLET THEATRE
San Mateo, California

Director-Choreographer, Anne Bena; Sets, Lila Vultee, Hu Pope, Paul Pratchanko; Costumes, Lorraine Lehre, Jeannette Owlett, Alice Weiner; Lighting Design, David Arrow; Stage Manager, Edward Bena; Press, Robert Burmister

COMPANY

Principals: Rosine Bena, Sam Weber; Soloists: Loretta Bartlett, Cathleen McCarthy, Karstyn McCoy, Linda Triplett, Anne Rosenberg, Margi Walsh, Diana Wayne; Corps: Misses Amarillo, Burwell, Butler, Freeman, Gaumer, Iverson, Kjolby, Kelley, Kortum, Lucia, Mann, Myers, Pratchenko, Rehbein, Messrs. Benthin, Cofer, Laaser, Pitterson

REPERTOIRE

"Nutcracker" (Tchaikovsky, Anne Bena), "Swan Lake" (Tchaikovsky, Sallie Wilson), "Roundabout" (Malcolm Arnold, Martin Buckner), and *Premieres* of "Springfest" (Brahms, Marc Wilde), "Vinasa" (Akutagowa, Marc Wilde), "Paging Mr. Stair" (Kern/Porter, Stan Kahn/Anne Bena)

PHYLLIS ROSE DANCE COMPANY
Rockaway Park, N. Y.

Company Director-Choreographer, Phyllis Rose; Composers, Richard Bunn, Jim Erwin, Eric Salzman; Costumes, Terry Leong; Sets, Ned Hallick; Lighting Design-Production Manager, Deanna Greenwood

COMPANY

Phyllis Rose

Ruth Botchan
Randy Howard
Craig Nazur

Diana Simkin
J. Edward Sydow
Dirk Van Tassel

REPERTOIRE

"Diversions" (None, Phyllis Rose), "Flamingo & Peacock" (Debussy, J. Edward Sydow), "Gotham Boogie" (Popular Themes, Diana Simkin), "Interweave" (Conga Drums, Rose), "Pollution" (Eric Salzman, Rose), "Santanna" (Pop/Rock, Erick Hodges), "The Romp" (Richard Bunn, Rose), "Rosie" (Popular, Rose), "Water Dance," (Water Sounds, Diana Simkin)

Erick Hodges, Ellen Kalmanoff, Joel Stahl
in "Diversions" *(Szabo Photo)*
Phyllis Rose Dance Company

PITTSBURGH BALLET THEATRE
Pittsburgh, Pennsylvania

Artistic Director, Nicolas Petrov (1969–1977), John Gilpin 1977); Co-Artistic Director, Frederic Franklin (1973–1977); General Manager, Kay S. Cushing; Music Director, Ottavio De Rosa; Ballet Master, Frano Jelincic; Lighting Designer, Pat Simmons; Scene and Costume Designers, Frank Childs, Henry Heymann, W. Oren Parker, Stephen Petipas, Rouben Ter-Arutunian; Production Manager, E. F. West; Stage and Company Manager, Martha Jacobs; Press, Mary R. Bensel

COMPANY

PRINCIPALS: Dagmar Kessler, JoAnn McCarthy, Alexander Filipov, Thierry Dorado
SOLOISTS: Jeanne Loomis, Susan Perry, Nancy Dickson, Gregory Slodowski, Gernot Petzold, Alexander Agadzhanov
CORPS: Michael Abbitt, Bruce Abjornson, Douglas Bentz, Sharon Bowditch, Thomas Christopher, Peter Degnan, Susan Degnan, Lisa Anne Ely, Kathryn Irey, Paul McRae, Roland Morrissette, Roberto Munoz, Nola Nolen, Paul Plesh, Kay Prud'Homme, Deidre Sayler, Mark Schneider, Cynthia Schowalter, Susa E. Stone, Patricia Sweeney, Roger Triplett, Valerie Windsor, Beth E. Zeldes
GUEST ARTISTS: Dinko Bogdanic, Alain Dubreuil, Kaleria Fedicheva, Christian Holder, Dennis Poole

REPERTOIRE

"Cinderella" (Prokofiev, Zakharov/Petrov), "Nutcracker" (Tchaikovsky, Ivanov/Petrov), "Spectre de la Rose" (von Weber, Fokine/Beriozoff), "Petrouchka" (Stravinsky, Fokine/Beriozoff), "Swan Lake" (Tchaikovsky, Petipa/Franklin/Petrov), "Dohnanyi Suite" (Dohnanyi, Taras), "Giselle" (Adam, Coralli/Franklin), "Pas de Dix" (Glazounov, Balanchine).
PREMIERES: "Othello" (Crum, Butler), "Maria Sabina" (Balada, Petrov), "Fantasia" (Serebrier, Petrov), "Reverences" (Corelli, Stuart Sebastian), "Pas de Deux Eclatant" (Shostakovich, Sebastian), "Tribute" (Franck, Franklin)

Right: "Giselle" Above: (L) JoAnn McCarthy, Alexander Filipov in "Othello" (R) Dagmar Kessler in "Cinderella" Top: JoAnn McCarthy, Dinko Bogdanic in "Swan Lake"

PREMIERE DANCE ARTS COMPANY
Denver, Colorado

Artistic Director-Choreographer, Gwen Bowen; Assistant Director-Choreographer, Dixie Turnquist; Costume Mistress, Joan Cope; Lighting Design, Charles Everitt; Sets, Gwen Bowen, Rod Miller; Press, Connie Claxton, Carol March; Technical Director, Rod Miller

COMPANY

SOLOISTS: Crystal Chapman, Holly Cope, Linda Jacoby, Valerie Thornburg
CORPS: Greg Ahrens, Tammy Barkdoll, Jenny Claxton, Vicky Fields, Robin Kassoff, Carol March, Carol McDowell, Susan Selner, Beth Shafer, Kara Zinn
GUEST ARTISTS: Melissa Lowe, Jory Hancock

REPERTOIRE

"Sorcerer's Apprentice" (Dukas, Bowen), "Holiday Waltz" (Strauss, Linda Jacoby), "Rags and Things" (Lamb/Joplin, Mark Schneider), "Coppelia Act II" (Delibes, Danilova/Mark Schneider), "Hansel and Gretel" (Humperdinck, Bowen), "Three Preludes" (Rachmaninoff, Stevenson), "Moldavian Suite" (Traditional, John Landovsky), "Zampa" (Herold, Bowen), "Sounds" (von Suppe, Bowen), "Pet Shop Jamboree" (Selected, Dixie Turnquist)
PREMIERES: "Tribute to Glenn Miller" (Miller, Crystal Chapman), "Curtains" (John, Rise Kelly) "Dancin' " (Murphy/Spheeris, Vicky Fields), "Images for 8" (Chorea/Abercrombie/Pepper, Jory Hancock/Melissa Lowe), "Celebration" (Tchaikovsky, Bowen), "Montage" (Fasch, Debra Norblom Sams), "Gypsy Village" (Brahms, Alexandra Geronikos), "Tsamiko" (Kotsaftis/Grives, Geronikos), "Hasapiko" (Xarhakos, Geronikos), "Waltz Fantasy" (Brahms, David Miller), "Winter Jewels" (Strauss, Miller), "Sea Anemone" (Copeland, Bowen)

"Montage"
(Premiere Dance Arts)

Dodie Pettit, David Anderson, Linda Edwards
in "Coppelia" (Princeton Ballet)

PRINCETON BALLET COMPANY
Princeton, N. J.

Director-Choreographer, Audree Estey; Ballet Mistress, Judith Leviton; Business Manager, L. Wendell Estey; Choreographer Alexei Yudenich; Lighting Design, Lowell Achziger, Richard Warwinsky; Costumes, Gloria Woodside, Bonnie Brienza, Ruth Pettit; Stage Manager, Peter Cook; Press, Jean B. Pariso

COMPANY

PRINCIPALS: Dodie Pettit, Justin Glodowski
SOLOISTS: Karen Carter, Sukey Cohen, Linda Edwards, Penn Kingan, Lorri Lee, Beatrice Neuwirth, Susan Olson, Shirin Stave
CORPS: Ruth Charney, Marian Gizzi, Betsy Guerin, Andrea Juris, Abigail Kaplan, Dania Myers, Elaine Quinet, Evelyn Richmond, Karen Russo, Karen Steinnagel, Robin Tantum
GUEST ARTISTS: Barbara Sandonato, Bruce Wells, Rober Glady, Felipe Da Lama, Paul Naegel, Roger Rouillier, David Anderson

REPERTOIRE

"The Nutcracker" (Tchaikovsky, Audree Estey/Lila Brunner) "Coppelia" (Delibes, Frederic Franklin/Judith Leviton), "Les Sylphides" (Chopin, Fokine/Barbara Sandonato/Judith Leviton), "Stars and Stripes Pas de Deux" (Sousa, Balanchine/Sara Leland), "To Unfurl the Fan" (Purcell/Blow, Myra Kinch), "Peter and the Wolf" (Prokofiev, Estey), "Circus" (Barnum & Bailey Band, Ne Jorgenson), "Hoedown" (Traditional, Ruth Langridge), and Premieres of "Corelli Concerto" (Corelli, Alexei Yudenich), "We Celebrate" (Selected, Joan Morton Lucas), "Tack Annie" (Gershwin Larry Clark)

RAM ISLAND DANCE COMPANY
Portland, Maine

Artistic Director-Choreographer, Andrea Stark; Company Manager, Victoria Nolan; Stage Manager, Alan Lovell

COMPANY

John Carrafa	Jan Peterson
Sam Costa	Sylvia Toffel
Sandra Iannicelli-Lovell	Andrea Stark

REPERTOIRE

"Motifs" (Bach, Andrea Stark), " Issue" (Ivanovici, Rachel Lampert), "Home" (Haydn, Lampert), and Premieres of "Unfinished Trio" (Monteverdi, Stark), "The Compulsory Rags" (Joplin/Muir/-Johnson/Matthews/Stark), "8 Etudes for 5 Dancers" (Elliott Carter, Stark), "Silent Moving" (None, Stark)
(No photos available)

Ram Island Dance Company

RHODE ISLAND DANCE REPERTORY COMPANY
Providence, R. I.

Artistic Director-Choreographer, Julie Strandberg; Designer, Peter Anderson; General Manager, Joanne Gomes

COMPANY

Skip Carter	Nancy Reichley
Janet Danforth	Marty Sprag
Richardson Lambertson	Julie Strandberg
and Lisa Guisbond, Alice Kaltman, Peter Shile, Jane Zalutsky	

REPERTOIRE

"Duet" (Weather Report, Ted Rotante), "Success" (Nora Guthrie) "Couples" (Terry Riley, Danny Grossman), "National Spirit" (Marches/Anthams, Grossman), "Festino" (Tartini, Julie Strandberg), "Physics Made Easy" (Gerald Shapiro, Kathy Eberstadt), "Aria" (Stravinsky, David Briggs)

Janet Danforth, Nancy Reichley (prone)
in "Success" (Rhode Island Dance Co.)

RIO GRANDE VALLEY CIVIC BALLET
McAllen, Texas

Artistic Director-Choreographer, Doria Avila; Administrative Director, Alfred J. Gallagher; Company Manager, Jeanne Ross; Ballet Mistress, Colette Ross; Sets, George Pettit, Peter Wolf Associates; Costumes, Michelle Munsch; Stage Manager-Lighting Design, Doria Avila; Sound, Alfred J. Gallagher; Press, Aurora Pena, Pat Patrick, Barbara Uhlaender, Joanne Anderson

COMPANY

PRINCIPALS: Colette Ross, Rosemary Cavazos, Linda Acevedo, Sheryl Uhlaender, Steve Lyssy
SOLOISTS: Yvette Martinez, Gergory Ortiz, David Kent, Jaime Perez
CORPS: Lisa Acevedo, Melissa Barrera, Linda Eanes, Linda Garza, Jackie Graham, Debra Handy, Linda Jaime, Dede Johnson, Jackie Linn, Venezia Mancilla, Wendy Patrick, Maritza Pena, Patty Putz, Polly Putz, Tracy Tarvin, Ann Williams, Ann Flores, Sherri Peters, Marie Gonzalez, Cynthia Dunnigan, Quita Hill, Kenneth Kelberlau, Michael Boggan, Malcolm Miranda, Audie Lea, Kelly Wooters, Monica Martinez, Stephanie Hall, Patricia Gurl
GUEST ARTIST: Anthony Sellers, Terri Hayes, Beth Eisleben, Homer Garza, Gary Rochelle

REPERTOIRE

(All choreography by Doria Avila) "The Nutcracker" (Tchaikovsky, Avila; Pas de Deux, Anthony Sellers), "Fiesta de Huapango" (Moncayo) "Feria en Espana" (Massenet) "Fiesta Mexicana!" (Popular) "Carnival of Death" (Menotti), "Celebration in the Sun" (Ginastera), "Caracole" (Lecocq), "America Hurrah!" (Sousa), "Green Mansions" (Villa-Lobos), "Misa Mariachi" (Traditional), "Variations on America" (Ives), and *Premieres* of "La Fille Mal Gardee" (Herold/Lanchbery, Avila) "Don Quixote Grand Pas de Deux" (Minkus, Petipa), "Capriccio Espanol" (Rimsky-Korsakov, Gisela Noriega), "Roots Suite" (Quincy Jones, Avila), "Texas Dance Party" (Gimble, Avila)

Rosemary Cavazos and Rio Grande Valley
Civic Ballet in "La Fille Mal Gardee"
(Earley Photo)

ROCKY MOUNTAIN BALLET
Colorado Springs, Colorado

Formerly Colorado Ballet Company; Director-Choreographer, Ilse Reese Gahart; Technical Director, Steve Dingmann; Costumes, Ilse Reese Gahart, Ursula Stack; Lighting Design, Don Shipman; Accompanist, Ben Gahart

COMPANY

SOLOISTS: Patricia Smith, Susan Kimler, Susan Carney, Melissa McGill, Marie Burgess, Cliff Cannon
CORPS: Bessie Frank, Anne Adams, Kathy Burgess, Gillie Cannon, Kristiina Hintgen, Mary Jo Hoover, Susie Linger, Nichola Ryan, Nancy Spielkamp, Jana Steele, Alice Segarra, Virginia Ellett
APPRENTICES: Beverly Cellini, Susi Hassell, Bruce Gomea, Tony Manteneri, Helen Trujillo, Andrew Metcalf, Bill Tilghman, Ginette Cole
GUEST ARTIST: Kirk Hathaway

REPERTOIRE

(All choreography by Ilse Reese Gahart) "Cinderella" (Prokofiev), "Firebird" (Stravinsky), "Chopin Festival" (Chopin), "Malaguena" (Lecuona)

Rocky Mountain Ballet Ensemble
in "Firebird"

RONDO DANCE THEATER
Bedford, N. Y.

Director-Choreographer, Elizabeth Rockwell; Lighting Design-Stage Manager, Ben Dolphin, Michael Smart; Costumes, Martha Yoshida; Musical Director, Eric Lewis

COMPANY

Hseuh-Tung Chen	Dennis Kosjan
Rosemary Newton	Tony Ndoga
Susan Osberg	Catherine Sullivan
Evan Williams	Andrew Quinlan-Krichels

REPERTOIRE: "Step to Step to Haydn" (Haydn, Paul Sanasardo), "Black Angels" (Crum, Kazuko Hirabayashi), "Incantation" (Copland, Susan Osberg), "Emperor of Ice Cream" (Stravinsky/Gershwin, Rockwell/Desoto/Osberg/Williams)

Kate Johnson, Dennis Kosjan in "Black Angels"
(Rondo Dance Theater)

SACRAMENTO BALLET

Sacramento, California

Artistic Director-Choreographer, Barbara Crockett; Associate Director-Choreographer, McGarry Caven; General Manager, Al Gallo; Conductor, Daniel Kingman; Lighting Design, Bruce Kelley, Steve Odehnal; Press, Jim Myers; Stage Manager, Bruce Kelley; Wardrobe, Marjorie Bader

COMPANY

Danielle Anderson, Sarah Arnold, Lorna Baer, Didi Boyer, Cheryl Chalmers, Jody Downes, Teresa Dryden, Margaret Francis, Shelley Gilchrist, Julie LeNeave, Barbara Nyland, Ronald Ortman, Ronald Shepherd, Sharon Ree, Karen Skelton, Jill Stewart, David Takacs, Elizabeth Thompson, John Tuttle, Suzann Tuttle
GUEST ARTISTS: Patricia McBride, Helgi Tomasson, Deborah Dobson, Jonas Kage, Allyson Deane, Michael Dwyer

REPERTOIRE

"Mobile" (Khachaturian, Tomm Ruud), "La Favorita" (Donizetti, Barbara Crockett), "Imaginary Dialogue" (John McLaughlin, McGarry Caven), "The Nutcracker" (Tchaikovsky, Crockett), "Coppelia" (Delibes, Alicia Alonso/Margarita DeSaa) "Pas de Quatre" (Pugni, Anton Dolin), and *Premieres* of "Guitar Concerto" (Malcolm Arnold, McGarry Caven), "The Wonder Phenomena" (Stanley Lunetta, Caven), "Souree Musicale" (Benjamin Britten, Ronn Guidi)

John Tuttle, Cheryl Chalmers
in "Soiree Musicale"

SAINT LOUIS CIVIC BALLET

St. Louis, Missouri

Artistic Director-Choreographer, Stanley Herbertt; Associate Artistic Director, Betty McRoberts; Associate Director, LaVerne Meyering; Conductor, Gerhard Zimmerman; Designers, Stanley Herbertt, Betty McRoberts, Gerri Stretz Meyer, Madonna Gross, Stage Managers, Mike Moody, George Kinney

COMPANY

Cindy Abernathy, Monica Albers, Barbara Bates, Ingrid Breyer, Ginny Burt, Amy Corday, Karen Cracchiola, Melody Dye, Kim Kuhlmann, Stephanie Kretow, Bonnie Luebbert, Owen Mueller, Tony Parise, Kim Reitz, Susu Rosenthal, Michelle Sapienza, Lisa Schallert, Diane Shamess, Patti Smith, Marilyn Szozepanik, Laura Webber, Kyle Wehmueller

REPERTOIRE

"The Nutcracker" (Tchaikovsky, Stanley Herbertt), "The History of Dance in America" (Miscellaneous, Herbertt), and *Premieres* of "Hungarian Dances" (Brahms, Betty McRoberts), "Escapade" (Contemporary, Gerri Stretz Meyer), "Le Premier Bal des Mesdemoiselles" (Strauss, Edward Pfeiffer), "Opus IV" (Contemporary, McRoberts/Meyer), "Star Bright, Star Light" (Miscellaneous, Carol Jones)

Mary Heidbreder, Laurie Bartram in "The Nutcracker"
(St. Louis Civic Ballet)
Art Vasterling Photo

ST. MARK'S DANCE COMPANY

Washington, D. C.

Director-Choreographer, Mary Craighill; Costumes, Cara Gargano; Stage Manager, Suzann Lamb; Company Managers, Cara Gargano, Nancy Mitchell

COMPANY

Rosetta Brooks	Veta Goler
James Caton,	Fred Lee
Mary Craighill	Tony Linnear
Stanley Fowler	Glynis Long
Cara Gargano	Jan Tievsky

REPERTOIRE: Passacaglia" (Bach, Craighill), "Benedictus" (Electric Prunes, Craighill), "Eugene Onegin" (Janacek, Craighill), "Peter and the Wolf" (Prokofiev, Craighill), "Africanus Brazilius" (Paul Winter, Jan Tievsky), "Rendezvous" (Jarreh, Gargano), "Kinetic Suite" (Watson, Craighill), "Spectrum" (Collage, Tievsky), and *Premieres* of "Gospel Suite" (Traditional, Rosetta Brooks), "Sarah" (Mahler, Gargano), "Christmas Carol" (Bartok, Craighill), "Victory" (Bodnar, Caton), "Fantasie and Passacaille" (Weiss, Craighill)

Mary Craighill (R) and St. Mark's Dance Company
in "Sarah" *(Jogues R. Prandoni Photo)*

SAN DIEGO BALLET COMPANY
San Diego, California

Director, Keith J. Martin; Ballet Mistress, Elaine Thomas; Musical Director, Charles Ketcham; Guest Conductor, Denis De Coteau; Technical Director, William S. Hepner III; Wardrobe Mistress, Linda Pierson; General Manager, Patrick L. Kelley

COMPANY

PRINCIPALS: Helen Dexter, Keith Martin, Monica Mudgett, Duncan Schute
CORPS: Toni D'Amelio, Arturo Fernandez, Anael-Kadosh Garza, Cathy Head, Regina Helmer, Suzan Kroll, Kathleen McHugh, James McArdle, Ellen Richards, Willow Storm, Diana Tennyson
GUEST ARTISTS: Galina Panov, Jillana

REPERTOIRE

"Les Sylphides" (Chopin, Fokine), "Technique de Ballet" (Czerny, Arova after Petipa), "Don Quixote Pas de Deux" (Minkus, Martin after Petipa), "Carmen" (Bizet, Arova), "La Bayadere" (Minkus, Arova after Petipa), "Dialogues and Images" (Stravinsky, Sutowski), "Le Corsaire Pas de Deux" (Drigo, Petipa), "Ouvertures Classique" (Berlioz, Sutowski), "Spring Waters" (Rachmaninoff, Messerer), "Pas de Quatre" (Pugni, Arova after Dolin), "Harp Concerto" (Boieldieu, Sutowski)
PREMIERES: "Swan Lake" (Tchaikovsky, Keith J. Martin after Petipa/Ivanov), "Nutcracker" (Tchaikovsky, Martin), "Firebird" (Stravinsky, Frantz), "Tarantella" (Gottschalk, Davis), "Trio" (Brahms, Davis), "Support" (Caliope Collage, Willis), "Poulenc Concerto" (Poulenc, Davis), "3 Studies in Jazz" (J. D. Power), "Lonely One" (Mahler, Martin), "Reflections of Don Juan" (Strauss, Zirra), "Song of Songs" (Penderecki, Pasqualetti)

Galina Panov, Keith Martin and San Diego Ballet
in "The Nutcracker"

SAN JOSE DANCE THEATRE
San Jose, California

Co-Directors, Paul Curtis, Shawn Stuart; Choreographer, Shawn Stuart; Lighting Design-Technical Director, James R. Earle, Jr.; Wardrobe Mistress, June Guy; Press, Richard Green, Jr.

COMPANY

Nancie Berridge, Joan Brobst, Mary Callahan, Mary Campbell, Jacqueline Kamber, Kae Guy, Jennifer Johnson, Sarah Clish, Kathleen Kane, Sonja Krusic, Sharon Nagle, Kelcey Poe, Ann Robinson, Sally Ross, Erin Silva, Melanie Spencer, Lynn Wingrove, Ellen Brunetto, Dorothy Faulds, Dee Robnett, Julie Soper
Audrey Berridge, Julie Burgio, Kim Gardner, Diana Hayes, Sandra Kimrey, Laura Rogers, Molly Story, Helen Voss, Robert Hall, Larry Kramer, Shawn Stuart, Steve Vickers

REPERTOIRE

"Courtly Dances" (Britten, Shawn Stuart), "The Nutcracker" (Tchaikovsky, Paul Curtis/Stuart), "Coronation" (Crum, Stuart), "Kuan Yin" (Bach, Stuart), "Carmina Burana" (Orff, Stuart), "Peter and the Wolf" (Prokofiev, Stuart), "Danzas de las Pulgas" (Traditional Mexican, Stuart), "Raymonda Pas de Deux" (Glazounov, Curtis)

San Jose Dance Theatre in "Coronation"
(Alissa Crandall Photo)

SAVANNAH BALLET
Savannah, Georgia

Artistic Director-Choreography, Bojan Spassoff; Assistant to Director, Stephanie Wolf; Conductor, George Trautwein; Costumes, Glen Glenn; Scenery, Angela Story; Lighting Design, Barbara Krisnsen

COMPANY

Bojan Spassoff, Stephanie Wolf, and Gaye Baxley, Kathleen Collins, Jenifer Grissette, Mary Hagan, Tara Harold, Lewis Hooten, George McGarvey, Heidi Mueller, Thomas Rahal, Steven Walker
GUEST ARTISTS: Suzanne Farrell, Peter Martins, Daniel Duell, Heather Watts, Kathleen Haigney

REPERTOIRE

"French Suite" (Bach, Bojan Spassoff), "Cinderella Act I" (Prokofiev, Spassoff), "Pas de Deux: A Promise" (Craig Shuler, Robert Weiss), "Suite for Flute and Jazz Piano" (Claude Bolling, Lewis Hooten), and *Premiere* of "The Legend of the Waving Girl" in 3 acts (Elgar/Sullivan/Tchaikovsky/Williams/David Matthew, Spassoff)

Stephanie Wolf, Bojan Spassoff
in "A Promise" (Savannah Ballet)   **163**

Sims Cosmopolitan Dance Troop

SIMS' COSMOPOLITAN DANCE TROOP

New York, N. Y.

Artistic Director-Choreographer, Jamie Sims; Managing Director, Chris Stamey; Technical Director, Greg Vines; Stage Manage Ann A. Hayek; Sets and Costume Designers, Greg Vines, Glen T

COMPANY

Austin Alexis	Djuna Morga
Heather Campbell	Jamie Sim
Pat Farmer	Glen T
Judy Kahn	Greg Vin

REPERTOIRE: "Les Saltimbanques" (Sims/Sousa, Jamie Sims "Les Femmes" (Spoken, Sims), "Bufon!" (silence, Sims "Musique!" (Dancers, Sims), "Giblets" (Spoken, Sims) and Premie of "Dance Dance" (Supremes/Temptations/Sam & Dave, Jam Sims)

SOUTHERN THEATRE BALLET COMPANY

Jacksonville, Florida

Founder-Artistic Director-Choreographer, Marta Jackson; Technical Director-Lighting and Set Designer, Leonardo Favela; Costumes, Mary Lovelace; Ballet Mistress, Virginia Pelegrin; Manager, Judy Barchelder; Press, Bobby Maduro; Guest Choreographers, Gayle Parmelee, Magda G. de Aunon, Earle Sieveling

COMPANY

Linda Bell, Nancy Bock, Sharon Booth, Neyda Castells, Lori Childers, Pam Davis, Susan Depadua, Susan Donziger, Pam Farber, Joy Farris, Cindy Goldsmith, Pamela Huelster, Gentry Linville, Ginny Markgraff, Melody McCombs, Susie McCall, Virginia Pelegrin, Mary Saltmarsh, Dane Smith, Sara Howell, Karena Richter, Kathy Bell, Tracy Cauley, Lisa Ossi, Lourdes Palomino, Cathy Peake, Ceci Perez, Barbara Spraggins, Karen Wood, Randy Wook, Susu Saltmarsh, Cindi Green

REPERTOIRE

"Solitude" (Ravel, Marta Jackson), "Isle of Loneliness" (Wagner, Jackson), "Quadrille" (Strauss, Jackson), "The River" (Smetana, Jackson), "Romance" (Dvorak, Sieveling), "Concerto" (Bach, de Aunon after Alonso), "Nutcracker" (Tchaikovsky, Parmelee), "Swan Lake Act II" (Tchaikovsky, Jackson/Petipa), "Grand Pas de Quatre" (Pugni, Jackson), "Aurora's Wedding" (Tchaikovsky, Jackson after Petipa), "El Amor Brujo" (DeFalla, Jackson), "Rochene" (Glazounov, Jackson), "Esprit" (Britten, Parmelee), "Ballet School," "Carmina Burana," "Sleeping Beauty"

Southern Theatre Ballet Company

SOUTHWEST BALLET

Fort Worth, Texas

Founder-Artistic Director, William Martin-Viscount; Presiden Parker Willson; Press, Susan Huston; Costumes, Minta Deitric Ellarose Sullivan; Pianists, Hildur Nelson, Lance Williams

COMPANY

Maria-Clara Salles de Almeida, Bridget Armstrong, Catherine Bay E. F. Bingham, Randy Bloss, Mark Borchelt, Krinna Brock, S Buck, Mark Bush, Rudy Calsoncin, Ana Lucia de Carvalho, Glad de Carvalho, Laurie Casserly, Susie Clark, Marcia Baptis Cruzeiro, Debbie Curtis, Theresa Dalton, Kathleen Dean, Anne Compiegne, Cyd Dewell, Johanna Dodson, Jenny Douglas, Pa Dowies, Glenn Edgerton, Leslie Finch, Tim Fox, Robin Friedber Kellie Gale, Rosie Gonzalez, Vincent Guerrero, Deirdre Hade, La rence Hall, Lynette Hall, Betsy Halvorsen, Penny Hatch, Mar Heath, Cathy Hebert, Laurin Huber, Holly Hughes, Sandra Hu man, Melinda Iverson, Rodney Jenkins, Michael Job, Cheryl Jon Karen Kaufman, Jeanne King, Kevin Maurer, Steven McBri Kerri McClatchy, Michelle McGlothin, Sally Miller, Megan Mu phy, Jill Murphy, Carolyn Muzny, Linda Nordvig, Lassie Ozal Sherrill Ozaki, Penny Parker, Saundra Parker, Laura Pasqual, D Anne Perry, Marjorie Ann Quast, Christine Rakela, Kathy Rake Marjorie Randazzo, Sara Randazzo, Tony Randazzo, Norr Reyna, Mark Rhodes, Rita Rivera, Tad Robichaux, Desiree Rutk Jesse Salazar, Augenija Sestokaite, Judith Sheinuff, Steve Shotro Judy Spinella, Ann Stroh, Linda Stuart, Marcie Teat, Rebec Thompson, Gerre Tipton, Kelly Van Patter, Barbara Vives, Cath ine Vives, Kelly Walker, Kelly Williamson, James Dan Young GUEST ARTISTS: Violette Verdy, Anne Burton, Ana Lucia Carvalho, Yurek Lazowski, Emilio Martins, Michael Job, Ma Borchelt

REPERTOIRE

"Giselle" (Adolphe Adam, Bill Martin-Viscount), "Les Sylphid (Chopin, Fokine/Martin-Viscount), "Rossini Pas de Trois" (R sini, Martin-Viscount), "Czerny Etudes" (Czerny, Martin-V count), "Spring Waters" (Rachmaninoff, Messerer), "Stars a Stripes Pas de Deux" (Sousa, Balanchine)

Violette Verdy, Bill Martin-Viscount in "Giselle" (Southwest Ballet)

Stanze Peterson

STANZE PETERSON DANCE THEATRE
San Francisco, California

Artistic Director-Choreographer-Costume Designer, Stanze Peterson; Technical Director-Lighting Design, Kevin Myrick; Stage Manager, Jody Mahoney

COMPANY

Stanze Peterson	Frances Parham
Janet Ross	Mimi Platner-Mills
Jose Corrales	Don McKing
Virginia Kester	Esther Platner

REPERTOIRE: "The Sameness Wheel" (Jones/Maldron/Nyro, Peterson), "Untitled Solo" (Rodrigo, Maclovia), "Lament for Things to Come" (Fontella Bass, Peterson), "Cortege" (John Lewis, Peterson), "Ships ..." (Olly Wilson, Peterson)

TANCE'S DANCERS
San Francisco, California

Artistic Director-Choreographer, Tance Johnson; Sound, Jeffrey Hughes; Lighting Design, Stewart Kipple; Costumes, Tance Johnson, Tom Sczepanski; Press, Lois Zanich

DANCERS

Susan Ashley, Thom Bessey, Gilbert Chun, Theresa de la Cruz, Betty Gamboa, Marie Goulis, Jeffrey Hughes, Gloria Makris, Lila Nevarez, Gary Poole, Yvonne Prucha, John Riley, Ercilia Santos, Rosa Wang
GUEST ARTISTS: Bruce Bain, Charles Butts, Peggy Davis, Kathy Puzan, Suplicio Wagner

REPERTOIRE

"The Chase" (Joe Simon, Evelyn Ante), "Ceremony of the Cords" (Xenakis, Tance Johnson), "Encounters" (Benson, Johnson), "Les Sylphides" (Chopin, Fokine), "Classical Symphony" (Prokofiev, Mercedes Quinterra), "Aleatoric Thing" (Orff, Johnson), "Ethnic Suite" (Stravinsky, Johnson), "Canticle" (Chopin, Johnson), and *Premieres* of "Fly Away" (John Denver, Ercilia Santos), "Turn That Beat Around" (Robinson, Johnson), "Joplin Suite" (Joplin, Johnson), "Rings and Shadows" (Harris, Johnson)

Right Center: Yvonne Prucha, John Riley, Tance Johnson, Marie Goulis, Ercilla Santos, Richard Goodwin, Lila Nevarez in "Joplin Suite"
(Pete Peters Photo)

THEATRE FLAMENCO
San Francisco, California

Artistic Director, Adela Clara; Assistant Director, Miguel Santos; Choreographers, Adela Clara, Miguel Santos, Dini Roman; Sets, Cal Anderson; Lighting Design, Keith Gonzales; Technical Director, Clive Shephard; Company Manger, Larry Campbell

COMPANY

PRINCIPALS: Adela Clara, Miguel Santos, Paula Caro, Ernesto Hernandez, Cruz Luna, Damita Prado, Dini Roman
CORPS: Ricardo Oriana, Paula Reyes, Monique Fournier, Rebeca Mauleon, Rodolfo Figueroa, Ricardo Mareno, Victor Salazar, Margaret Cuevas, Yvonne Flores, Julia Thomas, Amalia Victoria, guitarists Teo Greso, Rogelio Fuentes, Juan Moro, singers Isa Mura, Catalina Mejia, narrators Sergio Echeverria, Carol Rivera

REPERTOIRE

"Triana" (Albeniz, Vega), "La Cana" (Traditional, Santos), "Romance Sonambulo" (Traditional, Clara), "Vitaminas-Vitaminas" (Traditional, Eugenia), "Colombian Suite" (Traditional, Cartegena), "La Soltera" (de Falla, Roman), "Orgia" (Turina, Alba), "Leyenca" (Albeniz, Flores), "Viva la Jota" (Traditional, Santos), "Soledad" (Traditional, Merce), "Cordoba" (Albeniz, Eugenia), "Viva Navarra" (Larregla, Clara), "Misa Flamenca" (Traditional, Santos), "Romeras" (Traditional, Martinez), "La Vida Breve" (deFalla, Eugenia)
PREMIERES: "Al Amor" (Traditional, Clara), "Alma Dolorosa" (Traditional, Clara), "La Sultana" (Traditional, Clara), "Llanto" (Traditional, Merce), "Garrotin" (Traditional, Merce), "Sonata en D" (Albeniz, Clara), "Gigantes y Cabezudos" (Caballero, Roman), "Fiesta en Mexico" (Traditional, Zamarripa/Almendares, Santos), "Playera" (Granados, Clara) .

Theatre Flamenco in "Al Amor"

THELMA OLAKER YOUTH CIVIC BALLET

Petersburg, Virginia

Artistic Director-Choreographer, Christin Parks; Ballet Mistress, Karmon Oliver; Guest Choreographers, Mary Marshall, Heidi Robitshek, Bob Pemberton; Lighting Design, Mark Compton; Costumes and Set, Barbara Hebert

COMPANY

SENIORS: Teresa Adams, Patti Barnhill, Beverly Brown, Nancy Carter, Debra Hearington, Sherry Hebert, Kathy Hilsher, Elania Jemison, Debbie McMillan, Renee Moneyhun, Blake Strange, Guy Bilyeu, Steve King, Bruce Linnell, Brian Thomas
JUNIORS: Belinda Jo Anderson, Mary Kay Barnhill, Elizabeth Brockwell, Julie Cloninger, Pam Coleman, Laura McMillan, Carrie Sartor, Kim Thweat, Robin Trainer
APPRENTICES: A. P. Brown, Lisa Crescentini, Charlotte Daniel, Ginger Elmore, Ashley Enochs, Mandy Hamner, Rob Hebert, Lori Lewis, Stacey MaGee, Lisa Nicholas, Suzanne Powroznick, Nanette Robinson, Jeff Rogers, Suzanne Rogers, Selena Shriver, Jill Smith, Phil Strange, Deborah Whipp, Tamera Jones

REPERTOIRE

"A Musical Tom Sawyer" (Christin Parks, Parks/Karmon Oliver/-Mary Marshall/Rudy Garza/Jack Voorhees), "Bees . . . The Spirit of the Hive" (Ravel, Parks), "Ballet in a Barn" (Dvorak/Rodgers, Marshall/Heidi Robitshek/Bob Pemberton)

Guy Bilyeu, Sherry Hebert, Steve King
in "A Musical Tom Sawyer"
(Thelma Olaker Youth Civic Ballet)

THUNDERBIRD AMERICAN INDIAN DANCERS

New York, N. Y.

Artistic Director-Choreographer, Louis Mofsie

COMPANY

Jack Preston, Alan Brown, Sam Tarrant, Bill Cuellar, Louis Mofsie, Ivan Vasquez, Michael Tarrant, Kevin Tarrant, Grace Valdez, Rosemarie Richmond, Kitty Gabourel, Beverly Pallats, Marie Radice, Judy Tarrant, Terry Pickett, Jane Cuellar
GUEST ARTISTS: Margaret Martinez, Margo Hill, Becky Hill, Holly Thunderbird

REPERTOIRE

Eastern Woodlands/Iroquois tribal dances: Robin Dance, Fish Dance, Striking the Stick; Southwest/Hopi and Santo Domingo Pueblo dances: Hoop Dance, Eagle Dance, Thunder Dance; Plains/Sioux and Winnebago tribal dances: Rabbit Dance, Fancy Dance; Northwest/Kwakiutl dances: Initiation Ceremonial Dance

TOLEDO BALLET COMPANY

Toledo, Ohio

Founder-Artistic Director-Choreographer, Marie Bollinger Vogt; Conductor, Serge Fournier; Sets, William R. Smith; Lighting Design, Susan Blaser; Costumieres, Rosalind Gonia, Evelyn Davis; Business Manager, Carl Hibscher; Production Coordinator, Evelyn Brandman; President, Lynn Parquette

COMPANY

Craig Barrow, Polly Brandman, Kathleen Carter, Suzanne Carter, Nancy Davis, Ed Drill, Lisa Filzer, Rebecca Free, Kathleen Gorman, Ernst Hillenbrand, Nagwa Mikhail, Sarah Mott, Judith Nasatir, Kimberly Parquette, Fredericka Rapp, Hilary Sujkowski, Laura Wade, Renata Wolgast
GUEST ARTISTS: Marianna Tcherkassky, Terry Orr, Christine Sarry, Violette Verdy, Edward Villella, Soili Arvola, Leo Ahonen

REPERTOIRE

"The Nutcracker," "Giselle," "Water Music Suite," "Swan Lake," "Symphony for Fun" "Capriccio Espagnole," "Les Patineurs," "Italian Symphony," "Graduation Ball," "Les Sylphides," "Old King Cole," "American Dance Suite," "Red Pony," "Stars and Stripes"

Left Center: Jack Preston, Bill Cuellar, Sam Tarrant
in "Robin Dance" *(David Kutz Photo)*

Alison Booth, Steve Donahue, Kim Parquette,
Hillary Sujkowski of Toledo Ballet

TULSA CIVIC BALLET

Tulsa, Oklahoma

Artistic Directors, Roman Jasinski, Moscelyne Larkin; Manager, P. E. Burke; Conductors, Tom Lewis, Maurice Kaplow

COMPANY

Principals: Tim Fox, Donna Grisez; Soloists: Dorothy Bridwell, Hope Theodoras and Corps de Ballet of 32(names not submitted)
GUEST ARTISTS: Fernando Bujones, Veronica Tennant, Desmond Kelly, Patricia Ruanne, Joyce Knopick, Jeri Kumery

REPERTOIRE

"Pas de Quatre" (Pugni, Dolin/Krassovska), "Don Quixote Pas de Deux" (Minkus, Petipa), "Tchaikovsky Divertissement" (Tchaikovsky, Jasinski), "Nutcracker" (Tchaikovsky, Invanov/Jasinski/Larkin), "Swan Lake Act II" (Tchaikovsky, Ivanov/ Jasinski/Larkin), "Grande Tarantelle" (Gottschalk, Jasinski), "Classical Symphony" (Prokofiev, Jasinski), and *Premieres* of "Jigs and Reels" (Malcolm Arnold, Richard Englund), "A Polish Tribute" (Chopin, Roman Jasinski)

R. J. Kumery Photos

**Top Right: Jeri Kumery
in "Classical Symphony"**

Donna Grisez, Emily Palik, Timothy Fox
in "Grande Tarantelle"

Timothy Fox, Donna Grisez
in "A Polish Tribute"

UNIVERSITY CIVIC BALLET

El Paso, Texas

Artistic Director-Choreographer, Ingeborg Heuser; Ballet Master, John Gardner; Musical Director, Lawrence Gibson; Technical Director, Paul Enger

COMPANY

PRINCIPALS Andree Harper, Kathi Henderson, Roxan Lotspeich, Leticia Hernandez, Rene Segapeli, Mark Loomis, Ernest Tolentino
(no other names submitted)

REPERTOIRE

"The Nutcracker" (Tchaikovsky, McFall/Heuser), "Romeo and Juliet Pas de Deux" (Prokofiev, Lavrovsky), "Don Quixote Pas de Deux" (Minkus, Traditional)
PREMIERES: "A Reflection of Lilies" (Bach, Gardner), "Don Juan" (Gluck, Heuser), "Crown of Dreams" (Berg, Gardner), "The Unicorn, Gorgon and Manticore" (Menotti, Heuser), "Just for Fun" (Gershwin, Heuser)

**Leticia Hernandez, John Gardner
in "Don Juan"** *(B. A. Haag Photo)* **167**

VALENTINA OUMANSKY DRAMATIC DANCE ENSEMBLE
West Los Angeles, California

Artistic Director-Choreographer, Valentina Oumansky; Associate, Marilyn Carter; Lighting Design, Tom Rodgers, Sergio Alvarado

COMPANY

Valentina Oumansky
Paul Bucalstein
Beth Gage
Barrie Raffel

Marilyn Carter
Janet Dolan
Dellamaria Marino
Tarumi Takagi

REPERTOIRE: (All choreography by Valentina Oumansky) "A Bow Is a Bow Is a Bow" (Bach/Purcel), "Adoration" (Alan Hovhaness), "Afro-American Jazz Legend" (Jazz Compilation), "Cortez, the Conqueror" (Alberto Ginastera), "Conversations in Silence and Sound" (Kenneth Klauss), "El Popol Vuh" (Elisabeth Waldo), "Facade" (Sitwell/Walton), "Ghazals" (Hovhaness), "God in a Box" (Luciano Berio), "Homage to the Southwest Indian" (Herman Stein), "In the Hills" (Hovhaness), "Poe-Pourri" (Collage), "Rin Tin Tin Superstar" (Hovhaness), "With Apologies to Aesop the Horse" (Herman Stein), "Zen Zen", and *Premiere* of "Alice in Queryland" (Collage, Valentina Oumansky)

Top Right: Valentina Oumansky, Dellamaria Marino, Tarumi Takagi in "Poe-Pourri"

Virginia Beach Ballet in "Courtly Dancers"

VIRGINIA BEACH BALLET
Virginia Beach, Virginia

Artistic Director-Choreographer, Major H. Burchfield; Ballet Master, Colin Worth; Costume Mistress, Dona McCloud; Costumes, Phyllis M. Hale, John Jones, Gail Sedel, Janet Groom, Elizabeth Marquette; Stage Manager, Beth Hudson; Lighting Design, Maynard Allen, Beth Hudson; Audio, Ursula Jones

COMPANY

Gary Barton
Debby Benvin
Shelagh Gaffikin
Wade T. P. Goss

Ena Naranjo
Tony Pisacano
Heidi S. Robitshek

REPERTOIRE: "Courtly Dances" (16th Century, Major Burchfield), "Seagulls" (Copland, Burchfield), "Danse" (Stravinsky, Vija Martinsons Cunningham), "Black Swan Pas de Deux" (Tchaikovsky, Colin Worth), "Les Patineurs" (Meyerbeer, Worth), "The Snowflakes Are Falling" (Debussy, Burchfield)
PREMIERES: "Concerto" (Saint-Saens, Colin Worth), "A Boy, a Girl and a Chair" (Sor, Eef DeKievit), "Dying Swan" (Saint-Saens, Worth), "Razzmatazz and All That Jazz!" (Walter Murphy, Major Burchfield), "Carnival of the Animals" (Saint-Saens, Burchfield/-Worth), "Les Bijoux" (Vivaldi, Burchfield), "Autumn Leaves Pas de Deux" (Gounod, Worth), "The Tango" (Unknown, Burchfield)

VIRGINIA BEACH CIVIC BALLET
Virginia Beach, Virginia

Artistic Director-Choreographer, Colin Worth; Ballet Mistress, Sylvia Worth; Wardrobe Mistress, Dona McCloud; Stage Manager, Beth Hudson; Lighting, Maynard Allen; Audio, Ursula Jones; Sets, Judith Doyle

COMPANY

SOLOISTS: Debbie Jakubec, Ann Watkins, Nancylew Guarnieri, Ann Tate, Elizabeth Hurd, Dawn Dodson
CORPS: Valerie Willson, Lisa Hunt, Dottie Watkins, Audrey Bender, Sarah Bender, Katherine Caldwell, Monique McCloud, Andrea Michalos, Debra Campbell, Dena Bailey, Casey Ivey, Cynthia Tamayo Colleen Tamayo, Cecilia Tamayo, Julian Kaplan, Ellen Hylton, Hannah Stith, Valorie Gross, Julianna Holm, Susan Denby
REPERTOIRE: "Coppelia" (Delibes, Colin Worth), "The Old Skating Pond" (Meyerbeer, Worth), "Contra Dances" (Beethoven, Worth)

Virginia Beach Ballet in "Carnival of the Animals"
(Al Zaic Photo)

VIRGINIA BEACH COMMUNITY BALLET

Virginia Beach, Virginia

Artistic Director, Virginia Biggs; Ballet Mistresses, Betty Jean Walker, Janet Smith; Sets and Stage Design, Mike Bell; Wardrobe Mistress, Kim Crosby; Press, Mal Vincent, Mary Dissen

COMPANY

Janet Smith, Jody Norris, Terri Early, Shelia Francis, Melinda Sullivan, Garnett Nielson, Julie Cruser, Cathleen Callan, Karen Addison, George Slocom, Allan Clements, John Van Auken, Scott Hollifield, Bruce White
Junior Company: Susan Mohr, Katherine Baiker, Jennifer Scott, Ruth Hickson, Darlene Stevenson
GUEST ARTISTS: David Anderson, Dorothy Fiore

REPERTOIRE

"One by Two by Three" (Poulenc, Walker), "Pas Espagnol" (Massenet, Walker), "Variation Classique" (Glazounov, Biggs), "Expectation" (Quincy Jones, Smith), "The Attic" (Kabelevsky, Walker)

Terri Early in "Reach"
(David St. Clair Photo)

WASHINGTON DANCE THEATRE

Washington, D. C.

Artistic Director-Choreographer, Erika Thimey; Stage and Lighting Director, Guy LeValley; Conductor, William J. Akers; Costumes, Dagmar Wilson, Hertha Woltersdorf; Masks and Sets, David Komuro, E. Raye LeValley

COMPANY

Camille Bacon, Phil Cole, Miriam Cramer, Ellie Grayson, Julie Houghton, Lorraine Johnson, Stephen Johnson, E. Ray LeValley, Joanne Lynch, Brick Oberholzer, Carol O'Tolle, Diana Parson, Kevin Tolson

REPERTOIRE

"Bucket of Ashes" (Vernon Edwards), "Psalm" (Joseph Ott), "Ceremony of Carols" (Britten), "Playthings of the Wind" (Cassman/Sala), "First Totem Pole" (Lohoefer), and *Premieres* of "Meditation" (Massenet), "Lamentation of Jeremiah" (Ginastera), "Candle Procession" (Bach)

Howard Millard Photo

"The Lamentations of Jeremiah"
(Washington Dance Theatre)

WESTCHESTER BALLET COMPANY

Ossining, N. Y.

Director-Choreographer, Iris Merrick; Designer, Guy Smith; Financial Director, Dorothy L. Meinel; Press, Jackie Robie; Props, Mary Anne Rodino

COMPANY

PRINCIPALS: Lenore Meinel, Rhona Kastle
CORPS: Patty Morrissy, Heather Behling, Jill Robie, Phyliss Crower, Jane Brayton, Michele Brucellaria, Lynn Hanover, Larie Beckett, Susan Kenney, Nancy Wellman
GUEST ARTISTS: Michele Cichetti, Paulo Denubila, Richardo Mercado, Michele Ceballos, Peter Humphrey, Pianist Robert Levin, Peter Schabel

REPERTOIRE

Nutcracker" (Tchaikovsky, Iris Merrick), "Suite of Schubert Dances of Isadora Duncan" (Schubert, Merrick), "Cinderella" (Prokofiev, Merrick), "Seasons" (Chausson, Merrick)
PREMIERES: "Romeo and Juliet" (Tchaikovsky), "Holiday" (Anderson), "Le Retour" (Kabelevsky), "Sleeping Beauty" (Tchaikovsky), "Caprice" (Shostakovich), "Emperor Valse" (Strauss), "Peter and the Wolf" (Prokofiev), "East of the Sun" (Grieg), "The Tailer and the Doll" (Rossini/Britten), "Cry Baby Dolls" (Kabelevsky), "Come What May" (Riisager), "Star Maiden" (McDowell), "Swan Lake Act II" (Tchaikovsky), "Secret River" (Leyden), "Giselle" (Adam), "Tarkus" (Emerson Lake and Palmer)

Lenore Meinel
(Westchester Ballet)

169

Lydia Abarca   Leo Ahonen   Carolyn Adams   Reid Anderson   Charthel Arthur

BIOGRAPHIES OF DANCERS AND CHOREOGRAPHERS

ABARCA, LYDIA. Born Jan. 8, 1951 in NYC. Studied at Fordham U., Harkness House. Debut 1968 with Dance Theatre of Harlem.

ADAIR, TOM. Born in Venus, Tex. Joined American Ballet Theatre in 1963, elevated to soloist in 1966.

ADAMS, CAROLYN. Born in N.Y.C. Aug. 16, 1943. Graduate Sarah Lawrence Col. Studied with Schonberg, Karin Waehner, Henry Danton, Wishmary Hunt, Don Farnworth. Member of Paul Taylor Co. since 1965. Director of Harlem Dance Studio.

ADAMS, DIANA. Born in Stanton, Va. Studied with Edward Caton, Agnes de Mille. Made professional debut in 1943 in "Oklahoma!" Joined Ballet Theatre in 1944. N.Y.C. Ballet 1950. Now ballet mistress-teacher at School of American Ballet. N.Y.C.

AHONEN, LEO. Born June 19, 1939 in Helsinki, Finland. Studied at Kirov Theatre. Scandinavian School of Ballet. Joined company and rose to principal. Appeared with Bolshoi Ballet. Joined National Ballet of Holland as dancer and ballet master; Royal Winnipeg Ballet 1966; San Francisco Ballet 1968. Since 1972 principal and teacher with Houston Ballet.

AIELLO, SALVATORE. Born Feb. 26, 1944 in N.Y. Attended Boston Cons. Studied with Danielian, Stanley Williams. Rosella Hightower, Professional debut with Joffrey Co. in 1964, subsequently with Donald McKayle, Pearl Lang, Patricia Wilde, Alvin Ailey, Harkness Ballet, and in Bdwy musicals. Joined Royal Winnipeg Ballet 1971. Promoted to principal 1972.

AILEY, ALVIN. Born Jan. 5, 1931 in Rogers, Tex. Attended UCLA. Studied with Lester Horton, Hanya Holm, Martha Graham, Anna Sokolow, Karel Shook, and Charles Wiedman. Debut 1950 with Lester Horton Dance Theatre, and became choreographer for company in 1953. Formed own company in 1958 and has toured U.S. and abroad. Now N.Y. City Center based.

AITKEN, GORDON. Born in Scotland in 1928. Joined Saddler's Wells Ballet in 1954. Soloist with Royal Ballet.

ALBA, MARIA. Born in China of Spanish-Irish parentage. Began studies in Russian School of Ballet, Peking. Moved to Spain, studied with Regla-Ortega, and La Quica. After professional debut in teens, became one of world's foremost Spanish dancers at 21. Toured with Iglesias Co., and Ballet Espagnol. With Ramon de los Reyes, formed company in 1964 that has toured U.S., S. America and Europe.

ALBANO, JOSEPH. Born Dec. 29, 1938 in New London, Conn. Studied with Vilzak, Legat, Bartholin, Hightower, Danielian, Graham, Weidman, and Limon. Performed with Charles Wiedman Co., Ballet Russe, Martha Graham, Joos-Leeder, N.Y.C. Ballet. Founder-artistic director-choreographer of Hartford Ballet Co., Established Albano Ballet 1971. First dancer to serve as Commissioner for Conn. Commission for the Arts.

ALBRECHT, ANGELE. Born Dec. 12, 1942 in Frieburg, Ger. Studied at Royal Ballet, and with Lula von Sachnowsky, Tatjanti Granzeva, Rosella Hightower. Debut 1960 with Ntl. Theater Mannheim; Hamburg Staatsoper 1961-7; Ballet of 20th Century from 1967.

ALDOUS, LUCETTE. Born Sept. 26, 1938 in Auckland, N.Z. Studied at Royal Ballet School. Joined Rambert, London's Festival Ballet (1963), Royal Ballet (1966), Australian Ballet (1971).

ALENIKOFF, FRANCES. Born in N.Y.C.; graduate Bklyn Col. Studied with Graham, Limon, Horton, Anthony, Sanasardo, Humphrey, Sokolow, Barashkova, Dunham, Fort, Flores. Debut 1957. Since 1959 toured with own company, and as soloist. Has choreographed Bdwy musicals.

ALEXANDER, ROD. Born Jan. 23, 1922 in Colo. Studied with Cole, Holm, Maracci, Riabouchinska, Horton, Castle. Debut with Jack Cole Dancers, then in Bdwy musicals before forming own company and becoming choreographer for Bdwy and TV.

ALLEN, JESSICA. Born Apr. 24, 1946 in Bryn Mawr, Pa. Graduate UCol., NYU. Debut 1970 with Jean Erdman Dance Theatre. Also appeared with Gus Solomons, Matt Maddox.

ALLENBY, JEAN. Born Apr. 29, 1946 in Bulawayo, Rhodesia and began training there. Debut 1966 with Cape Ballet. Joined Stuttgart in 1971 and promoted to principal.

ALONSO, ALICIA. Born Alicia Martinez, Dec. 21 in Havana; married Fernando Alonso. Studied with Federova, and Volkova, and at School of American Ballet. Made debut in musicals. Soloist with Ballet Caravan 1939-40. Ballet Theatre 1941. In 1948 formed own company in Havana. One of world's greatest ballerinas.

ALUM, MANUEL. Born in Puerto Rico in 1944. Studied with Neville Black, Sybil Shearer, Martha Graham, Mia Slavenska. Joined Paul Sanasardo Company in 1962. Has appeared with The First Chamber Dance Quartet, and American Dance Theatre 1972. Also teaches and choreographs, and formed own company 1972.

ALVAREZ, ANITA. Born in Tyrone, Pa. in 1920. Studied with Martha Graham, and appeared with her company 1936-41. Since 1941 has appeared in Bdwy musicals.

AMOCIO, AMEDEO. Born in 1942 in Milan, Italy. Studied at LaScala, and joined company, rising to soloist. Has created many ballets and choreographed musicals and films.

AMMANN, DIETER. Born Feb. 5, 1942 in Passau, Ger. Attended Essen Folkway School. Joined Stuttgart Ballet in 1965.

ANAYA, DULCE. Born in Cuba; studied with Alonso, at School of Am. Ballet; joined Ballet Theatre at 15, Ballet de Cuba where she became soloist. In 1957 was prima ballerina of Stuttgart Opera before joining Munich State Opera Ballet for 5 years, Hamburg Opera for 3. Returned to U.S. and joined Michael Maule's Dance Variations, Ballet Concerto. Founder-Director of Jacksonville (Fla.) Ballet Theatre since 1970.

ANDERSON, CAROLYN. Born Apr. 28, 1946 in Salt Lake City. Graduate Univ. Utah. Studied with Willam Christensen, Patricia Wilde, Peryoslavic, Caton, Weisburger, Danilova, Vladimiroff. Principal dancer with Ballet West before joining Pa. Ballet as soloist.

ANDERSON, REID. Born Apr. 1, 1949 in New Westminster, BC, Can. Studied with Dolores Kirkwood, and Royal Ballet School. Appeared in musicals before joining London's Royal Opera Ballet 1967, Stuttgart Ballet 1969.

ANDERSSON, GERD. Born in Stockholm June 11, 1932. Pupil of Royal Swedish Ballet, and Lilian Karina. Joined company in 1948, became ballerina in 1958.

ANDROS, DICK. Born in Oklahoma City, March 4, 1926. Trained with San Francisco Ballet, American Theatre Wing, Ballet Arts, Met Ballet, Ballet Theatre, Ballet Russe. Has appeared with San Francisco Ballet, Irene Hawthorne, Marian Lawrence, John Beggs, Eve Gentry, Greenwich Ballet, Lehigh Valley Ballet, and Dance Originals. Now teaches.

ANTONIO. Born Antonio Ruiz Soler Nov. 4, 1922 in Seville, Spain. Studied with Realito, Pericet, and Otero. Made professional debut at 7. Became internationally famous with cousin Rosario as "The Kids From Seville." Formed separate companies in 1950's, his becoming Ballets de Madrid. Made N.Y. debut in 1955 and has returned periodically.

ANTONIO, JUAN. Born May 4, 1945 in Mexico City. Studied with Xavier Francis. Am. Ballet Center, Ballet Theatre School. Made debut 1963 in Mexico with Bellas Artes, N.Y. debut 1964 with Ballet Folklorico, subsequently danced with Glen Tetley, Louis Falco, Pearl Lang, Gloria Contreras, and Jose Limon. Now associate director of Falco Co.

ANTUNEZ, OSKAR. Born Apr. 17, 1949 in Juarez, Mex. Studied with Ingeborg Heuser, and at Harkness School. Made debut with Les Grands Ballets Canadiens in 1968. Joined Harkness Ballet in 1968.

APINEE, IRENE. Born in Riga, Latvia where she began training at 11. Moved to Canada; founded school in Halifax. Became leading dancer with National Ballet of Canada, and in 1956 became member of Les Ballets Chiriaeff, now Les Grands Ballets Canadiens. Soloist with Ballet Theatre in 1959. Rejoined Les Grands Ballets in 1965.

| Dick Andros | Annette av Paul | Richard Arve | Gladys Bailin | Frank Ashley |

APONTE, CHRISTOPHER. Born May 4, 1950 in NYC. Studied at Harkness House, and made debut in 1970 with the Harkness company.

ARMIN, JEANNE. Born in Milwaukee. Aug. 4, 1943. Studied with Ann Barzel, Stone and Camryn, Ballet Russe, and in Paris with Mme. Nora. Made debut with Chicago Opera Ballet in 1958, joined Ballet Russe (1959) American Ballet Theatre (1965). Has appeared on Bdwy.

ARMITAGE, KAROLE. Born Mar. 3, 1954 in Madison, WI. Attended UUtah. With Geneva Ballet (1973–74). Joined Merce Cunningham Co. 1975.

ARMOUR, THOMAS. Born Mar. 7, 1909 in Tarpon Springs, Fla. Studied with Ines Noel Armour. Preobrajenska, Egorova. Debut with Ida Rubenstein, followed by Nijinska's company, Ballet Russe, Ballet Russe de Monte Carlo. Founder-Artistic Director Miami Ballet.

ARNOLD, BENE. Born in 1935 in Big Springs, Tex. Graduate UUtah. Trained with Willam, Harold, and Lew Christensen at San Francisco Ballet. Joined company in 1950, becoming soloist in 1952, Ballet Mistress 1960–63. Joined Ballet West as Ballet Mistress 1963.

AROVA, SONIA. Born June 20, 1927 in Sofia. Bulgaria. Studied with Preobrajenska; debut 1942 with International Ballet, subsequently appearing with Ballet Rambert, Met Opera Ballet, Petit's Ballet, Tokyo-Kamaski Ballet, Ballet Theatre, Ruth Page Ballet Co., Norwegian State Opera Ballet. Co-Director San Diego Ballet from 1971.

ARPINO, GERALD. Born on Staten Island, N.Y. Studied with Mary Ann Wells. May O'Donnell, Gertrude Shurr, and at School of American Ballet. Made debut on Bdwy in "Annie Get Your Gun." Toured with Nana Gollner, Paul Petroff Ballet Russe; became leading male dancer with Joffrey Ballet, and NYC Opera. Currently choreographer and assistant director of Joffrey Ballet and co-director of American Ballet Center.

ARTHUR, CHARTHEL. Born in Los Angeles. Oct. 8, 1946. Studied with Eva Lorraine, and at American Ballet Center. Became member of Joffrey Ballet in 1965.

ARVE, RICHARD. Born in Clemson, S.C. Studied with Graham, Cunningham, Joffrey, Hayden; soloist with Ruth Page Ballet, Chicago Opera Ballet, Flower Hujer, Phyllis Sabold, Erica Tamar, Maggie Kast. Now teaches, and director of Richard Arve Dance Trio.

ARVOLA, SOILI. Born in Finland; began ballet studies at 8; joined Finnish Ballet at 18; San Francisco Ballet 1968–72; Houston Ballet 1972–. Also choreographs and appears with Ballet Spectacular.

ASAKAWA, HITOMI. Born Oct. 13, 1938 in Kochi, Japan. Studied and made professional debut in Nishino Ballet 1957. Joined Ballet of 20th Century 1967.

ASAKAWA, TAKAKO. Born in Tokyo, Japan, Feb. 23, 1938. Studied in Japan and with Martha Graham. Has appeared with Graham Co., and with Alvin Ailey, Donald McKayle, and Pearl Lang, and a revival of "The King and I." Now member of Graham company.

ASENSIO, MANOLA. Born May 7, 1946 in Lausanne, Switz. Studied at LaScala in Milan. Danced with Grand Theatre de Geneve (1963–4), Het Nationale Ballet (1964–6), NYC Ballet (1966–8), Harkness Ballet 1969–.

ASHLEY, FRANK. Born Apr. 10, 1941 in Kingston, Jamaica. Studied with Ivy Baxter, Eddy Thomas, Neville Black, Martha Graham. Has appeared with National Dance Theatre of Jamaica, Helen McGehee, Pearl Lang, Martha Graham, Yuriko, Eleo Pomare. Also choreographs for own company and teaches.

ASHTON, FREDERICK. Born in Guayaquil, Ecuador, Sept. 17, 1906. Studied with Massine and Marie Rambert. Joined Ida Rubinstein Co. in Paris in 1927, but soon left to join Rambert's Ballet Club for which he choreographed many works, and danced. Charles Cochran engaged him to choreograph for his cabarets. In 1933 was invited to create works for the newly formed Vic Wells Co. and in 1935 joined as dancer and choreographer. Moved with company to Covent Garden, and continued creating some of world's great ballets. Was knighted in 1962; first man so honored for services to ballet. After serving as associate director of Royal Ballet, became its director with the retirement of Dame Ninette de Valois in 1963. Retired in 1970.

ASTAIRE, FRED. Born Frederick Austerlitz in Omaha, Neb. May 10, 1899. Began studying at 5; was in vaudeville with sister Adele at 7; Bdwy debut in 1916 in "Over The Top." Appeared in many musicals and films.

ATWELL, RICK. Born July 29, 1949 in St. Louis, Mo. Studied with Dokoudovsky, Mattox, Krassovska, and Wilde. Joined Harkness Ballet in 1967 after appearing in several musicals.

AUER, MICHAEL. Born May 10, 1954 in Vienna, Austria. Studied at Vienna State Ballet School, Sch. of American Ballet, with Yuri Chatal, Viki Fedine, Sonya Tyven, Duncan Noble. Member Memphis Ballet (1969–72), Yuri Chatal Co. (1972–74), North Carolina Dance Theatre (1975–76), Eliot Feld Ballet (1977).

AUGUSTYN, FRANK. Born Jan. 27, 1953 in Hamilton, Ont., Can. Studied at Ballet School of Canada. Joined Natl. Ballet of Canada in 1970, rising to principal in 1972.

av PAUL, ANNETTE. (Wiedersheim-Paul). Born Feb. 11, 1944 in Stockholm. Studied at Royal Ballet School, and made debut with Royal Opera House Ballet. Appeared with Royal Winnipeg Ballet before joining Harkness Ballet in 1966. Now principal with Les Grands Ballets Canadiens.

AYAKO. (See Uchiyama. Ayako)

BABILEE, JEAN. Born Jean Gutman Feb. 2, 1923 in Paris. Studied at School of Paris Opera. In 1945 became premier danseur in Les Ballets des Champs-Elysees. Toured with own company. Guest artist with ABT.

BAGNOLD, LISBETH. Born Oct. 10, 1947 in Bronxville, N.Y. UCLA graduate. Studied with Gloria Newman, Limon, Nikolais, Murray Louis. Joined Nikolais Dance Theatre in 1971.

BAILIN, GLADYS. Born in N.Y.C. Feb. 11, 1930. Graduate Hunter Col. Studied with Nikolais and joined his company in 1955. Has also appeared with Murray Louis and Don Redlich.

BAKER-SCOTT, SHAWNEEQUA. Born in Bronx; attended Hunter Col., CCNY. Studied with Holm, Humphrey-Wiedman, NDG, Ailey, Beatty, Holder, Clarke, Graham. Debut 1952 with Donald McKayle, subsequently with Destine, New Dance Group, Ailey, Marchant, Dancers Theatre Co., Eleo Pomare.

BALANCHINE, GEORGE. Born Georges Malitonovitch Balanchivadze in St. Petersburg, Russia on Jan. 9, 1904. Graduate Imperial School of Ballet. Debut 1915 in "Sleeping Beauty." Began choreographing while still in school. Left Russia in 1924 to tour with own company. Became associated with Diaghilev in Paris where he choreographed more than 10 works. Thence to Copenhagen as Ballet Master of Royal Dutch Ballet, then joined newly formed Russes de Monte Carlo. Formed Les Ballets in 1933 and toured Europe. Invited to establish school in N.Y., and in 1934 opened School of American Ballet, followed by American Ballet Co. Choreographed for Met (1935–8). Bdwy musicals, and for such companies as Original Ballet Russe, Sadler's Wells Theatre Ballet, Ballet Russe de Monte Carlo, Ballet Theatre, and Ballet Society. Formed NYC Ballet which premiered in 1948, and won international acclaim under his direction and with his brilliant choreography.

BALLARD, MICHAEL. Born July 17, 1942 in Denver, Colo. Studied with Nikolais and Louis and made professional debut with Alwin Nikolais Co. in 1966. Joined Murray Louis Co. in 1968.

BALOUGH, BUDDY. Born in 1953 in Seattle, Wash. where he began studying at 9. Trained at ABT School, and in 1970 joined Am. Ballet Theatre, rising to soloist in 1973. Also joined Ballet of Contemporary Art in 1973, for which he choreographs.

BANKS, GERALD. Born Feb. 4 in NYC. Attended CCNY, American Ballet Center. Joined Dance Theatre of Harlem 1969.

BARANOVA, IRINA. Born in Petrograd, Russia in 1919. Studied with Olga Preobrajenska. Soloist with Opera; Ballet Russe 1932–40; ballerina with Ballet Theatre 1941–2. More recently has been appearing in plays and musicals, and teaching at Royal Academy.

BARI, TANIA. (formerly Bartha Treure). Born July 5, 1936 in Rotterdam. Studied with Netty Van Der Valk, Nora Kiss, Asaf Messerer. Joined Bejart's Ballet in 1955; principal from 1959.

BARKER, JOHN. Born in Oak Park, Ill., Nov. 20, 1929. Studied at Chicago U., and with Bentley Stone, Walter Camryn, Margaret Craske, Antony Tudor, Pierre Vladimiroff, Anatole Oboukoff, Valentina Perevaslavic, and Maria Nevelska. Made professional debut with Page-Stone Camryn Co. in 1951. Has appeared with Chicago Opera Ballet, Juilliard Dance Theatre, and Jose Limon Co.

BARNARD, SCOTT. Born Oct. 17, 1945 in Indianapolis, Ind. Graduate Butler U. Studied with Perry Bronson, Robert Joffrey, Gerald Arpino, Richard Englund, Hector Zaraspy. Debut 1963 with St. Louis Opera. Joined Joffrey Ballet in 1968, and now its ballet master.

BARNES, NERISSA. Born Feb. 2, 1952 in Columbus, Ga. Attended UIll. Debut 1969 with Julian Swain Inner City Dance Co. Joined Alvin Ailey company in 1972.

BARNETT, DARRELL. Born Sept. 24, 1949 in Miami, Okla. Attended Okla U. Studied with Mary Price, Ethel Winter, Betty Jones, Martha Graham. Debut in 1970 with Ethel Winter, subsequently with Yuriko, Mary Anthony, Pearl Lang, Erick Hawkins, Richard Gain, Kazuko Hirabayashi. Joined Harkness Ballet in 1971. Made soloist 1973.

BARNETT, ROBERT. Born May 6, 1925 in Okanogan, Wash. Studied with Nijinska, Egoroba, Preobrajinska, and at School of American Ballet. Made debut with Original Ballet Russe; joined NYC Ballet in 1950; Atlanta Ballet in 1958, and its director from 1963. Choreographs, and teaches.

BARREAU, PIERRE R. Born Aug. 30, 1952 in Haiti, WI. Graduate Juilliard School of Dance. With Allnations Co. (1972–74), Rush Dance Co. (1974–75), Raymond Johnson Dance Co. (1975–76), Contemporary Dance System (1975–), ChoreoMutation (1975–), Janet Soares Dance Co. (1975–).

BARREDO, MANIYA. Born Nov. 19, 1952 in Manila, PI. Attended St. Paul Col., American Ballet Center. Debut 1965 with Philippine Hariraya Dance Co. Joined Joffrey Ballet 1972.

BARTA, KAROLY. Born Aug. 5, 1936 in Bekescsaba, Hungary. Debut there at 11 with folk ensemble. Studied at Hungarian State Ballet Inst.; performed with Budapest opera and ballet. First choreographic work at 15. Joined Hungarian National Folk Ensemble before emigrating to U.S. in 1957. Attended Met Opera Ballet, and Stone-Camryn School. Joined Chicago Opera Ballet, and continued to choreograph for various groups. Co-founder of Hungarian Ballets Bihari, Barta Ballet Co., was teacher-director for Birmingham Civic Ballet, and now operates his own school in Washington, D.C.

BARYSHNIKOV, MIKHAIL. Born Jan. 27, 1948 in Riga, Latvia. Began training at Latvian Opera Ballet School. Moved to Kirov school and joined company at 18 as soloist. Was guest artist with Bolshoi Ballet in Toronto, Can., when he defected in 1974. Has appeared with ABT, Australian Ballet, Hamburg, Paris Opera, Eliot Feld Ballet.

BATES, JAMES. Born Feb. 8, 1949 in Dallas, Tex. Studied with Moreno, Nault, Danilova, Fallis, and Harkarvy. Joined Les Grands Ballets Canadiens in 1968.

BAUMAN, ART. Born in Washington, D.C. Studied at Juilliard, Met, and Martha Graham schools. Has danced with Lucas Hoving, Paul Sanasardo, Charles Weidman. Has choreographed numerous works and teaches. Is asst. director of DTW.

BAYS, FRANK. Born June 6, 1943 in Bristol, Va. Attended King Col. Studied with Perry Brunson, and at Am. Ballet Center. Debut with American Festival Ballet 1964; joined Joffrey Ballet 1965; First Chamber Dance Co. 1972.

BEALS, MARGARET. Born Mar. 5, 1943 in Boston. Studied with Mattox, Graham, Sanasardo, Slavenska. Has appeared in musicals, and with Valerie Bettis, Jean Erdman, Pearl Lang, Jose Limon, and Paul Sanasardo. Also choreographs, and performs in concert.

BEATTY, TALLEY. Made professional debut in Bdwy musicals. Joined Ballet Society in 1947. Has more recently toured, given solo performances, formed own company, choreographs, and teaches.

BECKER, BRUCE. Born May 28, 1944 in NYC. Graduate Utah State U. Studied at O'Donnell-Shurr, Graham, and Don Farnworth studios. Debut 1961 with Norman Walker, subsequently on Bdwy, with Tamiris-Nagrin, Limon, O'Donnell; joined Batsheva in 1969. Now performs with Jane Kosminsky.

BECKLEY, CHRISTINE. Born Mar. 16, 1939 in Stanmore, Eng. Studied at Royal Ballet School, joined company and advanced to solo artist.

BEJART, MAURICE. Born Jan. 1, 1927 in Marseilles, France. Studied at Opera Ballet School, and with Leo Staats. Danced with Opera Ballet until 1945; Ballets de Roland Petit (1947–49); International Ballet (1949–50); Royal Swedish Ballet (1951–2). In 1954 organized Les Ballets de l'Etoile and debuted as choreographer. Company became Ballet Theatre de Maurice Bejart. In 1959 appointed director of Theatre Royale de la Monnaie, Brussels, and its name was changed to Ballet of the 20th Century.

BELHUMEUR, CHANTAL. Born Mar. 20, 1949 in Montreal, Can. Studied with Graham, Les Grands Ballets Canadiens and became member 1965; joined Eleo Pomare in 1971.

BELIN, ALEXANDRE. Born Apr. 3, 1948 in Mulhouse, France. Made debut in 1966 with Les Grands Ballets Canadiens, promoted to principal.

BENJAMIN, FRED. Born Sept. 8, 1944 in Boston. Studied with Elma Lewis, ABT, Claude Thompson, Talley Beatty. Has danced in musicals, with Boston Ballet, and Talley Beatty Co. Also teaches and choreographs.

BENJAMIN, JOEL. Born Feb. 21, 1949 in NYC. Attended Juilliard, Columbia; studied with Alwin Nikolais, Martha Graham, and at American Ballet Center. Made debut in Paris in 1963. Formed own company in 1963. Director American Chamber Ballet.

BENNETT, CHARLES. Born Apr. 8, 1934 in Wheaton, Ill. Studied with Bentley Stone, made debut with Ruth Page's Ballet before joining American Ballet Theatre. Member of NYC Ballet before formation of First Chamber Dance Quartet, now First Chamber Dance Co.

BENNETT, MICHAEL. Born in 1943 in Buffalo, NY. Made Bdwy debut as dancer in 1961, and as choreographer in 1966.

BENTLEY, MURIEL. Born in NYC. Studied with Tomaroff, Tarasoff, Swoboda, Fokine, Ruth St. Denis, Dolin and at Met Opera School. Made debut with Ruth St. Denis in 1931. Has appeared with Jose Greco 1936–7, at Met 1938–9; joined Ballet Theatre in 1940. Has since danced with Jerome Robbins' Ballets: U.S.A.

BERG, BERND. Born Nov. 20, 1943 in East Prussia. Began training at 11 in Leipzig. Joined Stuttgart Ballet in 1964; became soloist in 1967.

BERG, HENRY. Born in Chicago, Apr. 4, 1938. Studied with DeRea, Morrelli, Lew Christensen. Made professional debut with Ballet Alicia Alonso in 1958, subsequently joining San Francisco Ballet (1962), and Joffrey Ballet (1967).

BERGSMA, DEANNE. Born Apr. 16, 1941 in South Africa. Studied with Royal Ballet and joined company in 1958. Became soloist in 1962, principal in 1967.

BERIOSOVA, SVETLANA. Born Sept. 24, 1932 in Lithuania. Came to U.S. in 1940; studied at Vilzak-Shollar School. Debut with Ottawa Ballet Co. in 1947. Appeared with Grand Ballet de Monte Carlo 1947; Met Opera 1948; Sadler's Wells 1950, and became ballerina in 1954 with Royal Ballet.

BERNAL, CHRISTINE. Born Nov. 3, 1945 in San Francisco. Graduate USan Diego. Studied with Lew Christensen, Elaine Thomas, Maggie Black. Joined San Francisco Ballet 1960, promoted to soloist; Pennsylvania Ballet 1973. Appears as guest artist for many companies.

BERTRAM, VICTORIA. Born Feb. 26, 1946 in Toronto, Can. Studied at National Ballet School and joined National Ballet of Canada in 1963. Promoted to soloist.

BESWICK, BOB. Born Nov. 11, 1945 in San Francisco. Studied with Cunningham, Sokolow, Waring, Louis, Bailin, Nikolais. Made debut in 1967 with Utah Repertory Dance Theatre, subsequently with Nikolais Co. Choreographer and teacher.

BETHEL, PEPSI. Born in Greensboro, NC. Attended Adelphi Col. Toured Africa and performed during 1969–70. Since 1971 has been artistic director-choreographer for Pepsi Bethel Authentic Jazz Dance Theatre.

BETTIS, VALERIE. Born in 1920 in Houston, Tex. Studied with Hanya Holm. Debut with Miss Holm's company in 1937, and as choreographer in 1941. Subsequently appeared as dancer-choreographer for several Bdwy productions, and own company that toured U.S. and abroad. Teaches in NYC.

BEWLEY, LOIS. Born in Louisville, Ky. Studied with Lilias Courtney. Made debut with Ballet Russe de Monte Carlo; subsequently with ABT, Ballets U.S.A., NYC Ballet.

BHASKAR. Born Bhaskar Roy Chowdhury in Madras, India, Feb. 11, 1930. Studied with G. Ellappa. Made debut in Madras in 1949 as concert dancer with own company which he brought to NYC in 1956. As dancer and/or choreographer, has appeared on Bdwy, and internationally.

BIEVER, KATHRYN. Born May 9, 1942 in Bryn Mawr, Pa. Studied in Ballet Russe School, Pa. Ballet School. Made debut in 1961 with American Festival Ballet before joining Pennsylvania Ballet. Joined Les Grands Ballets Canadiens 1972.

BILES, RICHARD. Born in Salem, Ore. Attended Ill. Inst. Tech., UWisc. Joined Dance Repertory Theater. With Nikolais Dance Theatre 1970–71. Formed own company with which he tours. Also teaches.

| Darrell Barnett | Lois Bewley | Pepsi Bethel | Karen Brown | Robert Brassel |

BIRCH, PATRICIA. Born in Englewood, N.J. Studied at School of Am. Ballet, Cunningham, and Graham schools. Made debut with Graham company. Has appeared in concert, on Bdwy, and with Donald Saddler, Valerie Bettis. Also choreographs.

BJORNSSON, FREDBJORN. Born in Copenhagen in 1926. Entered Royal Danish Ballet school 1935; graduated into company and became soloist in 1949; became one of great leading mimes and exponent of Bournonville style.

BLACKSTONE, JUDITH. Born May 10, 1947 in Iowa City, Iowa. Studied with Donya Feuer, Paul Sanasardo, Mia Slavenska, Karoly Zsedenyi. Debut with Sanasardo Co. in 1958.

BLANKSHINE, ROBERT. Born Dec. 22, 1948 in Syracuse, N.Y. Studied at American School of Ballet. Professional debut in 1965 with Joffrey Ballet which he left in 1968. Joined Berlin Opera Ballet in 1970.

BOARDMAN, DIANE. Born Jan. 17, 1949 in NYC. Bklyn. Col. graduate. Began training at 6, studying with Murray Louis, James Truitte, Wilson Morelli, and John Medicros. Has appeared with Murray Louis, Alwin Nikolais, Phyllis Lamhut companies. Also teaches and choreographs.

BOLENDER, TODD. Born in Canton, O. in 1919. Studied with Chester Hale, Vilzak, and at School of American Ballet. Soloist with Ballet Caravan in 1937, Littlefield Ballet in 1941; founder-director of American Concert Ballet in 1943; joined Ballet Theatre in 1944, Ballet Russe de Monte Carlo in 1945. First choreography in 1943. Became dancer-choreographer for Ballet Society, and has continued to choreograph for various companies; was director of Cologne and Frankfurt Opera Ballets.

BONNEFOUS, JEAN-PIERRE. Born Apr. 25, 1943 in Paris. Attended Paris Opera School of Dance. Made debut in 1964 with Opera Ballet and became premier danseur. Appeared with companies in Frankfort, Moscow, Milan, Berlin, Oslo, Toronto before joining NYC Ballet in 1970 as a principal.

BORIS, RUTHANNA. Born in 1918 in Brooklyn. Studied at Met Opera School, with Helene Veola, and Fokine. Member of American Ballet in 1935, Met soloist in 1936, and premiere danseuse 1939–43. Joined Ballet Russe de Monte Carlo in 1943. Has choreographed a number of works. Now teaches.

BORTOLUZZI, PAOLO. Born May 17, 1938 in Genoa, Italy. Debut 1958 with Italian Ballet. Joined Bejart Ballet in 1960, rising to principal dancer. Joined ABT in 1972 as principal.

BOUTILIER, JOY. Born in Chicago, Sept. 30, 1939. Graduate of U. Chicago. Studied at Henry St. Playhouse, and with Angelina Romett. Debut with Nikolais in 1964, subsequently with Mimi Garrard, Phyllis Lamhut, and Murray Louis. Has choreographed and appeared in own concerts.

BOWMAN, PATRICIA. Born in Washington, D.C. Studied with Fokine, Mordkin, Legat, Egorova, and Wallman. Ballerina at Roxy and Radio City Music Hall, with Mordkin Ballet in 1939, Ballet Theatre in 1940, and appeared with Chicago Opera, Fokine Ballet, and in musicals and operettas. Now teaches.

BRADLEY, LISA. Born in Elizabeth, N.J. in 1941. Studied at Newark Ballet Academy, American Ballet Center, and with Joyce Trisler. Appeared with Garden State Ballet before joining Joffrey Ballet in 1961. Invited to study classic roles with Ulanova. Joined First Chamber Dance Co. in 1969; Hartford Ballet 1972 where she also teaches. Returned to Joffrey 1976.

BRASSEL, ROBERT. Born Nov. 3, in Chicago. Attended Ind. U., American Ballet Center. Trained with Robert Joffrey, Hector Zaraspe, Lillian Morre. Joined Joffrey Ballet in 1965, ABT in 1968. 1976 principal with Royal Ballet de Wallonie in Belgium.

BREUER, PETER. Born in Tegernsee, Ger. Joined Munich Opera Ballet in 1961, Dusseldorf Ballet in 1965 as soloist. Has appeared with many companies as guest artist, including ABT 1976.

BRIANSKY, OLEG. Born in Brussels Nov. 9, 1929. Studied with Katchourovsky, Gsovsky, Volkova. Joined Les Ballets des Champs-Elysees; became lead dancer in 1946. Subsequently with Ballets de Paris, London Festival Ballet, Chicago Opera Ballet. Formed own company, and teaches.

BRIANT, ROGER. Born May 4, 1944 in Yonkers, N.Y. Studied at Joffrey Center, Martha Graham Studio, O'Donnell-Shurr Studio. Has appeared on Bdwy, and with Martha Graham, Glen Tetley, Donald McKayle, Norman Walker companies.

BROCK, KARENA. Born Sept. 21, 1942 in Los Angeles. Studied with Lanova, Lichine, Riabouchinska, DuBoulay, and Branitzska. Danced with Natl. Ballet of Netherlands before joining American Ballet Theatre in 1963. Became soloist in 1968, principal 1973. Has appeared in musicals and films.

BROOKS, ROMAN. Born July 5, 1950 in Millington, Tenn. Attended Harbor-Compton Jr. Col. Studied with Eugene Loring. Joined Dance Theatre of Harlem 1973.

BROWN, CAROLYN. Born in Fitchburg, Mass. in 1927. Graduate of Wheaton College. Studied with Marion Rice, Margaret Craske, Antony Tudor and Merce Cunningham. Professional debut with Cunningham in 1953 and appeared in almost entire repertoire of the company in roles she created. Left company in 1973 to choreograph.

BROWN, KAREN. Born Oct. 6, 1955 in Okmulgee, OK. Studied at American Ballet Center. Joined Dance Theatre of Harlem in 1973.

BROWN, KELLY. Born Sept. 24, 1928 in Jackson, Miss. Studied with Bentley Stone, Walter Camryn. Made professional debut with Chicago Civic Opera Ballet in 1946; soloist with Ballet Theatre (1949–1953). Has since appeared in films, musicals, and on TV.

BROWN, LAURA. Born Sept. 1, 1955 in San Francisco, Cal. Studied at Ballet Celeste, San Francisco Ballet. Joined Dance Theatre of Harlem 1972.

BROWN, SANDRA. Born Jan. 6, 1946 in Ft. Wayne, Ind. Studied with Tudor, Craske, Graham, Limon. Made Debut in Juilliard concert in 1967, subsequently dancing with DTW, James Clouser, James Waring, and Lucas Hoving.

BROWNE, LESLIE. Born in 1957 in Phoenix, AR. Graduate School of American Ballet. Joined ABT soloist 1976.

BRUHN, ERIK. Born Oct. 3, 1928 in Copenhagen. Attended Academie of Royal Danish Theatre, and received training with Royal Danish Ballet with which he made his debut in 1947. Became its leading male dancer, and has appeared on tour with the company, and as guest soloist with all leading companies throughout the world. For brief period was a principal dancer with American Ballet Theatre, and a permanent guest artist. Is considered one of world's greatest classical dancers. Appointed Director of Ballet of Royal Swedish Opera in 1967. Retired in 1972. Resident Producer National Ballet of Canada 1973.

BRYANT, HOMER. Born Mar. 29, 1951 in St. Thomas, VI. Attended Adelphi U. Debut 1970 with Manhattan Festival Ballet; Joined Dance Theatre of Harlem 1973.

BUCHTRUP, BJARNE. Born Aug. 11, 1942 in Copenhagen. Studied with Birger Bartholin. Leon Danielian. Appeared in musicals before joining West Berlin Ballet Co. in 1963. Danced with Manhattan Festival Ballet (1965–66) and joined American Ballet Theatre in 1967.

BUGLISI, JACQULYN. Born Feb. 19, 1951 in NYC. Attended HS of Performing Arts, Martha Graham School. Has appeared with Teatro Danza, Pearl Lang, Mary Anthony, Manuel Alum, Joyce Trisler, Martha Graham (1977).

BUIRGE, SUSAN. Born in Minneapolis, June 19, 1940. Graduate of U. Minn. Studied at Juilliard, Henry St. Playhouse, Conn. College. Made professional debut with Nikolais Co. in 1964. Has also appeared with Murray Louis, Mimi Garrard, Bill Frank, Juilliard Dance Ensemble, and Jose Limon. Also choreographs, and teaches.

BUJONES, FERNANDO. Born Mar. 9, 1955 in Miami, Fla. Attended Cuban Ntl. Ballet School, School of American Ballet, Juilliard. Debut 1970 with Eglevsky Ballet, followed by Ballet Spectacular 1971–2, American Ballet Theatre 1972. Raised to soloist 1973.

BURKE, DERMOT. Born Jan. 8, 1948 in Dublin, Ire. Studied at Royal School of Dance. Appeared with Royal Concert Group before joining Joffrey Company in 1966, National Ballet 1972. Rejoined Joffrey 1976.

BURNS, LOUISE. Born June 14, 1949 in Florida. Attended UHawaii; Studied with Merce Cunningham, Viola Farber, Betty Jones, Peter Saul. Danced with Merce Cunningham (1970, 1976–), Mel Wong 1976.

BURR, MARILYN. Born Nov. 20, 1933 in New South Wales. Studied at Australian Ballet School; made debut with Ntl. Ballet Co. in 1948. Joined London Festival Ballet in 1953 as soloist; became ballerina in 1955. Joined Hamburg State Opera Co. in 1963. Had danced with Natl. Ballet of Wash.

BUSHLING, JILISE. Born in 1957 in Santa Monica, Ca. Studied at American Ballet Theatre School, Sch. of Am. Ballet. Made debut in 1972 with Joffrey II Co. Joined NYCB in 1974.

BUSSEY, RAYMOND. Born Mar. 8, 1946 in Pawtucket, R. I. Studied with Perry Brunson, Tupine, and at Joffrey School. Made professional debut with American Festival Ballet in 1962. Joined Joffrey Company in 1964.

BUSTILLO, ZELMA. Born in Cartagena, Columbia, but came to N.Y.C. at 6. Graduate HS Performing Arts. Appeared with Thalia Mara's Ballet Repertory, at Radio City Music Hall, with American Festival Ballet, Joffrey Ballet Co. (1965), National Ballet (1970).

BUTLER, JOHN. Born in Memphis, Tenn., Sept. 29, 1920. Studied with Martha Graham and at American School of Ballet. Made debut with Graham company in 1947. Appeared in Bdwy musicals before becoming choreographer. Formed own company with which he toured.

CAL, SERGIO. Born Aug. 26, 1951 in Cuba. Studied at Joffrey School, N. Carolina Sch. of Arts, Harkness Sch. Debut 1972 with Harkness Ballet, subsequently with Ballet Rep. Co., Alvin Ailey company (1975–).

CALDWELL, BRUCE. Born Aug. 25, 1950 in Salt Lake City, U. Studied with Bene Arnold, Willam Christensen at UUtah. Joined Ballet West in 1967; became principal in 1973.

CALZADA, ALBA. Born Jan. 28, 1947 in Puerto Rico. UPR graduate. Studied in San Juan and made debut with San Juan Ballet in 1964. Was guest with Eglevsky and Miami Ballets before joining Pa. Ballet. in 1968. Now a principal.

CAMMACK, RICHARD L. Born Oct. 24, 1945 in Knoxville, Tenn. Graduate Butler U. Studied at Harkness House, American Ballet Theatre School. Joined ABT in 1969.

CAMPANERIA, MIGUEL. Born Feb. 5, 1951 in Havana, Cuba. Studied at Ntl. Ballet of Cuba, and made debut with company in 1968. Joined Harkness Ballet and became soloist in 1973.

CAMPBELL, SYLVESTER. Born in Oklahoma. Joined NY Negro Ballet 1956, and subsequently Het Netherlands Ballet 1960, Ballet of 20th Century, Royal Winnipeg Ballet 1972.

CAMRYN, WALTER. Born in Helena, Mont, in 1903. Studied with Bolm, Maximova, Swoboda, Novikoff, and Muriel Stuart. Appeared with Chicago Civic Opera Ballet. Page-Stone Ballet, and Federal Theatre as premier danseur and choreographer. Teacher at Stone-Camryn School, Chicago. Has choreographed more than 20 ballets.

CANDELARIA, SANSON. Born July 13, 1947 in Albuquerque, NMex. Joined Les Grands Ballets Canadiens 1965, Lisbon's Gulbenkian Ballet 1969, American Classical Ballet 1971, Boston Ballet 1972.

CARAS, STEPHEN. Born Oct. 25, 1950 in Englewood, N.J. Studied at American Ballet Center, School of American Ballet. Made debut in 1967 with Irene Fokine Co. Joined N.Y.C. Ballet in 1969.

CARLSON, CAROLYN. Born in Oakland, Calif., Mar. 7, 1943. Graduate U. Utah. Studied at San Francisco Ballet School, and Henry St. Playhouse. Professional debut in 1965 with Nikolais Co. Has also appeared with Murray Louis, and in New Choreographers Concert.

CARROLL, ELISABETH. Born Jan. 19, 1937 in Paris. Studied with Sedova, Besobrasova. Made debut in 1952 with Monte Carlo Opera Ballet; joined Ballet Theatre in 1954, Joffrey Ballet in 1962, and Harkness Ballet in 1964.

CARTER, RICHARD. Became principal male dancer of San Francisco Ballet in 1958. With wife, Nancy Johnson, performed in more than fifty countries. Was director and premier danseur of the San Diego Ballet Co. for which he created 14 ballets. Now with San Francisco Ballet.

CARTER, WILLIAM. Born in 1936 in Durant, Okla. Studied with Coralane Duane, Carmalita Maracci. Joined American Ballet Theatre in 1957, N.Y.C. Ballet in 1959. Helped to organize and appeared since 1961 with First Chamber Dance Co. Joined Martha Graham Co. 1972, ABT 1972. Promoted to principal 1977.

CARTIER, DIANA. Born July 23, 1939 in Philadelphia, Pa. Studied with Tudor, Doubrouska, Balanchine, Joffrey, Griffith, and Brunson, Debut 1960 with Met Opera Ballet, subsequently with John Butler, N.Y.C. Opera Ballet, Zachary Solov, and Joffrey Ballet since 1961. Joffrey ballet mistress.

CASEY, SUSAN. Born in April 1949 in Buffalo, N.Y. Studied at Ballet Russe, and Harkness Schools, and with Kravina, Danielian, Shollar, Vilzak, and Volkova. Joined American Ballet Theatre in 1965; became its youngest soloist in 1969.

CASTELLI, VICTOR. Born Oct. 9, 1952 in Montclair, N.J. Studied at Newark Ballet Acad., School of American Ballet. Appeared with Garden State Ballet, and Eglevsky Ballet before joining NYC Ballet in 1971.

CATANZARO, TONY. Born Nov. 10, 1974 in Bklyn. Studied with Norman Walker, Sanasardo, Danielian, Lillian Moore, Lang, Joffrey, Jaime Rogers. Debut 1968 in musicals, subsequently appearing with Norman Walker, Harkness Youth Ballet, N.J. Ballet, Boston Ballet; joined Joffrey in 1971. Returned to Boston Ballet 1973. Joined Dancers 1977.

CATON, EDWARD. Born in St. Petersburg, Russia. Apr. 3, 1900 Studied at Melidova's Ballet School, Moscow, and made professional debut in 1914. Joined Max Terptzt Co. (1918), Ourkransky-Pavley Co. (1919), Pavlova (1924), Chicago Opera Ballet (1926), American Ballet (1934), Catherine Littlefield (1935), Mikhail Mordkin (1938), Ballet Theatre (1940), retired in 1942 to teach and choreograph.

CAVRELL, HOLLY. Born Sept. 2, 1955 in NYC. Attended Hunter Col., studied with Pearl Lang, Patsy Birch, Rod Rodgers, Alwin Nikolais, American Dance Center, Debut 1972 with Ballet Players; Joined Martha Graham Co. 1973.

CEBRON, JEAN. Born in Paris in 1938. Made debut in 1956 in London. Joined Joos Folkwangballet. Tours world in concert.

CESBRON, JACQUES. Born May 10, 1940 in Angers, France. Studied at Paris Opera Ballet School, and joined company in 1958. Member of Harkness Ballet before becoming soloist with Pennsylvania Ballet in 1966. Left in 1969.

CHAIB, ELIE. Born July 18, 1950 in Beirut, Lebanon. Began studies in Beirut in 1966. Made debut 1969 as soloist with Beirut Dance Ensemble. Came to U.S. in 1970; appeared in Joffrey's "Petrouchka," Chamber Dance Ensemble before joining Paul Taylor Co. 1973.

CHAMBERLIN, BETTY. Born Nov. 10, 1949 in Madison, Wisc. Studied with Armour, LaVerne, Nault, Skibine, and at ABT. Joined American Ballet Theatre in 1969.

CHAMPION, GOWER. Born in Geneva, Ill., June 22, 1920. After appearing in vaudeville, night clubs, and on Bdwy, made debut as choreographer for "Lend An Ear" in 1946. Is now in great demand as choreographer and director of musicals, and films.

CHAPLINE, CLAUDIA. Born May 23, 1930 in Oak Park, Ill. Graduate George Washington U. Studied with Davis, Weidman, Hoving, Humphrey, Horst, Nikolais, Deitz, Limon, Graham, Cassan, Maracci, Rousellat. Debut 1948 with Evelyn Davis Co.; subsequently with Doris Humphrey, Gloria Newman, Instant Theatre, and in 1973 formed IDEA Co. for which she directs and choreographs.

CHARLIP, REMY. Born Jan. 10, 1929 in Brooklyn, NY. Attended Cooper Union, Reed Col. Studied at New Dance Group, with Merce Cunningham, Jean Erdman. Appeared with Cunningham for 11 years. Now choreographs.

CHASE, DAVID. Born June 18, 1948 in Mill Valley, Cal. Graduate URochester. Studied with Walter Nicks, Karl Shook, Graham School, Joffrey School, Nadia Potts, Norbert Vesak. Debut 1971 with Norbert Vesak, subsequently with Walter Nicks Co., Kazuko Hirabayashi; joined Martha Graham Co. 1972.

CHASE, LUCIA. Born March 24, 1907 in Waterbury, Conn. Studied at Theatre Guild School, and with Mikhail Mordkin. Became member of his company and danced title role in "Giselle" in 1937. Was principal dancer with Ballet Theatre when it was founded in 1939. In 1945 became co-director with Oliver Smith of American Ballet Theatre. In recent years has appeared only with her company in "Fall River Legend." "Swan Lake," and "Las Hermanas."

CHAUVIRE, YVETTE. Born Apr. 22, 1917 in Paris. Studied at Paris Opera School. Appeared with Paris Opera Ballet, London Festival Ballet, Royal Ballet (1959). In 1963 appointed director of Paris Opera Ballet School.

CHING, CHIANG. Born Jan. 26, 1946 in Peking, China. Graduate Peking School of Dance. Producer-Director of Great Wall Dancers of San Francisco. Also teaches and choreographs.

CHIRIAEFF, LUDMILLA. Born in 1924 in Latvia. Began training at early age in Berlin with Alexandra Nicolaieva. Joined de Basil's Ballets Russe, was soloist with Berlin Opera Ballet, and prima ballerina at Lausanne Municipal Theatre. Opened own academy in Geneva and choreographed for Ballet des Arts, Geneva. Moved to Canada in 1952 and organized own company, ultimately leading to her being founder and artistic director of Les Grands Ballets Canadiens.

CHOUTEAU, YVONNE. Born in Ft. Worth, Tex. in 1929. Studied with Asher, Perkins, Vestoff, Belcher, Bolm, at Vilzak-Shollar School of American Ballet. Made debut as child in American Indian dance company at Chicago's 1933 Fair. Joined Ballet Russe de Monte Carlo in 1943. Now teaches, makes guest appearances, and is Co-Director of Okla. Civic Ballet.

CHRISTENSEN, HAROLD. Born Dec. 24 in Brigham City, Utah. Studied with Balanchine. Appeared with Met Opera Ballet (1934), Ballet Caravan, San Francisco Opera Ballet, San Francisco Ballet. Retired to teach and direct San Francisco Ballet School.

Sanson Candelaria   Alba Calzada   Gary Chryst   Francesca Corkle   Winthrop Corey

CHRISTENSEN, LEW. Born May 9, 1906 in Brigham City, Utah. Studied with uncle Lars Christensen at American School of Ballet. Performer and choreographer since 1934, on Bdwy, for Met Opera, Ballet Caravan, American Ballet Co., and N.Y.C. Ballet. In 1938, with brothers Harold and Willam, founded San Francisco Ballet; has been general director since 1951.

CHRISTENSEN, WILLAM. Born Aug. 27, 1902 in Brigham City, Utah. Studied with uncle Lars Christensen, Nescagno, Novikoff, and Fokine. Made debut with Small Ballet Quartet in 1927, subsequently becoming choreographer, ballet master, director and teacher. With brothers Harold and Lew, formed San Francisco Ballet which he directed until 1951 when he established School of Ballet at U. of Utah. Is director-choreographer for Utah Civic Ballet which he organized in 1952, now Ballet West.

CHRISTOPHER, ROBERT. (formerly Robert Hall). Born Mar. 22, 1942 in Marion, Md. Studied with Harry Asmus, Vincenzo Celli, Celo Quitman. Made debut in 1960 with National Ballet of Venezuela; subsequently with Stuttgart Ballet, ABT, Anne Wilson, Valerie Bettis, Sophie Maslow; soloist and ballet master for Garden State Ballet, and appears with Downtown Ballet.

CHRYST, GARY. Born in LaJolla, Calif. Studied with Walker, Hoving, Limon, Jaime Rogers, Nina Popova, ABC. Debut at 16 with Norman Walker, subsequently with McKayle, Washington Ballet, N.Y.C. Opera, before joining Joffrey Ballet in 1968.

CLARE, NATALIA. Born in Hollywood, Calif. Studied with Nijinska, Egorova; joined de Basil's Ballet Russe, then Markova-Dolin Co., Ballet Russe de Monte Carlo. In 1956, established school in North Hollywood, and founded Ballet Jeunesse for which she is artistic director and choreographer.

CLARKE, THATCHER. Born Apr. 1, 1937 in Springfield, Ohio. Made professional debut with Met Opera Ballet in 1954, subsequently joined Ballet de Cuba, Ballet Russe de Monte Carlo, San Francisco Ballet, and American Ballet Theatre. Has appeared in several musicals.

CLAUSS, HEINZ. Born Feb. 17, 1935 in Stuttgart. Studied at Stuttgart Ballet School, and with Balanchine. Joined Stuttgart Ballet in 1967 after appearing with Zurich Opera Ballet, and in Hamburg.

CLEAR, IVY. Born in Camden, Maine, Mar. 11, 1948. Studied at Professional Children's School of Dance and School of American Ballet. Made professional debut in 1963 with N.Y.C. Ballet. Soloist with Joffrey Ballet from 1965 to 1969.

CLIFFORD, JOHN. Born June 12, 1947 in Hollywood. Studied at American School of Dance and School of American Ballet. Appeared with Ballet of Guatemala and Western Ballet before joining N.Y. City Ballet in 1966. Soloist since 1969. Choreographed 7 works for the company, in addition to works for other companies. Left in 1974 to become artistic director-choreographer for Los Angeles Ballet.

CLOUSER, JAMES. Born in 1935 in Rochester, N.Y. Studied at Eastman School of Music, Ballet Theatre School. Joined ABT in 1957, Royal Winnipeg Ballet in 1958, rising to leading dancer in 1959, subsequently choreographed, composed and designed for it, and became ballet master and assistant director. Has appeared in concert, taught, and tours with wife Sonja Zarek. Ballet master for Houston Ballet.

COCKERILLE, LILI. Born in Washington, D.C. Studied at Fokine School, Wash. School of Ballet and School of American Ballet. Made professional debut with N.Y.C. Ballet in 1963, joined Harkness Ballet in 1964, Joffrey Co. in 1969.

COFFMAN, VERNON. Born Dec. 5, 1947 in Tucson, Ariz. Studied with Lew and Harold Christensen. Made professional debut with San Francisco Ballet in 1964. Joined Joffrey Ballet in 1966, and American Ballet Theatre in 1967.

COHAN, ROBERT. Born in N.Y.C. in 1925. Soloist with Martha Graham Co. Opened own school in Boston, joined faculty of Harvard's Drama Center, made solo tours here and abroad, taught in Israel and choreographed for Batsheva Co. Now director of London Contemporary Dance Theatre.

COHEN, ZE'EVA. Born Aug. 15, 1940 in Israel. Studied at Juilliard, and appeared with its Dance Ensemble. Joined Anna Sokolow Co. 1961, subsequently with Pearl Lang, and in solo concerts. Choreographs and teaches.

COLEMAN, LILLIAN. Born Nov. 21, 1949 in N.Y.C. Attended SUNY, Harkness School. Made debut with New Dance Group.

COLL, DAVID. Born Mar. 20, 1947 in Chelsea, Mass. Studied with Vilzak. Nerden, Van Muyden, Fallis, Christensen. Made debut in 1965 with San Francisco Ballet. Joined American Ballet Co. in 1969. ABT in 1970. Became soloist in 1972.

COLLIER, LESLEY. Born Mar. 13, 1947 in Kent, Eng. Studied at Royal Academy of Dancing, Royal Ballet School. Joined Royal Ballet in 1965.

COLLINS, JANET. Born in New Orleans in 1917. Studied with Carmalita Maracci, Bolm, Lester Horton, Slavenska and Craske. Appeared in solo concerts before becoming premiere danseuse of the Met Opera Ballet (1951–54). Now teaches.

COLTON, RICHARD. Born Oct. 4, 1951 in N.Y.C. Attended Hunter Col., ABT School, American Ballet Center. Debut 1966 with James Waring Co.; joined Joffrey Ballet 1972.

COMELIN, JEAN-PAUL. Born Sept. 10, 1936 in Cannes, France. Studied at Cons. of Music and Art; made debut with Paris Opera Ballet in 1957. Soloist for London Festival Ballet in 1961, principal in 1962. Joined National Ballet 1967, Pa. Ballet in 1970; left in 1972. Now director Milwaukee Ballet.

CONDODINA, ALICE. Born in Phildelphia; graduate of Temple U. Studied with Tudor, Zaraspe, Danielian, and at Met Opera Ballet, Ballet Theatre, and American Ballet Schools. Danced with Ruth Currier, Lucas Hoving, Sophie Maslow, Jack Moore, and Jose Limon Companies. Director-choreographer for own company since 1967.

CONOVER, WARREN. Born Feb. 5, 1948 in Philadelphia, Pa. Studied with Peter Conlow, Harkness House. Debut 1966 with Pa. Ballet. Subsequently with Harkness Ballet, Eglevsky Ballet, Niagara Ballet, Richmond Ballet; joined ABT 1971, soloist 1973.

COREY, WINTHROP. Born in 1947 in Washington, D.C. Studied with Ntl. Ballet and appeared with company. Joined Royal Winnipeg Ballet in 1966; Ntl. Ballet of Canada 1972; principal 1973.

CORKLE, FRANCESCA. Born Aug. 2, 1952 in Seattle, Wash. Studied with Virginia Ryan, Perry Brunson, Robert Joffrey. Joined Joffrey Ballet in 1967.

CORKRE, COLLEEN. Born in Seattle, Wash. and began training at 4. Debut with Chicago Opera Ballet. Dancer and choreographer for several musicals. Formed own company that tours annually.

CORVINO, ALFREDO. Born in Montevideo, Uruguay, where he studied with Alberto Poujanne. Also studied with Margaret Craske, Antony Tudor. Was premier danseur, assistant ballet master, and choreographer for Municipal Theatre, Montevideo. Appeared with Jooss Ballet, Ballet Russe de Monte Carlo, Metropolitan Opera Ballet. Juilliard dance faculty since 1952.

COSI, LILIANA. Born in Milan, and entered LaScala School in 1950. Was exchange artist with Bolshoi; made debut as prima ballerina in 1965 in "Swan Lake" with Bolshoi. Named prima ballerina of LaScala in 1968, and Assoluta in 1970. Has appeared as guest artist with many companies.

COWEN, DONNA. Born May 2, 1949 in Birmingham, Ala. Studied with Gage Bush, Richard Englund, School of American Ballet, Joffrey. Made debut in 1968 with Huntington Dance Ensemble; joined Joffrey Ballet in 1969.

CRAGUN, RICHARD. Born in Sacramento, Cal. Studied in London's Royal Ballet School and in Denmark. Joined Stuttgart Ballet in 1962 and quickly emerged as principal.

CRANE, DEAN. Born Jan. 5, 1932 in Logan, Iowa. Made professional debut at 14 as aerialist with Pollock Circus. Studied with Nimura, Dokoudovsky, Tudor and Petroff. Became first dancer and choreographer with Ballet Arts Co. Has also appeared on Bdwy and in clubs, and teaches.

CRASKE, MARGARET. Born in England. Studied with Cecchetti. Appeared with Diaghilev Ballets Russe, de Valois group. Became Ballet Mistress for Ballet Theatre in 1946, subsequently joined Met Opera Ballet School staff and became its assistant director. Currently with Manhattan School of Dance.

CRAVEY, CLARA. Born July 1, 1950 in West Palm Beach, Fla. Trained at Harkness School, and made debut with company in 1968.

CRISTOFORI, JON. Born in Buzzard's Bay, Mass., and began training at 15. Became lead student dancer in National Ballet of Wash., and toured with it until joining Joffrey Ballet. Left in 1969.

CROLL, TINA. Born Aug. 27, 1943 in N.Y.C. Bennington Col. graduate. Studied with Cunningham, Fonaroff. Debut 1964 in Kaufmann Hall. Has danced and choreographed for DTW since 1965. Formed own company in 1970 for which she choreographs.

CROPLEY, EILEEN. Born Aug. 25, 1932 in London. Studied with Sigurd Leeder, Maria Fay, Martha Graham, Don Farnworth. Made debut in 1966 with Paul Taylor Co.

CUNNINGHAM, JAMES. Born Apr. 1, 1938 in Toronto, Can. Graduate UToronto, London Academy Dramatic Arts. Studied at Martha Graham School. Choreographed for and performed with own company from 1967.

CUNNINGHAM, MERCE. Born Apr. 16 in Centralia, Wash. Studied at American School of Ballet. Professional debut as soloist with Martha Graham in 1940; with company through 1945. Began choreographing in 1946; in 1952 formed own company that has toured extensively every year. Teaches in his N.Y. studio.

CUNNINGHAM, RON. Born in Chicago; graduate Roosevelt U. Studied with Robert Lunnon, Eric Braun, Wigman, Cunningham, Humphrey, Weidman. Debut 1965 with Allegro American Ballet. Subsequently with Lucas Hoving, Kazuko Hirabayashi, Daniel Nagrin, Lotte Goslar, Zena Bethune, Ballet Concepts, Boston Ballet 1972.

CURRIER, RUTH. Born in 1926 in Ashland, Ohio. Studied with Doris Humphrey and Elsa Kahl. Made debut in 1949 with American Dance Festival. Soloist with Jose Limon Co. 1949–63. Since 1956 has been director-choreographer for own company which has toured U.S. Also teaches. Is director of Jose Limon Co.

CUTLER, ROBYN. Born May 25, 1948 in Atlanta, Ga. Attended Juilliard. Made debut 1972 with Jose Limon Co.

DABNEY, STEPHANIE. Born July 11, 1958 in Philadelphia, PA. Studied at Youngstown Academy, Dance Theatre of Harlem whose company she joined in 1975.

d'AMBOISE, JACQUES. Born July 28, 1934 in Dedham, Mass. Joined N.Y.C. Ballet at 15 after 7 years at School of American Ballet; rapidly rose to premier danseur in 1953. Has appeared in films and on TV and choreographed.

DANA, JERILYN. Born in Portland, Me., where she began dancing at 6. Studied with Boston Ballet, and graduated into company. Became soloist in 1969.

DANIAS, STARR. Born Mar. 18, 1949 in N.Y.C. Studied at School of Am. Ballet. Debut 1968 with London Festival Ballet, subsequently joined Joffrey Ballet in 1970.

DANIELIAN, LEON. Born Oct. 31, 1920 in N.Y.C. Studied with Mordkin and Fokine. Debut with Mordkin Ballet in 1937. Appeared with Original Ballet Russe, Ballet Russe de Monte Carlo, Ballet Theatre, Ballet des Champs Elysees, and San Francisco Ballet. Was choreographer-director of Ballet de Monte Carlo. Now with American Ballet Theatre School.

DANIELS, DANNY. Born in 1924 in Albany, N.Y. Studied with Thomas Sternfeld, Jack Potteiger, Vincenzo Celli, Elisabeth Anderson-Ivantzova, Anatole Vilzak. Appeared in musicals, as soloist with orchestras, and as dancer for de Mille Dance Theatre before becoming choreographer for TV and Bdwy musicals.

DANILOVA, ALEXANDRA. Born Nov. 20, 1906 in Peterhof, Russia. Graduate of Imperial School of Ballet, and became member of company. Subsequently with Balanchine's company, Les Ballets Russes de Diaghilev, Ballet Russe de Monte Carlo (both de Basil's and Massine's). Made N.Y.C. debut in 1948 at Met with Massine's company. Has appeared with and choreographed for N.Y.C. Ballet. In 1954 formed and toured with own company, The Concert Dance Group; choreographer for Met 1961–62. Now teaches.

DANTE, SHARON. Born Jan. 8, 1945 in Torrington, Conn. Graduate UHartford. Studied with Graham, Limon, Weidman, ABT School. Appeared with Charles Weidman, Larry Richardson, Rudy Perez, Jose Limon. Founder-Director of Nutmeg Ballet.

D'ANTUONO, ELEANOR. Born in 1939 in Cambridge, Mass. Danced with Ballet Russe de Monte Carlo for 6 years before joining Joffrey Ballet in 1960. Became member of American Ballet Theatre in 1961; principal since 1963.

DAVIDSON, ANDREA. Born in 1955 in Montreal, Can. Studied at Ntl. Ballet School, and joined company in 1971; Promoted to soloist in 1972.

DAVIS, GARY. Born in Washington, D.C. Graduate UMd., UIll. Studied at National Academy of Dance. Debut 1954 with Charles Weidman, subsequently with Jeff Duncan, Tina Croll, NY Dance Collective, Mimi Garrard, Paul Taylor. Also choreographs.

DAVIS, MARTHA HILL. Born in East Palestine, O. Graduate Columbia, NYU. Debut with Martha Graham (1929–31). Director of Dance, Bennington (1934–42), NYU (1930–51), Juilliard since 1951. Founder Conn. Col. School of Dance and American Dance Festival.

DAVIS, ROBERT. Born March 13, 1934 in Durham, N.C. Studied at Wash. School of Ballet, and with Fokine, Franklin, and Joffrey. Debut in 1960 and has appeared as principal dancer with Washington Ballet, National Ballet of Canada, and Joffrey Ballet. Is also director and choreographer.

DEAN, LAURA. Born Dec. 3, 1945 on Staten Island, NY. Studied with Lucas Hoving, Muriel Stuart, Matt Mattox, Martha Graham, American Ballet Center, Mia Slavenska. Appeared with Paul Taylor, Paul Sanasardo. Formed own company in 1971.

DEANE, MICHAEL. Born Nov. 4, 1950 in NYC. Graduate UColo. Studied with Larry Boyette, Robert Christopher, Dan Wagoner, Joffrey School. Debut 1974 with Paul Taylor Co. Member Repertory Dance Theatre 1974–75.

DeANGELO, ANN MARIE. Born Oct. 1, 1952 in Pittston, Pa. Trained at San Francisco Ballet School and made debut with its company in 1970. Joined Joffrey 1972.

DE BOLT, JAMES. Born in Seattle, Wash. Studied with Marian and Illaria Ladre, and at U. Utah. Debut with Seattle's Aqua Theatre. Joined Joffrey Ballet in 1959, subsequently with N.Y.C. Opera Ballet, N.Y.C. Ballet 1961, Manhattan Festival Ballet 1965. Is also a costume designer and choreographer. Re-joined Joffrey Co. in 1968. Currently premier danseur with Oslo's Den Norske Opera.

DE GANGE, ANN. Born Sept. 22, 1952 in New London, Conn. Juilliard graduate. Studied with Corvino, Tudor, McGehee, Winters. Debut 1971 with Kazuko Hirabayashi, subsequently with Martha Graham Co. from 1972.

de JONG, BETTIE. Born in Sumatra, and moved to Holland in 1947. Made debut with Netherlands Pantomime Co. Studied with Martha Graham and joined company; subsequently with Pearl Lang and Lucas Hoving. Joined Paul Taylor in 1962.

DELAMO, MARIO. Born during January 1946 in Havana, Cuba. Studied with May O'Donnell, Gertrude Shurr, Norman Walker. Debut 1966 with Norman Walker Co.; Glenn Tetley 1969; Alvin Ailey 1970; Martha Graham Co. 1972.

DELANGHE, GAY. Born Aug. 21, 1940 in Mt. Clemens, Mich. Studied at Severo School. Professional debut in 1960 and toured with "The Dancemakers." Choreographer, performer and teacher since 1965. Joined Lucas Hoving Co. in 1967.

de LAPPE, GEMZE. Born Feb. 28, 1922 in Woodhaven, Va. Attended Hunter Coll. and Ballet Arts School. Studied with Duncan, Fokine, Nimura, Caton, and Nemtchinova. Has appeared with Ballet Theatre and Agnes de Mille Dance Theatre and in Bdwy productions.

de LAVALLADE, CARMEN. Born March 6, 1931 in Los Angeles. Attended LACC, and studied with Lester Horton. Professional debut with Horton Dance Theatre. Bdwy debut in 1954. Has appeared with John Butler, Met Opera, de Lavallade-Ailey, Donald McKayle, and Ballet Theatre.

DELZA, SOPHIA. Born in N.Y.C. Studied in China. Professional debut 1953 in program of Chinese dances. Has toured world in concert, and been choreographic consultant for Met Opera, LCRep. Theatre, and Bdwy musicals.

de MAYO, FRED DOUGLASS. Studied at Abbey Theatre, and with Fokine, Youskevitch, Pereyaslavec, and in Paris with Preabrajenska. Appeared with National Ballet, Met. Opera Ballet. Founder of Newburgh Ballet. Now Director of Dance at West Point, and teaches at New Paltz SUNY.

de MILLE, AGNES. Born in N.Y.C. in 1909. Graduate of UCLA. Studied with Kosloff, Rambert, Karsavina, Tudor, Sokolova, Caton, Craske, Stroganova, and Dolmetsch. Debut in 1928 in own dance compositions and toured with them in Europe. Became leading choreographer for Bdwy. Created first ballet "Black Ritual" for Ballet Theatre in 1940. In 1953 organized Agnes de Mille Dance Theatre which toured U.S. Has also choreographed for Ballet Russe de Monte Carlo, and Royal Winnipeg Ballet. In 1973 organized and choreographs for Heritage Dance Theatre.

DENARD, MICHAEL. Born Nov. 5, 1944 in Dresden, Germany. Studied in Toulouse and Paris. Has appeared with Berlin Opera, and Paris Opera Ballets, with Bejart, and joined ABT (1971) as principal.

DENVERS, ROBERT. Born Mar. 9, 1942 in Antwerp. Studied with Nora Kiss, Tania Grantzeva, Peretti; joined Bejart's Ballet in 1963; Ntl. Ballet of Canada.

De SOTO, EDWARD. Born Apr. 20, 1939 in The Bronx. Attended Juilliard, AADA, New Dance Group Studio. Danced with Gloria Contreras, Judith Willis, Sophie Maslow, Art Bauman, Valerie Bettis, before joining Limon Co. in 1966.

DESTINE, JEAN-LEON. Born in Haiti, March 26, 1928. Attended Howard U. Made professional debut at Jacob's Pillow in 1949. Formed own company and has toured U.S., Europe, and Japan. Also teaches.

DeVILLIERS, JOHN R. Born Apr. 22, 1951 in Sacramento, CA. Attended Chico State, UCal., American Ballet Center. Debut 1975 in "Nureyev and Friends."

| Matthew Diamond | Agnes deMille | Ulysses Dove | Linda Diamond | Michael Ebbin |

DIAMOND, LINDA. Born in Panama. Studied with Ana Ludmilla, Martha Graham, Merce Cunningham, New Dance Group. Performed with Stuart Hodes, Eleo Pomare, Fusion, and currently director-choreographer for her own company.

DIAMOND, MATTHEW. Born Nov. 26, 1951 in N.Y.C. Attended CCNY. Debut 1967 with Matteo and the Indo-American Dance Co. Subsequently with Norman Walker, N.Y.C. Opera, Louis Falco, Jose Limon 1975, own company 1976.

DI BONA, LINDA. Born July 21, 1946 in Quincy, Mass. Studied at Boston Ballet School and made debut with company in 1965. Joined Harkness Ballet 1972. Currently prima ballerina with Royal Ballet de Wallonie in Belgium.

DICKSON, CHARLES. Born June 30, 1921 in Bellwood, Pa. Studied with Fokine, Massine, Dolin, Tudor, Volkova, Preobrajenska, Egorova, Balanchine, Markova, Lôring, Nijinska. Debut 1938 with Ballet Russe de Monte Carlo; AmBalTh 1940–42; Alicia Alonso Ballet 1952–55; Borovansky Ballet of Australia 1955–58; ballet master London Festival Ballet 1958–61; artistic director-ballet master Ballet Municipal de Santiago 1963–76; from 1971 director Metropolitan Academy, and Metropolitan Ballet Co.

DISHONG, ZOLA. Born Aug. 4, 1945 in Albany, Cal. Studied with Lew Christensen, Anatole Vilzak, Michael Lland, Patricia Wilde. Debut 1962 with San Francisco Ballet, subsequently with ABT 1967.

DOBRIEVICH, LOUBA. Born Feb. 9, 1934 in Bajina Basta, Yugoslavia. Studied at Belgrade Academy of Dance. Debut 1954 with Opera Zagreb; subsequently with Paris Theatre Ballet 1958, Maurice Bejart Co. from 1959.

DOBRIEVICH, PIERRE. Born Dec. 27, 1931 in Veles, Yugoslavia. Studied at Etudes de Droit. Debut 1955 with Opera Zagreb; subsequently with Paris Theatre Ballet 1957, Ludmila Cherina 1958, Les Etoiles de Paris 1959, Maurice Bejart from 1960.

DOBSON, DEBORAH. Born June 23, 1950 in Sacramento, Ca. Studied at San Francisco Ballet Sch., Sch. of Am. Ballet. Debut 1968 with Andre Eglevsky Co., joined ABT in 1969; promoted to soloist in 1973; joined Stuttgart 1975.

DOKOUDOVSKY, VLADIMIR. Born in 1922 in Monte Carlo. Studied with Preobrajenska; made debut at 13; became soloist with Ballet Russe de Monte Carlo, Mordkin Ballet, Ballet Theatre. Premier danseur with Original Ballet Russe (1942–52). Has choreographed several ballets. Now teaches.

DOLIN, ANTON. Born Sydney Francis Patrick Chippendall Healey-Kay in Slinfold, Sussex, Eng. July 27, 1904. Studied with Astafieva, Nijinska. With Diaghileff Company 1921–9, principal dancer with Sadler's Wells 1931–5. Ballet Russe 1939, 1946–8. Founder, director, and dancer with Markova-Dolin Co. 1935–8, 1945, 1947–8. Danced, restaged, and choreographed for Ballet Theatre from inception to 1946. 1949 organized and danced with London Festival Ballet until 1961. Currently artistic adviser of Les Grands Ballets Canadiens.

DOLLAR, WILLIAM. Born Apr. 20, 1907 in East St. Louis, Mo. Studied with Fokine, Mordkin, Balanchine, Vladimiroff, and Volinine. Lead dancer with Philadelphia Opera, American Ballet 1936–7, Ballet Caravan 1936–8, Ballet Theatre 1940, American Ballet Caravan 1941, New Opera Co. 1942, Ballet International 1944, Ballet master for American Concert Ballet 1943, Ballet Society 1946, Grand Ballet de Monte Carlo 1948, N.Y.C. Ballet. Has choreographed many works, and teaches.

DONN, JORGE. Born Feb. 28, 1947 in Buenos Aires. Attended school of Teatro de Colon. Appeared in musicals before joining Bejart Ballet in 1963, rising to leading male dancer.

DORADO, THIERRY. Born in 1950 in Paris, France. Studied with Nina Tikanova, Paris Opera School. Debut with Paris Opera Ballet; appeared with Nice Opera Ballet, Ballets de Roland Petit, Stuttgart 1969–70). Joined Ballet West as principal 1973.

DOUGLAS, HELEN. Studied with Maggie Black, Karoly Zsedenyi, Vincenzo Celli, Margaret Craske. Debut 1966 with Met Opera Ballet. Joined Joffrey 1966–68; ABT 1968–71; Eliot Feld 1973. Also lecturer.

DOUGLAS, SCOTT. Born June 16, 1927 in El Paso, Tex. Studied with Lester Horton and Ruth St. Denis. Appeared with San Francisco Ballet, Ballets U.S.A., John Butler, Ballet Theatre, Nederlands National Ballet, Glen Tetley Co. Ballet Master for ABT.

DOWELL, ANTHONY. Born in London Feb. 16, 1943. Studied with June Hampshire, entered Royal Ballet School at 10. Debut as hunter in "Swan Lake" at Covent Garden Opera House. Joined Sadler's Wells Opera Ballet, and Royal Ballet in 1961. Is now a principal.

DOYLE, DESMOND. Born June 16, 1932 in South Africa. Joined Royal Ballet in 1951. Became soloist in 1953; is now a principal and teacher.

DRAPER, PAUL. Born 1909 in Florence, Italy. Began studies at early age, and became tap soloist, elevating it to ballet-tap concert form. Made debut in 1932 in London. Continues to give solo performances, teaches, and is photographer.

DRIVER, SENTA. Born Sept. 5, 1942 in Greenwich, Conn. Graduate Bryn Mawr, Ohio State U. Studied with Maggie Black, Don Farnworth, and at O'Donnell-Shur Studio. Joined Paul Taylor Company in 1967, left in 1973 to choreograph and direct Harry.

DU BOULAY, CHRISTINE. Born in 1923 in Ealing, Eng. Trained in Sadler's Wells Ballet School. Soloist with International Ballet before joining Sadler's Wells. Settled in U.S. in 1950, and with husband, Richard Ellis, became founders and directors of Illinois Ballet Co.

DUBREUIL, ALAIN. Born in Monte Carlo, Mar. 4, 1944. Studied at mother's ballet school until awarded scholarship at Arts Educational School (1960). Joined London Festival Ballet in 1962 and became soloist in 1964.

DUDLEY, JANE. Dancer-choreographer. Born in N.Y.C. in 1912. Studied with Martha Graham, Hanya Holm, Louis Horst. Leading dancer with Graham Co. (1937–44). With Sophie Maslow and William Bales, formed concert Dance Trio. Retired in 1954 to teach.

DUELL, DANIEL. Born Aug. 17, 1952 in Rochester, NY. Attended Fordham U., School of American Ballet. Debut 1971 with Edward Villella Co., subsequently with Eglevsky Ballet, Dayton Ballet, Lincoln Center Repertory Dancers, NYCB 1974; promoted to soloist 1977.

DUFFY, DIANE. Born in Philadelphia, Pa. Studied at Pa. Ballet Sch., Harkness House. Debut at 15 with Pennsylvania Ballet; joined Harkness, National, Eliot Feld Ballet (1973).

DUNCAN, JEFF. Born Feb. 4, 1930 in Cisco, Tex. Attended N. State Tex. U., studied with Holm, Nikolais, Limon, Cunningham, Schwetzoff, Tomkins, Joffrey. Assistant to Doris Humphrey and Anna Sokolow. Debut 1952 at Henry St. Playhouse. Has appeared with New Dance Group, Juilliard Dance Theatre, Anna Sokolow, Jeff Duncan Dance Co., and is founder-director of Dance Theatre Workshop. Has also appeared in Bdwy musicals and teaches.

DUNHAM, KATHERINE. Born June 22, 1912, in Chicago. Debut with Chicago Opera Co. in 1933. Bdwy debut 1940 in "Cabin In The Sky." Formed own company for which she choreographed; toured with it in 1943, and subsequently in 57 other countries. Founded Katherine Dunham School of Cultural Arts in N.Y.C. in 1943.

DUNNE, JAMES. Born in Waldwick, N.J. Studied with Irene Fokine, and at School of American Ballet, Harkness House. Joined Harkness Ballet for 4 years, then Joffrey Ballet.

EBBELAAR, HAN. Born Apr. 16, 1943 in Hoorn, Holland. Studied with Max Dooyes and Benjamin Harkarvy. Danced with Nederlands Dans Theater before joining American Ballet Theatre in 1968 as soloist; promoted to principal in 1969, Dutch Natl. Ballet (1970).

EBBIN, MICHAEL. Born June 5, 1945 in Bermuda. Studied at Patricia Gray's, National Ballet, American Ballet, American Ballet Center, and Harkness Schools. Has danced with Eleo Pomare, Cleo Quitman, Australian Dance Theatre, Anna Sokolow, Talley Beatty, and Rod Rodgers companies, and appeared on Bdwy. Joined Ailey company 1972.

177

EDWARDS, LESLIE. Born Aug. 7, 1916 in Teddington, Eng. Studied with Marie Rambert and at Sadler's Wells School. Debut 1933 with Vic-Wells Ballet, subsequently joined Ballet Rambert, Royal Ballet, Now teaches and makes guest appearances.

EGLEVSKY, ANDRE. Born in Moscow Dec. 21, 1917. Received training in France. At 19 joined Rene Blum's Ballet de Monte Carlo. Came to U.S. in 1937, and after appearing with all major companies, joined Ballet Theatre. In 1947 appeared with Grand Ballet du Marquis de Cuevas. In 1950 joined N.Y.C. Ballet and danced leading male roles until 1958, also created "Scotch Symphony" and other ballets for the company. In 1955, with his wife, prima ballerina Leda Anchutina, opened school in Massapequa, L.I., and in 1960 formed local classical ballet company which he directs.

EISENBERG, MARY JANE. Born Mar. 28, 1951 in Erie, Pa. Attended Hunter, New School. Studied at Graham, ABT, Harkness schools. Debut 1969 with Glen Tetley; subsequently with Keith Lee, Contemporary Dance Ensemble, Louis Falco.

ELLIS, RICHARD. Born 1918 in London. At 15 joined Vic-Wells Ballet which became Sadler's Wells Ballet. Important member of company until 1952. After touring U.S. with company in 1949–50, settled in Chicago. With wife, Christine Du Boulay, became founders and co-directors of Illinois Ballet Co.

ENCKELL, THOMAS. Born in Helsinki, Finland, Oct. 14, 1942. Studied with Margaret Craske. Professional debut with Met Opera Ballet in 1962. Joined Finnish Natl. Opera Ballet 1965. Manhattan Festival Ballet 1966.

ENGLUND, RICHARD. Born in Seattle, Wash. Attended Harvard, Juilliard. Studied with Tudor, Graham, Volkova. Appeared with Limon, Met Opera, Natl. Ballet of Canada, ABT, and in musicals. Currently teaches and choreographs. Director Ballet Repertory Co.

ENSMINGER, MORGAN. Born Dec. 14, 1949 in Washington, DC. Graduate Sarah Lawrence Col. Studied with Viola Farber, Jeff Slayton, Alfredo Corvino. Appeared with Rudy Perez, Jeff Slayton, Raymond Johnson, Kathy Bernson, Stormy Mullis.

ENTERS, ANGNA. Dancer, choreographer, and mime was born in 1907 in N.Y.C. Created own style of dance and pantomime that she has performed all over the world. Is also a writer and painter.

ERDMAN, JEAN. Born in Honolulu, Hawaii. Graduate of Sarah Lawrence College (1938). Studied at Bennington, American School of Ballet, Hisamatsu, Martha Graham, Pukui and Huapala Hawaiian Dance Schools. Professional debut 1938 with Martha Graham, and as a choreographer in 1942. Organized own company in 1950, and made annual tours through 1960. World tour 1963–5 with "The Coach With The Six Insides" which she conceived and staged. Head of NYU Dance Dept. for 5 yrs. Director of Open Eye Theatre.

ERICKSON, BETSY. Born in Oakland, Cal. Attended Cal. State U., San Francisco Ballet School. Debut with San Francisco Ballet. Joined American Ballet Theatre 1967; returned to SF Ballet 1973.

ESTELLE & ALFONSO. Born in N.Y.: trained with Haakon, Mattox, Juarez, LaSylphe, Nettles, Chileno, Wills, Thomas. Toured widely as team. Currently operate school in Poughkeepsie, N.Y., and artistic directors for Mid-Hudson Regional Ballet.

ESTNER, ROBERT. Born in North Hollywood, Calif. Attended Los Angeles City Valley Jr. Col. Studied with Robert Rossalatt, Natalie Clare, Andre Tremaine, Carmalita Maracci, and at ABC. Appeared with Ballet Concerto, Pacific Ballet, Ballet La Jeunesse, before joining Joffrey Co.

EVANS, BILL. Born Apr. 11, 1946 in Lehi, Utah. Graduate Univ. Utah. Studied at Harkness House, American Dance Center, ABT School. Made debut in 1966 with Ruth Page Ballet. Joined Repertory Dance Theatre in 1967 as dancer and choreographer.

EVERETT, ELLEN. Born in Springfield, Ill. June 19, 1942. Studied in Chicago and School of American Ballet. Professional debut 1958 with Ruth Page's Chicago Opera Ballet. Soloist with American Ballet Theatre from 1967. Raised to principal 1973. Has also appeared on Bdwy.

FADEYECHEV, NICOLAI. Born in Moscow in 1933. Studied at Bolshoi School and joined company in 1952; became soloist in 1953, and subsequently premier danseur.

FAISON, GEORGE. Born Dec. 21, 1945 in Washington, D.C. Attended Howard U. Studied with Louis Johnson, Claude Thompson, Alvin Ailey, Dudley Williams, Elizabeth Hodes. Appeared on Bdwy and with Universal Dance Experience (1971).

FALCO, LOUIS. Born in N.Y.C.; studied with Limon, Weidman, Graham, and at American Ballet Theatre School. Danced, choreographed, and toured with Jose Limon, Co., as principal dancer for 10 years, choreographed for other groups, and own company which he formed in 1967.

FALLET, GENEVIEVE. Born Aug. 2, 1943 in Switzerland. Studied at Royal Ballet, and with Yuriko, Cunningham, Wagoner, DTW. Has danced with London and Paris companies, with Frances Alenikoff, and solo.

FALLIS, BARBARA. Born in 1924 in Denver, Colo. Moved to London in 1929. Studied at Mona Clague School, Vic-Wells and Vilzak-Shollar Schools. Debut 1938 in London. With Vic-Wells Ballet 1938–40; Ballet Theatre in 1941; Ballet Alicia Alonso (1948–52), N.Y.C. Ballet (1953–58). Now teaches.

FARBER, VIOLA. Born in Heidelberg, Ger., Feb. 25, 1931. Attended American U. and Black Mt. College. Studied with Katherine Litz, Merce Cunningham, Alfredo Corvino, and Margaret Craske. Debut 1952 with Merce Cunningham, subsequently with Paul Taylor, and Katherine Litz. More recently, choreographing, and guest artist with Merce Cunningham. Director of own company.

FARRELL, SUZANNE. Born Roberta Sue Ficker Aug. 16, 1945 in Cincinnati. Began ballet studies in Cincinnati, subsequently attending School of American Ballet. After 15 months joined N.Y.C. Ballet, and became a principal dancer in 1965. Joined National Ballet of Canada in 1970, Bejart (1970), returned to NYCB in 1975.

FAXON, RANDALL. Born Sept. 26, 1950 in Harrisburg. Pa. Studied with Elizabeth Rockwell. Martha Graham, Paul Sanasardo, Alfredo Corvin, and at Juilliard. Debut 1969 with Ethel Winter; joined Lucas Hoving in 1970, Gus Solomons 1975.

FEDICHEVA, KALERIYA. Born in Leningrad in July 1937. Attended Kirov School; joined company in 1956; Resigned in 1974 and came to U.S. in 1975. Appeared with Terpsichore Co.

FEDOROVA, NINA. Born Apr. 24, 1958 in Philadelphia, Pa. Studied at Pa. Ballet School, Sch. of Am. Ballet. Made Debut with NYC Ballet in 1974.

FEIGENHEIMER, IRENE. Born June 16, 1946 in N.Y.C. Attended Hunter Col. Studied with Holm, Graham, Cunningham, ABC. Debut 1965 with Met Opera Ballet, subsequently danced with Merry-Go-Rounders, Ruth Currier, Anna Sokolow, Cliff Keuter, Don Redlich.

FEIN, RICHARD. Born in Los Angeles where he studied with Don Hewitt, Joey Harris, and performed with the Harris Co. Joined National Ballet of Canada 1972, Eliot Felt Ballet 1974.

FEIT, VALERIE. Born July 17, 1956 in Johannesburg, SAf. Studied at Harkness and ABT schools. Joined Eliot Feld company 1974, Alvin Ailey 1975.

FELD, ELIOT. Born 1943 in Brooklyn. Studied with Richard Thomas and at School of American Ballet. Appeared with N.Y.C. Ballet, and on Bdwy before joining American Ballet Theatre in 1963. Co-founder (1969), director, dancer, and choreographer for American Ballet Co. Rejoined ABT in 1971. Debuted Eliot Feld Ballet 1974.

FERNANDEZ, ROYES. Born July 15, 1929 in New Orleans. Studied with Lelia Hallers and Vincenzo Celli. Appeared with Ballet Russe, Markova-Dolin, Ballet Alicia Alonso, de Cuevas' Ballet, before joining Ballet Theatre. Premier danseur since 1957. Retired in 1973 to teach. Has appeared with several companies as guest artist.

FIBICH, FELIX. Born May 8, 1917 in Warsaw, Poland; attended dance and theatre schools, and made professional debut there in 1936. Became dancer-choreographer in 1939. Formed own company that has toured widely with Israeli and Chassidic dancers. Also teaches.

FIFIELD, ELAINE. Born in Sydney, Aust. Studied at Sadler's Wells, RAD. Debut 1948 with Sadler's Wells Co., subsequently appeared with Royal Ballet, Australian Ballet.

FIGUEROA, ALFONSO. Born May 24, 1947 in N.Y.C. Graduate Boston Cons. Studied with Virginia Williams, Thomas-Fallis, Pearl Lang. Debut 1967 with Boston Ballet; subsequently Pearl Lang, American Ballet 1968, Alvin Ailey 1970, Boston Ballet 1971.

FILENE, SHARON. Born Nov. 4, 1951 in Norristown, PA. Graduate NCar. Sch. of Arts. Studied with Martha Graham, Kazuko Hirabayashi, Jane Dudley, Richard Gain, Pauline Koner, Valerie Bettis. Appeared with Hirabayashi Dance Theatre, Kathryn Posin Dance Co., Marcus Shulkind Dance Co., Koner Dance Consort, before joining Martha Graham Co. 1977.

FILIPOV, ALEXANDER. Born Mar. 19, 1947 in Moscow. Studied at Leningrad Kirov School. Debut with Moiseyev Ballet, defected and appeared with Pa. Ballet, Eglevsky Ballet, ABT (1970), Pittsburgh Ballet 1971, San Francisco Ballet 1974.

FISERA, VICKI. Born Aug. 2, 1942 in Berwyn, IL. Studied with Edna McRae, Maggie Black, Hector Zaraspe, William Dollar, Patricia Wilde. With Chicago Lyric Opera and Chicago Opera Ballet (1961–65), Metropolitan Opera Ballet (1966–).

FISHER, NELLE. Born Dec. 10, 1920 in Berkeley, Cal. Appeared with Martha Graham Co., in Bdwy musicals; choreographs and teaches.

FITZGERALD, HESTER. Born Oct. 1, 1939 in Cleveland, O. Trained with Nedjedin, Levinoff, and at Ballet Russe, American, and Ballet Theatre schools. Debut with Ballet Russe 1956; subsequently with N.Y.C. Ballet, ABT, and Harkness Ballet.

FLINDT, FLEMMING. Born Sept. 30, 1936 in Copenhagen. Entered Danish Royal Ballet School at 10; became member at 18. Invited by Harald Lander to appear in London; returned to Danish Ballet and became leading dancer before joining Paris Opera as danseur etoile, and choreographing. Ranks among world's greatest male dancers, and has achieved recognition as choreographer. Became director of Royal Danish Ballet in 1966. Resigned 1977.

FLINDT, VIVI. Born Feb. 22, 1944 in Copenhagen, Den. Studied at Royal Danish Ballet and joined company in 1965.

FONAROFF, NINA. Born in N.Y.C. in 1914. Studied with Martha Graham, at School of American Ballet. Danced with Graham (1937–46) before forming own company in 1945. Is now teacher, choreographer.

| Ingrid Fraley | Frederic Franklin | Brenda Garratt | Tom Fowler | Charlene Gehm |

FONTEYN, MARGOT. Born May 18, 1919 in Surrey, Eng. Began training at 14 with Astafieva, and a few months later entered Sadler's Wells School. Solo debut with company in 1934 in "The Haunted Ballroom." In 1935, succeeded to ballerina roles of Markova. Unrivaled in roles of Aurora and Chloe. Made Dame of British Empire by Queen Elizabeth. Guest star of Royal Ballet, and considered Prima Ballerina Assoluta of the world.

FOREMAN, DONLIN. Born July 22, 1952 in Cambellsville, KY. Attended UMontevallo, UUtah, ABT. Debut 1974 with Ballet West, subsequently with National Ballet of Ill., Joyce Trisler Co., joined Martha Graham Co. 1977.

FOREMAN, LAURA. Born in Los Angeles. U. Wisc. graduate. Danced with Tamiris-Nagrin, Marion Scott, Harriet Anne Gray, Ann Halprin. Director of Laura Foreman Dance Company; Founder/Director of Choreographers Theatre/ChoreoConcerts; director New School Dance Dept.

FOSSE, BOB. Born in Chicago June 23, 1927. Appeared in musicals and clubs before becoming outstanding choreographer for Bdwy, films, and TV.

FOSTER, RORY. Born Feb. 3, 1947 in Chicago, Ill. Attended Ill. Benedictine Col. Studied with Robert Lunnon, Doreen Tempest, Vincenzo Celli. Debut 1962 with Allegro American Ballet; joined American Ballet Theatre 1970.

FOWLER, TOM. Born Feb. 18, 1949 in Long Beach, Cal. Graduate U. Cin. Studied with David Howard, Claudia Corday, David McLean, Margaret Black, Richard Thomas, Harkness House. Debut 1971 with American Ballet Company. Joined Joffrey 1974.

FOX, LISA. Born Aug. 29, 1950 in New Jersey. Attended UCal. Studied with Margaret Jenkins, San Francisco Ballet. Debut 1977 with Merce Cunningham Co.

FRACCI, CARLA. Born Aug. 20, 1936 in Milan, Italy. Began training at 8 at La Scala with Edda Martignoni, Vera Volkova, and Esmee Bulnes. Became prima ballerina of La Scala in 1958; joined London Festival Ballet as guest artist. Now permanent guest artist with American Ballet Theatre.

FRALEY, INGRID. Born Nov. 1, 1949 in Paris, France. Studied at San Francisco Ballet, and made debut with company in 1964. Subsequently with Kiel-Lubeck Opera Ballet, Fokine Ballet, Eglevsky Ballet, joined American Ballet Theatre 1969; Joffrey 1975.

FRANKEL, EMILY. Born in N.Y.C. Studied with Weidman, Holm, Graham, Craske, Tudor, and Daganova. Professional debut 1950. Founder, director, choreographer, and dancer with Dance Drama Co. since 1955. Has made 8 transcontinental tours, a State Dept. sponsored tour of Europe, and British Arts Council tour of England and Scotland.

FRANKLIN, FREDERIC. Born in Liverpool, Eng. in 1914. Studied with Legat, Kyasht, and Pruzina. Made debut as child dancer; went to London at 17; appeared in music halls, night clubs, and musicals before joining Markova-Dolin Co. 1935–7. Premier danseur with Ballet Russe de Monte Carlo from 1938; became its ballet master in 1944. Artistic Adviser ABT (1961). Director National Ballet (1962–74); Artistic Director Pittsburg Ballet Theatre 1974–1977.

FRAZER, SUSAN. Born in NYC. Studied at Sch. of Am. Ballet, and with Jean Hamilton, Vladimir Dokoudovsky. Joined National Ballet 1968; promoted to soloist 1972. Joined ABT 1974, Joffrey Ballet 1976.

FREDERICK, JULIA. Born in Boston. Studied and performed with Boston Ballet, Harkness Ballet, N.Y.C. Ballet. Also danced with Penn. Ballet, Garden State Ballet, and N.Y.C. Opera Co. Resident soloist with Hartford Ballet.

FREEDMAN, LAURIE. Born July 7, 1945 in N.Y.C. Graduate Bennington Col. Studied with Graham, Cunningham, Zena Rommett. Debut 1967 with Merry-Go-Rounders, subsequently with Batsheva Dance Co. (1968).

FREEMAN, FRANK. Born July 16, 1945 in Bangalore, India. Studied at Royal Ballet School. Joined company in 1963. Joined London Festival Ballet as soloist in 1971.

FUENTE, LUIS. Born in 1944 in Madrid where he began studies at early age. Joined Antonio's Ballets de Madrid in 1963; Joffrey Ballet 1964–1970. National Ballet (1970) as principal; London Festival Ballet 1972. Rejoined Joffrey 1976. Organized own company in Madrid.

FUERSTNER, FIONA. Born Apr. 24, 1936 in Rio de Janeiro. Attended San Francisco State College. Studied at San Francisco Ballet School (debut with company 1952). School of American Ballet, Ballet Rambert, Royal Ballet, Ballet Theatre schools. Has danced with Les Grands Ballets Canadiens, San Francisco, N.Y.C. Center, and Philadelphia Opera ballet companies. Principal dancer with Pennsylvania Ballet. Became Ballet Mistress in 1974.

GABLE, CHRISTOPHER. Born 1940 in London, began studies at Royal Ballet School. At 16 joined Sadler's Wells Opera Ballet, and next year Covent Garden Opera Ballet. In 1957 became member of Royal Ballet and at 19 advanced to soloist. Retired in 1967 to act.

GAIN, RICHARD. Born in Belleville, Ill. Jan. 24, 1939. Studied with Lalla Baumann, and Martha Graham. Professional debut with St. Louis Municipal Opera, followed by musicals. Became member of Graham Co. in 1961, also danced with Jazz Ballet Theatre, Lotte Goslar, Sophie Maslow, and Pearl Lang, and formed concert group "Triad" that performed in N.Y. and on tour. Joined Joffrey Co. in 1964; ABT in 1967. Teaches at N.C. School of Arts.

GARDNER, BARBARA. Born June 7, 1940 in Lynbrook, NY. Graduate Stanford U. Studied with Wigman, Sanasardo, Cunningham. Has appeared with Nikolais, Marion Scott, Phoebe Neville, Elina Mooney, and her own company. Also teaches.

GARRARD, MIMI. Born in Gastonia, N.C. Attended Sweet Briar College. Studied at Henry St. Playhouse, with Julia Barashkova. Angelina Romet. Has appeared with Alwin Nikolais and Murray Louis companies, and own company for which she choreographs.

GARRETT, BRENDA. Born Jan. 25, 1954 in Georgetown, Guiana. Studied at London's Royal Ballet School. Joined Dance Theatre of Harlem in 1973.

GARTH, MIDI. Born in N.Y.C. Studied with Francesca de Cotelet, Sybil Shearer, Louis Horst. Has choreographed and performed solo concerts in N.Y. and on tour. Also teaches.

GARY, M'LISS. Born Nov. 8, 1951 in Lisbon, Port, Graduate Natl. Ballet Academy. Studied with Oleg Tupine, Richard Thomas, Barbara Fallis. Debut 1969 with National Ballet, joined American Ballet Co. in 1971.

GAYLE, DAVID. Born July 10, 1942 in Yorkshire, Eng. Appeared in Covent Garden opera ballets before joining Royal Ballet. Left in 1970 to teach in Buffalo, NY.

GEHM, D. CHARLENE. Born Dec. 14, 1951 in Miami, FL. Studied with George Milenoff, Thomas Armour, Harkness Sch., ABT Sch., Am. Ballet Center. Debut 1970 with Harkness Ballet. With National Ballet (1971–74), Chicago Ballet (1974–5), Joffrey Ballet (1976–).

GENNARO, PETER. Born 1924 in Metairie, La. Studied at American Theatre Wing. Debut with Chicago San Carlo Opera 1948, and Bdwy bow same year. After several musicals and TV, choreographed "Seventh Heaven" in 1955. Is much in demand as dancer and choreographer on television.

GENTRY, EVE. Born Aug. 20, in Los Angeles. Used own name Henrietta Greenhood until 1945. Studied with Holm, Graham, Humphrey, Weidman, Tamiris, Barashkova, at Ballet Arts Studio, and American Ballet Center. Debut with Hanya Holm. Since 1949, director-choreographer-soloist with own company.

GERMAINE, DIANE. Born July 5, 1944 in N.Y.C. Studied with Martha Graham. May O'Donnell, Norman Walker, Paul Sanasardo. Debut with Sanasardo in 1963. Has appeared in concert with Norman Walker, Manuel Alum, Cliff Keuter, Donya Feuer; also teaches and choreographs.

GEVA, TAMARA. Born 1908 in St. Petersburg, Russia. Studied at Maryinsky Theatre. Joined Diaghilev. Came to U.S., signed by Ziegfeld, subsequently appeared in musicals and films and with American Ballet.

GIELGUD, MAINA. Born Jan. 14, 1945 in London. Studied with Karsavina, Idzikovski, Egorova, Gsovsky, Hightower. Debut 1961 with Petit Ballet, subsequently with Ballet De Marquis de Cuevas, Miskovitch, Grand Ballet Classique, joined Bejart Ballet in 1967.

GILMORE, RICHARD. Born in Franklin, PA. Attended Butler U. Studied at Harkness House. Joined Eliot Feld Ballet in 1973.

GILPIN, JOHN. Born in 1930 in Southsea, Eng. Was child actor; joined Ballet Rambert 1945, London's Festival ballet 1950, becoming artistic director and principal dancer. Guest artist with ABT and Royal Ballet. Resigned as artistic director Festival Ballet but remained premier danseur. 1977 artistic director Pittsburgh Ballet Theatre.

GIORDANO, GUS. Born July 10, 1930 in St. Louis. Graduate U. Mo. Debut at Roxy N.Y.C., 1948, subsequently appeared in musicals on TV before becoming choreographer. Currently director of Giordano Dance Studio in Evanston, Ill., and his own company.

GLADSTEIN, ROBERT. Born Jan. 16, 1943 in Berkeley, Calif. Attended San Francisco State College, and studied at San Francisco Ballet School. Became member of San Francisco Ballet in 1960 and choreographed 13 ballets. Joined American Ballet Theatre in 1967, became soloist in 1969. Rejoined S.F. Ballet 1970.

GLASSMAN, WILLIAM. Born 1945 in Boston and began dance studies at 7. Scholarship to School of American Ballet. Studied with Alfredo Corvino and Margaret Craske. Appeared in musicals, with N.Y.C. Opera, and on TV, before joining American Ballet Theatre in 1963. Promoted to soloist 1965. With Niagara Frontier Ballet.

GLENN, LAURA. Born Aug. 25, 1945 in N.Y.C. Graduate Juilliard. Joined Limon Co. in 1964. Has also performed with Ruth Currier, Sophie Maslow, Valerie Bettis, and Contemporary Dance Sextet.

GLUCK, RENA. Born Jan. 14, 1933. Juilliard graduate. Studied with Graham, Tudor, Horst, Blanche Evans. Founding member of Batsheva Dance Co. in 1963. Also choreographs.

GLUSHAK, NANETTE. Born Dec. 31, 1951 in NYC. Studied at School of Am. Ballet. Made debut with American Ballet Theatre in 1967. Promoted to soloist 1973.

GODREAU, MIGUEL. Born Oct. 17, 1946 in Ponce, P.R. Studied at Joffrey Ballet Center, School of American Ballet, Ballet Russe, and with Martha Graham. Debut 1964 with First American Dance Co., subsequently with Ailey, McKayle, and Harkness Ballet. After appearing on Bdwy, organized and danced with own company in 1969. Returned to Ailey Co. in 1970. Left to appear in London. Principal with Birgit Cullberg Co. in Sweden.

GODUNOV, ALEKSANDR. Born in 1950 on the island of Sakhalin, north of Japan. Began training in Riga, Latvia. Debut at 17 with Igor Moiseyev's Young Classical Ballet. Made debut with Bolshoi in 1970 as principal.

GOLLNER, NANA. Born 1920 in El Paso, Texas. Studied with Kosloff. Soloist with American Ballet 1935, de Basil's Ballet Russe 1935–6. Blum's Ballet Russe 1936–7. Ballet Theatre 1939–48. Only American to achieve rank of ballerina in foreign country.

GOODMAN, ERIKA. Born Oct. 9 in Philadelphia. Trained at School of American Ballet, and American Ballet Center. Debut with N.Y.C. Ballet 1965. Appeared in Pa. Ballet, and Boston Ballet before joining Joffrey Ballet in 1967.

GOPAL, RAM. Born Nov. 20. Hindu dancer, came to U.S. in 1938, and with own company has toured world as its soloist. Operates own school.

GORDON, LONNY JOSEPH. Born in Edinburg, Tex. Graduate of U.Tex and U.Wisc. Studied at Grand Kabuki Theatre in Tokyo, and with Koisaburo Nishikawa, Richo Nishikawa. Has given solo performances throughout Japan and U.S. Director Southern Repertory Dance Theatre, and teacher.

GORDON, MARVIN. Born in N.Y.C. Graduate Queens Col. Studied with New Dance Group, Met Opera Ballet, Graham, Humphrey, and Weidman. Appeared on Bdwy and TV, in concert with Doris Humphrey, and Pearl Lang. Choreographed before becoming founder-director of Ballet Concerts, that has appeared in N.Y. and on tour throughout U.S.

GORDON, MEG ELIZABETH. Born May 6, 1953 in NYC. Attended New School, NYC Ballet. Joined Alvin Ailey Co. 1973.

GORRISSEN, JACQUES. Born Apr. 21, 1945 in Ghent, Bel. Studied at Ballet School Royal Flemish Opera. Debut 1962 with Ballet Royal Flemish Opera. Joined National Ballet of Canada in 1968. Promoted to soloist.

GOSLAR, LOTTE. Born in Dresden, Ger. Studied at Mary Wigman School. Toured Europe as dance mime before coming to U.S. in 1937. Formed own pantomime company for tours of U.S. and Europe. Also teaches.

GOVRIN, GLORIA. Born Sept. 10, 1942 in Newark, N.J. Studied at Tarassof School, American Ballet Academy, School of American Ballet. Joined N.Y.C. Ballet in 1957. Promoted to soloist at 19.

GOYA, CAROLA. Born in N.Y.C. Studied with Fokine, Otero, LaQuica, Maria Esparsa. Danced with Met Opera before solo debut as Spanish dancer in 1927. Appeared with Greco before partnership with Matteo in 1954.

GRAHAM, MARTHA. Born May 11, 1893 in Pittsburgh. Studied at Denishawn School of Dance; made debut with its company in 1919, and danced with them until 1923. First choreographed and appeared in N.Y.C. in a program of 18 original works in 1926, followed by annual concerts until 1938. A founder of Bennington (Vt.) Dance Festival where she staged several premieres of her works. Formed own company with which she has made numerous successful tours throughout world. Founded Martha Graham School of Contemporary Dance in 1927, and remains its director. Has created over 100 dances.

GRANT, ALEXANDER. Born Feb. 22, 1925 in Wellington. New Zealand. Entered Sadler's Wells School in 1946, and five months later joined company. Has created more major roles than any other male dancer with Royal Ballet. Appointed Director National Ballet of Canada in 1976.

GRAY, DIANE. Born May 29, 1944 in Painesville, Ohio. Attended Juilliard. Studied with Graham, Tudor, Youskevitch, Schwezoff, Melikova, Hinkson, Winter, McGehee, Ross. Debut 1964 with Martha Graham Co. Has also appeared with Helen McGehee, Yuriko, Pearl Lang, Sophie Maslow, Jeff Duncan.

GRECO, JOSE. Born Dec. 23, 1919 in Montorio-Nei-Frentani, Compobasso, Italy. Studied with Mme. Veola in N.Y.C. Argentinita and La Quica in Madrid. Debut as soloist 1935 with Salmaggi Opera Co. Partner with La Argentinita 1943–4. Pilar Lopez 1946–8, before organizing own company in 1949, with which he has become internationally famous.

GREENFIELD, AMY. Born July 8, 1940 in Boston. Studied with Graham, Cunningham, Fonaroff, Robert Cohan, American Ballet Center. Made debut in 1965. Has appeared in concert and with DTW.

GREGORY, CYNTHIA. Born July 8 in Los Angeles where she studied with Lorraine, Maracci, Panaieff, and Rossellat. Danced with Santa Monica Civic Ballet, L.A. Civic Light Opera in 1961 joined San Francisco Ballet, subsequently S.F. Opera Ballet, and American Ballet Theatre in 1965, became principal in 1968; Resigned in 1975. Returned 1976.

GREY, BERYL. Born in Highgate, England, June 11, 1927. Began studies at Sadler's Wells Ballet School, and at 15 danced "Swan Lake" with its company. Left in 1957 but returned for guest appearances. Appointed in 1966 to head Arts Education School, London. Director London Festival Ballet, made Commander British Empire in 1973.

GRIFFITHS, LEIGH-ANN. Born Dec. 5, 1948 in Johannesburg, S.A. Studied at Royal Ballet School. Joined Stuttgart Ballet in 1968.

GRIGOROVICH, YURI. Born in Leningrad Jan. 2, 1927. Graduated from Leningrad Ballet School and became one of leading soloists with Kirov Co. In 1964 became choreographer for Moscow Bolshoi Ballet Co.

GROMAN, JANICE. Born in New Britain, Conn. Joined N.Y.C. Ballet at 16. Later with ABT, and First Chamber Dance Quartet.

GROSSMAN, DANIEL WILLIAMS. (formerly Daniel Williams) Born in 1943 in San Francisco, CA. Studied with Welland Lathrop, Gloria Unti, May O'Donnell, Gertrude Shurr, Nina Fonaroff, Wishmary Hunt, Paul Taylor. Joined Taylor company 1963 for 10 years. 1973 joined Toronto Dance Theatre, and is now its teacher-dancer-choreographer director.

GUERARD, LEO. Born Jan. 18, 1937 in Boston, Mass. Studied at School of American Ballet. Debut 1952 with ABT; subsequently with Grand Ballet de Cuevas 1957, Skandinavian Ballet 1960, Royal Winnipeg Ballet 1963, Western Theatre Ballet 1964, Intl. Ballet Caravan 1968, Boston Ballet 1968.

GUNN, NICHOLAS. Born Aug. 28, 1947 in Bklyn. Studied with Ellen Segal, Helen McGehee, June Lewis, Don Farnworth. Appeared with Stuart Hodes Co. Joined Paul Taylor Co. in 1969.

GUTELIUS, PHYLLIS. Born in Wilmington, Del. Studied with Schwetzoff, Tudor, Graham. Joined Graham Company in 1962. Has appeared on Bdwy, with Glen Tetley, Yuriko, Sophie Maslow, John Butler.

GUTHRIE, NORA. Born Jan. 2, 1950 in N.Y.C. Studied with Marjorie Mazia, Martha Graham, and at NYU. Debut 1970 with Jean Erdman Co.

GUZMAN, PASCHAL. Born in Arecibo, P.R. Attended Harkness, National Ballet, Graham, Dalcroze schools. Debut 1964 with National Ballet, subsequently with Baltimore Ballet, Washington Dance Repertory, Penn. Ballet, New America Ballet, Ballet Concerto, Downtown Ballet.

GYORFI, VICTORIA. Born in Wenatchee, Wash. Studied at San Francisco Ballet, and made debut with its company. Appeared with Munich Ballet, Bayerische Staats Oper, and returned to SF Ballet.

HAAKON, PAUL. Born in Denmark in 1914 Studied at Royal Danish Ballet School, with Fokine, Mordkin, and at School of American Ballet. Debut with Fokine in 1927. Danced and toured with Anna Pavlova. Became premier danseur with American Ballet in 1935. Appeared in musicals and nightclubs. In 1963 became ballet master and instructor of Jose Greco Co.

HACKNEY, PEGGY. Born Dec. 28, 1944 in Miami, Fla. Graduate Duke U., Sarah Lawrence Col. Has performed with Deborah Jowitt, Micki Goodman, Jose Limon Co., Tina Croll, and Jeff Duncan Teaches extensively.

| Maina Gielgud | John Gilpin | Laura Glenn | Alexander Grant | Lisa Hess |

HAGGBOM, NILS-AKE. Born Apr. 20. 1942 in Stockholm, Swed. Studied at Royal Swedish Ballet, with Raymond Franccetti, Vera Volkova, Erik Bruhn, William Griffith, Stanley Williams, Royal Ballet. Joined Royal Opera Ballet in 1959, quickly rising to danseur noble. Guest artist with many companies.

HAISMA, RICHARD. Born Aug. 6, 1945 in Grand Rapids, Mich. Studied with Nancy Hauser and appeared with her company before joining Murray Louis Co. in 1973.

HALL, YVONNE. Born Mar. 30, 1956 in Jamaica, WI. Studied at Dance Theatre of Harlem and made debut with company in 1969.

HAMILTON, PETER. Born in Trenton, N.J. Sept. 12, 1915. Attended Rutgers. Danced in Broadway musicals before becoming choreographer and teacher.

HAMMONS, SUZANNE. Born Aug. 26, 1938 in Oklahoma City. Attended San Francisco Ballet, American Ballet Center, and Harkness schools. Debut in 1958 with San Francisco Ballet; subsequently joined Harkness, and Joffrey Ballet companies.

HANITCHAK, LEONARD R., JR. Born July 24, 1944 in Oklahoma City. Studied with Ethel Butler, Graham, and Cunningham. Has danced with DTW, and Rudy Perez Co.

HANKE, SUSANNE. Born in 1948 near Berlin. Studied with Anneliese Morike, Anne Woolliams, and at Royal Ballet School. Debut 1963 in Wuerttemberg State Theatre Ballet. Joined Stuttgart Ballet in 1966.

HARKARVY, BENJAMIN. Born in N.Y.C. in 1930. Studied with Chaffee, Caton, Preobrajenska, and at School of Am. Ballet. Made debut with Bklyn. Lyric Opera, for which he also choreographed. Opened school in 1955 and formed concert group. Ballet master for Royal Winnipeg, and Nederlands Ballet. Artistic Director of Pa. Ballet 1972.

HARKNESS, REBEKAH. Born in St. Louis, Mo. Promoted American dancers for several years before establishing Harkness Ballet in 1965, and Harkness Ballet School.

HARPER, LEE. Born Nov. 10, 1946 in Hickory, N.C. Juilliard graduate. Studied with Tudor, Limon, Koner, Lindgren, Cunningham, Alvin Ailey.

HARPER, MEG. Born Feb. 16, 1944 in Evanston, Ill. Graduate of U. Ill. Studied with Merce Cunningham and made professional debut with his company in 1968.

HARRIS, RANDAL. Born in Spokane, Wash. Attended Pacific Lutheran U. Studied with Joffrey, Edna McRae, Jonathan Watts ABC. Joined Joffrey Ballet in 1970.

HART, DIANA. Born Apr. 21, 1952 in Lansing, Mich. Attended Juilliard, and Martha Graham schools. Made debut 1973 with Graham Company. Has also appeared with Saeko Ichinohe Co.

HART, JOHN. Born in London in 1921. Studied with Judith Espinosa, and at Royal Acad. Joined Sadler's Wells in 1938, and rose to principal. Became ballet master in 1951, asst. director in 1962.

HARUM, EIVIND. Born May 24, 1944 in Stavanger, Nor. Attended Utah State U. Debut 1959 with Stuart Hodes company, and subsequently with Helen Tamiris, Harkness Ballet, Alvin Ailey Co., Martha Graham (1975). Has also appeared in several musicals.

HARVEY, DYANE. Born Nov. 16, 1951 in Schenectady, N.Y. Studied with Marilyn Ramsey, Paul Sanasardo. Appeared with Schenectady Ballet, Dance Uptown, Miguel Godreau, Eleo Pomare, Movements Black, Story Time Dance Theatre.

HARWOOD, VANESSA. Born June 14, 1947 in Cheltenham, Eng. Studied with Betty Oliphant, Ntl. Ballet School, Rosella Hightower. Debut 1965 with National Ballet of Canada; became principal in 1970.

HASH, CLAIRE RISA. Born May 18, 1946 in Norwich, Conn. Studied at U. Colo. and NYU. Debut 1970 with Jean Erdman Co.

HAUBERT, ALAINE. Born in N.Y.C. Attended U. Utah. Studied with Helen Averell, Raoul Pause, Kira Ivanovsky, Dorothy Dean, Alan Howard, William Griffith. Debut with Monterey Peninsula Ballet, subsequently with Pacific Ballet, ABT, Joffrey Ballet.

HAUPERT, LYNN. Born Aug. 16, 1954 in Syracuse, NY. Studied with Paul Sanasardo, Dance Theatre of Harlem. Debut 1972 with Paul Sanasardo Dance Co.

HAWKINS, ERICK. Born in Trinidad, Colo. Studied at School of American Ballet. Appeared with American Ballet 1934–7, Ballet Caravan 1936–9, and with Martha Graham, before becoming choreographer, teacher, and director of his own company.

HAYDEE, MARCIA. Born April 18, 1940 in Rio de Janeiro. Studied at Royal Ballet School, London. Debut with Marquis de Cuevas Ballet. Joined Stuttgart Ballet in 1961, becoming its prima ballerina, and in 1976 its artistic director.

HAYDEN, MELISSA. Born in Toronto, Can. April 25, 1923, where she received early training before becoming charter member of N.Y.C. Ballet in 1949. Has appeared with Natl. Ballet of Canada, Ballet Theatre, and Royal Ballet. In great demand as educator and lecture-demonstrator. Has also appeared on Bdwy. Director "Ballet Festival." Retired 1973 to teach. 1976 artistic director Pacific Northwest Dance Co. Resigned 1977.

HAYMAN-CHAFFEY, SUSANA. Born Jan. 31, 1948 in Tenterden, England, Studied at Sadler's Wells School, and with Lepeshinskaya, Graham, Cunningham. Made debut in 1968 with Merce Cunningham.

HAYWARD, CHARLES SUMNER. Born May 2, 1949 in Providence, R.I. Attended Juilliard. Debut in 1968 with Jose Limon Company.

HEINEMAN, HELEN. Born Aug. 13, 1947 in Highland Park, Ill. Attended Hunter Col. Studied with Sybil Shearer, Mme. Swoboda. Debut 1963 with National Ballet; became soloist before leaving in 1966. Ballet Russe 1967; Nederlands Dans Theater 1968–9; Harkness Ballet 1970.

HELPMANN, ROBERT. Born April 9, 1909 in Mt. Gambier, Austl. Attended King Alfred Col.; studied with Laurent Novikov. Debut in Austl. musicals; in 1933 joined Sadler's Wells (now Royal Ballet), and rose to soloist from 1933–50. Became choreographer, and created ballet "Hamlet" in 1942. Recently has devoted time to acting, guest performances, and directing Australian Ballet from which he resigned. Made Commander of British Empire in 1964.

HERBERTT, STANLEY. Born in Chicago in 1919. Studied with Tudor, Caton, Ivantzova. Member of Polish Ballet, Littlefield, Chicago and San Carlo Opera Ballets before joining Ballet Theatre in 1943. Founder-Director of St. Louis Ballet. Also teaches and choreographs.

HERMANS, EMERY. Born June 25, 1931, in Seattle. Studied with Vaunda Carter, and at Henry St. Playhouse. Debut 1968 with Nikolais Co. Has danced with Carolyn Carlson, Al Wunder, and in own works.

HESS, LISA CAMILLE. Born in Amarillo, TX. Studied at School of American Ballet; joined NYC Ballet in 1975; appeared with "Nureyev and Friends."

HIATT, JOHN. Born Oct. 5, 1939 in St. George, U. Studied at UUtah, and became charter member and principal of Ballet West in 1963.

HIGHTOWER, ROSELLA. Born Jan. 30, 1920 in Ardmore, Okla. Studied at Perkins School. Appeared with Ballet Russe de Monte Carlo 1938–41. Ballet Theatre 1941–5. Markova-Dolin 1946. Original Ballet Russe 1946–7. Teaches in Cannes and makes guest appearances.

HILL, CAROLE. Born Jan. 5, 1945 in Cambridge, Eng. Studied at Royal Ballet School and made debut with Royal Ballet Co. in 1962.

HILL, MARTHA. (see DAVIS, MARTHA HILL)

HINKSON, MARY. Born in Philadelphia, March 16, 1930. Graduate of U. Wisc. Studied with Graham, Horst, Shook, June Taylor, Schwezoff. Debut with Graham Co. in 1952. Also danced with John Butler, N.Y.C. Opera, and N.Y.C. Ballet.

HODES, STUART. Born in 1924. Studied with Graham, Lew Christensen, Ella Daganova, and at School of American Ballet. Leading dancer with Graham (1947–58), appeared in Bdway musicals, and as soloist in own works. Choreographer and instructor with Harkness Ballet. Now teaches, and heads NYU Dance Dept.

HOFF, ALEXIS. Born Aug. 31, 1947 in Chicago. Studied with Melba Cordes, Betty Gour, Edna MacRae and at Stone-Camryn School. Made debut with Chicago Lyric Opera Ballet in 1961. Joined Harkness Ballet in 1965, becoming soloist in 1968.

HOFF, STEVEN-JAN. Born June 24, 1943, in Hilversum, Holland. Studied at Amsterdam Academie of Dance. Appeared in musicals before joining American Ballet Theatre in 1966. Became soloist in 1969. Joined Garden State Ballet 1970. Formed own "Film and Dance Theatre" in 1971.

HOFFMAN, PHILLIP. Born in Rochester. N.Y. Attended Miami Dade Jr. Col. Studied with Thomas Armour, and at Harkness House, ABC. Joined Joffrey Ballet in 1969.

HOGAN, JUDITH. Born Mar. 14, 1940 in Lincoln. Neb. Studied with Martha Graham. Made debut with Bertram Ross in 1964. Danced with Glen Tetley before joining Graham Co. in 1967.

HOLAHAN, WILLIAM. Born Mar. 19, 1950 in Philadelphia, PA. Graduate York U. Studied at Graham School, with Helen McGeehee, Robert Cohan, Sandra Neals, Gus Solomons. Debut 1973 with Contemporary Dancers, subsequently with Manuel Alum, Kazuko Hirabayashi, Pearl Lang, Murray Louis.

HOLDEN, RICHARD. Born Aug. 8 in Braintree, Mass. Graduate of London Inst. of Choreology. Appeared with George Chaffee Ballet, Met Opera, Ballets Minerva. Choreologist for Harkness Ballet, and director of Tucson Civic Ballet.

HOLDEN, STANLEY. Born in London, Jan. 27, 1928. Studied with Marjorie Davies Romford. Made professional debut in 1944 with Royal Ballet and remained until 1969. Now teaches, and makes guest appearances.

HOLDER, CHRISTIAN. Born 1950 in Trinidad. Studied in London, and with Martha Graham, Bella Malinka, ABC, Joined Joffrey Ballet.

HOLDER, GEOFFREY. Born in Port-of-Spain, Trinidad, Aug. 1, 1930. Attended Queens Royal College. With brother's dance company in Trinidad, later its director. With own company, made first U.S. appearance in 1953. Besides touring, and giving annual concerts with his group, has appeared on Bdwy, with Met opera, and John Butler Co., also choreographs and designs.

HOLM, HANYA. Born in 1898 in Worms-am-Rhine, Germany. Attended Hoch Conserv., Dalcroze Inst., Wigman School. U.S. debut with own company in 1936, followed by annual performances and transcontinental tours. Came to U.S. in 1931 to found N.Y. Wigman School of Dance which became her school in 1936. Has choreographed musicals and operas in U.S. and London.

HOLMES, GEORGIANA. Born Jan. 5, 1950 in Vermont. Studied with Pauline Koner, Duncan Noble, Job Sanders, Boston School of Ballet. Debut 1969 with Norman Walker; subsequently with Pearl Lang, Louis Falco, Paul Sanasardo, Manual Alum. Also teaches.

HONDA, CHARLOTTE. Born June 2, 1940 in San Jose, Calif. Graduate Ohio State U. Studied with Cunningham, Graham, Hoving, Limon, Sanasardo, Farnworth. Debut in 1967 with Larry Richardson; subsequently with Katherine Litz, ChoreoConcerts, and Laura Foreman.

HORNE, KATHRYN. Born in Ft. Worth, Tex., June 20, 1932. Studied with Margaret Craske, Antony Tudor. Debut 1948 with Ft. Worth Opera Ballet. Appeared with American Ballet Theatre as Catherine Horn (1951–56), a principal dancer Met Opera Ballet (1957–65), Manhattan Festival Ballet (1963–8), also ballet mistress and teacher for MFB.

HORVATH, IAN. Born in Cleveland, O., June 3, 1945. Studied with Danielian, Joffrey. Appeared in musicals, and on TV before joining Joffrey Ballet. With ABT from 1967, soloist in 1969. Director Cleveland Ballet.

HOSKINS, PAUL. Born Sept. 5, 1952 in Collinsville, Ill. Attended Southern Ill. U. Studied with Katherine Dunham. Joined Alvin Ailey Co. 1972.

HOULIHAN, GERRIE. Born June 13, 1945 in Ft. Lauderdale, FL. Attended Juilliard, and studied with Edna Veralle, Antony Tudor, Mary Hinkson, Margaret Black, Marjorie Mussman. Debut 1966 with Met. Opera Ballet. With Paul Sanasardo (1968–71), Manuel Alum (1973), Lar Lubovitch (1972–).

HOULTON, LOYCE. Born in Duluth, MN. Graduate Carleton Col., NYU. Studied with Louis Horst, Martha Graham, Doris Humphrey, Jose Limon, Nina Fonaroff. In 1962 founded Contemporary Dance Playhouse which in 1969 became Minnesota Dance Theatre and for which she is teacher-choreographer-artistic director.

HOVING, LUCAS. Born in Groningen, Holland. Attended Dartington Hall, and Kurt Jooss School. Professional debut with Kurt Jooss Ballet in 1942. Has appeared with Graham, Limon, and his own company. Has also appeared in Bdwy musicals.

HOWARD, ALAN. Born in Chicago. Studied with Edna MacRae and in Europe. Joined Ballet Russe de Monte Carlo in 1949 and became premier danseur. Appeared with N.Y.C., and Met Opera Ballets before being appointed director of Academy of Ballet in San Francisco. Founded and was artistic director of Pacific Ballet.

HOWELL, JAMES. Born in Yakima, Wash. Attended U. Wash. Studied with Else Geissmar, Martha Graham, Doris Humphrey, Mary Wigman, Margaret Craske, Alfredo Corvino, Robert Joffrey. Original member of Joffrey Ballet.

HUANG, AL. Born in Shanghai, came to U.S. in 1955. Attended Oregon State U., Perry-Mansfield School, graduate UCLA and Bennington. Studied with Carmelita Maracci. Appeared with Lotte Goslar before forming own co., with which he tours when not teaching.

HUGHES, KENNETH. Born in Norfolk, Va. attended NC School of Arts, School of Am. Ballet. Debut 1969 with American Ballet; subsequently with Lar Lubovitch, American Classical Ballet, Les Grands Ballets Canadiens, ABT 1972, Eliot Feld Ballet.

HUGHES, MICHAELA. Born Mar. 31, 1955 in Morristown, NJ. Made debut 1973 with Houston Ballet. Joined Eliot Feld Co. in 1974.

HUHN, HILLER. Born in New Orleans, LA. Danced with Royal Winnipeg Ballet; joined National Ballet (Washington, DC) as principal in 1971. Now ballet master of Houston Ballet.

HUJER, FLOWER. Born in Hollywood, Calif. Studied with Theodore Kosloff, Charles Weidman. Has toured in solo concerts and choreographs.

HUNTER, JENNY. Born Aug. 20, 1929 in Modesto, Calif. Studied with Merce Cunningham, Charles Weidman, Marjorie Sheridan. Debut 1951 with Halprin-Lathrop Co. With Dancers' Workshop Co. until 1958 when she left to found, direct, and choreograph for own company, Dance West.

HYND, RONALD. Born in London, April 22, 1931. Studied with Marie Rambert, Angela Ellis, Volkova, Idzikowski, and Pereyaslavee. Professional debut 1949 with Ballet Rambert. Joined Royal Ballet in 1951, and graduated from corps to principal dancer.

ICHINO, YOKO. Born in Los Angeles, CA. Studied with Mia Slavenska, Sara Neece, Margery Mussman, Mme. Besobrazsova. Has been member of Stuttgart Ballet, Joffrey Ballet (1971–75). Now appears as guest artist and teacher.

ICHINOHE, SAEKO. Born Sept. 13 in Tokyo, Japan. Graduate Juilliard 1971. Studied with Ishii Baku, Martha Graham. Dalcroze Sch. Debut 1955 with Ishii Baku Co. (Tokyo), Takahashi Hyo Ballet (1967), Va. Ballet Theatre (1975), Joan Miller (1975). Began choreographing in 1963, also teaches and performs in concert.

INDRANI. Born in Madras, India. Studied with Pandanallur Chokkalingam Pillai, Sikkil Ramaswami Pillai, Devas Prasad Das, Narasimha. First dancer to present Orissi classic dance outside India. Tours extensively in solo and with company.

IRION, CYNTHIA. Born in Montclair, NJ. Studied at NJ School of Ballet, and joined NJ Ballet. Joined Eliot Feld Ballet in 1975.

ISAKSEN, LONE. Born Nov. 30, 1941 in Copenhagen where she studied with Edithe Feifere Frandson. Accepted in Royal Danish Ballet School at 13. In 1959 joined group organized by Elsa Marianne Von Rosen and Allan Fredericia, and shortly elevated to soloist. In 1961 studied at Joffrey's American Ballet Center, and appeared with his company. In 1965 joined Harkness Ballet, and became one of its principal dancers until 1970, when she joined Netherlands Natl. Ballet.

ISRAEL, GAIL. Born in Paterson, N.J. Studied with Alexandra Fedorova. Rose to soloist with Ballet Russe before joining American Ballet Theatre in 1962.

JACKSON, DENISE. Born in N.Y.C.: attended ABC. Danced with N.Y.C. Opera Ballet, joined Joffrey Ballet in 1969.

JAGO, MARY. Born in 1946 in Henfield, Eng. Trained at Royal Ballet School. Joined Covent Garden Opera Ballet in 1965; Natl. Ballet of Canada 1966; now a principal.

JAMES, JANICE. Born Feb. 14, 1942 in Salt Lake City, U. Studied with Willam and Lew Christensen; Joined NYC Ballet in 1963; joined Ballet West 1965, and is now a principal, and teacher.

JAMISON, JUDITH. Born in 1944 in Philadelphia. Studied at Judimar School, Phila. Dance Acad., Joan Kerr's School, Harkness School, and with Paul Sanasardo. Debut 1965 with ABT. Joined Ailey Co. in 1965, Harkness Ballet in 1966, and rejoined Ailey in 1967.

JAYNE, ERICA. Born Aug. 8, 1945 in Amersham, Eng. Studied at Royal Ballet School, RAD. Debut 1962 with Royal Opera Ballet. Currently principal with Les Grands Ballets Canadiens.

JEANMAIRE, RENEE ZIZI. Born Apr. 29, 1924 in Paris. Studied at L'Opera de Paris with Volinine, and with Boris Kniaserf. Debut with Ballet de Monte Carlo in 1944. Joined Ballet Russe de Colonel de Basil (1945–47), Petit's Ballets de Paris in 1948. Has appeard in musicals and films.

JENNER, ANN. Born March 8, 1944 in Ewell, Eng. Began studies at 10 with Royal Ballet School. Debut with Royal Ballet in 1962. Became soloist in 1966, principal in 1970.

JENSEN, CHRIS. Born Jan. 24, 1952 in Los Angeles, Cal. Studied with Albert Ruiz, Harriet DeRea, Carmelita Maracci, and at School of Am. Ballet. Debut 1970 with Ballet du Grand Theatre de Geneve; joined Harkness Ballet 1972.

JERELL, EDITH. Studied with Antony Tudor, Margaret Craske, Dokoudovsky, Brenna, Pereyaslavee, Joffrey, Popova, Gentry, Norman Walker, Nona Schurman, Nancy Lang. Lazowski, Dunham, and Nimura. Appeared with Met Opera Ballet as principal or solo dancer for 10 years. Is now teacher, concert and guest artist, and on staff of Joffrey Ballet.

| Gregory Huffman | Loyce Houlton | Kenneth Hughes | Deborah Jowitt | Louis Johnson |

JHUNG, FINIS. Born May 28, 1937 in Honolulu where he began training. Gradute of U. Utah. Appeared on Bdwy before joining San Francisco Ballet in 1960. Advanced to soloist then joined Joffrey Ballet in 1962. Joined Harkness Ballet as soloist in 1964. Now teaches.

JILLANA. Born Oct 11, 1936 in Hackensack. N.J. After studying from childhood at School of American Ballet, joined N.Y.C. Ballet in teens, rising rapidly to ballerina. With ABT (1957–8) returned to NYCB (1959). Retired in 1966. Is active in teaching and touring U.S. Artistic Adviser for San Diego Ballet.

JOFFREY, ROBERT. Born Dec. 24, 1930 in Seattle, Wash. Began studies with Mary Ann Wells, later attended School of American Ballet, and studied with May O'Donnell and Gertrude Shurr. Debut as soloist with Petit's Ballets de Paris. Appeared with O'Donnell company, and taught at HS Performing Arts and Ballet Theatre School before starting his own American Ballet Center in 1950. Formed first company in 1952 that was resident co. of N.Y. Opera, and made tours in his own works in the U.S. and abroad. Reorganized group appeared in 1965 and has been internationally acclaimed. Is now City Center company.

JOHNSON, BOBBY. Born Oct. 26, 1946 in San Francisco. Studied at Harkness House and with Joffrey, Mattox, Jack Cole, Fokine. Has appeared on Bdwy and with Fred Benjamin Co.

JOHNSON, LOUIS. Born in Statesville, N.C. Studied with Doris Jones, Clara Haywood, and at School of American Ballet. Debut with N.Y.C. Ballet in 1952. Appeared in musicals before forming, choreographing for, and dancing with own group. Teaches, and on staff of Negro Ensemble Co.

JOHNSON, NANCY. Born in 1934 in San Francisco. Studied with Harold and Lew Christensen at San Francisco Ballet School, eventually becoming principal dancer of S.F. Ballet Co. With Richard Carter, toured world, appearing in fifty nations. Was prima ballerina with San Diego Ballet Co.

JOHNSON, PAMELA. Born in Chicago where she studied with Richard Ellis and Christine Du Boulay. Made debut with their Illinois Ballet Co. Joined Joffrey Ballet in 1966, American Ballet Theatre 1972.

JOHNSON, RAYMOND. Born Sept. 9, 1946 in N.Y.C. Graduate Queens Col. Studied with Alwin Nikolais, Murray Louis, Gladys Bailin, Phyllis Lamhut. Debut 1963 with Nikolais, joined Murray Louis in 1968; subsequently with Rod Rodgers, Joy Boutilier, Rudy Perez. Also teaches and choreographs for his own company.

JOHNSON, VIRGINIA. Born Jan. 25, 1950 in Washington, DC. Attended NYU, Washington School of Ballet. Debut 1965 with Washington Ballet; joined Capitol Ballet 1968: Dance Theatre of Harlem 1971.

JOHNSON, WILLIAM. Born Aug. 13, 1943 in Ashland, Kan. Attended San Francisco City Col., SF Ballet School. Debut 1961 with San Francisco Ballet; joined NYC Ballet 1970.

JONES, BETTY. Born in Meadville, Pa. Studied with Ted Shawn, Alicia Markova, La Meri, Doris Humphrey, and Jose Limon. Debut 1947 with Limon Co. and toured world with it. Has own lecture-performance, and teaches master classes throughout U.S. Has appeared in Bdwy musicals.

JONES, MARILYN. Born Feb. 17, 1940 in Newcastle, Australia. Studied with Tessa Maunder, Lorraine Norton, Royal Ballet School. Debut 1956 with Royal Ballet, subsequently with Borovansky Ballet, Marquis de Cuevas, London Festival, and Australian Ballets.

JONES, SUSAN. Born June 22, 1952 in York, Pa. Studied at Washington School of Ballet. Joined Joffrey company 1968, NYC Opera Ballet 1969, Am. Ballet Theatre 1971.

JORGENSEN, NELS. Born in New Jersey in 1938. Studied with Rose Lischner, and toured with her co. before beginning studies at School of American Ballet in 1953. Appeared in musicals and on TV before joining Joffrey Ballet as soloist in 1958. Artistic director Louisville Ballet.

JURKOWSKI, KRYSTYNA. Born June 15, 1954 in Nottingham, Eng. Appeared with Joffrey II, NJ Ballet, before joining City Center Joffrey Ballet in 1973.

JURRIENS, HENNY. Born Feb. 21, 1949 in Arnhem, Holland. Trained at Arnhem Dance Academy. Debut 1966 with Norkse Opera, Oslo, joined Dutch National Ballet 1970.

KAGE, JONAS. Born in Stockholm, Swed. Began training at 9 in Royal Swedish Ballet School, and joined company in 1967. Joined ABT in 1971, rising to principal in 1973; Stuttgart 1975.

KAHN, ROBERT. Born May 31, 1954 in Detroit, Mich. Attended NYU. Made debut 1975 with Jose Limon Co., subsequently joined Paul Taylor Co.

KAHN, WILLA. Born May 4, 1947 in NYC. Attended Bklyn Col., CCNY. Studied with Paul Sanasardo, Mia Slavenska, Karoly Zsedenyi. Debut 1959 with Paul Sanasardo Dance Co.

KAIN, KAREN. Born Mar. 28, 1951 in Hamilton, Ontario, Can. Trained at Ntl. Ballet School, and joined Ntl. Ballet of Canada in 1969; promoted to principal in 1971.

KARNILOVA, MARIA. Born in Hartford, Conn., Aug. 3, 1920. Studied with Mordkin, Fokine, and Craske. First appeared with Met corps de ballet (1927–34). Became soloist with Ballet Theatre, and Met Opera Ballet. Recently in Bdwy musicals.

KATAYEN, LELIA. Born in N.Y.C.: studied with Francesca de Cotelet, Sybil Shearer, Nanette Charisse, Joseph Pilates. In 1960 formed Katayen Dance Theatre Co, for which she is director-choreographer. Head of Southampton College Dance Dept.

KATO, MIYOKO. Born Sept. 26, 1943 in Hiroshima, Japan. Studied at Tachibana Ballet School. Made U.S. debut in 1965 with Met. Opera Ballet. Member of Harkness Ballet; joined Joffrey 1975.

KAYE, NORA. Born in N.Y.C. Jan. 17, 1920. Studied at Ballet School of Met Opera, and with Michel Fokine. Debut at 7 with Met's children's corps de ballet. Joined American Ballet Theatre as soloist in 1940 and N.Y.C. Ballet in 1950. Now assistant to her husband, choreographer and director, Herbert Ross.

KEHLET, NIELS. Born in 1938 in Copenhagen where he began studies at 6, subsequently going to Royal Danish Ballet School. Teachers include Vera Volkova, Stanley Williams, Nora Kiss, and Melissa Hayden. First solo at 16 in Royal Danish Ballet's "Sleeping Beauty." Made concert tour of Africa, and guest artist with de Cuevas' Ballet, London Festival Ballet, and ABT (1971).

KEHR, DOLORES. Born May 11, 1935 in Boston. Studied with Fokine, Danielian, Doukodovsky, Vikzak. Made debut in 1952 with Ballet Russe; former ballerina with National Ballet. Now has school in Ft. Lauderdale, Fla., and is director of "Classiques," Denver Civic Ballet.

KEIL, BIRGIT. Born Sept. 22, 1944 in Kowarschen, Sudetanland. Studied at Royal Ballet School. Made debut 1961 with Stuttgart Ballet.

KELLY, DESMOND. Born in 1945 in Bulawayo, Rhodesia. Studied at London's Royal Acad. Joined London Festival Ballet, becoming principal in 1963; subsequently with New Zealand Ballet, Zurich Opera Ballet, National Ballet 1968, Royal Ballet as principal in 1970.

KELLY, GENE. Born Aug. 23, 1912 in Pittsburgh. Graduate of U. Pittsburgh. Teacher and choreographer before appearing in Bdwy musicals and films. Currently choreographing and directing films.

KELLY, KAREN. Born Feb. 1, 1951 in Philadelphia. Trained at Thomas-Fallis School. Debut 1969 with American Ballet Co.

KENT, ALLEGRA. Born Aug. 11, 1938 in Los Angeles where she began her studies. At 13 went to School of American Ballet, and 2 years later joined N.Y.C. Ballet. Quickly rose to one of company's leading ballerinas.

KENT, HELEN. Born Dec. 30, 1949 in N.Y.C. U. Wisc. graduate. Studied with Waring, Cunningham, Nikolais. Made debut in 1971 with Murray Louis Co.

KENT, LINDA. Born Sept. 21, 1946 in Buffalo, N.Y. Juilliard graduate. Studied with Graham, Limon, Sokolow, Craske, Corvino, Tudor. Joined Alvin Ailey Co. in 1968, Paul Taylor Co. 1975.

KESSLER, DAGMAR. Born in 1946 in Merchantville. N.J. Studied with Thomas Cannon. Joined Penn. Ballet 1965, Hamburg State Opera 1966, London's Festival Ballet in 1967, Pittsburgh Ballet 1973.

KEUTER, CLIFF. Born in 1940 in Boise, Idaho. Studied with Welland Lathrop, Graham, Farnworth, Slavenska, Sanasardo. Debut in 1962 with Tamiris-Nagrin Co. Formed own company in 1969 for which he choreographs.

KIDD, MICHAEL. Born in N.Y.C. Aug. 12, 1919. Attended City College, and School of American Ballet. Studied with Blanche Evan, Ludmilla Scholler, Muriel Stewart, and Anatole Vitzak. Appeared as soloist with Ballet Caravan in 1938, and with Eugene Loring Co. Solo dancer with Ballet Theatre (1942–47), before becoming popular choreographer for musicals and films.

KIM, HAE-SHIK. Born Apr. 29, 1944 in Seoul, Korea. Graduate of Ewha U. Studied at Royal Ballet, London. Made debut in 1959 with Lim Sung Nam: subsequently with Zurich Opera Ballet (1967) and from 1969 with Les Grands Ballets Canadiens; promoted to soloist in 1970.

KIMBALL, CHRISTINA. Born Dec. 22, 1954 in Otsu, Japan. Debut 1972 with Alvin Ailey Co.

KINCH, MYRA. Born in Los Angeles. Graduate of U. of Calif. Solo and concert dancer, and choreographer of satirical ballets. Also teaches.

KING, BRUCE. Born in Oakland, Calif. Graduate of U. Calif. and NYU. Studied at Holm, Met Opera Ballet and Cunningham Schools. Debut 1950 with Henry St. Playhouse Dance Co. Toured with Merce Cunningham and is choreographer and teacher.

KIRBY, CHARLES. Born Apr. 28, 1926 in Little Rock, AR. Attended Little Rock U. Studied with Vera Nemtchinova, Hitchins, Nijinska, Agullo. Joined National Ballet of Canada in 1965 as soloist and character dancer.

KIRKLAND, GELSEY. Born in 1953 in Bethlehem, Pa. Studied at School of American Ballet. Joined N.Y.C. Ballet in 1968, promoted to soloist in 1969, principal in 1972. Joined ABT 1974.

KIRPICH, BILLIE. Born in N.Y.C., graduate of NYU. Studied with Graham, and at American School of Ballet. Debut 1942 with Pittsburgh Dance Co. Has appeared with New Dance Group, NYC Opera Ballet, on TV, and in musicals.

KITCHELL, IVA. Born in Junction City, Kan., March 31, 1912. Appeared with Chicago Opera Ballet before making solo debut as dance satirist in 1940. Has continued as concert artist and teacher.

KIVITT, TED. Born in Miami, Fla., Dec. 21, 1942. Studied with Alexander Gavriloff, Thomas Armour, Jo Anna Kneeland, and George Milenoff. Debut 1958 in night club revue. Appeared in Bwdy musicals before joining American Ballet Theatre in 1961. Elevated to soloist in 1964, principal dancer in 1967.

KLOS, VLADIMIR. Born July 1, 1946 in Prague. Studied at Koncervatory Prag. Joined Stuttgart Ballet and quickly rose to principal.

KNAPP, MONICA. Born Jan. 23, 1946 in Germany. Made debut in 1963, and appeared with several companies before joining Stuttgart Ballet in 1971; promoted to principal.

KOESUN, RUTH ANN. Born May 15, 1928 in Chicago. Studied with Suoboda, Nijinksa, Tudor, and Stone-Camryn. Debut with Ballet Theatre in 1946, and became one of its principal dancers. Retired in 1968 but makes guest appearances.

KOLPAKOVA, IRINA. Born in 1933 in Leningrad. Studied with Kirov company and made debut at 18. Elevated to principal ballerina. Now prima ballerina for Leningrad Kirov Co.

KOMAR, CHRIS. Born Oct. 30, 1947 in Milwaukee, WI. Graduate UWisc. Studied with Myron Nadel, Merce Cunningham, Richard Thomas. Joined Cunningham company 1972.

KONDRATYEVA, MARINA. Born Feb. 1, 1933 in Kazan, Russia. Enrolled in Bolshoi School in 1943; graduated into company in 1953. One of company's principal ballerinas.

KONER, PAULINE. Born 1912 in NYC. Studied with Fokine, Michio Ito, Angel Cansino. Debut 1926 with Fokine Ballet. Debut as choreographer-solo dancer 1930. Formed own company (1949–1964). In addition to solo-performances, now teaches and choreographs.

KONING, LEON. Born July 5, 1947 in Zandvoort, Netherlands. Studied with Peter Leoneff, Benjamin Harkarvy, Richard Gibson, Hans Brenner. Debut 1967 with Netherlands Dance Theater.

KOSMINSKY, JANE. Born in Jersey City, N.J. in 1944. Attended Juilliard, CCNY. Debut 1960 with May O'Donnell. Joined Paul Taylor Co. in 1965. Has appeared with Helen Tamiris, Daniel Nagrin, and Norman Walker.

KOVICH, ROBERT. Born Jan. 17, 1950 in San Jose, CA. Attended Bennington Col. Joined Merce Cunningham Co. in 1973.

KRASSOVSKA, NATHALIE. Born June 3,1918 in Leningrad. Studied with Preobrajenska, Fokine, Massine, Balanchine, and Nijinska. Prima ballerina with Ballet Russe de Monte Carlo and London Festival Ballet. Currently teaches and dances with Dallas Civic Ballet, and appears with other companies as guest artist.

KRONSTAM, HENNING. Born in Copenhagen in 1934. Studied at Royal Danish Ballet School and joined company in 1952. Became premier danseur in 1956. Has appeared as guest artist with many companies.

KRUPSKA, DANIA. Born Aug. 13, 1923 in Fall River, Mass. Studied at Ethel Phillips, and Mordkin Ballet Schools. Began dancing at 6 in Europe as Dania Darling. On return to U.S., joined Catherine Littlefield Ballet. Became member of American Ballet Co. in 1938. More recently has been busy as choreographer.

KUCHERA, LINDA M. Born Jan. 28, 1952 in Monongahela, Pa. Studied at Wash. School of Ballet. Debut 1970 with NYC Opera Ballet; Joffrey II 1970, Ballet Brio 1972–3, ABT 1973.

KUNI, MASAMI. Started career in Japan at 13. Gained international fame in solo recitals throughout Europe. Graduate of German Dance College, and studied with Mary Wigman and Max Terpis. Has taught and choreographed in Berlin, London, Copenhagen, Italy, Argentina, and Israel. Is currently director of Kuni Inst. of Creative Dance in Tokyo and Los Angeles.

LAERKESEN, ANNA. Born in 1942 in Copenhagen. Studied at Royal Danish Ballet School and joined company in 1959. Became soloist in 1961.

LaFONTSEE, DANE. Born Nov. 9, 1946 in Lansing, Mich. Studied at School of Am. Ballet. Debut in 1966 with National Ballet; joined Pa. Ballet in 1967, promoted to soloist in 1972.

LaFOSSE, EDMUND. Born in 1954 in Beaumont, TX. Danced with National Ballet of Washington before joining Eliot Feld Ballet in 1974.

LAING, HUGH. Born in 1911 in Barbados, B.W.I. Studied in London with Craske and Rambert. Long career with Ballet Rambert, and Ballet Theatre, before joining N.Y.C. Ballet in 1950. Now a commercial photographer.

LA MERI. Born Russell Meriwether Hughes in Louisville, Ky., May 13, 1899. Professional debut in 1928. Annual tours throughout world until 1957. Established Ethnologic Dance Center and Theater in 1943, which she closed in 1956, and retired in 1960. Has written several books on dance, and teaches. Organized Festival of Ethnic Dance 1970.

LAMHUT, PHYLLIS. Born Nov. 14, 1933 in N.Y.C. where she began her studies in Henry St. Settlement Playhouse. Also studied with Cunningham, and at American Ballet Center. Debut in title role of Nikolais' "Alice in Wonderland." In 1957 gave concert of own works, and has appeared with Murray Louis. In addition to dancing, teaches and choreographs for her company.

LAMONT, DENI. Born in 1932 in St. Louis, Mo. Appeared in musicals before joining Ballet Russe de Monte Carlo in 1951, Ballet Theatre 1953, N.Y.C. Ballet in 1954, now soloist.

LANDER, TONI. Born June 19, 1931 in Copenhagen, and studied there with Leif Ornberg, and in School of Royal Danish Ballet. Became member of its company at 17. In 1951, joined Paris Opera Ballet. Later joined London Festival Ballet, Ballet Theatre Francais. ABT in 1960 becoming principal ballerina. Rejoined Royal Danish 1971.

LANDON, JANE. Born Jan. 4, 1947 in Perth, Australia. Attended Royal Ballet School, London. Joined company in 1963 rising to principal dancer in 1969. Member of Stuttgart Ballet from 1970.

LANG, HAROLD. Born Dec. 21, 1920 in Daly City, Calif. Debut with S.F. Opera Co., subsequently dancing with Ballet Russe de Monte Carlo, and Ballet Theatre. More recently has appeared in musicals, and teaches.

LANG, PEARL. Born May 29, 1922 in Chicago. Attended U. of Chicago, and studied at Frances Allis, Martha Graham, American Ballet, Nenette Charisse, and Vicente Celli Schools. Debut with Ukrainian Folk Dance Co. in 1938, subsequently appearing with Ruth Page, Martha Graham companies before forming her own. Became active choreographer and teacher and has appeared on Bdwy.

LANNER, JORG. Born Mar. 15, 1939 in Berlin. Studied with Kurt Jooss, Nora Kiss, Menia Martinez. Debut 1958 in Ballet Babilee; joined Bejart in 1959.

LANOVA, MERRIEM. Born in California. Attended San Francisco State, and U. Cal. Studied with Nijinska, Lichine, Danilova, and at School of Am. Ballet, and Ballet Arts. Appeared with Ballet International, and Ballet Russe de Monte Carlo. Now operates own school, choreographs for and directs Ballet Celeste International.

LAPZESON, NOEMI. Born in Buenos Aires, Argentina, June 28, 1940. Studied at Juilliard, and with Corvino, Tudor, Limon, Nikolais, and Graham. Debut in Buenos Aires in 1955. Has appeared with Yuriko, Sophie Maslow, Helen McGehee, Bertram Ross, and Martha Graham. Has appeared in several musicals, and teaches.

LARSEN, GERD. Born in Oslo in 1921. Studied with Tudor. Debut with London Ballet, followed with Ballet Rambert, International Ballet, Sadler's Wells (now Royal) becoming soloist in 1954. Also teaches.

LASCOE, MATTI. Born Feb. 24, 1932. Graduate UCal. Trained with New Dance Group, Merce Cunningham, Herbert Ross. Premiered her own Dance Theatre Co. in 1972.

LATIMER, LENORE. Born July 10, 1935 in Washington, D.C. Graduate Juilliard. Joined Jose Limon Co. in 1959. Has appeared with Valerie Bettis, Anna Sokolow. Also teaches.

LAVROVSKY, MIKHAIL. Born Oct. 29, 1941. Studied at Bolshoi and graduated into company, rapidly rising to principal.

LAYTON, JOE. Born May 3, 1931 in N.Y.C. Studied with Joseph Levinoff. Bdwy debut in 1947. After many musicals, joined Ballet Ho de George Reich in Paris (1945–6). Returned to N.Y. and has become popular director and choreographer.

La Meri

Vladimir Klos

Sara Leland

Daniel Lewis

Susan Lovelle

LECHNER, GUDRUN. Born Nov. 7, 1944 in Stuttgart, Ger. Studied at Stuttgart, and Royal Ballet School, London. Debut 1962 with Stuttgart Ballet; promoted to principal.

LEDIAKH, GENNADI. Born in 1928 in Russia. Entered Bolshoi School in 1946, and was graduated into company in 1949.

LEE, ELIZABETH. Born Jan. 14, 1946 in San Francisco. Studied with Harriet DeRea. Wilson Morelli, Richard Thomas. Debut 1964 with Pennsylvania Ballet. Joined American Ballet Theatre in 1967. American Ballet Co. 1969. Rejoined ABT in 1971; Eliot Feld Ballet 1974.

LEE, KEITH. Born Jan. 15, 1951 in the Bronx. Studied at Harkness, and Ballet Theatre Schools. Has danced with Norman Walker, Harkness Youth Co., and own company. Joined ABT in 1969; became soloist in 1971.

LEES, MICHELLE. Born Mar. 18, 1947 in Virginia. Studied at Wash. School of Ballet. Made debut 1964 with National Ballet.

LEIGH, VICTORIA. Born July 3, 1941, in Brockton, Mass. Studied with Georges Milenoff and at JoAnna-Imperial Studio. Debut 1958 with Palm Beach Ballet. Joined American Ballet Theatre in 1961, and became soloist in 1964.

LELAND, SARA. Born Aug. 2, 1941 in Melrose, Mass. Studied with E. Virginia Williams, Robert Joffrey, and at School of Am. Ballet. Debut with New England Civic Ballet, and subsequently with N.Y.C. Opera (1959), Joffrey Ballet (1960), N.Y.C. Ballet from 1960. Appointed principal in 1972.

LERITZ, LAWRENCE ROBERT. Born Sept. 26, 1955 in Alton, Ill. Trained with Harkness, Joffrey, and School of Am. Ballet. Debut 1974 with Harkness Ballet. With NY Dance Ensemble (1974–75), American Chamber Ballet 1975. Hamburg Ballet 1976.

LERNER, JUDITH. Born in Philadelphia, Dec. 30, 1944. Attended Hunter College, American Ballet School, Ballet Theatre School, and studied with Nenette Charisse and Antony Tudor. Debut as soloist with Eglevsky Ballet in 1961, and joined American Ballet Theatre same year.

LESINS, MARCIS. Born Jan. 6, 1946 in Neustadt, WGer. Studied with Elisabeth Curland, Helen Uraus-Natschewa, Leonid Gonta. Debut 1963 with Munich Opera Ballet; joined Stuttgart Ballet 1970; promoted to principal.

LEVANS, DANIEL. Born Oct. 7, 1953 in Ticonderoga, N.Y. Studied at HS Performing Arts, N.Y. School of Ballet. Debut in 1969 with American Ballet Co. Joined ABT in 1971, promoted to soloist in 1972, principal 1973. Joined NYCB 1974, U.S. Terpischore Co. 1975. Also teaches.

LEVINE, MICHELLE. Born Jan. 24, 1946 in Detroit, Mich. NYU graduate. Studied with Nenette Charisse, Gladys Bailin, Jean Erdman. Debut 1970 with Erdman Co.

LEVINSON, ANDREW. Born July 28, 1954 in Pittsburgh, PA. Studied with Vern Nerden, Penelope Johnson, Paul Sanasardo, Am. Ballet Center. Debut 1965 with Oakland Metropolitan Ballet, Sanasardo Co. 1972, Joffrey Ballet 1976.

LEWIS, DANIEL. Born July 12, 1944 in Bklyn. Juilliard graduate. Joined Limon Co. in 1963. Has appeared with Ruth Currier, Felix Fibich, Anna Sokolow companies.

LEWIS, JAMES J. Born July 30, 1946 in Denver, Colo. Graduate U. Mich. Studied with Sandra Severo. Debut 1969 with Boston Ballet. Joined American Ballet Co. in 1970.

LEWIS, MARILYN. Born June 15, 1947 in Winnipeg, Can. Attended United Col. Debut in 1966 with Royal Winnipeg Ballet; subsequently with Deutsche Operam Phein, and Wuppertal Opera in Germany, Netherlands Dans Theatre.

LIEPA, MARIS. Born July 27, 1930 in Riga, Latvia. Studied at Riga, and Bolshoi schools. Joined Bolshoi in 1961, quickly rising to principal.

LINDEN, ANYA. Born Jan. 3, 1933 in Manchester, Eng. Studied in U.S. with Theodore Koslov, entered Sadler's Wells School in 1947; joined company (now Royal) in 1951; ballerina in 1958. Now retired.

LINDGREN, ROBERT. Born in 1923 in Vancouver, Can. Studied with Vilzak, Swoboda, Preobrajenska. Joined Ballet Russe in 1942, N.Y.C. Ballet in 1957. Retired to teach.

LINN, BAMBI. Born in Brooklyn. April 26, 1926. Studied with Mikhail Mordkin, Helen Oakes, Hanya Holm, Agnes de Mille, and Helene Platava. Debut 1943 in "Oklahoma!" Subsequently danced with Ballet Theatre, Met Opera Ballet, Dance Jubilee Co., and American Ballet Co.

LISTER, MERLE. Born in Toronto, Can., where she began training and had own dance troupe. After moving to N.Y.C., organized dance company in 1964 with which she has appeared in N.Y. and on tour. Also teaches.

LITTLEMAN, ANITA. Born Jan. 4, 1952 in San Francisco, CA. Attended UHawaii, UWash. Trained with Jack Claus, Robert Joffrey. Joined Joffrey company in 1970. Has appeared with Donald McKayle, George Faison, Eleo Pomare, currently with Alvin Ailey.

LITZ, KATHERINE. Born in 1918 in Denver, Colo. Studied with Humphrey, Weidman, Horst, Platova, Thomas. Debut with Humphrey-Weidman Co. in 1936. Soloist with Agnes de Mille Co. (1940–42), and in Bdwy musicals. Debut as choreographer in 1948 in Ballet Ballads, followed by solo and group works. Also teaches.

LLAND, MICHAEL. Born in Bishopville, S.C. Graduate U.S. Car. Studied with Margaret Foster. Debut 1944 in "Song of Norway." Joined Teatro Municipal Rio de Janeiro (1945), ABT (1948) rising to principal in 1957, Ballet Master Houston Ballet (1968), ABT (1971).

LOKEY, BEN. Born Dec. 15, 1944 in Birmingham, Ala. Graduate U. Utah. Studied with Wm. Christensen, Caton, Peryoslavic, Weisberger, Morawski, Patricia Wilde. Made debut in 1966. Principal with Ballet West, and soloist with Pa. Ballet.

LOMBARDI, JOAN. Born Nov. 18, 1944 in Teaneck, N.J. Parsons graduate. Studied with Raoul Gelebert, Igor Schwezoff, Paul Sanasardo, Richard Thomas. Debut 1967 with Sanasardo Co. Has appeared with N.Y.C. Opera Ballet, and John Butler.

LOMMEL, DANIEL. Born March 26 in Paris. Studied with Joseph Lazzini, Nora Kiss. Made debut in 1966 with Grand Ballet Marquis de Cuevas. Joined Bejart Ballet in 1967 and is now a principal dancer.

LORING, EUGENE. Born in Milwaukee in 1914. Studied at School of American Ballet, and with Balanchine, Muriel Stuart, Anatole Vilzak, and Ludmilla Schollar. Debut 1934 in "Carnival." Subsequently with Met Opera Ballet, and Ballet Caravan, for whom he choreographed and starred in "Billy The Kid." Has become a leading choreographer for all media. Owns and operates American School of Dance in Hollywood.

LORRAYNE, VYVYAN. Born April 20, 1939 in Pretoria, South Africa. Entered Royal Ballet School in 1956 and company in 1957. Became principal in 1967.

LOUIS, MURRAY. Born Nov. 4, 1926 in N.Y.C. Graduate of NYU. Studied with Alwin Nikolais, and made debut in 1953. Has appeared annually in concerts and on tour with Nikolais, and own company, for which he also choreographs. Co-director of Chimera Foundation for Dance.

LOUTHER, WILLIAM. Born 1942 in Brooklyn. Attended Juilliard. Studied with Kitty Carson, Martha Graham, May O'Donnell, Antony Tudor, Gertrude Schurr. Debut with O'Donnell Co. in 1958. Has appeared in musicals, and with Donald McKayle Co. Joined Graham Co. in 1964. Artistic director Batsheva Co. 1972.

LOVE, EDWARD. Born June 29, 1950. Graduate Ohio U. Debut 1973 with Alvin Ailey Dance Theatre.

LOVELLE, LAURA. Born May 6, 1958 in Brooklyn, NY. Studied at Dance Theatre of Harlem and made debut with company in 1973.

LOVELLE, SUSAN. Born May 22, 1954 in NYC. Attended Barnard, SUNY. Studied at Dance Theatre of Harlem, and made debut with company in 1968.

LOWSKI, WOYTEK. Born Oct. 11, 1939 in Brzesc, Poland. Studied in Warsaw and Leningrad. Debut 1958 with Warsaw Ballet, joined Bejart Ballet 1966, Cologne Ballet 1971, Roland Petit Co. in 1972; Boston Ballet 1973 as premier danseur.

LOYD, SUE. Born May 26, 1940 in Reno, Nev. Studied with Harold and Lew Christensen, Vilzak, Scolar, Danielian, Zerapse, Bruson, and Joffrey. Debut with San Francisco Ballet in 1954. Joined Joffrey Ballet in 1967. Ballet Mistress for Cincinatti Ballet.

LUBOVITCH, LAR. Born in Chicago; attended Art Inst., U. Iowa, Juilliard, ABT School, and studied with Martha Graham, Margaret Black. Debut 1962 with Pearl Lang, subsequently with Glen Tetley, John Butler, Donald McKayle, Manhattan Festival Ballet, Harkness, before forming own company. Also designs and choreographs for other companies.

LUCAS, JONATHAN. Born Aug. 14, 1922 in Sherman, Tex. Gradute of Southern Methodist U. Studied at American Ballet School. Debut 1945 in "A Lady Says Yes," followed by many Bdwy musicals. Became choreographer in 1956.

LUCCI, MICHELLE. Born Apr. 26, 1950 in Buffalo, NY. Studied at Banff School, with Joffrey, Caton, Lazowski, and Harkarvy. Debut 1968 with Royal Winnipeg Ballet. Joined Pennsylvania Ballet in 1969.

LUDERS, ADAM. Born Feb. 16, 1950 in Copenhagen, Den. Trained at Royal Danish Ballet School, and was graduated into company. Joined London Festival Ballet (1972), NYC Ballet as a principal in 1975.

LUDLOW, CONRAD. Born in Hamilton, Mont. in 1935. Began studies in San Francisco, and became member of its ballet company where he attained rank of soloist before joining N.Y.C. Ballet in 1957. Retired in 1973.

LUPPESCU, CAROLE. Born April 18, 1944 in Brooklyn. Attended Ind. U. Studied at Met Opera Ballet School. Joined Pennsylvania Ballet in 1964. Has performed with Ballet Rambert. Now retired.

LUSBY, VERNON. Born in New Orleans, La. Studied with Leila Haller, Dolin, Caron, Craske, Nijinska, Tudor. Appeared with ABT, Grands Ballets de Marquis de Cuevas, Natl. Ballet of Brazil. Also dancer and choreographer on Bdwy. Now associate director Royal Winnipeg Ballet.

LYMAN, PEGGY. Born June 28, 1950 in Cincinnati, Ohio. Studied at Stone-Camryn, Martha Graham, and Joffrey schools. Debut 1969 with NYC Opera Ballet. Joined Martha Graham Co. in 1973.

LYNN, ENID. Born in Manchester, Conn. Studied with Joseph Albano, Martha Graham, Sigurd Leeder. Director-Choreographer for Hartford Modern Dance Theatre, and Hartford Ballet.

LYNN, ROSAMOND. Born Dec. 31, 1944 in Palo Alto, Calif. Studied with Bill Griffith, Vincenzo Celli, Richard Thomas, Patricia Wilde. Debut 1964 with Philadelphia Lyric Opera, subsequently with ABT (1965), Alvin Ailey Co. (1970)

MACDONALD, BRIAN. Born May 14, 1928 in Montreal, Canada where he began choreographing for television. In 1958 became choreographer for Royal Winnipeg Ballet, and commuted to Norwegian and Royal Swedish Ballets where he held positions as director. Joined Harkness Ballet as director in 1967, left in 1968.

MacLEARY, DONALD. Born in Iverness, Scot., Aug. 22, 1937. Trained at Royal Ballet School. Joined company in 1954, became soloist in 1955 and premier danseur in 1959. Has partnered Beriosova on most of her appearances.

MacMILLAN, KENNETH. Born Dec. 11, 1930 in Scotland. Studied at Sadler's Wells and joined company (now Royal) in 1948. Debut as choreographer with Sadler's Wells Choreographers Group in 1953 with "Somnambulism." Subsequently created dances for Theatre Ballet, Royal Ballet, American Ballet Theatre, Royal Danish, Stuttgart, and German Opera Ballet. Perhaps most famous are "Romeo and Juliet" and "The Invitation." Director Royal Ballet from 1970–1976.

MADSEN, EGON. Born Aug. 24, 1944 in Copenhagen. Appeared with Pantomime Theatre and Scandinavian Ballet before joining Stuttgart Ballet in 1961. Promoted to soloist in 1963. Now principal.

MADSEN, JORN. Born Dec. 7, 1939 in Copenhagen. Studied at Royal Danish Ballet School; joined company in 1957; appointed soloist in 1961. Guest with Royal Ballet in 1965. Now retired.

MAGNO, SUSAN. Born in 1946 in Melrose, Mass. Studied with Margaret Craske, Alice Langford, Virginia Williams. Appeared with Boston Ballet before joining Joffrey Ballet in 1965. Lar Lubovitch Co. in 1972.

MAGUIRE, TERRILL. Born May 2, 1947 in Pasadena, CA. Graduate UCLA. Studied with Richard Oliver, Donald McKayle, Donald Hewitt, Marie Marchowsky, Stefan Wenta, Sandra Neals, Gus Solomons. Has performed with Richard Oliver, Charles Weidman, Marie Marchowsky, Sandra Neals, and formed own company in 1973.

MAHLER, RONI. Born in N.Y.C. in 1942. Studied with Maria Swoboda and at Ballet Russe School. Debut with Ballet Russe de Monte Carlo in 1960. Joined National Ballet in 1962 and became leading soloist in 1966. Joined ABT as soloist in 1969.

MAIORANO, ROBERT. Born Aug. 29, 1946 in Brooklyn, NY. Studied at School of American Ballet. Joined NYC Ballet in 1962.

MAJORS, DALIENNE. Born Feb. 26, 1950 in San Antonio, TX. Juilliard graduate. Studied with Martha Graham, Maggie Black, Alfredo Corvino, Marjorie Mussman. Appears with Elizabeth Keen and Frances Alenikoff companies.

MAKAROVA, NATALIA. Born Nov. 21, 1940 in Leningrad. Studied at Kirov School and joined company in 1959. Had triumph with her first "Giselle" in 1961. Defected and joined ABT in 1970 as principal; made debut in "Giselle."

MALONEY, JULIE. Born in Newark, NJ. Debut 1970 with Charles Weidman. Joined Jan Wodynski company in 1972, and formed own company in 1975.

MANN, BURCH. Born in Texas: Studied with Adolph Bolm, Mordkin, and Fokine. Operates studio in Pasadena, Calif. Organized "Burch Mann Concert Group" that has become The American Folk Ballet.

MARCEAU, MARCEL. Born March 22, 1923 in Strasbourg, France. Studied with Charles Dullen and Etienne Decroux. Debut with Barrault-Renaud Co. in 1946. In 1947 formed own company, and among other works, presented "Bip" with whom he has become identified. Subsequently toured Europe, and U.S.

MARCHOWSKY, MARIE. Studied with Martha Graham: became member of company 1934–40. With own company, and as soloist, performing own choreography, has appeared in U.S. and abroad.

MARCU, REMUS. Born in Rumania where he danced with Rumanian State Opera before coming to U.S. in 1970. Has danced with Pittsburgh Ballet, Boston Ballet, Pennsylvania Ballet. Joined Eliot Feld Ballet in 1974.

MARINACCIO, GENE. Born 1931 in Newark, NJ. Studied with Bupesh Guha, Michael Brigante. Appeared with Lichine's Ballet, Petit's Ballet de Paris, Ballet Russe Monte Carlo, Ballet de Cuba. Now teaches and formed own company American Concert Ballet.

MARKHAM, DIANNE. Born June 1, 1949 in Springwater, NY. Graduate UOre. Trained at Louis-Nikolais School. Debut 1975 with Murray Louis Dance Co.

MARKO, IVAN. Born Mar. 29, 1947 in Hungary. Studied at Allami Ballet Intezet. Debut 1967 with Budapest Opera Ballet. Joined Ballet of 20th Century 1968.

MARKOVA, ALICIA. Born in London, Dec. 1, 1910. Studied with Seraphine Astafieva and Enrico Cecchetti. Appeared with Diaghilieff Ballet (1925–29). Vic-Wells Ballet (1932–5), Markova-Dolin Ballet (1935–7), Monte Carlo Ballet Russe (1938–41), prima ballerina Ballet Theatre (1941–5). Original Ballet Russe 1946, Markova-Dolin Co. (1947–8), co-founder and prima ballerina London Festival Ballet (1950–2), and has appeared as guest artist with companies throughout the world. Director of Met Opera Ballet 1963–9. Teaches at U. Cinn.

MARKS, BRUCE. Born in N.Y.C. in 1937 and studied at Met Opera School of Ballet with Tudor and Craske. Joined Met Opera Ballet in 1957, rising to rank of first dancer; joined American Ballet Theatre in 1961 as a principal dancer, and became premier danseur. Appeared as guest in 1963 with Royal Swedish Ballet, and in 1963 with London Festival Ballet. Joined Royal Danish Ballet 1971. ABT 1974 summer season. Associate director Ballet West 1976.

MARKS, J. Born in Los Angeles, Feb. 14, 1942. Founder of San Francisco Contemporary Dancers Foundation. Has choreographed over 200 works. Founder-Director of First National Nothing.

MARSICANO, MERLE. Born in Philadelphia. Studied with Ethel Phillips, Mordkin, Ruth St. Denis, Mary Wigman, Martha Graham, Louis Horst. Debut with Pennsylvania Opera. Since 1952 has presented own program of solos which she choreographs.

MARTIN, KEITH. Born June 15, 1943 in Yorkshire, Eng. Joined Royal Ballet School in 1958 and company in 1961. Appointed soloist in 1967. Joined Pa. Ballet in 1971, and now a principal.

MARTIN, YON. Born Sept. 12, 1945 in Washington, D.C. Studied with Erika Thimey, Paul Sanasardo, and at Washington School of Ballet. Debut with Dance Theatre of Wash. Joined Sanasardo Co. in 1966.

MARTINEZ, ENRIQUE. Born 1926 in Havana, Cuba where he studied with Alonso and danced with Ballet Alicia Alonso. In addition to appearing with American Ballet Theatre has created several ballets, and in 1964 served as ballet master of Bellas Artes de Mexico.

MARTINEZ, MENIA. Born Sept. 27, 1938 In Havana, Cuba. Studied at Alonso School. Made debut with Alicia Alonso Ballet in 1954 subsequently with Bolshoi (1965), Kirov (1966), and Bejart from 1969.

MARTINS, PETER. Born 1947 in Copenhagen. Trained at Royal Danish Ballet School and joined company in 1965. Granted leave to appear with N.Y.C. Ballet. Joined company in 1970 as principal.

MARTIN-VISCOUNT, BILL. Born in Winnipeg, Can. Began study at 12 with Royal Winnipeg Ballet, subsequently studied at Royal Ballet, American Ballet Theatre, and Bolshoi Schools. Joined Royal Winnipeg Ballet in 1959; took leave to appear with London Festival Ballet, and returned in 1962. Appeared with Joffrey as principal in 1969, Rio de Janeiro Ballet in 1970. In demand as guest artist with regional companies. Artistic director Memphis Ballet 1974. Southwest Ballet 1975.

Adam Luders **Susan McLain** **Enrique Martinez** **Carol Jean Messmer** **Hector Mercado**

MASLOW, SOPHIE. Born in N.Y.C. where she studied with Blanche Talmund, and Martha Graham. Joined Graham company and became soloist. Debut as choreographer 1934. Joined Jane Dudley, William Bales to form Dudley-Maslow-Bales Trio. Helped found American Dance Festival at Conn. College. Has choreographed and appeared in many of her works. On Board of Directors and teaches for New Dance Group Studio.

MASON, KENNETH. Born April 17, 1942 in Bartford, Eng. Attended Royal Ballet School and joined company in 1959. Became principal in 1968.

MASON, MONICA. Born Sept. 6, 1941 in Johannesburg, S.A. Studied at Royal Ballet School, and joined company in 1958, rising to soloist, and principal in 1967.

MASSINE, LEONIDE. Born in Moscow, Aug. 9, 1896. Studied at Imperial Ballet School and with Domashoff Checchetti, and Legat. Discovered by Diaghilev; joined his company in 1914; became principal dancer and choreographer; Ballet de Monte Carlo 1932–41; Ballet National Theatre 1941–4, organized Ballet Russe Highlights 1945–6; subsequently appearing as guest artist and/or choreographer with almost every important company, and in films.

MASTERS, GARY. Born Oct. 17, 1948 in St.Paul, MN. Attended Juilliard, and trained with Hanya Holm. Debut 1969 with Ethel Winter company; joined Limon in 1970; promoted to soloist 1972. Also danced with Pennsylvania Ballet.

MATHEWS, FRED. Born July 10, 1945 in Pueblo, CO. Attended UCo., Bennington, Stephens Col. Joined Jose Limon Co. in 1973.

MATHIS, BONNIE. Born Sept. 8, 1942 in Milwaukee, Wisc. Attended Juilliard. Studied with Tudor and Anderson. Performed with Radio City Ballet, Paul Taylor, Norman Walker, before joining Harkness Ballet. ABT (1971) as soloist; promoted to principal in 1974.

MATTEO (Vittucci). Born in Utica, N.Y. Graduate of Cornell. Studied at Met Opera School, with La Meri, LaQuica, Esparsa, Azuma, Guneya, Balasaraswati. Member Met Opera School (1947–51); solo debut in 1953; formed partnership with Carola Goya in 1954. Teaches, and organized EthnoAmerican Dance Theater with which he appears.

MATTHEWS, LAURENCE. Born June 12, 1949 in Hollywood, Cal. Studied with Lew and Harold Christensen, Anatole Vizak, Ted Howard, Paul Curtis, Richard Gibson, Royal Cons. Den. Debut with San Francisco Ballet 1968. Joined Penn. Ballet 1973 as soloist; NYCB 1974.

MATTOX, MATT. Born Aug. 18, 1921 in Tulsa, Okla. Attended San Bernardino College; studied with Ernest Belcher, Nico Charisso, Eugene Loring, Louis Da Pron, Evelyn Bruns, Teddy Kerr, and Jack Cole. Debut 1946 in "Are You With It?," subsequently appearing in many musicals. First choreography in 1958 for "Say, Darling," followed by several Bdwy productions, and Met Opera Ballet.

MAULE, MICHAEL. Born Oct. 31, 1926 in Durban, S.Af. Studied with Vincenzo Celli and made debut in 1946 in "Annie Get Your Gun." Joined Ballet Theatre, then Ballet Alicia Alonso (1949–50), N.Y.C. Ballet (1950–53), Ballets; U.S.A. (1959), Ballet Ensemble (1960–61). In 1964 organized own touring group. Now teaches.

MAULE, SARA. Born June 27, 1951 in Tokyo, Japan. Studied at UCal., San Francisco Ballet School. Joined SFB in 1965; became soloist 1970; Am. Ballet Theatre 1972.

MAXIMOVA, YEKATERINA. Born in Russia in 1939. Entered Bolshoi School at 10, and joined company in 1958, rising to ballerina.

MAXWELL, CARLA. Born Oct. 25, 1945 in Glendale, Calif. Juilliard graduate; debut 1965 with Limon Co. (now soloist), also appears with Louis Falco, and in concert with Clyde Morgan.

MAYBARDUK, LINDA. Born Feb. 22, 1951 in Orlando, Fla. Studied at Natl. Ballet School of Canada and graduated into company in 1969; promoted to soloist.

MAZZO, KAY. Born Jan. 17, 1947 in Chicago. Studied with Bernadene Hayes, and at School of American Ballet. In 1961 appeared with Ballets U.S.A. before joining N.Y.C. Ballet corps in 1962, became soloist in 1965, ballerina in 1969.

McBRIDE, PATRICIA. Born Aug. 23, 1942, in Teaneck, N.J., and studied at School of American Ballet. Joined N.Y.C. Ballet in 1959 and became principal dancer before leaving teens; ballerina in 1961.

McCONNELL, TEENA. Born in Montclair, NJ. Attended Columbia U. Studied at School of Am. Ballet. Joined NYCBallet in 1961; promoted to soloist in 1966.

McFALL, JOHN. Born in Kansas City, Mo.; studied at San Francisco Ballet, and joined company in 1965.

McGEHEE, HELEN. Born in Lynchburg, Va. Graduate Randolph-Macon College. Studied at Graham School and joined company; became first dancer in 1954. Among her choreographic works are "Undine," "Metamorphosis," "Nightmare," "Cassandra," and "Oresteia." Also teaches, and dances with own company.

McKAYLE, DONALD. Born in N.Y.C., July 6, 1930. Attended NYCC; studied at New Dance Group Studio, Graham School, with Nenette Charisse, Karel Shook, and Pearl Primus. Debut with New Dance Group in 1948, subsequently appeared with Dudley-Maslow-Bales, Jean Erdman, N.Y.C. Dance Theatre, Anna Sokolow, and Martha Graham. Formed own company in 1951, and in addition to choreographing, teaches.

McKENZIE, KEVIN. Born Apr. 29, 1954 in Burlington, Vt. Trained at Washington School of Ballet. Debut 1972 with National Ballet. Joined Joffrey Ballet 1974.

McLAIN, SUSAN. Born Apr. 27, 1953 in New Haven, CT. Graduate CCNY. Studied with May O'Donnell, Norman Walker, Paul Sanasardo, Am. Dance Center, Pearl Lang, Martha Graham. Debut 1972 with Pearl Lang, also with Larry Richardson, joined Martha Graham Co. 1977.

McLEOD, ANNE. (formerly Anne Ditson) Born Dec. 20, 1944 in Baton Rouge, La. Graduate UCLA. Studied at Louis-Nikolais School. Joined Murray Louis Co. 1970.

McKINNEY, GAYLE. Born Aug. 26, 1949 in NYC. Attended Juilliard. Made debut 1968 with Dance Theatre of Harlem.

McLERIE, ALLYN ANN. Born Dec. 1, 1926 in Grand Mere, Can. Studied with Nemchinova, Caton, De Mille, Yeichi Nimura, Holm, Graham, and Forte. First performed in ballet corps of San Carlo Opera in 1942. Bdwy debut 1943 in "One Touch of Venus" followed by many musicals. Now in films.

MEAD, ROBERT. Born April 17, 1940 in Bristol, Eng. Studied at Royal Ballet School, and joined company in 1958. Made principal dancer in 1967. Joined Hamburg Opera Ballet in 1971.

MEDEIROS, JOHN. Born June 5, 1944 in Winston Salem, N.C. Studied at Boston Cons., with Ailey, Beatty, and Segarra. Has appeared in musicals and with Alvin Ailey Co.

MEEHAN, JOHN. Born May 1, 1950 in Brisbane, Aust. Trained at Australian Ballet School and joined company in 1970.

MEEHAN, NANCY. Born in San Francisco. Graduate U. Cal. Studied with Halprin, Lathrop, Graham, and Hawkins. Debut 1953 with Halprin company. Joined Erick Hawkins in 1962.

MEISTER, HANS. Born in Schaffhausen on the Rhine. Studied at Zurich Opera Ballet, Royal Ballet, Leningrad Kirov Schools. Joined Ntl. Canada 1957; Met Opera Ballet (1962–6); Zurich Opera 1966; founder-member Swiss Chamber Ballet; principal and teacher for Finnish Natl. Opera Ballet; director Zurich Ballet 1975.

MENENDEZ, JOLINDA. Born Nov. 17, 1954 in NYC. Studied at Ntl. Academy of Ballet. Made debut with Ballet Repertory Co. Joined American Ballet Theatre 1972; promoted to soloist 1974.

MERCADO, HECTOR. Born in NYC in 1949. Studied at HS of Performing Arts, Harkness Ballet. Joined Ailey company in 1970, left in 1975. Has appeared on Bdwy.

MERCIER, MARGARET. Born in Montreal. Studied at Sadler's Wells School, graduating into company in 1954. Joined Les Grands Ballets Canadiens in 1958; Joffrey Ballet 1963; Harkness Ballet 1964.

MERRICK, IRIS. Born in 1915 in N.Y.C. Studied with Fokine, Fedorova, Vladimiroff, Decroux, Egorova. Is now director and choreographer of Westchester Ballet Co. which she founded in 1950.

MESSMER, CAROL JEAN. Born Dec. 18, 1955 in New Orleans, LA. Studied at Joffrey School and joined company in 1975.

MEYER, LYNDA. Born in Texas. Studied at San Francisco Ballet School and joined company in 1962. Became principal dancer in 1966.

MILLER, BUZZ. Born in 1928 in Snowflake, Ariz. Graduate Ariz. State College. Debut 1948 in "Magdalena." In addition to Bdwy musicals, has appeared with Jack Cole Dancers, Ballets de Paris, and is choreographer.

MILLER, JANE. Born Mar. 19, 1945 in NYC. Studied at School of American Ballet. Debut 1964 with Pennsylvania Ballet; subsequently with Harkness Ballet, National Ballet as principal; Co-Director-principal with Eglevsky Ballet.

MILLER, LINDA. Born Sept. 7, 1953 in Washington, DC. Attended N.C. School of Arts, School of Am. Ballet. Debut 1972 with North Carolina Dance Theatre. Joined Eliot Feld Co. in 1974.

MINAMI, ROGER. Born in Hawaii, reared in Calif. Left Long Beach State College to attend Eugene Loring's American School of Dance. Became member of Loring's Dance Players, and now teaches in Loring's school.

MITCHELL, ARTHUR. Born in N.Y.C. Mar. 27, 1934. Studied at School of American Ballet. Joined N.Y.C. Ballet in 1955 and rapidly rose to principal. Was choreographer at Spoleto, Italy, Festival for one season. Founder-director-choreographer for Dance Theatre of Harlem.

MITCHELL, GREGORY. Born Dec. 9, 1951 in Brooklyn, NY. Graduate Juilliard. With National Ballet of Canada (1972–3), Shekinah Co., Eliot Feld Ballet 1976.

MITCHELL, JAMES. Born Feb. 29, 1920 in Sacramento, Calif. Graduate of LACC. Debut 1944 in "Bloomer Girl." Joined Ballet Theatre in 1950, subsequently danced with Met Opera, De Mille Dance Theatre, and on Bdwy.

MITCHELL, LUCINDA. Born Feb. 18, 1946 in Takoma Park, Md. Graduate Smith Col. Studied with Martha Graham. Debut 1970 with Bertram Ross Co.; Kazuko Hirabayashi Dance Theatre 1971; Martha Graham Co. 1972.

MLAKAR, VERONIKA. Born in 1935 in Zurich, Switzerland. Appeared with Roland Petit, Ruth Page, Milorad Miskovitch, Janine Charat, John Butler, and Jerome Robbins before joining American Ballet Theatre in 1964.

MOCCIA, JODI. Born Oct. 24, 1954 in NYC. Trained at Am. Dance Center. Joined Alvin Ailey company in 1974.

MOFSIE, LOUIS. Born in N.Y.C., May 3, 1936. Graduate of SUNY at Buffalo. Training on Hopi and Winnebago Indian reservations. Debut at 10. In 1950, organized, directed and appeared with own group performing native Indian dances, both in N.Y.C. and on tour.

MOLINA, JOSE. Born in Madrid, Spain, Nov. 19, 1937. Studied with Pilar Monterde. Debut 1953 with Soledad Mirales Co., subsequently joined Pilar Mirales, Jose Greco, and in 1962 premiered own company in the U.S. has since made international tours.

MONCION, FRANCISCO. Born in Dominican Republic, July 6. Studied at School of American Ballet. Danced with New Opera Co., Ballet International, Ballet Russe de Monte Carlo, and Ballet Society which became N.Y.C. Ballet. Is now a principal. First choreographic work "Pastorale" performed by company in 1957. Is also a painter.

MONK, MEREDITH. Born Nov. 20, 1943 in Lima, Peru. Graduate of Sarah Lawrence. Studied with Tarassova, Slavenska, Cunningham, Graham, Mata and Hari. Debut 1964, subsequently choreographed for herself and company.

MONTALBANO, GEORGE. Born in Bklyn. Studied with Mme. Deinitzen, Natalia Branitska., ABC. Appeared with Westchester Ballet, and in musicals, before joining Joffrey Ballet; Eliot Feld Ballet 1974.

MONTE, ELISA. Born May 23 in Brooklyn, NY. Trained with Vladimir Dokoudovsky, Maggie Black, Martha Graham. Joined Pearl Lang (1968), Baku (1971), Lar Lubovitch (1972), Marcus Schulkind (1975), Martha Graham (1974).

MONTERO, LUIS. Born in Granada in 1939. Debut at 15 with Mariemma company. Joined Pilar Lopez, then Jose Greco, Victor Albarez. Became first dancer with Jose Molina Bailes Espanoles in 1961; also choreographs for company.

MOONEY, ELINA. Born Nov. 28, 1942 in New Orleans. Attended Sara Lawrence Col. Studied with Evelyn Davis, Weidman, Cunningham, Tamiris, Sanasardo. Debut 1961 with Tamiris-Nagrin Co., subsequently with Weidman, Marion Scott, Paul Sanasardo, Cliff Keuter, Don Redlich, and own company.

MOORE, CHARLES. Born May 22, 1928 in Cleveland, OH. Studied with Eleanor Frampton, Charles Weidman, Katherine Dunham, Pearl Primus. Before starting own company, appeared with Primus, Destine, Holder, McKayle, Beatty, Ailey, and Olatunji. Also appeared on Bdwy.

MOORE, GARY. Born Jan. 29, 1950 in Washington, D.C. Studied with Mavis Murry, Tania Rousseau, Oleg Tupine. Debut with Harkness Youth Co. in 1969, after which joined Pa. Ballet.

MOORE, JACK. Born Mar. 18, 1926 in Monticello, Ind. Graduate U. Iowa. Studied at Graham School, School of American Ballet, Conn. College, and Cunningham Studio. Debut 1951, subsequently with Nina Fonaroff, Helen McGehee, Pearl Lang, Katherine Litz, Martha Graham, Anna Sokolow, and NYC Opera, in musicals, and his own works annually since 1957. Has taught at Conn. College, Bennington, Juilliard, UCLA, and Adelphi.

MORALES, HILDA. Born June 17, 1946 in Puerto Rico. Studied at San Juan Ballet School and American School of Ballet. Debut with N.Y.C. Ballet, then joined Penn. Ballet in 1965, becoming principal. Guest with Les Grands Ballets Canadiens, ABT 1973 as soloist.

MORAWSKI, MIECZYSLAW. Born Jan. 1, 1932 in Wilno, Poland. Studied at Warsaw Ballet School, Bolshoi and Kirov schools, and graduated as teacher. Now director of Virginia Beach Ballet.

MORDAUNT, JOANNA. Born Feb. 13, 1950 in London. Trained at Royal Ballet School; joined company in 1968; London Festival Ballet in 1970.

MORDENTE, TONY. Born in Brooklyn in 1935. Studied with Farnworth. Has appeared on Bdwy and TV, and been assistant to Gower Champion and Michael Kidd. Has also directed and choreographed musicals.

MORE, VICTORIA. Born in Los Angeles. Attended School of American Ballet. Debut with N.Y.C. Opera and joined Joffrey Ballet in 1969.

MORGAN, CLYDE. Born Jan. 30, 1940 in Cincinnati. Graduate Cleveland State Col. Studied at Bennington, Karamu House, Ballet Russe, New Dance Group. Debut 1961 with Karamu Dance Theatre; joined Limon 1965 (now soloist), also appears with Anna Sokolow, Pearl Lang, Olatunji, and in concert with Carla Maxwell.

MORGAN, EARNEST. Born Dec. 3, 1947 in Waihjwa, Hawaii. Attended Northwestern U. Studied with Jene Sugano, Gus Giordano, Ed Parish. Debut 1966 with Gus Giordano Co., subsequently in musicals before joining Paul Taylor Co. in 1969.

MORGAN, VICTORIA. Born Mar. 18, 1951 in Salt Lake City, U. Graduate UUtah with training under Willam Christensen. Joined Ballet West in 1970; principal since 1972.

MORISHITA, YOKO. Born in 1949 in Hiroshima, Japan. Began career at 4; attended Tachibana School, Matsuyama School. Joined Tokyo Matsyyama Ballet and rose to prima ballerina. Has been guest artist with many companies, including ABT in 1976.

MORRICE, NORMAN. Born in Agua Dulca, Mexico in 1931. Studied at Royal Academy, London, Rambert School. Joined Rambert Ballet 1953 eventually becoming principal dancer and choreographer. Director of Royal Ballet 1977.

MORRIS, MARK. Born Aug. 29, 1956. Studied with Verla Flowers, Perry Brunson, Marjorie Mussman, Jacques Patarozzi, Pedro Azorin, Maria Magdalena. Joined Eliot Feld Ballet 1976.

MORRIS, MARNEE. Born Apr. 2, 1946 in Schenectady, N.Y. Studied with Phyllis Marmein, Cornelia Thayer, Vladimir Dokoudovsky, and at School of Am. Ballet. Joined N.Y.C. Ballet in 1961. Is now a soloist.

MORRIS, MONICA. Born Sept. 23, 1946 in Eustis, Fla. Attended Oglethorpe U. Debut 1966 with Harkness Ballet; subsequently with Martha Graham Co., Paul Taylor Co. 1972.

MORROW, CARL. Born June 12, 1953 in Sydney, Aust. Studied at Australian Ballet School. Joined Stuttgart Ballet in 1972.

MOYLAN, MARY ELLEN. Born in 1926 in Cincinnati. Studied at School of American Ballet, and made debut at 16 as leading dancer in operetta "Rosalinda." In 1943 joined Ballet Russe de Monte Carlo as soloist. In 1950 became ballerina with Ballet Theatre. Retired in 1957.

MUELLER, CHRISTA. Born Dec. 20, 1950 in Cincinnati, O. Studied with Merce Cunningham, Ben Harkarvy, Harkness House. Debut 1972 with Dance Repertory Co. Joined Alvin Ailey Co. 1973.

MULLER, JENNIFER. Born Oct. 16, 1944 in Yonkers, N.Y. Graduate Juilliard. Studied with Limon, Graham, Lang, Tudor, Corvino, Craske, Horst, Sokolow. Has danced with Pearl Lang, Sophie Maslow, N.Y.C. Opera, Frances Alenikoff, Louis Falco. Member of Jose Limon Company from 1963. Teaches, and choreographs. Associate director of Falco Co.

MUMAW, BARTON. Born in 1912 in Hazelton, Pa. Studied with Ted Shawn; debut with Shawn's company in 1931 and danced with group until it disbanded. Now makes guest appearances, teaches, and appears in musicals.

MUNRO, RICHARD. Born Aug. 8, 1944, in Camberley, Eng. Trained at Hardie Ballet School. Debut with Zurich Opera Ballet, subsequently with London Festival Ballet, American Ballet Co. Now co-director of Louisville Ballet and teacher.

MURPHY, SEAMUS. Born in Hong Kong. Attended Juilliard. Appeared on Bdwy before forming own company. Also teacher.

MURRAY-WHITE, MELVA. Born May 24, 1950 in Philadelphia, Pa. Attended Md. State, Ohio State U. Studied with Marion Cuyjet, Bettye Robinson. Debut 1971 with Dance Theatre of Harlem.

MUSGROVE, TRACI. Born Feb. 7, 1948 in Carlysle, Pa. Graduate SMU. Studied with Graham, Limon, Hoving, Kuch, Yuriko. Debut 1970 with Yuriko, subsequently with Pearl Lang, Martha Graham.

MUSIL, KARL. Born Nov. 3, in Austria. Studied at Vienna State Opera School; joined company in 1953; promoted to soloist in 1958. Has appeared as guest artist with many companies.

MUSSMAN, MARJORIE. Born Feb. 19, 1943 in Columbus, O. Attended Smith College, and Sorbonne, Paris. Studied with Reznikoff, Marmein, Limon, and Joffrey. Debut with Paris Festival Ballet in 1964, and U.S. debut with Jose Limon in 1964. Member of Joffrey Ballet 1965. Joined First Chamber Dance Co.

Jane Miller

Jack Moore

Pamela Nearhoof

Gary Norman

Mary Ann Niles

NAGRIN, DANIEL. Born May 22, 1917 in N.Y.C., graduate of CCNY. Studied with Graham, Tamiris, Holm, and Sokolow. Debut in 1945 in "Marianne," followed by several Bdwy musicals and choreography for Off-Bdwy productions. Now appears in solo concerts, and teaches.

NAGY, IVAN. Born Apr. 28, 1943 in Debrecen, Hungary. Studied at Budapest Opera Ballet School and joined company. Came to U.S. and National Ballet in 1965. One season with N.Y.C. Ballet; joined ABT in 1968 as soloist. Became principal in 1969.

NAHAT, DENNIS. Born Feb. 20, 1947 in Detroit, Mich. Studied at Juilliard. Debut 1965 with Joffrey Ballet. Appeared and choreographed on Bdwy before joining ABT in 1968; Soloist 1970, Principal 1973. Co-director Cleveland Ballet.

NAMTALASHVILI, ILIA. Born in Russia in 1933. Began studies in province of Georgia at 8. Immigrated to Israel in 1972 and is founder-director-choreographer of Georgian Dancers of Israel.

NAULT, FERNAND. Born Dec. 27, 1921 in Montreal, Can. Studied with Craske, Tudor, Preobrajenska, Volkova, Pereyaslavic, Leese. Debut with American Ballet Theatre in 1944, for which he has been ballet master 20 years. Artistic Director of Louisville Ballet, and associate director of Les Grands Ballets Canadiens.

NEARHOOF, PAMELA. Born May 12, 1955 in Indiana, Pa. Studied at American Ballet Center, Sulik School. Joined Joffrey Ballet 1971.

NEARY, COLLEEN. Born May 23, 1952 in Miami, FL. Trained at School of American Ballet. Joined NYC Ballet in 1969, becoming soloist in 1974.

NEARY, PATRICIA. Born Oct. 27, 1942 in Miami, Fla. Studied with Georges Milenoff and Thomas Armour, at Natl. Ballet School, School of American Ballet. From 1962 to 1968 was soloist with N.Y.C. Ballet. Now makes guest appearances. Co-director Berlin State Opera Ballet 1970. Director Le Grand Theatre du Geneve 1972.

NEELS, SANDRA. Born Sept. 21, 1942 in Las Vegas, Nev. Studied with Nicholas Vasilieff, Martha Nishitani, Richard Thomas. Debut with Merle Marsicano in 1962. Teacher at Cunningham School since 1965.

NELSON, TED. Born May 17, 1949 in San Pedro, Cal. Studied at San Francisco Ballet, School of American Ballet. Debut 1970 with San Francisco Ballet. Joined Joffrey Ballet 1973.

NERINA, NADIA. Born Oct. 21, 1927 in Cape Town, South Africa where she received training. Joined Sadler's Wells Ballet in 1946, subsequently becoming one of its leading ballerinas. Now retired.

NEUMEIR, JOHN. Born Feb. 24, 1942 in Milwaukee. Studied at Stone-Camryn, and Royal Ballet (London) schools, and with Sybil Shearer, Vera Volkova. Debut 1961 with Sybil Shearer. With Stuttgart Ballet from 1963. Director Frankfurt Opera Ballet 1969; Hamburg Opera Ballet 1973.

NIELSEN, DOUGLAS. Born June 8, 1948 in St. Paul, MN. Graduate Augburg Col. Trained with Bella Lewitzky, Donald McKayle, Mia Slavenska, Pearl Lang, Paul Sanasardo. Debut 1973 with Gus Solomons company. Has also danced with Sanasardo Co., Pearl Lang.

NIGHTINGALE, JOHN. Born Oct. 21, 1943 in Salisbury, Southern Rhodesia. Studied at London School of Contemporary Dance. Joined Paul Taylor Company in 1967.

NIKOLAIS, ALWIN. Born Nov. 25, 1912 in Southington, Conn. Studied with Graham, Humphrey, Holm, Horst, Martin, and at Bennington Summer Dance School. Professional debut 1939. Designs, composes, and choreographs for own company that tours U.S. and abroad. Was co-director of Henry St. Playhouse School of Dance and Theatre. Now co-director of Chimera Foundation for Dance.

NILES, MARY ANN. Born May 2, 1935 in N.Y.C. Studied with Nenette Charisse, Ernest Carlos, Frances Cole, and Roye Dodge. Appeared with American Dance Theatre in U.S. and Europe. Was half of Fosse-Niles dance team that toured U.S. and appeared in Bdwy musicals. Currently teaching, dancing and choreographing.

NILLO, DAVID. Born July 13, 1917 in Goldsboro. N.C. Debut with Ballet Theatre in 1940, then with Ballet Caravan, and Chicago Opera Ballet before appearing in and choreographing musicals.

NIMURA, YEICHI. Born in Suwa, Japan March 25, 1908. First appeared with Operetta Taza. Soloist Manhattan Opera House 1928. Choreographed for musicals and Met Opera. Currently teaches.

NOBLE, CHERIE. Born Dec. 11, 1947 in Philadelphia. Studied with Ethel Phillips, Michael Lopuszanski, Edmund Novak, Pa. Ballet School. Debut with Novak Ballet in 1961 before joining Pennsylvania Ballet in 1962. Now artistic director Delaware Regional Ballet.

NORMAN, GARY. Born May 11, 1951 in Adelaide, Aust. Studied with Australian Ballet and joined company in 1970; National Ballet of Canada 1975.

NUCHTERN, JEANNE. Born in N.Y.C. Nov. 20, 1939. Studied with Craske, and Graham. Debut 1965 in "The King and I" followed by appearances with Martha Graham. Yuriko, Sophie Maslow, and Bertram Ross.

NUREYEV, RUDOLF. Born Mar. 17, 1938 in Russia; reared in Tartary, Bashkir. Admitted to Kirov Ballet school at 17; joined company and became premier danseur. Defected during 1961 appearance in Paris. Invited to join Royal Ballet as co-star and partner of Margot Fonteyn in 1962. Has choreographed several ballets. Considered by many as world's greatest male dancer. Has appeared with ABT, National Ballet of Canada, Australian Ballet, Paul Taylor.

O'BRIEN, SHAUN. Born Nov. 28, 1930. Studied with Fokine, Schwezoff, Diaghilev, Balanchine, School of American Ballet. Debut 1944 with Ballet International, subsequently with Ballet for America, Grand Ballet de Monte Carlo, Ballet Da Cuba, Conn. Ballet. N.Y.C. Ballet from 1949.

ODA, BONNIE. Born Sept. 15, 1951 in Honolulu, Hawaii. Graduate UHawaii. Appeared with UHawaii Dance Theater (1968–73), Ethel Winter (1971), Met. Opera Ballet (1971). Joined Martha Graham Co. 1973.

O'DONNELL, MAY. Born in Sacramento, Calif., in 1909. Debut with Estelle Reed Concert Group in San Francisco; lead dancer with Martha Graham Co. 1932–44. Formed own school and company for which she dances and choreographs.

OHARA, ORIE. Born June 18, 1945 in Tokyo. Studied at Tokyo Ballet School. Debut 1960 with Tokyo Ballet before joining Bejart Ballet.

OHMAN, FRANK. Born Jan. 7, 1939 in Los Angeles. Studied with Christensens in San Francisco, and appeared with S.F. Ballet. Joined N.Y.C. Ballet in 1962. Now soloist.

OLRICH, APRIL. Born in Zanzibar, E. Africa in 1931. Studied with Borovsky, and Tchernicheva. Joined Original Ballet Russe in 1944. Appeared on Bdwy.

O'NEAL, CHRISTINE. (formerly Christine Knoblauch) Born Feb. 25, 1949 in St. Louis, Mo. Made debut in 1966 with St. Louis Municipal Opera. Subsequently joined National Ballet, and Harkness Ballet as principal; ABT 1974.

ONSTAD, MICHAEL. Born Feb. 18, 1949 in Spokane, Wash. Studied with Robert Irwin, Anatol Joukowski, Willam Christensen, Gordon Paxman, Philip Keeler. Joined Ballet West as soloist in 1966.

ORIO, DIANE. Born Feb. 9, 1947 in Newark, N.J. Trained at Newark Ballet Academy, School of American Ballet, American Ballet Center. Joined Joffrey Ballet in 1968. Currently ballet mistress.

ORMISTON, GALE. Born April 14, 1944 in Kansas. Studied with Hanya Holm, Shirlee Dodge, and at Henry St. Playhouse. Debut 1966 with Nikolais Co. Appeared with Mimi Garrard, and formed own company in 1972.

ORR, TERRY. Born Mar. 12, 1943 in Berkeley, Calif. Studied at San Francisco Ballet School; joined company in 1959; American Ballet Theatre in 1965, became principal in 1972.

OSATO, SONO. Born Aug. 29, 1919 in Omaha, Neb. Studied with Egorova, Oboukhoff, Caton, Bolm and Bernice Holmes. Member of corps de ballet and soloist with Ballet Russe de Monte Carlo (1934–40), Ballet Theatre (1940–43), followed by Bdwy musicals.

OSBORNE, AARON. Born Oct. 16, 1947 in Lakeview, Ore. Graduate Juilliard. Studied with Maggie Black, Merce Cunningham, Pearl Lang, Jose Limon, Martha Graham, Antony Tudor, Alfredo Corvino. Debut 1970 with Jose Limon, Pearl Lang (1970–72), Lar Lubovitch (1975–).

OSSOSKY, SHELDON. Born Brooklyn, June 10, 1932. Attended Juilliard, and studied with Nikolais, Graham, Limon, Tudor, and Craske. Debut 1950, subsequently appeared in musicals and with Pearl Lang, Sophie Maslow, Fred Berke, and at Henry St. Playhouse.

OSTERGAARD, SOLVEIG. Born Jan. 7, 1939 in Denmark. Studied at Royal Danish Ballet School; joined company in 1957; appointed soloist in 1962.

OUMANSKY, VALENTINA. Born in Los Angeles; graduate of Mills College. Studied with Oumansky, de Mille, Vladimiroff, Horst, Cunningham, Graham, and Maracci. Debut with Marquis de Cuevas' Ballet International, subsequently on Bdwy musicals, before devoting full time to choreography, concert work, and teaching.

OWENS, HAYNES. Born in Montgomery, Ala. Studied with Elinor Someth, Molly Brumbly; appeared with Montgomery Civic Ballet. Attended ABC, and joined Joffrey Ballet in 1966.

OXENHAM, ANDREW. Born Oct. 12, 1945 in London, Eng. Studied with Gwenneth Lloyd, Rosella Hightower, Franchetti. Debut 1964 with Ntl. Ballet of Canada; joined Stuttgart Ballet 1969; National Ballet of Canada 1973 as soloist.

PADOW, JUDY. Born Jan. 10, 1943 in N.Y.C. Studied with Don Farnworth, Marvis Walter, Trisha Brown Schlicter, Ann Halprin. Has danced with Yvonne Rainer, and in own works.

PAGE, ANNETTE. Born Dec. 18, 1932 in Manchester, Eng. Entered Royal Ballet School in 1945, and joined company in 1950. Became ballerina in 1959. Has toured with Margot Fonteyn, and made guest appearances at Stockholm's Royal Opera. Retired in 1967.

PAGE, RUTH. Born in Indianapolis, Ind. Studied with Cecchetti, Bolm, and Pavlowa. Debut 1919 with Chicago Opera Co. Toured S. America with Pavlowa, leading dancer on Bdwy, and premier danseuse with Met Opera. Danced with Diaghilev Ballet Russe, and Ballet Russe de Monte Carlo. Formed own company with Bently Stone and toured U.S., Europe, and S. America for 8 years. In Chicago, has been first dancer, choreographer, director for Allied Arts, Grand Opera Co., Federal Theatre, Ravinia Opera Festival. Currently ballet director of both Chicago Opera Ballet and Lyric Opera of Chicago, and Chicago Ballet.

PAGELS, JURGEN. Born Apr. 16, 1925 in Luebeck, Ger. Studied with Lescevskis, Harmos, Vestena, Legat, Preobrajenska, Roje, Volinin, Rausch. Debut 1946 with Luebeck Atlantic Theatre; subsequently with Dortmond Opera, Ballet Theatre, Ballet Legat, and guest artist with many companies. Now teaches at Indiana U.

PANAIEFF, MICHAEL. Born in 1913 in Novgorod, Russia. Studied with Legat, Egorova. Debut with Belgrade Royal Opera Ballet, becoming first dancer in two years; later joined Blum Ballet, Ballet Russe, and Original Ballet Russe. Now has school and performing group in Los Angeles.

PANETTA, JANET. Born Dec. 12, 1949 in NYC. Attended City Col. Studied with Margaret Craske, Antony Tudor, Alfredo Corvino. Debut 1966 with Manhattan Festival Ballet; subsequently with Met Opera Ballet, ABT, Gloria Contreras, Paul Sanasardo, Hirabayashi Dance Theatre.

PANOV, VALERY. Born in 1939 in Vilnius, Lithuania. Made debut at 15. Joined Leningrad Maly Ballet 1958; Kirov 1963 and became its lead dancer. U.S. debut 1974.

PAPA, PHYLLIS. Born Jan. 30, 1950 in Trenton, N.J. Studied at Joffrey, Harkness, and Ballet Theatre schools. Debut with Harkness Ballet in 1967. Joined ABT in 1968. Royal Danish Ballet 1970.

PAREDES, MARCOS. Born in Aguascalientes, Mex. Trained at Academia de la Danza. Danced with Ballet Contemperaneo, and Ballet Classico de Mexico before joining American Ballet Theatre in 1965. Became soloist 1968, principal 1973.

PARK, MERLE. Born Oct. 8, 1937 in Salisbury, Rhodesia. Joined Sadler's Wells (now Royal) Ballet in 1954, becoming soloist in 1958. Now a leading ballerina.

PARKER, ELLEN. Born Feb. 18 in Columbus, O. Attended N.C. School of Arts, and U. Pa. Studied with Tatiana Akinfieva, Josephine Schwarz, Oleg Briansky, Deborah Jowitt, Sonja Tyven, Job Sanders, Pauline Koner, Duncan Noble, Edward Caton. Appeared in musicals before joining Pa. Ballet in 1968,; left in 1972.

PARKES, ROSS. Born June 17, 1940 in Sydney, Australia. Studied with Valrene Tweedie, Peggy Watson, Audrey de Vos, Martha Graham. Debut 1959 with Ballet Francais. Has danced with Ethel Winter, Bertram Ross, Helen McGehee, Martha Graham, Sophie Maslow, Glen Tetley, Mary Anthony, Carmen de Lavallade, Jeff Duncan companies. Joined Pennsylvania Ballet in 1966; Martha Graham 1973. Associate Director Mary Anthony Dance Co.

PARKINSON, GEORGINA. Born Aug. 20, 1938 in Brighton, Eng. Studied at Sadler's Wells School. Joined Royal Ballet in 1957, became soloist in 1959. Now a principal ballerina.

PARKS, JOHN E. Born Aug. 4, 1945 in the Bronx. Studied at Juilliard. Teacher-dancer-choreographer for Movements Black: Dance Repertory Theatre. Joined Alvin Ailey Co. in 1970; left in 1974 for Bdwy musical.

PARRA, MARIANO. Born in Ambridge, Pa. Mar. 10, 1933. Studied with La Meri, Juan Martinez, La Quica, and Luisa Pericet in Spain. Debut 1957. Has organized and appeared with own company in N.Y.C. and on tour.

PATAROZZI, JACQUES. Born Apr. 28, 1947 in Ajallio, France. Studied with Paul Sanasardo and joined his company in 1972.

PAUL, MIMI. Born in Nashville, Tenn., Feb. 3, 1943. Studied at Washington (D.C.) School of Ballet and School of American Ballet. Debut 1960 in N.Y.C. Ballet in "Nutcracker" and became soloist in 1963. Joined ABT in 1969 as principal.

PEARSON, JERRY. Born Mar. 17, 1949 in St. Paul, Minn. Attending UMinn. Studied and appeared with Nancy Hauser before joining Murray Louis Co.

PEARSON, SARA. Born Apr. 22, 1949 in St. Paul, Minn. Attended UMinn. Studied and appeared with Nancy Hauser before joining Murray Louis Co.

PENNEY, JENNIFER. Born Apr. 5, 1946 in Vancouver, Can. Studied at Royal Ballet School, London, and graduated into company. Is now a principal.

PEREZ, RUDY. Born in N.Y.C. Studied with New Dance Group, Graham, Cunningham, Hawkins, Anthony, on faculty at DTW. Choreographer-Director Rudy Perez Dance Theatre, and artist-in-residence at Marymount Manhattan Col.

PERI, RIA. Born Aug. 20, 1944 in Eger, Hungary. Trained at Hungary State Ballet School, London Royal Ballet School. Debut 1964 with Royal Ballet.

PERRY, PAMARA. Born Feb. 8, 1948 in Cleveland, Ohio. Studied at School of American Ballet. Debut 1966 with Western Ballet Association of Los Angeles. With Eglevsky Ballet (1966–7), joined Joffrey Ballet in 1967. Retired in 1969.

PERRY, RONALD. Born Mar. 17, 1955 in NYC. Studied at Dance Theatre of Harlem, and made debut with company in 1969.

PERUSSE, SONIA. Born in 1954 in Longueil, Quebec, Can. Attended Ntl. Ballet School, and graduated into company in 1972. Promoted to soloist 1973.

PETERS, DELIA L. Born May 9, 1947 in N.Y.C. Attended School of American Ballet. Joined N.Y.C. Ballet in 1963.

PETERSON, CAROLYN. Born July 23, 1946 in Los Angeles. Studied with Marjorie Peterson, Irina Kosmouska, Carmelita Maracci, and at School of American Ballet. Debut 1966 with N.Y.C. Ballet.

PETERSON, STANZE. Born in Houston, Tex. Has appeared with Syvilla Fort, Edith Stephen, Charles Weidman, Eve Gentry, and Gloria Contreras. In 1963 organized Stanze Peterson Dance Theatre with which he has appeared in N.Y.C., San Francisco, and on tour.

PETIT, ROLAND. Born in Paris Jan. 13, 1924. Studied at Paris Opera School; became member of corps in 1939, and began choreographing. In 1945 was co-founder, ballet master, and premier danseur of Les Ballets des Champs-Elysees. In 1948 formed own company Les Ballets de Paris, for which he danced and choreographs.

PETROFF, PAUL. Born in Denmark: Studied with Katja Lindhart; Debut 1930 with Violet Fischer. Became premier danseur of de Basil's Ballet Russe; later joined Original Ballet Russe, Ballet Theatre (1943) and International Ballet. Now teaches.

PETROV, NICOLAS. Born in 1933 in Yugoslavia; studied with Ureobrajenska, Gsowsky, Massine. Appeared with Yugoslav Ntl. Theatre, Ballet de France, Theatre d'Art Ballet; lead dancer with Massine Ballet. Came to U.S. in 1967 and founded Pittsburgh Ballet Theatre; also teaches.

PHIPPS, CHARLES. Born Nov. 23, 1946 in Newton, Miss. Studied with Graham, Cunningham, and at Ballet Theatre School. Debut 1968 with Pearl Lang, subsequently with Louis Falco, Lucas Hoving.

PIERSON, ROSALIND. Born in Salt Lake City. Bennington graduate. Studied at Thomas-Fallis School, American Ballet Center. Has appeared with Ruth Currier, Charles Weidman, Ballet Concepts, Anne Wilson, DTW, Garden State Ballet.

PIKSER, ROBERTA. Born Sept. 3, 1941 in Chicago. Graduate U. Chicago. Studied with Erika Thimey, Paul Sanasardo. Debut 1951 with Dance Theatre of Washington; subsequently with Edith Stephen, Paul Sanasardo, Eleo Pomare.

PINNOCK, THOMAS. Born in Jamaica where he studied with Rex Nettleford, Eddy Thomas, Neville Black, and became principal with National Dance Theatre Co. Also studied with Martha Graham and is principal with Rod Rodgers Co. Is co-founder of Choreo-Mutations for which he choreographs.

PINCUSOFF, REVA. Born in Montreal, Can. Studied in London's Royal Ballet Sch. Has danced with Les Grands Ballets Canadiens, Pennsylvania Ballet, Eliot Feld Ballet.

PLATOFF, MARC. Born in Seattle, Wash., in 1915. Debut with de Basil's Ballet Russe; soloist with Ballet Russe de Monte Carlo 1938–42 and choreographed for them. As Marc Platt made Bdwy bow in 1943, subsequently in and choreographing for films. Was director of Radio City Ballet.

PLEVIN, MARCIA. Born Oct. 26, 1945 in Columbus, O. Graduate U. Wisc. Studied with Lang, Graham, Cohan, Yuriko. Debut 1968 with Pearl Lang, subsequently with Sophie Maslow, New Dance Group, Ethel Winter.

| Ronald Perry | Mimi Paul | Thomas Pinnock | Maya Plisetskaya | Albert Reid |

PLISETSKAYA, MAYA. Born in Russia Nov. 20, 1925. Began studies at Moscow State School of Ballet at 8 and joined Bolshoi company in 1943, rising to premiere danseuse. Internationally famous for her "Swan Lake." Awarded Lenin Prize in 1964. In addition to dancing with Bolshoi, is now teaching. Considered one of world's greatest ballerinas.

PLUMADORE, PAUL. Born Nov. 5, 1949 in Springfield, Mass. Studied at NYU and with Kelly Holt, Jean Erdman, Nenette Charisse, Gladys Bailin. Debut 1969 with Katherine Litz, with Jean Erdman in 1970, and in concert.

POMARE, ELEO. Born in Cartagena, Colombia Oct. 22, 1937. Studied with Jose Limon, Luis Horst, Curtis James, Geoffrey Holder, and Kurt Jooss. In 1958 organized and has appeared with the Eleo Pomare Dance Co. in N.Y.C., abroad, and on tour in the U.S.

POOLE, DENNIS. Born Dec. 27, 1951 in Dallas, Tex. Trained at Harkness School, and joined company in 1968; soloist 1970; National Ballet 1971–74 as principal; Joffrey Ballet 1975, principal 1977.

POPOVA, NINA. Born in 1922 in Russia. Studied in Paris with Preobrajenska and Egorova. Debut 1937 with Ballet de la Jeunesse. Later with Original Ballet Russe, Ballet Theatre, and Ballet Russe de Monte Carlo. Now teaches.

POSIN, KATHRYN. Born Mar. 23, 1944 in Butte, Mont. Bennington graduate. Studied with Fonaroff, Cunningham, Graham, Thomas-Fallis. Debut with Dance Theatre Workshop in 1965. Has danced with Anna Sokolow, Valerie Bettis, Lotte Goslar, American Dance Theatre, and in own works.

POURFARROKH, ALI. Born Nov. 27, 1938 in Iran. Studied at Tehran Consv. Joined ABT (1959–63), Met Opera Ballet 1963, Harkness 1964–67, 1971–72, Joffrey 1967, Frankfurt Ballet 1968, Associate Artistic Director-Ballet Master Ailey company 1973. Director Iranian National Ballet 1976.

POWELL, GRAHAM. Born in Cardiff, Wales. Aug. 2, 1948. Studied at Royal Ballet School; joined company in 1965, then Australian Ballet

POWELL, ROBERT. Born in Hawaii in 1941; graduate of HS Performing Arts. Has been featured dancer with all major American modern dance companies, and appeared with N.Y.C. Opera Ballet. Soloist with Graham Co., associate artistic director 1973.

PRICE, MARY. Born May 20, 1945 in Fort Bragg, N.C. Graduate U. Okla. Studied with Mary Anthony, Martha Graham. Debut 1970 with Mary Anthony, subsequently with Pearl Lang, Richard Gain, Larry Richardson.

PRIMUS, PEARL. Born Nov. 29, 1919 in Trinidad, B.W.I. N.Y. Debut at YMHA in 1943; first solo performance 1944. Has since choreographed and performed in West Indian, African, and primitive dances throughout the world. Also teaches.

PRINZ, JOHN. Born in Chicago May 14, 1945. Studied with Comiacoff, Allegro School, American Ballet Center, School of American Ballet. Joined N.Y.C. Ballet in 1964; Munich Ballet, then ABT in 1970. Appointed principal in 1971.

PROKOVSKY, ANDRE. Born Jan. 13, 1939 in Paris, and achieved recognition in Europe with Grand Ballet du Marquis de Cuevas and London Festival Ballet; made world tour with "Stars of the French Ballet." Joined N.Y.C. Ballet as principal dancer in 1963; London's Festival Ballet in 1967.

PROVANCHA, LEIGH. Born Mar. 22, 1953 in St. John's, Newfoundland. Studied at Wash. Ntl. School of Ballet, NC Sch. of Arts, Sch. of Am. Ballet. Debut 1972 with Ballet Repertory Co. Joined ABT 1973.

QUITMAN, CLEO. Born in Detroit. Attended Weinstein U. Studied with Martha Graham, Alfredo Corvino, Maria Nevelska. Formed N.Y. Negro Ballet Co. that toured Europe. Had appeared with Joffrey Ballet and is founder-director-choreographer of Cleo Quitman's Dance Generale.

RADIUS, ALEXANDRA. Born July 3, 1942 in Amsterdam, Holland. Studied with Benjamin Harkarvy. Debut with Nederlands Dans Theatre in 1957. Joined American Ballet Theatre in 1968 as soloist. Became principal in 1969. Joined Dutch National Ballet in 1970.

RAGOZINA, GALINA. Born in 1949 in Archangel, Russia. Joined Kirov Ballet in 1967, and rose to soloist. U.S. debut 1974.

RAIMONDO, ROBERT. Born June 18, 1945 in Jersey City, NJ. Studied at Harkness House, American Ballet Theatre School. Debut 1965 with American Festival Ballet; with Garden State Ballet (1967–70), Houston Ballet from 1972.

RAINER, YVONNE. Born in 1934 in San Francisco. Studied with Graham, Cunningham, Halprin, Stephen. Has performed with James Waring, Aileen Passloff, Beverly Schmidt, Judith Dunn. Started Judson Dance Workshop in 1962, and choreographs for own company.

RAINES, WALTER. Born Aug. 16, 1940 in Braddock, Pa. Attended Carnegie-Mellon U. Studied at Pittsburgh Playhouse, School of American Ballet, Dance Theatre of Harlem. Debut 1952 with Pittsburgh Opera Ballet; subsequently with Pennsylvania Ballet 1962, Stuttgart Ballet 1964, Dance Theatre of Harlem 1969.

RALL, TOMMY. Born Dec. 27, 1929 in Kansas City, Mo. Attended Chouinard Art Inst. Studied with Carmelita Maracci, David Lichine, and Oboukhoff of School of American Ballet. Joined Ballet Theatre in 1944, and became soloist in 1945. Has appeared in musicals, films, and choreographed for TV.

RANDOLPH, MARY. Born in Chicago, IL. Studied with Finis Jhung, Gabriella Darvash. Joined Eliot Feld Ballet 1976.

RAPP, RICHARD. Born in Milwaukee, Wisc. Studied with Adele Artinian, Ann Barzel, School of American Ballet. Joined N.Y.C. Ballet in 1958; became soloist in 1961.

RAUP, FLORITA. Born in Havana, Cuba; attended school in Springfield, O. Has studied with Holm, Limon, Humphrey, Tamiris, and Julia Berashkova. Debut in 1951. Has appeared in concert and with own group since 1953, in N.Y.C. and on tour.

REBEAUD, MICHELE. Born Jan. 24, 1948 in Paris, France. Debut 1972 with Paul Sanasardo Co.

REDLICH, DON. Born in Winona, Minn., Aug. 17, 1933. Attended U. Wisc., studied with Holm, and Humphrey. Debut in 1954 musical "The Golden Apple." Has danced with Hanya Holm, Doris Humphrey, Anna Sokolow, Murray Louis, John Butler, and in own concert program. Is teacher, choreographer, and tours with own Co.

REED, JANET. Born in Tolo, Ore., Sept. 15, 1916. Studied with Willam Christensen, Tudor, and Balanchine. Member of San Francisco Ballet 1937–41, Ballet Theatre 1943–6, N.Y.C. Ballet from 1949. Has been teaching since 1965.

REESE, GAIL. Born Aug. 13, 1946 in Queens, N.Y. Studied with Syvilla Fort, Hector Zaraspe, Marianne Balin. Debut with Cleo Quitman in 1967, and then with Talley Beatty, Lar Lubovitch, and Alvin Ailey from 1970.

REID, ALBERT. Born July 12, 1934 in Niagara Falls, N.Y. Graduate Stanford U. Studied with Nikolais, Cunningham, Lillian Moore, Richard Thomas, Margaret Craske. Debut 1959 with Nikolais Co., with Murray Louis, Erick Hawkins, Katherine Litz, and Yvonne Rainer.

REIN, RICHARD A. Born May 10, 1944 in N.Y.C. Attended Adelphi U. School of Am. Ballet. Debut 1965 with Atlanta Ballet, subsequently with Ruth Page's Chicago Ballet, Pa. Ballet, joined ABT in 1970, Pa. Ballet 1973.

REISER, WENDY. Born Aug. 11, 1953 in Hamilton, Can. Attended National Ballet School; joined Natl. Ballet of Canada in 1971. Promoted to soloist.

REMINGTON, BARBARA. Born in 1936 in Windsor, Can. Studied with Sandra Severo, School of American Ballet, Ballet Theatre School, Royal Ballet School. Joined Royal Ballet in 1959, followed by American Ballet Theatre, Joffrey Ballet.

RENCHER, DEREK. Born June 6, 1932 in Birmingham, Eng. Studied at Royal Ballet school and joined company in 1952, rising to principal in 1969.

REVENE, NADINE. Born in N.Y.C. Studied with Helen Platova. In musicals before joining Ballet Theatre. Subsequently member of N.Y.C. Ballet, prima ballerina of Bremen Opera in Germany, and First Chamber Dance Quartet. Joined Pa. Ballet in 1970 as soloist. Now assistant ballet mistress.

REY, FRANK. Born in 1931 in Tampa, Fla. Made debut with Chicago Opera Ballet. Founder-Director Florida Dance Camp, Choreographer-in-residence for Florida Ballet Theatre. Is noted as choreographer for outdoor dramas.

REYES, RAMON DE LOS. Born in Madrid and started dancing at 9. Debut at 17 after studying with Antonio Marin. Formed own company and toured Spain, Europe, and U.S. Joined Ximenez-Vargas Co., later Roberto Iglesias Co. as leading dancer. With Maria Alba, formed Alba-Reyes Spanish Dance Co. in 1964.

REYN, JUDITH. Born Dec. 28, 1943 in Rhodesia. Studied at Royal Ballet School, London, and joined in 1963. Member of Stuttgart Ballet since 1967; promoted to principal.

REYNOLDS, GREGORY C. Born July 18, 1952 in Washington, DC. Graduate Sarah Lawrence Col. Studied with Batya Heller, Erica Thimey, Paul Taylor. Joined Taylor company in 1973.

RHODES, CATHRYN. Born in 1958 in Westchester, NY. Studied with Iris Merrick, Don Farnworth, at Manhattan Ballet School, Manhattan School of Dance, Am. Ballet Theatre School. Joined ABT 1973.

RHODES, LAWRENCE. Born in Mt. Hope, W. Va., Nov. 24, 1939. Studied with Violette Armand. Debut with Ballet Russe de Monte Carlo. Joined Joffrey Ballet in 1960, Harkness Ballet in 1964. Became its director in 1969. Joined Netherlands National Ballet in 1970, Pa. Ballet 1972. Appeared with Eliot Feld Ballet 1974.

RIABOUCHINSKA, TATIANA. Born May 23, 1916 in Moscow. Studied with Alexandre Volinin, and Mathilda Kchesinska. Debut in London in 1932. With Monte Carlo Ballet Russe de Basil (1933-43), Ballet Theatre, London Festival Ballet, Theatre Colon (Buenos Aires, 1946-47). Also appeared in musicals. Now teaches.

RICHARDSON, DORENE. Born in N.Y.C., Oct. 5, 1934. Studied at NYU and Juilliard. Debut in 1953. In addition to musicals has appeared with Natanya Neumann, Sophie Maslow, Donald McKayle, and Alvin Ailey.

RICHARDSON, LARRY. Born Jan. 6, 1941 in Minerva, O. Graduate of Ohio State U. Studied with Louis Horst, Jose Limon. Has danced in Kauffman Hall, Hunter College, in musicals, and with Pearl Lang. Also choreographs and tours own company.

RIOJA, PILAR. Born Sept. 13, 1932 in Torreon, Mex. Studied with Pericet, Estampio, Ortega, Tarriba. Debut 1969 in Madrid, Spain; Carnegie Hall 1973. Tours with her own company.

RIVERA, CHITA. Born Jan. 23, 1933 in Washington, D.C. Studied at School of American Ballet. Has become popular star of musicals, and TV.

RIVERA, LUIS. Born in Los Angeles. Studied with Michael Brigante, Martin Vargas, Luisa Triana, Mercedes & Albano, Alberto Lorca. Appeared with several companies before forming his own.

ROBBINS, JEROME. Born Oct. 11, 1918 in N.Y.C. Attended NYU. Studied with Daganova, Platova, Loring, Tudor, New Dance League, and Helen Veola. Debut in 1937 with Sandor-Sorel Co. Subsequently in musicals before joining Ballet Theater in 1940, for which he first choreographed "Fancy Free." Joined N.Y.C. Ballet in 1949 and became its associate artistic director in 1950. Formed Ballets: U.S.A. which toured Europe and U.S. (1958-1961). Has choreographed and directed many Bdwy productions and ballets.

ROBERSON, LAR. Born May 18, 1947 in Oakland, Calif. Attended Cal. State College, and Graham School. Debut 1968 with Sophie Maslow Company. Joined Graham Company in 1969. Also appeared with Pearl Lang.

ROBINSON, CHASE. Born in Panama City, Fla. Graduate of Fla. State U. Studied with Aubry Hitchins, Don Farnworth. Debut in 1956. Has since appeared with Natl. Ballet of Canada, Joffrey, Limon, Graham, Lang, Butler, Cunningham, and Hoving. Also teaches.

ROBINSON, NANCY. Born Aug. 28, 1945 in Los Angeles. Studied with Andre Tremaine, Michael Panaieff, San Francisco Ballet, joined company in 1964. Became soloist in 1964 with American Ballet Theatre in 1967, Joffrey Co. in 1968.

RODGERS, ROD. Born in Detroit where he began his studies. Member of Erick Hawkins Dance Co., and dance supervisor of Mobilization for Youth project. Has also appeared in concert of own works and with own company for which he choreographs.

RODHAM, ROBERT. Born Sept. 2, 1939 in Pittston, Pa. Studied with Barbara Weisberger, Virginia Williams, and at School of American Ballet. Joined N.Y.C. Ballet in 1960. Ballet master, choreographer, and principal with Pennsylvania Ballet from 1963.

RODRIGUEZ, ZHANDRA. Born Mar. 17, 1947 in Caracas. Ven. Debut 1962 with Ballet National Venezuela; joined American Ballet Theatre in 1968; soloist 1970, principal 1973.

ROESS-SMITH, JULIE. Born July 28, 1947 in Brooksville, FL. Attended American U. Studied with Merce Cunningham, Viola Farber, Dan Wagoner. Joined Cunningham company in 1973.

ROHAN, SHEILA. Born Nov. 20, 1947 in Staten Island, N.Y. Studied with Vincenzo Celli, Phil Black, James Truitte. Debut 1970 with Dance Theatre of Harlem.

ROMANOFF, DIMITRI. Born in Tsaritzin, Russia. Came to U.S. in 1924 to attend Stanford U. and study with Theodore Kosloff. First dancer with American Ballet Theatre when it was organized in 1940. Now directs school in San Jose, Calif.

ROMERO, RAFAEL. Born Apr. 2, 1945 in Puerto Rico. Studied at School of American Ballet, Natl. Ballet, and American Ballet Center. Has appeared with Ballets de San Juan, Westchester Ballet, Pilar Gomez, National Ballet, Joffrey Ballet, N.Y.C. Opera Ballet (1970).

RON, RACHAMIM. Born Nov. 15, 1942 in Cairo. Studied with Gertrude Kraus, Donald McKayle, Glen Tetley, Pearl Lang, Martha Graham. Debut 1963 with Batsheva Dance Co. of Israel. Joined Donald McKayle Co. in 1967 and Martha Graham in 1968. Rejoined Batsheva 1970.

ROOPE, CLOVER. Born 1937 in Bristol, Eng. Studied at Royal Ballet School and joined company in 1957. Debut as choreographer in 1958. Also appeared with Helen McGehee.

ROSARIO. Born Rosario Perez in Seville Nov. 11, 1920. Cousin of Antonio with whom she achieved international fame. Studied with Realito. With Antonio, became known as "The Kids From Seville" and toured world together until they separated in 1952. Formed own company, but changed to dance recitals. Has returned to guest star with Antonio and his Ballets de Madrid.

ROSS, BERTRAM. Born in Brooklyn, Nov. 13, 1920. Leading male dancer of the Martha Graham Co., appeared in almost every work in the active repertoire. Has appeared with own company and choreography. Now teaches.

ROSS, DONNA. Born May 17, 1956 in Midland, TX. Attended URochester, Ballet Center of Buffalo, American Ballet Center. With Festival Ballet (1971-73), joined Joffrey Ballet in 1976.

ROSS, HERBERT. Born May 13, 1927 in Brooklyn. Studied with Doris Humphrey, Helene Platova, and Laird Leslie. Debut in "Follow the Girls" in 1944. In 1950 choreographed and appeared with Ballet Theatre in "Caprichos," subsequently choreographing for Bdwy musicals, Met Opera Ballet, American Ballet Theatre, and danced with own company in 1960. Now a film director.

ROSS, REBECCA. Born March 31, 1949 in Orlando, FL. Studied with Edith Royal, and Joffrey School. Debut 1969 with NYC Opera Ballet, subsequently Hamburg Opera Ballet (1970-71), Deutsch Oper Berlin (1971-73), Grand Theatre de Geneve (1973-4), He Nationale Ballet Amsterdam (1974-).

ROSSON, KEITH. Born Jan. 24, 1937 in Birmingham, Eng. Studied at Royal Ballet School. Joined Covent Opera Ballet in 1954 and Royal Ballet in 1955. Became soloist in 1959, and principal dancer in 1964.

ROTANTE, THEODORE. Born Feb. 23, 1949 in Stamford, Conn. Studied with Nenette Charisse, Kelly Holt, Jean Erdman, Glady Bailin, Matt Mattox, Donald McKayle. Debut in 1970 with Jean Erdman Dance Theatre.

ROTARDIER, KELVIN. Born Jan. 23, 1936 in Trinidad, W. I. Studied at London's Sigurd Leder School, Jacob's Pillow, and International School of Dance. Appeared in musicals before joining Alvin Ailey Co. in 1964. Now teaches.

ROTHWELL, CLINTON. Born Mar. 1, 1945 in Guildforn, Eng. Attended Royal Ballet School. Debut with Royal Opera Ballet; subsequently San Francisco Ballet, Ntl. Ballet of Holland, and Ntl Ballet of Canada where he is soloist.

ROWE, SUSAN A. Born July 4, 1955 in Cheyenne, WY. Attended N. Carolina School of Arts. Debut 1974 with Agnes deMille Heritage Dance Theater; joined Eliot Feld Ballet 1977.

ROZOW, PATRICIA. Born Feb. 18, 1947 in Brooklyn, NY. Graduate Butler U. Studied at Harkness School. Joined Ballet West in 1969. Promoted to soloist in 1971; principal in 1973.

RUDKO, DORIS. Born Oct. 18, in Milwaukee. Graduate U. Wis. Studied with Humphrey, Weidman, Limon, Graham, Holm, Hors Daganova, Platova, Joffrey, and Fonaroff. Debut on Bdwy 1946 i "Shooting' Star." Concert performer and choreographer since 194 Formed own company in 1957. Is also a teacher.

RUIZ, BRUNILDA. Born in Puerto Rico June 1, 1936. Studie with Martha Melincoff, and Robert Joffrey before joining his tourin group in 1955, and his company in 1961. Appeared with Philadel phia and N.Y.C. Opera companies. Joined Harkness Ballet in 196

RUSHING, SHIRLEY. Born in Savannah, Ga. Attended Juilliar Bklyn Col. Studied with O'Donnell, Shurr, Bronson, Limon, Tudo Graham. Has appeared with Eleo Pomare, Rod Rodgers, Loui Johnson, Gus Denizulu. Co-founder of Choreo-Mutations.

RUSSELL, PAUL. Born Mar. 2, 1947 in Texas. Studied at Scho of American Ballet, Dance Theatre of Harlem. Debut 1970 wi Hartford Ballet; subsequently with Garden State Ballet, Syracu Ballet Theatre; joined Dance Theatre of Harlem 1971.

| Rod Rodgers | Donna Ross | Clinton Rothwell | Suki Schorer | Peter Schaufuss |

RUUD, TOMM. Born in 1943 in Pasadena, Cal. Graduate UUtah. Studied with Willam Christensen, Bene Arnold, Gordon Paxman. Joined Ballet West 1963; made soloist 1965, principal 1969. Teaches and makes guest appearances with other companies. Joined San Francisco Ballet 1975.

RYBERG, FLEMMING. Born Nov. 24, 1940 in Copenhagen, Den. Studied at Royal Theatre in Copenhagen; made debut 1958 with Royal Danish Ballet.

SABLE, SHERRY. Born Sept. 4, 1952 in Philadelphia. Studied at Phila. Dance Academy, Graham School. Debut 1970 with Pearl Lang, subsequently with DTW, Richard Gain.

SABLINE, OLEG. Born in 1925 in Berlin. Studied with Preobrajenska, Egorova, Colinine, Ricaus; danced with Grand Ballet de Monte Carlo, l'Opera Comique Ballet, Grand Ballet du Marquis de Cuevas. Came to U.S. in 1958. Formed and toured with own group Ballet Concertante. Currently teaches.

SADDLER, DONALD. Born Jan. 24, 1920 in Van Nuys, Calif. Attended LACC. Studied with Maracci, Dolin, and Tudor. Debut in 1937, subsequently appearing with Ballet Theatre (1940–3, 1946–7), and in Bdwy musicals. First choreography "Blue Mountain Ballads" for Markova-Dolin Co. in 1948. Performed with own company in 1949. Assistant artistic director of Harkness Ballet 1964–1970. Has choreographed several Bdwy productions.

SAMPSON, ALLEN. Born Oct. 1, 1957 in NYC. Made debut with Dance Theatre of Harlem in 1972.

SAMPSON, RONDA CAROL. Born June 26, 1953 in Roanoke, Va. Made debut with Atlanta Ballet in 1968. Joined Dance Theatre of Harlem in 1969.

SAMPSON, ROSLYN. Born May 8, 1955 in Nashville, Tenn. Appeared with Atlanta Ballet; joined Dance Theatre of Harlem 1969.

SANASARDO, PAUL. Born Sept. 15, 1928 in Chicago. Attended Chicago U. Studied with Tudor, Thimey, Graham, and Slavenska. Debut in 1951 with Erika Thimey Dance Theatre; subsequently with Anna Sokolow, and Pearl Lang. In 1958 established, and directs Studio For Dance, a school for his own company that presents concerts throughout the U.S., Canada, and BWI. Choreographer and dancer on TV. Director of Modern Dance Artists (N.Y.C.), and School of Modern Dance (Saratoga, N.Y.).

SANCHEZ, MIGUEL. Born Feb. 21, 1951 in Puerto Rico. Studied at School of American Ballet, and with Anne Wooliams. Debut 1969 with Stuttgart Ballet. Is guest artist with Ballets de San Juan, P.R.

SANDERS, JOB. Born in Amsterdam in 1929. Studied with Gavrilov, and at School of American Ballet. Debut with Ballet Society. Subsequently with Ballet Russe de Monte Carlo, ABT, Ruth Page's Ballet, American Festival Ballet, Netherlands Ballet, Netherlands Dance Theatre. Began choreographing in 1956. Also teaches.

SANDONATO, BARBARA. Born July 22, 1943 in Harrison, N.Y. Studied at Lorna London School, and School of American Ballet. Debut with N.Y.C. Ballet, danced with Gloria Contreras Co., before joining Pennsylvania Ballet in 1964 and rising to principal; Canadian Ntl. Ballet 1972–3; returned to Pa. Ballet 1973.

SANJO, MARIKO. Born June 12, 1933 in Tokyo, Japan. Studied with Martha Graham, Alvin Ailey, Zena Rommett. Has appeared in concert, and with Donald McKayle (1962), Ailey company (1962–64).

SANTANGELO, TULY. Born May 30, 1936 in Buenos Aires. Studied at Opera Theatre, with Martha Graham, Alwin Nikolais. Debut 1956 with Brazilian Co., subsequently with Nikolais, Don Redlich (1970).

SANTIAGO, ANTHONY. Born Jan. 7, 1942 in Cartagena, Col. Studied with Craske and Tudor. Joined Les Grand Ballets Canadiens 1963–65, Met Opera Ballet 1965–72, 1974–76, Houston Ballet 1973–74.

SAPIRO, DANA. Born Jan. 2, 1952 in N.Y.C. Studied with Karin Irvin, Joffrey, and at American Ballet Center. Debut 1970 with Joffrey Ballet. Joined Alvin Ailey company 1972.

SAPPINGTON, MARGO. Born in Baytown, Tex., July 30, 1947. Studied with Camille Hill, Matt Mattox, and at American Ballet Center. Debut with Joffrey Ballet in 1965. Also appeared in musicals, and choreographs.

SARRY, CHRISTINE. Born in Long Beach, Calif. in 1947. Studied with Silver, Howard, Maracci, Oumansky, Fallis, Thomas. Joined Joffrey Ballet in 1963. American Ballet Theatre in 1964. American Ballet Co. (1969), rejoined ABT as soloist in 1971; Eliot Feld Ballet 1974.

SARSTADT, MARIAN. Born July 11, 1942 in Amsterdam. Studied at Scapino School, with Mme. Nora, Audrey de Vos. Debut in 1958 with Scapino Ballet. Joined de Cuevas Co. in 1960. Netherlands Dance Theatre in 1962.

SATINOFF, JEFF. Born Nov. 6, 1954 in Philadelphia, Pa. Attended N.C. School of Arts. Debut 1972 with North Carolina Dance Theatre. Joined Eliot Feld Co. 1974.

SATO, SHOZO. Born May 18, 1933 in Kobe, Japan. Graduate Tokyo U. Debut with Classical Ballet in 1948. Has appeared around the world in concert and lecture demonstrations since 1964.

SAUL, PETER. Born Feb. 10, 1936 in N.Y.C. Studied with Craske, Tudor, and Cunningham. Appeared with Met Opera Ballet 1956–7, International Ballet 1960–61, American Ballet Theatre 1962–4, Les Grands Ballets Canadiens 1964–5, Merce Cunningham 1966–7.

SCHANNE, MARGRETHE. Born in Copenhagen Nov. 21, 1921. Graduate of Royal Danish Ballet school; joined company, in mid-1940's, rapidly rising to premiere danseuse and the epitome of the Bournonville style. Briefly joined Petit's Ballets des Champs-Elysses in Paris and in 1947 made London debut with it before returning to Royal Danish Ballet where she became synonymous with "La Sylphide." Made N.Y. debut in it in 1956, and danced it for her farewell performance in N.Y. and Copenhagen in 1966. Now teaches.

SCHAUFUSS, PETER. Born Apr. 26, 1950 in Copenhagen, Denmark. Trained at Royal Danish Ballet School. Joined company at 17. With National Ballet of Canada (1969), London Festival Ballet (1970–74), NYC Ballet as a principal 1974.

SCHEEPERS, MARTIN. Born in 1933 in Arnheim, Holland. Studied with Georgi, Adret, Crofton, Lifar, Gsovsky, Kiss. Debut in 1948 with Amsterdam Opera. Joined Champs-Elysses and London Festival Ballets before American Ballet Theatre in 1960.

SCHORER, SUKI. Born in Cambridge, Mass. Attended U. Cal. Studied at San Francisco Ballet School and joined company. In 1959 joined N.Y.C. Ballet, becoming soloist in 1963, ballerina in 1969. Retired in 1971 and teaches.

SCHRAMEK, TOMAS. Born in Bratislave, Czech. Began training at 9. Graduate Musical and Theatrical Academy. Joined Slovak Character Dance Co. 1959, rising to principal. Left Czech. in 1968 to join National Ballet of Canada. Promoted to principal 1973.

SCHULKIND, MARCUS. Born Feb. 21, 1948 in N.Y.C. Graduate Goddard Col. Studied at Juilliard. Debut 1968 with Pearl Lang, then with Norman Walker, Felix Fibich; joined Batsheva in 1970.

SCOTT, MARION. Born July 24, 1922 in Chicago. Studied with Graham, Humphrey, Weidman, Horst, Tamiris, and Slavenska. Debut with Humphrey-Weidman Co. in 1942. Danced with Tamiris, and in 1964 formed own company for which she choreographs. Also teaches.

SCOTT, WILLIAM. Born Nov. 3, 1950 in N.Y.C. Studied with Martha Graham, Harkness House, Richard Thomas. Debut 1968 with Harkness Youth Co. Joined Dance Theatre of Harlem in 1970. Is also ballet master and teacher.

SEGARRA, RAMON. Born Nov. 26, 1939 in Mayaguez, P.R. Studied with Chafee, Malinka, Moore, Pereyaslavec, Vilzak, Oboukoff, Vladimiroff, Eglevsky, and Zaraspe. Debut 1954 with Ballet Chafee, subsequently appearing as soloist with May O'Donnell Co. (1956–8), Ballet Russe de Monte Carlo (1958–61), N.Y.C. Ballet (1961–4), and ballet master of Ailey Co. from 1970. Ballet Master Hamburg Stage Opera Ballet 1972; Ballet Hispanico 1972.

SEIGENFELD, BILLY. Born Oct. 15, 1948 in Mt. Vernon, N.Y. Graduate Brown U. Studied with Nikolais. Debut 1970 with Don Redlich Co., subsequently with Elina Mooney.

SEKIL, YAROSLAV. Born in Ukrania in 1930. Entered Bolshoi School in 1949, and joined company in 1951. Became one of leading character dancers.

SELF, JIM. Born Mar. 6, 1954 in Greenville, AL. Studied with Edward Parish, Shirley Mordine, Merce Cunningham. With Chicago Dance Troupe (1972), Moming (1974–5), Merce Cunningham (1977–).

SELF, KEVIN. Born Apr. 21, 1955 in Denton, Tex. Attended NC School of Arts. Debut 1973 with Agnes DeMille Heritage Dance Theatre. Joined ABT 1974.

SELLERS, JOAN. Born Sept. 21, 1937 in N.Y.C. Studied with Graham, Cunningham, Thomas, Fallis, Farnworth. Debut 1960 with Dance Theatre, subsequently with DTW, James Cunningham Co.

SERAVALLI, ROSANNA. Born March 9, 1943 in Florence, Italy. Trained and performed in Italy before joining American Ballet Theatre in 1963.

SERGAVA, KATHERINE. Born in Tiflis, Russia. Studied with Kehessinska, Fokine, Kyasht, Mendes. Danced with Mordkin Ballet, Ballet Theatre (1940), Original Ballet Russe. More recently appeared in musicals.

SERRANO, LUPE. Born Dec. 7, 1930 in Santiago, Chile. Studied in Mexico City with Dambre and joined Mexico City Ballet Co. Organized Mexican Academy of Modern Dance. After studying with Celli and Tudor, performed with Ballet Russe, and Ballet Theatre (since 1953).

SERRANO, RAYMOND. Born Apr. 19, 1950 in Vieques, P.R. Studied at Thalia Mann Sch., Sch. of Am. Ballet. Debut 1968 with National Ballet. Appeared with Eglevsky Co., Ballet Concerto, Ballet Repertory Co. before joining ABT 1975.

SETTERFIELD, VALDA. Born Sept. 17, 1934 in Margate, Eng. Studied with Rambert, Karsavina, Waring, Cunningham. Debut with Ballet Rambert in 1955. Since, with James Waring, Aileen Pasloff, Katherine Litz, David Gordon, Merce Cunningham.

SEYMOUR, LYNN. Born 1939 in Wainwright, Alberta, Canada. Studied at Royal Ballet School, London graduating into company. Besides appearing as dramatic ballerina with Royal Ballet, has made guest appearances with Stuttgart, and Canadian National Ballet. Guest artist with Ailey Co. 1970–71. Rejoined Royal Ballet 1970.

SHANG, RUBY. Born Nov. 16, 1948 in Tokyo where she began studies at 6. Attended Pembroke Col. Studied with Julie Strandberg, Martha Graham, Iehige Reiko. Joined Paul Taylor Co. in 1971.

SHANKAR, UDAY. Born in Udayapur, India, in 1902. Had such success helping his father produce Hindu plays and ballets, that Anna Pavlova requested his help, and he appeared with her in "Radha-Krishna." At her insistence, pursued dance career. Organized own company and toured U.S. in 1931, 1952, 1962, and 1968. Has been more responsible than any other dancer for arousing interest in Indian dance.

SHAW, BRIAN. Born June 28, 1928 in Golear, Yorkshire, Eng. At 14 entered Sadler's Wells School, and joined company 2 years later, becoming one of Royal Ballet's outstanding principal dancers.

SHEARER, MOIRA. Born in Dunfermline, Scotland. Jan. 17, 1926. Studied with Legat and Preobrajenska; joined International Ballet at 15, transferring to Sadler's Wells and became ballerina in 1944. More recently has appeared on stage and films.

SHEARER, SYBIL. Born in Toronto, Can. Studied in France and Eng. Before forming and choreographing for own group, appeared with Humphrey Weidman Co., and Theatre Dance Co. Also teaches.

SHELLMAN, EDDIE. Born May 10, 1956 in Tampa, FL. Studied with Herbert Lehman, Alvin Ailey, NY Sch. of Ballet. Debut 1975 with Dance Theatre of Harlem.

SHELTON, SARA. Born Dec. 17, 1943. Studied at Henry St. Playhouse. Debut 1966 with Bill Frank Co., subsequently with Nikolais, Louis Murray, Mimi Garrard, Raymond Johnson. Also teaches and choreographs.

SHERMAN, HOPE (a.k.a. Asha Devi, Antonia Esperanza, Sha'Ana). Born in 1944 in Leonia, NJ. Studied at Met Opera School, in India, Japan, Spain, Columbia U. Gives solo concerts and teaches.

SHERWOOD, GARY. Born Sept. 24, 1941, in Swindon, Eng. Studied at Royal Ballet School; joined company in 1961; Western Theatre Ballet 1965; London's Festival Ballet 1966; returned to Royal Ballet in 1967.

SHIMIN, TONIA. Born Sept. 16, 1942 in N.Y.C. Attended Met Opera Ballet, Royal Ballet, Graham schools. Debut 1965 with Martha Graham, subsequently with Pearl Lang, Gus Solomons, Anna Sokolow, Mary Anthony. Joined Jose Limon Co. 1975.

SHIMOFF, KAREL. Born in Los Angeles where she began studies with Irina Kosmovska. Appeared with L.A. Junior Ballet and N.Y.C. Ballet's "Nutcracker" in L.A. in 1961. Studied at School of American Ballet, and joined N.Y.C. Ballet for 2 years, before returning as principal dancer with Ballet of Los Angeles.

SHOEMAKER, PAUL. Born July 18, 1949 in Dayton, OH. Attended Butler U. Has performed with Dance Repertory Co., Radio City Music Hall, Joffrey Ballet.

SHULER, ARLENE. Born Oct. 18, 1947 in Cleveland, O. Studied at School of American Ballet, and American Ballet Center. Debut with N.Y.C. Ballet in 1960, and joined Joffrey Ballet in 1965.

SHURR, GERTRUDE. Born in Riga, Latvia. Studied at Denishawn, and with Humphrey, Weidman, and Graham. Has appeared with Denishawn Co., Humphrey-Weidman Concert Co., and Martha Graham. Now teaches.

SIBLEY, ANTOINETTE. Born in Bromley, Eng., Feb. 27, 1939. Studied at Royal Ballet School, and made debut with them in 1956, becoming soloist in 1959, principal in 1960.

SIDIMUS, JOYSANNE. Born June 21 in NYC. Attended Barnard Col., School of Am. Ballet, Joffrey School. Debut 1958 with NYC-Ballet. Subsequently with London Festival Ballet, National Ballet of Canada, Pennsylvania Ballet. Ballet Mistress Grands Ballets de Geneve (1971), Ballet Repertory Co. from 1973. Also teaches.

SIMMONS, DANIEL. Born in Edinburg, Tex. Studied at Pan American U., San Francisco Ballet School. Debut with SF Ballet 1967.

SIMON, VICTORIA. Born in 1939 in N.Y.C. Studied at School of American Ballet, American Ballet Center, Ballet Theatre School. Joined N.Y.C. Ballet in 1958, promoted to soloist in 1963.

SIMONE, KIRSTEN. Born July 1, 1934 in Copenhagen. Studied at School of Royal Theatre; made debut with Royal Danish Ballet in 1952, subsequently becoming principal dancer. Has appeared with Ruth Page Opera Ballet, Royal Winnipeg Ballet, Royal Swedish Ballet.

SIMONEN-SVANSTROM, SEIJA. Born in Helsinki, Finland, Sept. 7, 1935. Studied at Finnish Natl. Opera Ballet School, and with Nikitina, Baltazcheva, Semjonowa, Lopuchkina, Karnakoski, Stahlberg, Northcote, Franzel, and Craske. Debut 1952 with Helsinki Natl. Opera. Has appeared with Finnish Natl. Ballet, and London Festival Ballet.

SINGLETON, SARAH. Born Apr. 21, 1951 in Morgantown, WVa. Graduate Stephens Col. Studied with Susan Abbey, Rebecca Harris, Karel Shook, Paul Sanasardo. Debut 1972 with Sanasardo Dance Co.

SINGLETON, TRINETTE. Born in Beverly, Mass., Nov. 20, 1945. Studied with Harriet James, and at American Ballet Center. Debut with Joffrey Ballet in 1965.

SIZOVA, ALLA. Born in Moscow in 1939. Studied at Leningrad Ballet School. Joined Kirov Co. in 1958, and became its youngest ballerina.

SKEAPING, MARY. Born in Woodford, Eng. Studied with Novikov, Cecchetti, Trefilova, Egorova, Craske. Toured with Anna Pavlova (1925–31) and the Nemtchnivoa-Dolin Co. Became teacher, choreographer. Ballet Mistress for Sadler's Wells (1948–51), director Royal Swedish Ballet (1953).

SKIBINE, GEORGE. Born Jan. 17, 1920 in Russia. Studied with Preobrajenska, and Oboukhoff. Debut with Ballet de Monte Carlo in 1937, and with company until 1939. Original Ballet Russe (1939–40). American Ballet Theatre (1940–1942). Marquis de Cuevas Grand Ballet (1947–56), Theatre National de Opera Paris (1956–64), artistic director of Harkness Ballet 1964–66. Currently works with regional companies. Director Dallas Civic Ballet.

SLAGLE, LISA. Born Oct. 3, 1955 in Ft. Worth, TX. Studied at Houston Academy of Ballet, Joffrey School. With Houston Ballet (1972), Joffrey Ballet (1974–).

SLAVENSKA, MIA. Born in 1916 in Yugoslavia. At 12 made debut and toured Europe with Anton Vyanc, subsequently with Lifar and Dolin, and prima ballerina with Ballet Russe de Monte Carlo, before forming own company Ballet Variant that toured Americas and Europe. Has worked with many regional companies, toured with Slavinska-Franklin Co. Currently teaches at UCLA.

SLAYTON, JEFF. Born Sept. 5, 1945 in Richmond, Va. Attended Adelphi U. Studied with Merce Cunningham and made debut with his company in 1968. Appears with Viola Farber Co.

SLEEP, WAYNE. Born July 17, 1948 in Plymouth, England. Attended Royal Ballet School, and was graduated into the company in 1966.

SMALL, ROBERT. Born Dec. 19, 1949 in Moline, Ill. UCLA graduate. Studied with Gloria Newman. Murray Louis, Nikolais, and at Am. School of Ballet. Debut in 1971 with Murray Louis Co.

SMALLS, SAMUEL. Born Feb. 17, 1951 in N.Y.C. Attended CCNY. Studied with Lester Wilson, Jamie Rodgers, Harkness House. Debut 1969 with Dance Theatre of Harlem.

SMUIN, MICHAEL. Born Oct. 13, 1938 in Missoula, Mont. Studied with Christensen brothers, William Dollar and Richard Thomas. Joined San Francisco Ballet in 1957, and made choreographic debut in 1961. Has choreographed for Harkness and Ballet Theatre. Principal with American Ballet Theatre 1969–1973. Associate director San Francisco Ballet 1973.

SNIJDERS, RONALD. Born Aug. 15, 1937 in Alkmaar, Netherlands. Trained at Kennemer Ballet School, and with Mme. Ortovskaya, Karel Shook, Leonid Massine. Danced with Netherlands Ballet, Het National Ballet. Retired in 1977 to teach in Arnhem Conservatory.

SOKOLOW, ANNA. Born in 1912 in Hartford, Conn. Studied with Graham and Horst. Became member of Graham Co. but left to form own in 1938. Internationally known as choreographer, and her works include many modern classics. Formed Lyric Theatre Co. in Israel in 1962. Has taught at major studios and universities, and choreographed for Broadway, TV, and opera.

SOLINO, LOUIS. Born Feb. 7, 1942 in Philadelphia. Studied with Graham, O'Donnell, Schurr, Walker, Anthony, Farnworth. Has performed with Glen Tetley, Mary Anthony, Sophie Maslow, Norman Walker, Arthur Bauman, Seamus Murphy, and Jose Limon.

| Lupe Serrano | Paul Shoemaker | Lisa Slagle | Ronald Snijders | Estelle Spurlock |

SOLOMON, ROBERT. Born Feb. 13, 1945 in The Bronx. Studied at Henry Street Playhouse. Has appeared with Henry Street Playhouse Company, and Nikolais.

SOLOMON, RUTH. Born June 10, 1936 in N.Y.C. Studied with Jean Erdman and joined company in 1957, still appears with her between teaching. Now head of Dance-Theatre program at U. Cal. at Santa Cruz.

SOLOMONS, GUS, Jr. Born in Boston where he studied with Jan Veen and Robert Cohan. Danced with Donald McKayle, Joyce Trisler, Pearl Lang, Martha Graham, Merce Cunningham. Formed own company in 1971.

SOLOV, ZACHARY. Born in 1923 in Philadelphia. Studied with Littlefield, Preobrajenska, Carlos, Holm, and Humphrey and at American Ballet School. Debut with Catherine Littlefield Ballet Co. Later joined American Ballet, New Opera Co., Loring Dance Players, and Ballet Theatre. In 1951 became choreographer for Met Opera Ballet. Toured own company 1961–1962. Also appeared on Bdwy and with regional companies.

SOMBERT, CLAIRE. Born in 1935 in Courbevoie, France. A pupil of Brieux, made debut in 1950. Has appeared with Ballets de Paris. Ballets Jean Babilee, Miskovitch Co. Toured U.S. with Michel Bruel.

SOMES, MICHAEL. Born Sept. 28, 1917 in Horsley, Eng. Attended Sadler's Wells School; joined company (now Royal) in 1937, and became lead dancer in 1938. For many years, partner for Margot Fonteyn, and creator of many famous roles. In 1962 appointed assistant director of company, and still performs character roles.

SOWINSKI, JOHN. Born in Scranton, PA. Began studies at 5. Has danced with NYC Ballet, Pennsylvania Ballet, ABT (1965–69), American Ballet Co., Eliot Feld Ballet (1974–).

SORKIN, NAOMI. Born Oct. 23, 1948 in Chicago. Studied at Stone-Camryn School. Debut with Chicago Lyric Opera Ballet in 1963. Joined ABT in 1966; promoted to soloist in 1971. Joined San Francisco Ballet 1973; Eliot Feld Ballet 1974.

SPASSOFF, BOJAN. Born in Oslo, Norway. Appeared with Ntl. Ballet of Holland, Royal Danish Ballet, ABT, and joined San Francisco Ballet 1973.

SPIZZO, CHRISTINE. Born Apr. 3, 1953 in Belleville, Ill. Attended N.C. School of Arts, San Francisco Ballet Sch., Sch. of Am. Ballet. Debut 1971 with National Ballet; joined ABT 1974.

SPOHR, ARNOLD. Born in Saskatchewan, Can. Joined Winnipeg company in 1945, rising to leading dancer, and appeared in England partnering Markova. Began choreographing in 1950. In 1958 was appointed director of Royal Winnipeg Ballet for which he choreographs.

SPURLOCK, ESTELLE. Born May 9, 1949 in Jersey City, N.J. Graduate Boston Cons. Studied with Sonia Wilson, Lar Lubovitch, James Truitte. Debut 1971 with Alvin Ailey Co.

STACKHOUSE, SARAH. (formerly Sally). Born in Chicago, Graduate U. Wisc. Studied with Arrby Blinn, Steffi Nossen, Perry-Mansfield School, John Begg, Limon, Graham, and Nagrin. Joined Limon company in 1959. Also appeared with Alvin Ailey Co. Teaches at Juilliard and Conn. College.

STARBUCK, JAMES. Born in Albuquerque, New Mex. Attended College of Pacific. Debut 1934 with Ballet Modern, subsequently appearing with San Francisco Opera Ballet. Ballet Russe de Monte Carlo (1939–44). On Bdwy in musicals before first choreography for "Fanny." Has since choreographed and directed for theatre and TV.

STEELE, MICHAEL. Born in Roanoke, Va. Studied at American Ballet School, and made debut with N.Y.C. Ballet.

STEELE, ROBERT. Born June 22, 1946 in Erie, Pa. Attended Boston Cons. Studied with Statia Sublette, Virginia Williams, Stanley Williams, Vera Volkova. Debut 1974 with Boston Ballet; subsequently with Pennsylvania Ballet 1964, American Festival Ballet 1965, Royal Danish Ballet 1966, Boston Ballet 1968.

STEFANSCHI, SERGIU. Born Mar. 2, 1941 in Roumania. Graduate of Academie Ballet. Debut 1962 with Bucharest Opera Ballet; subsequently with Theatre Francais de la Dance, National Ballet of Canada 1971 as principal.

STEPHEN, EDITH. Born in Salamanca, N.Y. Studied with Doris Humphrey, Jose Limon, Mary Wigman, Rudolf Laban. Debut in 1962 with own company and choreography. Has toured U.S. and Europe.

STEVENSON, BEN. Born April 4 in Portsmouth, Eng. Was principal dancer for many years with London's Festival Ballet. Retired to teach but makes guest appearances. Directed Harkness Youth Co., National Ballet, Chicago Ballet, Houston Ballet (1975).

STEWART, DELIA WEDDINGTON. Born in Meridian, Miss. Studied at Ballet Arts Center, Ballet Theatre, and International Dance Schools. Appeared in Bdwy musicals. Director of Dixie Darling Dance Group. In 1963 became artistic director of Mississippi Coast Ballet.

STIRLING, CRISTINA. Born May 22, 1940 in London. Trained at Audrey de Vos and Andrew Hardie School. Debut with Sadler's Wells Opera Ballet. Subsequently with Netherlands Ballet, London Festival Ballet, American Ballet Co. Now co-director of Louisville Ballet and teacher.

STOCK, GAILENE. Born Jan. 28, 1946 in Ballarat, Aust. Studied with Paul Hammond, Rosella Hightower, and at London's Royal Ballet School. Debut 1962 with Australian Ballet; subsequently with Grande Ballet Classique de Paris (1963), Teatro del Balletto di Roma (1964), Ntl. Ballet of Canada (1973).

STONE, BENTLEY. Born in Plankinston, S.Dak. Studied with Severn, Caskey, Albertieri, Novikoff, and Rambert. After dancing in musicals joined Chicago Civic Opera, becoming premier danseur. Also danced with Ballet Rambert, Ballet Russe, and Page-Stone Ballet for which he choreographed many works.

STORNANT, VIC. Born in Lansing, MI. Graduate Mich. State U. Studied with Phyllis Lamhut, Paul Sanasardo, May O'Donnell, Zena Rommett. Joined Lamhut company (1971–), Diane Boardman (1972–5), Mimi Garrard (1971–73), Emery Hermans (1971–73). Also choreographs and teaches.

STRICKLER, ILENE. Born July 5, 1952 in NYC. Studied at Met Opera Ballet School. Debut 1969 with Manhattan Festival Ballet; subsequently with Yuriko Co., Boston Ballet 1973.

STRIPLING, JAN. Born Sept 27, 1947 in Essen, Ger. Studied with Volkova, Tudor, Jooss, Hoving, and Jean Lebron. Joined Stuttgart Ballet in 1963; promoted to principal.

STRIZAK, CAROL-MARIE. Born Jan. 8. 1957 in Chicago, IL. Studied at School of American Ballet. Made debut 1974 with NYC Ballet.

STROGANOVA, NINA. Born in Copenhagen, and studied at Royal Danish Ballet with Preobrajenska and Dokoudovsky. Appeared with Ballet de L'Opera Comique Paris, Mordkin Ballet, National Ballet de Basil's Original Ballet Russe, Ballet Russe de Monte Carlo, and Danish Royal Ballet. Was co-director and ballerina of Dokoudovsky-Stroganova Ballet. Is now a teacher.

STRUCHKOVA, RAISSA. Born in 1925 in Moscow; graduate of Bolshoi School in 1944. Became soloist in 1946 with company; now a prima ballerina. Has appeared in almost every ballet performed in Bolshoi repertoire.

SUKANYA. Born Nov. 14, 1946 in Calcutta, India. Trained with Deva Prasad Das, Raja Reddy, and at Pan Dan Allur School. Tours in solo concerts.

SULTZBACH, RUSSELL. Born in Gainesville, Fla. Studied at Royal School, and American Ballet Center. Debut 1972 with Joffrey Ballet.

SUMNER, CAROL. Born Feb. 24, 1940 in Brooklyn. Studied with Eileen O'Connor and at School of American Ballet. Joined N.Y.C. Ballet, becoming soloist in 1963.

SURMEYAN, HAZAROS. Born Jan. 21, 1943 in Skopje, Yugo. Began training at 13. Made debut with Skopje Opera Ballet; subsequently with Belgrade Opera Ballet, Mannheim Opera Ballet, Cologne Opera Ballet. Joined National Ballet of Canada in 1966. Is now a principal and teacher.

SUTHERLAND, DAVID. Born Sept. 18, 1941 in Santa Ana, Cal. Studied with Michael Panaieff, Aaron Girard. Debut 1959 with Ballet de Cuba. Joined Stuttgart Ballet in 1965; promoted to principal. Ballet master Netherlands Dans Theater 1977.

SUTHERLAND, PAUL. Born in 1935 in Louisville, Ky. Joined Ballet Theatre in 1957, subsequently dancing with Royal Winnipeg Ballet, and Joffrey Ballet. Rejoined American Ballet Theatre as soloist in 1964; promoted to principal 1966; Harkness in 1969, Joffrey 1971.

SUTOWSKI, THOR. Born in Trenton, NJ. in Jan. 1945. Studied with Rosella Hightower, Franchette, Williams, Franklin, Tupine, Pereyaslavec. Debut with San Diego Ballet; then with San Francisco Ballet, National Ballet, Hamburg Opera Ballet, Norwegian Opera Ballet where he became premier soloist. Now co-director of San Diego Ballet.

SUZUKI, DAWN. Born in Slocan, B.C., Can. Graduate U. Toronto; studied at Canadian Royal Academy of Dance, Banff and Martha Graham Schools. Debut with Yuriko in 1967, followed by performances with Pearl Lang. Joined Graham Co. in 1968.

SVETLOVA, MARINA. Born May 3, 1922 in Paris. Studied with Trefilova, Egorova, and Vilzak. With Original Ballet Russe (1939–41). Ballet Theatre (1942), prima ballerina Met Opera Ballet (1943–50), N.Y.C. Opera (1950–52), own concert group (1944–58), and as guest with most important European companies, Artistic Director of Dallas Civic Ballet; choreographer for Dallas, Seattle, and Houston Operas; Teaches at Indiana U.

SWANSON, BRITT. Born June 6, 1947 in Fargo, N.Dak. Studied at S.F. Ballet Sch., N.Y. School of Ballet. Debut 1963 with Chicago Opera Ballet, subsequently with S.F. Ballet, on Bdwy, with Paul Sanasardo, Paul Taylor (1969).

SWAYZE, PATRICK. Born in Houston, TX. Studied at Harkness House. Joined Eliot Feld Ballet 1975.

TALIAFERRO, CLAY. Born Apr. 5, 1940 in Lynchburg, Va. Attended Boston Consv. Debut 1964 with Emily Frankel Co. Has appeared with companies of Donald McKayle, Sophie Maslow, Buzz Miller, Stuart Hodes, Jose Limon.

TALLCHIEF, MARIA. Born Jan. 24, 1925 in Fairfax, Okla. After studying with Nijinska, joined Ballet Russe de Monte Carlo in 1942, and became leading dancer. In 1948 joined N.Y.C. Ballet as prima ballerina, and excelled in classic roles. Has appeared as guest artist with Paris Opera and other European companies. Retired in 1965.

TALLCHIEF, MARJORIE. Born Oct. 19, 1927 on Indian reservation in Oklahoma. Studied with Nijinska, and Lichine. Debut with American Ballet Theatre in 1945, subsequently with Marquis de Cuevas Ballet (1947–56), Theatre National Opera de Paris (1956–64), Bolshoi (1964), and Harkness Ballet in 1964. Resigned in 1966. Now teaches. Associate director Dallas Civic Ballet.

TALMAGE, ROBERT. Born June 24, 1943 in Washington, D.C. Attended S.F. State Col. Studied with Eugene Loring. Appeared with Atlanta Ballet, in musicals, before joining Joffrey Ballet in 1968.

TANNER, RICHARD. Born Oct. 28, 1949 in Phoenix, Ariz. Graduate U. Utah. Studied at School of Am. Ballet. Made debut with N.Y.C. Ballet in 1968.

TARAS, JOHN. Born in N.Y.C. Apr. 18, 1919. Studied with Fokine, Vilzak, Shollar, and at School of American Ballet. Appeared in musicals and with Ballet Caravan, Littlefield Ballet, American Ballet, and Ballet Theatre with which he became soloist, ballet master, and choreographed first ballet "Graziana" in 1945. Joined Marquis de Cuevas' Grand Ballet in 1948. Returned to N.Y.C. Ballet in 1959 as assistant to Balanchine. Has created and staged ballets for companies throughout the world.

TAVERNER, SONIA. Born in Byfleet, Eng., in 1936. Studied at Sadler's Wells, and joined company before moving to Canada where she became member of Royal Winnipeg Ballet, developing into its premiere danseuse. Joined Pa. Ballet as principal in 1971; left in 1972.

TAYLOR, BURTON. Born Aug. 19, 1943 in White Plains, N.Y. Studied with Danielian, and at Ballet Theatre School. Debut with Eglevsky Ballet in 1959 before joining American Ballet Theatre, Joffrey Co. in 1969.

TAYLOR, GWYNN. Born Sept. 4, 1956 in Los Angeles, CA. Attended Mt. San Antonio Col. Studied with Gene Marinaccio, Stanley Holden, Andre Tremaine, Finis Jhung. With Gene Marinaccio Ballet (1971–74), Pacific Ballet Theater (1974–76), Eliot Feld Ballet (1976–).

TAYLOR, JUNE. Born in 1918 in Chicago. Studied with Merriel Abbott. Debut in "George White's Scandals of 1931." Choreographer for June Taylor Dancers and director of own school.

TAYLOR, PAUL. Born in Allegheny County, Pa., July 29, 1930. Attended Syracuse U., Juilliard, Met Opera Ballet, and Graham Schools. Studied with Craske and Tudor. Member of Graham Co. for 6 years, and appeared with Merce Cunningham, Pearl Lang, Anna Sokolow, and N.Y.C. Ballet. In 1960 formed and choreographs for own company that tours U.S. and Europe annually.

TCHERINA, LUDMILLA. Born in Paris in 1925. Trained with d'Allesandri, Clustine, Preobrajenska. Has appeared with Monte Carlo Opera, Ballets des Champs-Elysees. Nouveau Ballet de Monte Carlo. Toured with own company, and now appears in films.

TCHERKASSKY, MARIANNA. Born 1955 in Glen Cove, N.Y. Studied with her mother Lillian Tcherkassky; made debut with Eglevsky Ballet; joined ABT in 1970; soloist in 1972.

TENNANT, VERONICA. Born Jan. 15, 1947 in London, Eng. Studied in Eng., and Ntl. Ballet School of Canada. Debut 1964 with Ntl. Ballet of Canada, and rapidly rose to principal.

TEPSIC, JEAN. Born July 15, 1948 in Sanford, FL. Graduate Tex. Christian, Fla. State. Studied at Cincinnati Consv. Artistic director Atlantic Dance Co., teacher.

TETLEY, GLEN. Born Feb. 3, 1926 in Cleveland, Ohio. Attended Franklin and Marshall College, and NYU graduate. Studied with Holm, Graham, Tudor, and Craske. Debut in 1946 in "On The Town," subsequently with Hanya Holm (1946–9), John Butler (1951–9), N.Y.C. Opera (1951–66), Robert Joffrey (1955–6), Martha Graham (1957–60). American Ballet Theatre (1958–60), Ballets U.S.A. (1960–1), Nederlands Dans Theatre (1962–5). Formed own company in 1961, and choreographs. Director of Stuttgart Ballet 1974–1975.

THARP, TWYLA. Born in Portland, IN. in 1941. Graduate Barnard College. Studied with Collonette, Schwetzoff, Farnworth, Louis, Mattox, Graham, Nikolais, Taylor, and Cunningham. Debut with Paul Taylor in 1965. Has organized, choreographed, and appeared with own company in N.Y.C. and on tour.

THOMAS, RICHARD. Born in Paintsville, KY. Studied with Bronislava Nijinska. After appearing on Bdwy, joined Ballet Theatre in 1946. With his wife, former ballerina Barbara Fallis, operates NY School of Ballet.

THOMAS, ROBERT. Born Mar. 5, 1948 in Iowa City. Studied with Anne Kirksen, and at Harkness School. Joined Harkness Ballet in 1968. Joffrey Ballet 1970.

THOMPSON, BASIL. Born in Newcasle-on-Tyne, Eng. Studied at Sadler's Wells. Joined Covent Garden Ballet in 1954, the Royal Ballet, ABT in 1960. Currently ballet master of Joffrey Ballet.

THOMPSON, CLIVE. Born in Kingston, Jamaica, B.W.I., Oct. 20. Studied with and joined Ivy Baxter's Dance Co. Attended Soohih School of Classical Dance, and University College of West Indies. Came to U.S. in 1960, studied with Graham, and joined company in 1961. Also with Talley Beatty, Pearl Lang, Yuriko, Geoffrey Holder, and Alvin Ailey.

THORESEN, TERJE. Born in 1945 in Stockholm. Debut in 1959 Appeared with Royal Dramatic Theatre, Stockholm Dance Theatre Syvilla Fort African Dance Group.

TIMOFEYEVA, NINA. Born in 1935 in Russia. Entered Leningrad Ballet School and graduated into Kirov Co. in 1953. Joined Bolshoi in 1956 and is a principal ballerina.

TIPPET, CLARK. Born Oct. 5, 1954 in Parsons, Kan. Trained at National Academy of Ballet. Made debut with American Ballet Theatre 1972.

TODD, CAROLINE A. Born Mar. 29, 1944 in Savannah, GA. Trained at School of Am. Ballet, Am. Ballet Theatre, Am. Ballet Center. Debut 1965 with Am. Ballet Theatre; joined NYC Ballet 1967.

TOMASSON, HELGI. Born Oct. 8, in Reykjavik, Iceland. Studied with Sigidur Arman, Erik Bidsted, Vera Volkova, and American Ballet School. Debut in Copenhagen's Pantomine Theatre in 1958 In 1961 joined Joffrey Ballet; Harkness Ballet in 1964; N.Y.C. Ballet in 1970, becoming principal.

TOMLINSON, MEL A. Born Jan. 3, 1954 in Raleigh, NC. Attended NC School of Arts, Dance Theatre of Harlem. Debut 1973 with Agnes deMille's Heritage Dance Theatre. Joined Dance Theatre of Harlem 1974.

TORRES, JULIO. Born in Ponce, PR. Attended NY High School of Performing Arts. Appeared with Jose Greco, Carmen Amaya, Vienna Volksopera, Pilar Lopez. Founder-Director-Choreographer of Puerto Rican Dance Theatre.

TOTH, EDRA. Born in 1952 in Budapest, Hungary. Trained with Alda Marova, E. Virginia Williams. Joined Boston Ballet in 1965, rising to principal.

TOUMANOVA, TAMARA. Born in 1919. Protege of Pavlowa, danced first leading role with Paris Opera at 10; ballerina with Ballet Russe de Monte Carlo at 16. Joined Rene Blum Co. in 1939; returned to Paris Opera in 1947, and to London with de Cuevas Ballet in 1949. More recently in films.

TRACY, PAULA. Born Feb. 25 in San Francisco where she studied with Lew and Harold Christensen. Debut with San Francisco Ballet in 1956. Joined American Ballet Theatre in 1967, San Francisco Ballet 1973.

TRISLER, JOYCE. Born in Los Angeles in 1934. Graduate of Juilliard. Studied with Horton, Maracci, Tudor, Holm, Joffrey, Caton. Debut with Horton Co. in 1951. Became member of Juilliard Dance Theater, and performed with own group, for which she choreographed. Has also choreographed for musicals and operas. Now teaches.

TROUNSON, MARILYN. Born Sept. 30, 1947 in San Francisco Graduated from Royal Ballet School and joined company in 1966 Joined Stuttgart as principal.

| Burton Taylor | Tamara Toumanova | Antony Tudor | Violette Verdy | Marc Verzait |

TUDOR, ANTONY. Born Aug. 4, 1908 in London. Studied with Marie Rambert, and made debut with her in 1930, when he also choreographed his first work. Joined Vic-Wells Ballet (1933–5), and became choreographer. Formed own company, London Ballet, in N.Y. in 1938. In 1940 joined American Ballet Theatre as soloist and choreographer. Has produced ballets for N.Y.C. Ballet, Theatre Colon, Deutsche Opera, and Komaki Ballet. Was in charge of Met Opera Ballet School (1957–63); artistic director Royal Swedish Ballet 1963–64. Considered one of world's greatest choreographers. Associate director Am. Ballet Theatre 1974.

TUNE, TOMMY. Born Feb. 28, 1939 in Wichita Falls, Tex. Graduate UTex. Has been featured dancer in films and on Bdwy.

TUPINE, OLEG. Born in 1920 aboard ship off Istanbul. Studied with Egorova and made debut with her company. Joined Original Ballet Russe in 1938, Markova-Dolin Co. in 1947. Ballet Russe de Monte Carlo in 1951, then formed own company. Now teaches.

TURKO, PATRICIA. Born May 22, 1942 in Pittsburgh. Studied at School of American Ballet. Danced with Pittsburgh and Philadelphia Opera companies and in musicals before joining Pennsylvania Ballet in 1964. Now retired.

TURNEY, MATT. Born in Americus, Ga. Joined Martha Graham Co. in 1951. Also danced with Donald McKayle, Alvin Ailey, Paul Taylor, and Pearl Lang.

TUROFF, CAROL. Born Jan. 14, 1947 in New Jersey. NYU graduate; studied with Jean Erdman, Erick Hawkins. Debut 1968 with Hawkins Co., subsequently appearing with Jean Erdman, and in concert.

TUZER, TANJU. Born May 17, 1944 in Istanbul, Turkey. Trained at State Conservatory. Made debut with Turkish State Ballet 1961. Joined Hamburg State Opera Ballet 1969, Harkness Ballet 1972.

TYERS, SHARON. Born June 11, 1950 in Snoqualmie, WA. Attended UWash., UCLA. Studied with Ruthanna Boris, Mia Slavenska, Martha Graham. Danced with L. A. City Ballet, Seattle Opera Ballet, Choreographers Dance Co.; joined Martha Graham Co. 1977.

UCHIDA, CHRISTINE. Born in Chicago, Ill. Studied with Vincenzo Celli, School of American Ballet, American Ballet Center. Debut 1972 with Joffrey Ballet.

UCHIYAMA, AYAKO. Born in Hokkaido, Japan in 1925. Began studies in Tokyo with Masami Kuni, Aiko Yuzaki and Takaya Eguchi. In 1950 organized Uchiyama Art Dance School. Awarded scholarship to study in U.S. with Graham, Horst, Limon, Cunningham, Joffrey, Ballet Russe School, and Luigi's Jazz Center. Has given many concerts and recitals in Japan, and U.S. under sponsorship of Japan and Asia Societies.

ULANOVA, GALINA. Born in Russia, Jan. 8, 1910. Studied with Vagonova. Graduate of Leningrad State School of Ballet. Joined Bolshoi Company and became Russia's greatest lyric ballerina. Now in retirement, but coaches for Bolshoi.

ULLATE, VICTOR. Born in Spain. Studied with Rosella Hightower, Maria de Avila. Debut with Antonio. At 18 joined Bejart Ballet.

URIS, VICTORIA. Born Nov. 28, 1949 in NYC. Graduate NYU. Studied with May O'Donnell, Viola Farber, Martha Graham, Nenette Charisse. Debut 1971 with Norman Walker company, and subsequently with NY Dance Collective Sandra Neels, Rosalind Newman, Paul Taylor Dance Co. (1975).

UTHOFF, MICHAEL. Born in Santiago, Chile, Nov. 5, 1943. Graduate of U. Chile. Studied at Juilliard, School of American Ballet, American Ballet Center, and with Tudor, and Limon. Debut with Limon's company in 1964. Appeared with American Dance Theatre before he joined Joffrey Ballet in 1965, First Chamber Dance Co. (1969). Since 1972 artistic director of Hartford Ballet, and teacher at SUNY in Purchase N.Y.

VALDOR, ANTONY. Began career with Marquis de Cuevas Company, subsequently appearing with Jose Torres' Ballet Espagnol, Opera de Marseille, Theatre du Chatelet, Theatre Massimo de Palermo. Currently ballet master of San Francisco Ballet.

VALENTINE, PAUL. Born March 23, 1919 in N.Y.C. Began career at 14 with Ballet Russe de Monte Carlo, subsequently as Val Valentinoff with Fokine Ballet, and Mordkin Ballet. Since 1937 has appeared in theatre, TV, and night clubs.

VALLESKEY, CAROLE. Born Jan. 6, 1956 in Detroit, MI. Studied at Severo Ballet, ABT, Harkness Schools. Debut 1974 with Houston Ballet; joined Joffrey Ballet 1976.

VAN DANTZIG, RUDI. Born in Amsterdam in 1933. Studied with Sonia Gaskell. With Het Nederlands Ballet as dancer-choreographer (1954–59), Het Nederlands Dans Theater (1959–60), Dutch National Ballet and became its director-choreographer in 1971.

VAN DYKE, JAN. Born April 15, 1941, in Washington, D.C. Studied with Ethel Butler, Martha Graham, Merce Cunningham, and at Conn. College, Henry St. Playhouse. Dancer-choreographer-director of Church St. Dance Co., and appeared with DTW.

VAN HAMEL, MARTINE. Born Nov. 16, 1945 in Brussels. Attended Natl. Ballet School of Canada. Debut 1963 with Natl. Ballet of Can. Guest with Royal Swedish Ballet, Royal Winnipeg Ballet, Joffrey Ballet, before joining ABT. Became soloist in 1971, principal 1973.

VARDI, YAIR. Born May 29, 1948 in Israel. Studied at Batsheva Dance Studio, and joined Batsheva Dance Co.

VARGAS, GEORGE. Born Apr. 19, 1949 in Barranquilla, Col. Studied with Thomas Armour, School of American Ballet. Debut 1968 with Eglevsky Ballet; joined Boston Ballet 1969.

VASSILIEV, VLADIMIR. Born in Russia in 1940. Studied at Bolshoi School and joined company in 1958, becoming soloist in 1959, then principal.

VEGA, ANTONIO. Born in Huelva, Spain. Studied with Pericet and Antonio Marin. Has danced with Jose Molina, Luisillo, Marienna, Antonio, and Jose Greco. Joined Ballet Granada in 1968 as soloist.

VERDON, GWEN. Born Jan. 13, 1926 in Culver City, CA. Studied with Ernest Belcher, Carmelita Maracci. Danced with Aida Brodbent, Jack Cole companies. Became assistant to Cole, before becoming star of Bdwy musicals.

VERDY, VIOLETTE. Born in Brittany, Dec. 1, 1933. Debut in 1944 with Roland Petit. Danced with Royal Ballet, Paris Opera Ballet before joining ABT in 1957. Joined NYC Ballet as principal in 1958. Director Paris Opera Ballet 1977.

VERE, DIANA. Born Sept. 29, 1942 in Trinidad. Studied at Royal Ballet School and joined company in 1962; promoted to soloist in 1968, principal 1970.

VERED, AVNER. Born Feb. 3, 1938 in Israel. Debut 1965 with Bertram Ross, subsequently with Jose Limon, Pearl Lang.

VERSO, EDWARD. Born Oct. 25, 1941 in N.Y.C. Studied with Vincenzo Celli. Appeared on Bdwy and with Ballets U.S.A., before joining American Ballet Theatre in 1962, Joffrey Ballet in 1969. Directs his own school, and Festival Dance Theatre in N.J.

VERZAIT, MARC. Born July 25, 1948 in East Orange, NJ. Attended Rutgers Col. Studied with Fred Danieli, John Barker, William Dollar, Patricia Wilde. Debut 1967 with Garden State Ballet; joined Metropolitan Opera Ballet 1969.

VESAK, NORBERT. Born Oct. 22, 1936 in Vancouver, Can. Studied at Royal Acad., with Craske, Shawn, Volkova, Cunningham, Koner, La Meri. Director San Francisco Opera Ballet 1971–74. Guest choreographer for many companies. Director-choreographer Met Opera Ballet 1976.

VEST, VANE. Born in Vienna. Studied with Larry Boyette. Debut with Denver Civic Ballet; subsequently with Ballet Theatre Players, ABT 1968, San Francisco Ballet 1972.

VETRA, VIJA. Born Feb. 6 in Latvia. Studied in Vienna, and India. Debut 1945 in Burgertheatre, Vienna. Since 1955 has toured world in solo concerts, and teaches in own N.Y. studio.

VIKULOV, SERGEI. Trained at Leningrad Ballet School. Joined Kirov Company in 1956.

VILLELLA, EDWARD. Born Oct. 1, 1936, in Bayside, Queens, N.Y. Began studies at School of American Ballet at 10. Graduate of Maritime College. Joined N.Y.C. Ballet in 1957, and rapidly rose to leading dancer. First male guest artist to appear with Royal Danish Ballet. Appeared in N.Y.C. Center productions of "Brigadoon," and on TV. Recently choreographed for N.Y.C. Ballet and own ensemble.

VODEHNAL, ANDREA. Born in 1938 in Oak Park, Ill. Studied at Ballet Russe School, and School of American Ballet, and with Semenova and Danilova. Joined Ballet Russe de Monte Carlo in 1957, and became soloist in 1961. Joined National Ballet in 1962 as ballerina.

VOLLMAR, JOCELYN. Entered native San Francisco Ballet School at 12 and joined company at 17 in 1943. Later with N.Y.C. Ballet, American Ballet Theatre, de Cuevas Ballet, and Borovansky Australian Ballet. Rejoined S.F. Ballet in 1957, and has choreographed several ballets.

VON ARÓLDINGEN, KARIN. Born July 9, 1941 in Germany. Studied with Edwardova, Gsovsky. Debut 1958 in Frankfurt. Joined N.Y.C. Ballet in 1961, soloist 1967, principal 1972.

VONDERSAAR, JEANETTE. Born May 17, 1951 in Indianapolis, Ind. Trained at Harkness School, and made debut with company in 1969.

WAGNER, RICHARD. Born Jan. 30, 1939 in Atlantic City, N.J. Studied with Antony Tudor. Debut with Ballet Russe de Monte Carlo in 1957; joined American Ballet Theatre in 1960, and Harkness Ballet in 1964 as dancer and choreographer.

WAGONER, DAN. Born July 13, 1932 in Springfield, W.Va. Attended U.W.Va. Studied with Ethel Butler, Martha Graham. Debut 1958 with Graham, subsequently with Merce Cunningham, Paul Taylor, and own choreography and company.

WALKER, DAVID HATCH. Born Mar. 14, 1949 in Edmonton, Can. Studied at Natl. Ballet School, Toronto Dance Theatre, Martha Graham. Debut 1968 with Ballet Rambert, London, subsequently with Donald McKayle, Lar Lubovitch, Martha Graham.

WALKER, NORMAN. Born in N.Y.C. in 1934. Studied at HS Performing Arts. Appeared with May O'Donnell, Yuriko, Pauline Koner, and Pearl Lang. Began choreographing while in army, and afterward taught at Utah State U., Choreographed for musicals and festivals throughout U.S. Appears with own company, and choreographs for it as well as others. Also teaches, and was artistic director of Batsheva Co., and Jacob's Pillow.

WALL, DAVID. Born in London, March 15, 1946. Attended Royal Ballet School, and made debut with company in 1962. Now a principal.

WALLSTROM, GAY. Born Mar. 9, 1949 in Beaumont, Tex. Studied at American Ballet Center and joined Joffrey Ballet in 1968.

WARD, CHARLES. Born Oct. 24, 1952 in Los Angeles, Cal. Studied with Audrey Share, Stanley Holden, Michael Lland, Ballet Theatre School, Gene Marinaccio. Debut 1970 with Houston Ballet; joined ABT 1972; promoted to soloist 1974.

WARDELL, MARCIA. Born Dec. 22, 1948 in Lansing, Mich. Studied with Elizabeth Wiel Bergmann, Betty Jones, Ethel Winter, Alfredo Corvino, Murray Louis, Nikolais, Gladys Bailin. Debut in 1971 with Murray Louis Co.

WARNER, DENISE. Born Mar. 24, 1951 in Meriden, Conn. Studied with Vera Nikitins, American Ballet Theatre School. Debut 1968 with Hartford Ballet; joined ABT 1972.

WARREN, GRETCHEN. Born Apr. 7, 1945 in Princeton, N.J. Attended Aparri School, School of Ballet, Royal Ballet, and National Ballet Schools. Debut in 1964 with Covent Garden Opera Ballet; subsequently with Icelandic Natl. Opera Ballet, National Ballet (1964–5), Pa. Ballet from 1965. Made soloist in 1968.

WARREN, VINCENT. Born Aug. 31, 1938 in Jacksonville, Fla. Studied at Ballet Theatre School. Debut 1957 with Met Opera Ballet, subsequently with Santa Fe Opera, James Waring, Aileen Pasloff, Guatemala Natl. Ballet, Penn. Ballet, Cologne Opera Ballet, Les Grands Ballets Canadiens.

WATANABE, MIYOKO. Born in Japan and began training at 6. Joined all-girls Kabuki Troupe and became one of its leading performers. Came to U.S. in 1960 as announcer-interpreter for Kabuki troupe, and remained to perform in concert and teach classic Japanese dances.

WATSON, ELBERT. Born Jan. 15, 1951 in Norfolk, VA. Attended Norfolk State Col. Joined Alvin Ailey company in 1973.

WATTS, JONATHAN. Born in 1933 in Cheyenne, Wyo. Studied with Joffrey, Shurr, and O'Donnell. Debut with Joffrey before joining N.Y.C. Ballet in 1954, Australian Ballet 1962, and Cologne Opera Ballet as premier danseur in 1965. Now director Am. Ballet Center.

WAYNE, DENNIS. Born July 19, 1945 in St. Petersburg, Fla. Debut 1962 with Norman Walker Co.; subsequently with Harkness Ballet 1963, Joffrey Ballet 1970; ABT as soloist 1974. Resigned 1975 to form own company, DANCERS.

WEBER, DIANA. Born Jan. 16, in Passaic, N.J. Studied at Ballet Theatre School. Joined ABT in 1962; became soloist in 1966; San Francisco Ballet 1973.

WEBER, SUSAN. Born Nov. 8, 1951 in Chicago, IL. Graduate UCLA. Studied with Maggie Black, Jack Cole, Mia Slavenska. Joined Lar Lubovitch Company in 1974.

WEISS, JEROME. Born in Florida; graduate Juilliard. Debut with Miami Ballet; subsequently with Atlanta Ballet, Netherlands Dans Theatre 1968, Harkness Ballet 1971, San Francisco Ballet 1973.

WEISS, ROBERT. Born Mar. 1, 1949 in NYC. Studied at School of Am. Ballet. Joined NYC Ballet in 1966; promoted to soloist in 1972, principal 1977.

WELCH, GARTH. Born Apr. 14, 1936 in Brisbane, Aust. Studied with Phyllis Danaher, Victor Gzovsky, Anna Northcote, Zaraspe, Martha Graham. Debut 1955 with Borovansky Ballet, subsequently with Western Theatre Ballet, Marquis de Cuevas Ballet, Australian Ballet (1962).

WELLS, BRUCE. Born Jan. 17, 1950 in Tacoma, Wash. Studied with Patricia Cairns, Banff School, School of American Ballet. Joined N.Y.C. Ballet in 1967, dancing soloist and principal roles since 1969.

WELLS, DORREN. Born June 25, 1937 in London. Studied at Royal Ballet School and made debut with company in 1955, rising to ballerina.

WENGERD, TIM. Born Jan. 4, 1945 in Boston. Graduate U. Utah. Studied with Elizabeth Waters, Yuriko, Ethel Winter, Merce Cunningham, Viola Farber, Donald McKayle. Debut in 1966 with Ririe-Woodbury Co. Dancer-choreographer with Repertory Dance Theatre from 1966. Joined Graham Co. 1972.

WESCHE, PATRICIA. Born Oct. 13, 1952 in West Islip, N.Y. Attended American Ballet Theatre School. Debut 1969 with ABT.

WESLOW, WILLIAM. Born Mar. 20, 1925 in Seattle, Wash. Studied with Mary Ann Wells. Appeared on Bdwy and TV before joining Ballet Theatre in 1949. Joined N.Y.C. Ballet in 1958.

WHELAN, SUSAN. Born Feb. 26, 1948 in N.Y.C. Studied with Eglevsky, at Ballet Theatre, and Harkness schools. Joined Harkness Ballet in 1966, ABT 1971.

WHITE, FRANKLIN. Born in 1924 in Shoreham, Kent, Eng. After 3 years with Ballet Rambert, joined Royal Ballet in 1942. Is also well known as lecturer on ballet.

WHITE, GLENN. Born Aug. 6, 1949 in Pittsburg, Calif. Studied at Norfolk Ballet Academy. American Ballet Center, Debut 1968 with N.Y.C. Opera, joined Joffrey Company in 1969.

WHITE, ONNA. Born in 1925 in Cape Breton Island, Nova Scotia. Debut with San Francisco Opera Ballet Co. Became assistant choreographer to Michael Kidd, and subsequently choreographer for Bdwy, Hollywood, and London productions.

WHITENER, WILLIAM. Born Aug. 17, 1951 in Seattle, Wash. Studied with Karen Irvin, Mary Staton, Hector Zarasppe, Perry Brunson. Debut 1969 with City Center Joffrey Ballet.

WILDE, PATRICIA. Born in Ottawa, Can. July 16, 1928 where she studied before joining Marquis de Cuevas' Ballet International and continuing studies at School of American Ballet. Joined N.Y.C. Ballet in 1950 and became one of its leading ballerinas, having danced almost every role in the company's repertoire. Director of Harkness School. Ballet mistress for ABT. Teaches.

WILLIAMS, ANTHONY. Born June 11, 1946 in Naples, Italy. Studied with Virginia Williams and Joffrey. Debut 1964 with Boston Ballet. Joined Joffrey company 1968; rejoined Boston Ballet in 1969. Soloist with Royal Winnipeg Ballet 1973.

WILLIAMS, DANIEL. (see Daniel Williams Grossman).

WILLIAMS, DEREK. Born Dec. 14, 1945 in Jamaica, WI. Studied at Harkness House, Martha Graham School. Debut with Jamaican Ntl. Dance Co. Joined Dance Theatre of Harlem 1968.

WILLIAMS, DUDLEY. Born in N.Y.C. where he began dance lessons at 6. Studied with Shook, O'Donnell, Tudor, Graham, and at Juilliard. Has appeared with May O'Donnell, Martha Graham, Donald McKayle, Talley Beatty, and Alvin Ailey from 1964.

WILLIAMS, KERRY. Born in Philadelphia; studied at San Francisco Ballet School, and made debut with company. Joined American Ballet Co., and returned to SF Ballet in 1972.

WILLIAMS, STANLEY. Born in 1925 in Chappel, Eng. Studied at Royal Danish Ballet and joined company in 1943. Became soloist in 1949. Teacher and guest artist since 1950. Ballet master and leading dancer with Ballet Comique (1953–4). Knighted by King of Denmark. Since 1964, on staff of School of Am Ballet.

WILSON, ANNE. Born in Philadelphia. Graduate of U. of Chicago. Studied with Fokine, Tudor, Weidman, Elizabeth Anderson, Étienne Decroux, and Heinz Poll. Debut 1940 with American Ballet Theatre. Also with Weidman, and in 1944 formed own co. Noted for solo concert-lecture "The Ballet Story" which she has toured extensively.

WILSON, JOHN. Born in 1927 in Los Angeles. Studied with Katherine Dunham. Toured with Harriette Ann Gray, appeared in concert with own group, and Joyce Trisler. Joined Joffrey Ballet in 1956, Harkness Ballet in 1964.

WILSON, PAUL. Born Oct. 19, 1949 in Carbondale, Pa. Studied with Barbara Doerffer, Charles Weidman, Zena Rommett. Joined Weidman Co. 1971. Also danced with Jan Wodynski, Jeff Duncan, Xoregos Co. Formed Theatre-dance Asylum 1975. Also teaches.

| **Elbert Watson** | **Donna Wood** | **Glenn White** | **Lynda Yourth** | **Peter Woodin** |

WILSON, SALLIE. Born Apr. 18, 1932 in Ft. Worth, Tex. Studied with Tudor and Craske. Joined American Ballet Theatre in 1959, and in 1963 became principal dancer. Has also appeared with Met Opera and N.Y.C. Ballets.

WILSON, ZANE. Born Feb. 25, 1951 in Elkton, Md. Attended UMd. Trained at Harkness School and joined Harkness Ballet in 1970.

WINTER, ETHEL. Born in Wrentham, Mass., June 18, 1924. Graduate of Bennington College, Soloist with Martha Graham Co. since 1964. Has taught Graham Method in various schools in Eng. and appeared as lecture-demonstrator. Her own choreography has received recognition, and is included in repertoire of Batsheva Co. Also appeared with N.Y.C. Opera, and Sophie Maslow.

WINTZ, JODI CAROL. Born Oct. 29, 1954 in Binghamton, NY. Studied with Natalia Clare, Joffrey School. Joined Joffrey Ballet in 1975.

WITHAM, MELINDA. Born Dec. 29, 1954 in Mobile, AL. Studied at School of Am. Ballet Theatre. Appeared with Boston Ballet before joining Stuttgart Ballet.

WOLENSKI, CHESTER. Born Nov. 16, 1931 in New Jersey. Attended Juilliard, and American School of Ballet. Debut 1956 with Jose Limon, subsequently with Anna Sokolow, Donald McKayle, John Butler, American Dance Theatre, Juilliard Dance Theatre, Jack Moore, Bill Frank and Ruth Currier. Also appeared in musicals.

WONG, MEL. Born Dec. 2, 1938 in Oakland, Cal. Graduate UCLA. Studied at Academy of Ballet. SF Ballet School, School of Am. Ballet, Cunningham Studio. Debut in 1968 with Merce Cunningham Co.

WOOD, DONNA. Born Nov. 21, 1954 in NYC. Joined Alvin Ailey Dance Theatre 1972.

WOODIN, PETER. Born in Tucson, Ariz. Graduate Wesleyan U. Debut 1971 with Lucas Hoving Co.; subsequently with Utah Repertory Dance Theatre, Gus Solomons, Chamber Arts Dance Players, Alvin Ailey Dance Theatre 1973.

WRIGHT, CHRISTINE. Born Mar. 3, 1957 in Tokyo, Japan. Trained at Washington Sch. of Ballet. Has appeared with Marcus Schulkind Co., Kazuko Hirabayashi Dance Theater, Eglevsky Ballet, Saeko Ichinohe, Lar Lubovitch Co.

WRIGHT, KAREN. Born Oct. 25, 1956 in Denver, CO. Studied at Dance Theatre of Harlem and joined company in 1975.

WRIGHT, REBECCA. Born Dec. 5, 1947 in Springfield, Ohio. Studied with David McLain and Josephine Schwarz. Joined Joffrey Ballet in 1966; ABT 1975 as soloist.

WYATT, JOSEPH. Born Jan. 23, 1950 in Trinidad, WI. Attended State U. of NY. Joined Dance Theatre of Harlem in 1973.

YOHN, ROBERT. Born Sept. 23, 1943 in Fresno, Calif. Studied at Fresno State Col., New Dance Group, and with Charles Kelley, Perry Brunson. Has appeared with New Dance Group, Bruce King, and joined Erick Hawkins Company in 1968.

YOUNG, CYNTHIA. Born Dec. 16, 1954 in Salt Lake City, U. Studied with Carol Reed, Ben Lokey, Willam Christensen, Anatole Vilzak, Gordon Paxman. Joined Ballet West in 1970; promoted to soloist 1973; principal 1974.

YOUNG, GAYLE. Born Nov. 7, in Lexington, Ky. Began study with Dorothy Pring at U. Calif. Studied at Ballet Theatre School, and joined Joffrey Ballet. Appeared on Bdwy and with N.Y.C. Ballet before joining American Ballet Theatre in 1960. Became principal in 1964.

YOURTH, LINDA. Born in Maplewood, N.J. in 1944. Studied at Sch. of Am. Ballet, rising to soloist. Joined Ballet du Grand Theatre de Geneve (1968–71). Returned to NYCB in 1971.

YOUSKEVITCH, IGOR. Born in Moscow, Mar. 13, 1912. Studied with Preobrajenska. Debut in Paris with Nijinska company; joined De Basil's Ballet, then, Ballet Russe de Monte Carlo. In 1946 became premier danseur with Ballet Theatre. Currently operating own school in N.Y.C.

YOUSKEVITCH, MARIA. Born Dec. 11, 1945 in N.Y.C. Studied with father, Igor Youskevitch, and made debut with his company in 1963. Appeared with Met Opera Ballet before joining American Ballet Theatre in 1967. Promoted to soloist 1973.

YUAN, TINA. Born Oct. 9, 1947 in Shanghai, China. Attended Juilliard, Martha Graham School. Debut 1969 with Pearl Lang; subsequently Yuriko 1970, Chinese Dance Co. 1972, Alvin Ailey Co. 1972.

YUDENICH, ALEXEI. Born July 5, 1943 in Sarajevo, Yugoslavia. Studied at Sarajevo Opera Ballet School, and made debut with company. Guest artist with Sagreb Opera Ballet before joining Pennsylvania Ballet in 1964 as principal dancer; retired in 1973 and now teaches.

YURIKO. Born Feb. 2, 1920 in San Jose, Calif. Began professional career at 6 with group that toured Japan for 7 years. Studied with Martha Graham, and joined company in 1944, becoming soloist, and choreographer. Formed own company in 1948 with which she has appeared in N.Y. and on tour. Also appeared in musicals.

ZAMIR, BATYA. Studied with Alwin Nikolais, Gladys Bailin, Phyllis Lamhut, Murray Louis, Mimi Garrard, Rachel Fibish, Joy Boutilier, and in own concerts and choreography. Also teaches.

ZHDANOV, YURI. Born in Moscow in 1925. Began career at 12 before attending Bolshoi School. Joined Company in 1944, became Ulanova's partner in 1951. Is now retired.

ZIDE, ROCHELLE. Born in Boston, Ap. 21, 1938. Studied with Hoctor, Williams, Pereyaslavic, Joffrey, Danielian, and at Ballet Russe School. Debut in 1954 with Ballet Russe de Monte Carlo, subsequently appearing with Joffrey Ballet (1958), Ballets U.S.A. (1961), American Dances (1963), N.Y.C. Opera Ballet (1958–63), Ballet Spectaculars (1963), and became ballet mistress of Joffrey Ballet in 1965.

ZIMMERMANN, GERDA. Born Mar. 26, in Cuxhaven, Ger. Studied with Georgi, Wigman, Horst, Zena Rommett. Soloist with Landestheater Hannover 1959–62. Choreographer from 1967. Solo recitals in U.S. from 1967 and in Ger. Formed Kammertanz Theatre. Teaches.

ZINA, JOE. Born Feb. 19, 1949 in Ludlow, MA. Graduate Penn State U. Joined Nikolais Dance Theatre in 1975.

ZITO, DOROTHY. Born in Jersey City, N.J. Attended Juilliard. Studied at Graham, Harkness schools, and N.Y. School of Ballet. Debut 1969 with New Dance Group, subsequently with Pearl Lang.

ZOMPAKOS, STANLEY. Born in N.Y.C. May 12, 1925. Studied with Balanchine and at School of American Ballet. Debut 1942 with New Opera Co. In Bdwy musicals, with Ballet Russe de Monte Carlo (1954–6), and became artistic director of Charleston, S.C., Civic Ballet.

ZORINA, VERA. Born Jan. 2, 1917 in Berlin, Ger. Studied with Edwardova, Tatiana and Victor Gsovsky, Dolin, and Legat. Debut 1930 in Berlin. Toured with Ballet Russe de Monte Carlo (1934–6). Made N.Y.C. debut in "I Married An Angel" in 1938. Joined Ballet Theatre in 1943. Subsequently, appeared in Bdwy productions, films. 1977 became general director and artistic administrator of Norwegian Opera in Oslo.

ZORITCH, GEORGE. Born in Moscow June 6, 1919. Studied in Lithuania, Paris, and N.Y., with Preobrajenska, Vilzak, Vladimiroff, and Oboukhoff. Debut 1933 with Ida Rubenstein Co. in Paris. Joined de Basil Ballet Russe 1936. Ballet Russe de Monte Carlo 1938, Grand Ballet de Marquis de Cuevas (1951–8), Marina Svetlova Co. (1961), then formed own company. A favorite teacher and choreographer for regional ballet companies. Head of UAriz. dance dept.

ZSEDENYI, KAROLY. Born in Hungary; studied in Paris with Lubov Egorova. Made debut with Royal Opera Ballet of Budapest, becoming first dancer, and later director. 1948 became director of Royal Opera House Ballets in Brussels and Antwerp. In 1951 organized Ballet Experimental in Chile. Came to NYC in 1964 and started his school and the Zsedenyi Ballet.

OBITUARIES

HARRY ASMUS, 57, choreographer, teacher, and former dancer, was found stabbed to death in his Dover, DE., home on March 24, 1977, apparently a murder victim. His career began in Hollywood musicals, but he later appeared on Broadway, and joined American Ballett Theatre for five seasons. His teaching credits include ABT School, High School of Performing Arts, June Taylor School, and for three years was choreographer and ballet master for the Ballet Nacional de Venezuela in Caracas. At his death he was operating his own school, and was artistic director of the Dover Ballet Theatre. Surviving is his estranged wife, former Radio City Music Hall Ballet dancer, Judith Panzer.

BETTY BALIN, 61, former professional dancer, died Nov. 18, 1976 in New York City. She is survived by her daughter, actress Ina Balin, and a son, actor Richard Balin.

EHUD BEN-DAVID, 38, Israel's finest male dancer, and a principal with the Batsheva Company, died in an automobile accident on April 5, 1977. In 1971 he received the Gold Medal at the Paris International Festival of Dance for best male dancer. He performed with the Batsheva company from the time it was organized in 1964 until 1975 when he left to open his own school in his native Natania, Israel. He was also active in tv. He leaves his widow, dancer Linda Hodes of the Martha Graham Company, and a daughter.

GEORGE BOYCE, 77, former dancer, choreographer, and actor, died Feb. 4, 1977 in Hollywood, CA. He appeared in vaudeville before becoming a choreographer, and in films from 1937–1969. He is survived by his son and daughter.

THOMAS CANNON, 66, ballet master and choreographer for the Philadelphia Grand Opera, died Jan. 21, 1977 after a short illness. He had been premier danseur and choreographer for the Littlefield Ballet, guest artist with the Chicago Opera Ballet and Ballet Russe de Monte Carlo, and before his retirement last year was ballet master and choreographer for the Connecticut Opera and the Opera Guild of Greater Miami. No reported survivors.

PAUL CLARKE, 28, a principal dancer with London's Festival Ballet, died Sept. 12, 1976 of a heart attack in London. He joined the Festival Ballet in 1973 after having performed with the Royal Ballet. No reported survivors.

KAREN CONRAD, 59, an original member of American Ballet Theatre, and co-artistic director of the Southern Ballet in Atlanta, died July 24, 1976 in Atlanta, GA. Her professional career began as a soloist with the Littlefield Ballet in Philadelphia, and subsequently she danced with the Mordkin Ballet until 1939 when she joined Ballet Theatre, as a leading soloist. She created the role of the Woman in His Past in "Lilac Garden" and the French Ballerina in "Gala Performance," among others. She was probably best known for her Mazurka in "Les Sylphides." In 1944, after her marriage to Pittman Corry, she left the company, and with her husband established a school in Atlanta and the Southern Ballet for which she choreographed, and frequently danced. She retired in 1959. Surviving are her husband and four children.

IGOR DEGA, age unreported, former dancer and film actor, died July 5, 1976 of a heart attack in Burbank, CA. He had been a featured dancer for Earl Carroll, and toured the world with his act. His partners included Grace Poggi and Mimi Dega, to whom he was once married. No reported survivors.

TIMMY EVERETT, 38, dancer, choreographer and actor, died in his sleep March 4, 1977 apparently a heart failure. After several Broadway productions, he became a popular teacher and choreographer for many dance organizations. Surviving are his parents, and two sisters, actresses Sherry and Tanya Everett.

ALEX FISHER, age unreported, an employee of Dance Magazine, and former half of the well known Harrison and Fisher dance team, died in his sleep June 9, 1976 in NYC. With his wife Ruth Harrison, he danced throughout Europe and at the Lido in Paris for several years. His wife died in 1974. A sister survives.

ESTEBAN FRANCES, 61, Spanish-born ballet designer, died Sept. 20, 1976 following a fall while on a visit at Barcelona, Spain. He came to the U.S. in 1944 and eventually designed for such NYC Ballet productions as "Le Renard," "Til Eulenspiegel," "Con Amore," "La Sonnambula," and "Don Quixote." No reported survivors.

JURY GOTSHALKS, age unreported, Latvian-born teacher and original artistic director of the Milwaukee Ballet, died July 15, 1976 in his home in Milwaukee, WI. He had appeared with the National Ballet of Canada, Les Grands Ballets Canadiens, and the NYC Opera Ballet. Since 1968 he had been teaching at the Univ. of Wisc. No reported survivors.

STANISLAS IDZIKOWSKI, 82, Polish-born retired teacher and former dancer with Ballets Russes, died Feb. 12, 1977 in a London nursing home. He danced with Anna Pavlova's company from 1910–1914, Serge Diaghilev's Ballets Russes 1915–1928, and was a guest artist with the Vic-Wells Ballet (now Royal) in the early 1930's. He was co-author with the late Cyril Beaumont of "A Manuel of Classical Theatrical Dancing." No reported survivors.

MAC JOHNSTON, 71, comedy dancer, died March 22, 1977 in Mt. Vernon, MO. He worked alone, and as part of the team of Hamel and Johnston in vaudeville. He also taught tap dancing for several years. A son survives.

FIORELLA KEANE, age unreported, English-born ballet mistress and former dancer, died June 9, 1976 in NYC. She began her career in the 1940's with the Sadlers Wells Co. (now Royal), with whom she danced for 7 years. She came to NYC to join the faculty of Juilliard, and eventually was ballet mistress for Richard Englund and Alvin Ailey companies, and for American Ballet Theatre since 1974. She is survived by her parents and two sons.

JULIA LUMET, 69, former dancer and choreographer, and teacher, died Oct. 18, 1976 of cancer in Los Angeles, CA. She had also been head of the dance department at the Dallas Institute of Performing Arts. Surviving are her husband, actor Baruch Lumet, a son, director Sidney Lumet, and two daughters.

NICHOLAS MAGALLANES, 54, an original member and favorite dancer of the New York City Ballet, died May 2, 1977 of cancer in his home in North Merrick, L.I. Born in Mexico, he studied at the School of American Ballet and began his professional career with Balanchine's Ballet Caravan. He was with the Littlefield Ballet in 1942, Ballet Russe de Monte Carlo from 1943–46 when he joined Ballet Society which became the New York City Ballet. His last performance was with the company in 1976 in "Don Quixote." Some of his most memorable performances were in dramatic roles. He created the Poet in "Night Shadow" and in "Illuminations," the title role in "Orpheus," and the chief victim in "The Cage," and danced leading roles in many other ballets. No reported survivors.

MARTHA MANNERS, age unreported, English-born dancer and teacher, died March 28, 1977 in NYC. After making her professional debut at 14, she danced with the Marquis de Cuevas Company, Ballet Russe, and was soloist with the Russian Opera Ballet and the Metropolitan Opera Ballet. She had taught at Newark Ballet Academy, Birmingham Civic Ballet, and Birmingham Southern College. Recently she had been teaching private classes in NYC. She was the widow of Nicholas DeRose.

NATALIA ROSLAVLEVA, 69, a leading Soviet dance historian and critic, died of cancer Jan. 3, 1977 in Moscow. She was born Natalia Rene in the Ukraine. She was the author of "Era of the Russian Ballet," the most popular English-language history of the Russian ballet. No reported survivors.

ANGEL SOLER, age unreported, Spanish dancer, died Jan. 24, 1977 in Honolulu after stomach surgery. After leaving his native Peru, he performed with Jose Greco before forming his own act with Gisela Lorca. The team toured the world for many years. A sister and brother survive.

YURI SOLOVIEV, 36, one of the world's great classic dancers, was found Jan. 16, 1977 shot to death in his country home outside Leningrad, an apparent suicide. After graduating from the Leningrad School he joined the Kirov Ballet in 1958 and rapidly rose to stardom. He made his debut in 1961 in the West in the Prokofiev/Gregoriev ballet "The Stone Flower," to great critical acclaim. He leaves his widow, dancer Tatiana Legat, and a daughter.

NATALIE BRANITZKA von HOYER, 68, dancer and teacher, died March 8, 1977 in Flushing, NY. Born in St. Petersburg, Russia, she joined the Ballets Russes and retired from it in 1940, and came to the U.S. with her husband, Jan von Hoyer. She established the Branitzka Ballet School in NYC. A son survives.

TRUDL DUBSKY ZIPPER, age unreported, teacher and former dancer, died July 3, 1976 in California. A graduate of the State Academy in Vienna, she had been a member of the Bodenwieser Dance Group, the Harold Kreutzberg, and Jooss Groups. She taught in England, the Univ. of the Philippines, New York, Chicago and Los Angeles. Surviving is her husband, Herbert Zipper.

209

210

211

213

219

224